Modern East Asia: From 1600

A Cultural, Social, and Political History
Second Edition

PATRICIA EBREY
University of Washington–Seattle

ANNE WALTHALL
University of California–Irvine

JAMES PALAIS
Late of University of Washington–Seattle

WADSWORTH
CENGAGE Learning™

Australia • Brazil • Japan • Korea • Mexico • Singapore • Spain
United Kingdom • United States

WADSWORTH
CENGAGE Learning

Modern East Asia: From 1600
A Cultural, Social, and Political History,
Second Edition
Patricia Ebrey, Anne Walthall and James Palais

Publisher: Suzanne Jeans

Senior Sponsoring Editor: Nancy Blaine

Senior Marketing Manager: Katherine Bates

Senior Developmental Editor: Tonya Lobato

Senior Project Editor: Jane Lee

Art and Design Manager: Jill Haber

Cover Design Director: Tony Saizon

Senior Photo Editor: Jennifer Meyer Dare

Composition Buyer: Chuck Dutton

New Title Project Manager: James Lonergan

Editorial Assistant: Stacey Walker

Marketing Associate: Lauren Bussard

Editorial Assistant: Anne Finley

Cover image: *Woman in Kimono Holding a Battledore with an Actor Portrait*, Japanese, Taisho—early Showa era, color lithograph. Credit: Museum of Fine Arts, Boston. Leonard A. Lauder Collection of Japanese Postcards.

Text credits appear after page 528.

For product information and technology assistance, contact us at
Cengage Learning Customer & Sales Support, 1-800-354-9706

For permission to use material from this text or product,
submit all requests online at **www.cengage.com/permissions**
Further permissions questions can be e-mailed to
permissionrequest@cengage.com

Library of Congress Catalog Number: 2008926851

ISBN-13: 978-0-547-00536-2

ISBN-10: 0-547-00536-9

Wadsworth
20 Channel Center Street
Boston, MA 02210
USA

Cengage Learning is a leading provider of customized learning solutions with office locations around the globe, including Singapore, the United Kingdom, Australia, Mexico, Brazil, and Japan. Locate your local office at **www.cengage.com/global**

Cengage Learning products are represented in Canada by Nelson Education, Ltd.

To learn more about Wadsworth, visit **www.cengage.com/wadsworth**

Purchase any of our products at your local college store or at our preferred online store **www.CengageBrain.com**

Printed in the United States of America
4 5 6 13 12 11

CONTENTS

MAPS AND FIGURES

PREFACE

There are many reasons to learn about East Asia. A fifth of the world's population lives there. Every day newspapers carry articles on the rapid transformations of the world economy that make China, Japan, and Korea a growing presence in our lives. Globalization means that not only are people crossing the Pacific in ever increasing numbers, but also that American popular culture draws from many sources in East Asia, from Korean martial arts to Japanese anime and Chinese films.

But why approach East Asia through its history, rather than, say, its economy or contemporary culture? Many reasons can be offered. One cannot gain an adequate understanding of modern phenomena without knowing the stages and processes that led up to them. Moreover, all of the countries of East Asia are strongly historically minded. To a much greater extent than in the United States, people know and identify with people and events of a thousand or more years ago. In all three countries, people still read for pleasure *The Three Kingdoms,* a novel written in fourteenth-century China about the leaders of three contending states in third-century China. Historical consciousness also underlies the strong sense of separate identities among the people of China, Korea, and Japan. The fact that time and again Korea was able to protect its independence despite the attempts of both China and Japan to conquer it is a central part of Korean identity today. Yet another reason to learn about East Asia in the past is its comparative value. As a region that developed nearly independently of the West, East Asia sheds light on the variety of ways human beings have found meaning, formed communities, and governed themselves, expanding our understanding of the human condition.

When the three authors of this volume were students themselves (in the 1960s and 1970s), the fullest and most up-to-date textbook on East Asia was the two-volume set published in 1960 and 1965 by Cengage Learning, *East Asia: The Great Tradition* and *East Asia: The Modern Transformation,* written by Edwin O. Reischauer, John K. Fairbank, and Albert M. Craig. Not only did we learn the basic political chronology from these books, but they introduced us to such central issues as the dynastic cycle, the interplay of the Chinese and "barbarians," the ways Korea and Japan adapted features of the Chinese model, the challenge posed by the West in the nineteenth century, and modern revolutionary movements. When it came time for us to develop our own research agendas, these books still cast a shadow as we pursued questions that they did not pose or delved more deeply into topics that they covered only superficially.

It was because we respected these books that we were willing to listen when Nancy Blaine of Cengage Learning approached us about doing a new history of East Asia for the current generation of students. We knew that the task would be daunting. Could we take into account the wealth of scholarship that had been published in the forty-odd years since the original *East Asia* books and yet produce the leaner, more visual book requested by students and teachers today? As we discussed how to meet these challenges, we came up with a plan for this book.

COMPARABLE COVERAGE OF KOREA

The growth of Korean studies over the last quarter-century now makes it possible to give Korea comparable coverage to China and Japan (we ended up giving China about 50 percent of the space, Japan 30 percent, and Korea 20 percent). We know that many teachers have been frustrated in their attempts to cover Korea in their East Asia courses for lack of suitable materials and hope that our efforts prove useful to both them and their students.

A BROAD FOCUS: *CONNECTIONS* CHAPTERS

A second key decision we made was to search for ways to keep in mind the larger whole as we told the separate stories of China, Korea, and Japan. Our solution was to periodically zoom out to look at the wider region from a global or world-historical perspective. Thus, after every few chapters we have inserted a mini-chapter on developments that link the societies of East Asia both to each other and to the larger global context. We have labeled these mini-chapters "Connections" because they put their emphasis on the many ways each society was connected to what went on outside it. For instance, the origins and spread of Buddhism are of great importance to all of the societies of East Asia, but much of the story can be told as a common story that connects East Asia with the rest of Asia. Similarly, many books write about World War II in East Asia in entirely different ways from in their China and Japan chapters. By stepping back and writing about the war from a more global perspective, we can help students see the larger picture.

BALANCED CULTURAL, SOCIAL, AND POLITICAL HISTORY

Even though the volume of scholarship on East Asia has increased manyfold since the original *East Asia* set was written, we decided to honor its example of striving for balanced coverage of the different strands of history. A basic political narrative is essential to give students a firm sense of chronology and to let them think about issues of change. Moreover, there is no denying that the creation of state structures has much to do with how people lived their lives. Even the fact that people think of themselves as "Chinese," "Korean," or "Japanese" is largely a by-product of political history.

We also believed that students should gain an understanding of the philosophies and religions of East Asia. Confucianism and Buddhism have both been of great importance throughout the region, but in very diverse ways, as the historical context has

continually changed. Other elements of high culture also deserve coverage, such as the arts of poetry and calligraphy.

Yet we did not want to neglect topics in social, cultural, and economic history, where much of our own work has been concentrated. Even if the state is important to understanding how people lived, so were families, villages, and religious sects. We also wanted to bring in the results of scholarship on those who had been marginalized in the traditional histories, from laborers and minorities to women at all social levels.

A NARROW FOCUS: BIOGRAPHIES, DOCUMENTS, AND MATERIAL CULTURE

The danger of trying to cover so much is that we would have to stay at a high level of generalization. To keep our readers engaged and bring our story down to earth, we decided to devote three or four pages per chapter to closer looks at specific people, documents, and material objects.

Biographies

Most chapters have a one-page biography, often about someone who would not normally be mentioned in a history book. Although we found few truly ordinary people to write about for the earlier periods, we still ended up with a diverse set of individuals. The people sketched range from the most accomplished (such as the eminent Chinese poet Du Fu and the Korean admiral Yi Sunsin) to remarkably ordinary people (such as a woman whose job was to mind the neighborhood telephone). Three military men are portrayed; others were physicians, entrepreneurs, and founders of religious sects. We also have included some agitators and revolutionaries, and even a winning volleyball coach.

Documents

In our chapters we frequently cite short passages from primary sources, but we thought that students would also benefit from texts long enough for them to get a sense of the genre, the author's point of view, and the circumstances described. A few of those we have included were written by famous writers, such as Fukuzawa Yūkichi and Lu Xun. Some are excerpted from well-known pieces of literature, such as the play *The Peony Pavilion*. Others will be less familiar to teachers and students alike. Legal documents have been selected for what they reveal of ordinary people's lives. Religious texts of several sorts were chosen to help us see religion and popular beliefs in action. Many authors are utterly serious, complaining bitterly of war or corruption, for instance; others have well-developed senses of humor. All of the documents selected prompt active involvement and critical interpretation because they get readers to listen to the concerns of people of the past.

Material Culture

Texts are not our only sources for reconstructing the past; there is much to be discovered from material remains of many sorts. To give focus to this dimension of history, for each chapter we have selected one element of material culture to describe in some detail. These range from the most mundane—food, drink, clothing, houses, and means of transportation—to objects of art, including specific paintings, sculptures, or performing arts. Many of the objects discussed have economic significance—for example, fertilizers and the Grand Canal. Most of the features for the late nineteenth or twentieth century bring out ways material culture has changed along with so much else in modern times—from changes in the food people eat to new ways to amuse themselves.

THINKING LIKE A HISTORIAN

The "Documents" and "Material Culture" features challenge students to draw inferences from primary materials much the way historians do. Another way we have tried to help students learn to think like historians is to present history as a set of questions

more than a set of answers. What historians are able to say about a period or topic depends not only on the sources available, but also the questions asked. To help students see this, we begin each chapter with a brief discussion of the sorts of questions that motivate contemporary historians to do research on the time period. Most of these questions have no easy answers; these are not questions students will be able to answer simply by reading the chapter. Rather they are real questions, ones interesting enough to motivate historians to sift through recalcitrant evidence in their efforts to find answers. The earliest chapter on Korea, for instance, poses the question of how the three states on the Korean peninsula were able to survive in the face of Chinese power. The chapter on early-nineteenth-century Japan points out that historians have studied the period for clues to the causes of the Meiji Restoration, wanting to know the relative weight to assign to foreign pressure and domestic unrest. For the chapter dealing with China under the Nationalists, readers are told that the desire to explain the Communist victory in 1949 has motivated historians to ponder such questions as why May Fourth Liberalism lost its appeal and whether the economic politics of the Nationalists could have brought prosperity to China if Japan had not invaded. We hope that posing these questions at the beginning of each chapter will help readers see the significance of the topics and issues presented in the chapter.

USING THIS TEXT IN CLASS

East Asian history is commonly taught either as a one-term or one-year course. To fit both schedules, this text is available both as a single volume and divided chronologically. Since those who divide chronologically might prefer to break at the end either at 1600 or at 1800, the period 1600 to 1800 appears in both of the chronologically divided volumes.

Those who wish to supplement this text with other readings will find many suggestions on the website: **college.cengage.com/pic/ebrey2e**. Professors can also find art and photos from the text, downloadable for use in the classroom.

SECOND EDITION

Based on the advice and suggestions of teachers and students who used the first edition of this book, Anne Walthall and Patricia Ebrey revised it in the summer of 2007. Users seemed uniformly to like the features we had included—the Connections mini-chapters, the documents, biographies, and material culture features. Readers did, however, notice cases of uneven treatment, the inadvertent result of dividing responsibility for the chapters among the three authors.

For the first edition of this book, the three authors divided the work primarily by country of specialization, with Patricia Ebrey writing the parts on China, Anne Walthall those on Japan, and James Palais those on Korea. The Connections chapters we divided among ourselves chronologically, with Patricia Ebrey taking the early ones (on Prehistory, Buddhism, Cultural Contact Across Eurasia, and the Mongols), Anne Walthall taking the early modern and modern ones (on Europe Enters the Scene, Western Imperialism, and World War II), and James Palais doing the final one on East Asia in the Twenty-First Century.

Very sadly, James Palais fell ill during the preparation of the first edition and was not able to revise his chapters according to our original plan. He passed away shortly after the book was printed in summer 2006. At least he did get to see the book in print, and he proudly showed it to visitors.

For this revision, Patricia Ebrey revised James Palais's chapters covering up to 1800 and Anne Walthall the remainder. In our revisions we made every effort to achieve greater consistency in emphasis and level of detail across the three countries. We hope that we have honored Jim's long commitment to the study of Korean history by making his work more accessible to a larger audience.

Making Comparisons

For the second edition, we have shortened the book a little, and we have added something new. To help students think about similarities and differences among the cultures of China, Korea, and Japan, we have added some explicit comparisons of specific elements in their cultures, including women's situations, Neo-Confucianism, popular religion, and food. Because the comparisons deal with long spans of time, they appear mostly in the second half of the book.

ACKNOWLEDGMENTS

Many people have contributed to the shaping of this book. The three authors have been teaching about the societies of East Asia for two or three decades, and the ways they approach their subjects owe much to questions from their students, conversations with their colleagues, and the outpouring of scholarship in their fields. As we worked on this text, we received much advice from others, from early suggestions of possible collaborators to critiques of our original proposal and reviews of the drafts of our chapters. The reviewers' reports prompted us to rethink some generalizations, urged us not to weigh the book down with too much detail, and saved us from a number of embarrassing errors. We appreciate the time and attention the following reviewers gave to helping us produce a better book:

James Anderson, University of North Carolina at Greensboro; R. David Arkush, University of Iowa; Charles Armstrong, Columbia University; Craig N. Canning, College of William and Mary; Henry Chan, Minnesota State University; Alan Christy, University of California, SC; Sue Fawn Chung, University of Nevada, Las Vegas; Parks Coble, University of Nebraska; Anthony DeBlasi, University of Albany; Ronald G. Dimberg, University of Virginia; Franklin M. Doeringer, Lawrence University; Alexis Dudden, Connecticut College; Susan Fernsebner, Mary Washington College; Karl Friday, University of Georgia; James Gao, University of Maryland; Karl Gerth, University of South Carolina; Andrew Goble, University of Oregon; John B. Henderson, Louisiana State University; Jeff Hornibrook, SUNY Plattsburgh; William Johnston, Wesleyan University; Fujiya Kawashima, Bowling Green State University; Sun Joo Kim, Harvard University; Ari Daniel Levine, University of Georgia; Huaiyin Li,

University of Missouri-Columbia; Angelene Naw, Judson College; Steve Phillips, Towson University; Jonathan Porter, University of New Mexico; Wesley Sasaki-Uemura, University of Utah; Edward Slack, Eastern Washington University; S. A. Thornton, Arizona State University; Constantine Vaporis, University of Maryland, BC; Lu Yan, University of New Hampshire; Ka-che Yip, University of Maryland, Baltimore County; Theodore Jun Yoo, University of Hawaii at Manoa.

We also are grateful for all the work put into this book by the editorial staff at Cengage Learning: Nancy Blaine originally convinced us to take on this job; Tonya Lobato handled editing; Linda Sykes secured the photos; Janet Theurer handled the design and the art program; and Jane Lee managed the production details.

CONVENTIONS

Throughout this book names are given in East Asian order, with family name preceding personal name. Thus Mao Zedong was from the Mao family, Ashikaga Takauji from the Ashikaga family, and Yi Sŏnggye from the Yi family.

Both Japanese and Korean have phonetic scripts (Japanese a syllabary, Korean an alphabet), though Japanese additionally makes extensive use of Chinese characters. There are standard ways to transcribe these scripts into our alphabet. Here we have used the Hepburn system for transcribing Japanese. For Korean, we have used the McCune-Reischauer system with a few modifications, primarily placing priority on pronunciation rather than orthography.

Chinese does not have a phonetic script. In this book the pinyin system of romanization has been adopted.

The basic vowels, *a, e, i, o,* and *u* in all three languages are pronounced as in Italian, German, and Spanish.

> *a* as in f*a*ther
> *e* as in *e*nd
> *i* as the first *e* in *e*ve
> *o* as in *o*ld (shorter in length and with less of the *ou* sound of English)
> *u* as in r*u*de (shorter in length than English)

Diacritical marks over vowels change the pronunciations:

ŏ in Korean is like the *o* in r*o*t, except shorter in length than English

ŭ in Korean is something like the *oo* in f*oo*t

The macron over the ō or ū in Japanese indicates that the vowel is "long," taking twice as long to say, as though it were doubled. Macrons have been omitted from common place names well known without them, such as Tokyo and Kyoto.

ü in Chinese (used only after *l* or *n*) is like the German *ü*

The three languages are not so similar when one vowel follows another. In the case of Japanese, each vowel is pronounced as a separate syllable. In Chinese, they create a (one-syllable) diphthong (e.g., *mei,* which is pronounced like may). In Korean, two vowels also form diphthongs, but with some special pronunciations; *ae* is like the *a* in *a*dd; *oe* like the ö of German; and *ŭi* like the *uee* in q*uee*r.

Consonants for Japanese romanization are close enough to English to give readers little difficulty. In the case of Korean, voiced consonants (*j, g, b, d*) are like English. However, aspirated consonants (*ch', k', p', t'*) marked by a marked exhalation of air, and unaspirated consonants (*ch, k, p, t*) are like English but without any aspiration at all. In the Chinese case, divergence between how an English speaker would guess a pronunciation and how the word is actually pronounced is even greater. The most confusing consonants are listed below:

c	ts in tsar
z	dz in adze
zh	j in jack
q	ch in chin
x	sh

In the case of Chinese, the romanization system does not convey tones, which are also an important element in pronunciation.

For both Chinese and Korean, other ways of romanizing the language are also widely used. The South Korean government has recently adopted a system of romanization referred to as the Revised Romanization system or the Ministry of Culture romanization system. It does not use apostrophes or diacritical marks. Comparisons of the two systems of romanization can be found at **http://www.eki .ee/wgrs/rom2_ko.pdf.**

In the case of Chinese, pinyin only became the standard system of romanization in recent decades. Some earlier spellings were based on dialects other than Mandarin (Peking, Canton, Sun Yat-sen). More often the Wade-Giles system of romanization was employed. From context, if nothing else, most readers have inferred that Mao Zedong is the same person whose name used to be spelled Mao Tse-tung, or that Wang Anshi is the pinyin form of Wang An-shih. Two older spellings have been retained in this book because they are so widely known (Sun Yatsen and Chiang Kaishek). Charts for converting pinyin to Wade-Giles and vice versa are widely available on the Internet, should anyone want verification of their guesses (see, for instance, **http://www.loc.gov/ catdir/pinyin/romcover.html**; **http://www.library.ucla .edu/libraries/eastasian/ctable2.htm**; or **http://oclccjk .lib.uci.edu/wgtopy.htm**).

Europe Enters the Scene

TRADE ROUTES FLOURISHED BETWEEN NORTH-east and Southeast Asia long before European merchants and Catholic missionaries entered the South China Sea. Lured by Asian silks, ceramics, and spices, ships under the Portuguese flag were the first to risk the voyage in the early sixteenth century. The Spanish, British, and Dutch followed. In early seventeenth-century Japan, early eighteenth-century China, and early nineteenth-century Korea, rulers put a stop to missionary activities, albeit for different reasons. Trade between Europe and East Asia continued, but it was confined to Guangzhou in China and Nagasaki in Japan.

Hemmed in by Spain, Portugal relied on trade to fill royal coffers. At the beginning of the fifteenth century, Portuguese ships started exploring the west coast of Africa in search of gold. African gold then financed a voyage around the Cape of Good Hope in 1488. From there, the Portuguese established a colony at Goa on the west coast of India and followed Muslim and Indian trade routes to the Spice Islands of Indonesia. Once Queen Isabella and her husband, Ferdinand, captured Grenada, the last Muslim emirate in Spain, in 1492, they funded Christopher Columbus's voyage across the Atlantic in hopes of finding an alternative route to China. In 1494, the pope divided the world beyond Europe between Spain and Portugal. Spain's sphere included most of the Western Hemisphere except Brazil; Portugal went east.

China's contact with Portugal began in 1511 when Admiral Alfonso de Albuquerque captured the Chinese entrepôt of Malacca near the tip of the Malay Peninsula. With this as a base, the first official Portuguese embassy followed traders to China in 1517. The embassy behaved badly by refusing to conform to Chinese customs. Ship captains acted more like pirates than traders. Few Portuguese were willing to risk the long voyage in tiny ships around the Horn of Africa, across the wide expanse of the Indian Ocean, and through the Strait of Malacca to Macao. Most were neither officials dispatched from the Portuguese court nor explorers seeking glory and territory. What they had in limited resources and manpower had to go toward making a profit in competition with local traders (see Map C5.1).

Periodic prohibitions on maritime travel by Ming emperors at Beijing did not stop the Portuguese or seafaring people on the south China coast who made little distinction between trade, smuggling, and piracy. In 1521, the Ming tried to ban Portuguese from China. Two years later, an expeditionary force commissioned by the Portuguese king and charged with negotiating a friendship treaty defeated its mission by firing on Chinese warships near Guangzhou. In 1557, without informing Beijing, local Chinese officials decided that the way to regulate trade was to allow the Portuguese to build a trading post on uninhabited land near the mouth of the Pearl River. This the Portuguese called Macao. It became the first destination for all Europeans going to China until the nineteenth century, and it remained a Portuguese settlement until 1999.

The only significant products Portuguese traders brought to networks that had already developed in East Asia were firearms and New World crops such as corn, sweet potatoes, chili peppers, and tobacco. They reached Japan by accident in 1543 when a typhoon blew a ship with a mixed crew of Southeast Asians to a small island called Tanegashima. Among the goods exchanged for Japanese silver was the matchlock, a type of musket. The island's ruler ordered his retainers to study its operation and manufacture and distributed samples to more powerful mainland warlords. In 1570, Japanese troops deployed the Tanegashima matchlock in battle. In the meantime, Portuguese traders profited from the Ming ban on Japanese ships because they had raided the coast. The Portuguese carried 20 metric tons of Japanese silver a year to China in exchange for silk, sugar, medicine, and dye.

Trade between China and Europe increased in the late sixteenth century through an economic conjuncture that included the Americas following the discovery by Andrés de Urdaneta of a return route to Mexico. China needed foreign silver because its monetary system depended on it and domestic production had declined after 1430. China bought Japanese silver carried on Portuguese ships. China also absorbed 50 percent of silver mined in Mexico and Bolivia and carried in Spanish ships to Manila, founded in 1571 when Spain made the Philippines a colony. Disruptions in the flow of silver from Japan and the Western Hemisphere in 1639 contributed to the fall of the Ming. Spanish silver bought manufactured goods— Chinese silk, porcelain, and lacquer—that dominated the luxury trade in Europe and funded Spain's wars against multiple enemies for generations.

Portuguese merchants seeking profits in East Asia faced competition from their government when the Portuguese viceroy at Goa made the Japan trade a royal monopoly in 1550. The Ming approved because their officials also wanted to see trade regularized. Each year, a captain major appointed by the crown sent ships to Japan, where warlords competed to attract the ships to their ports. (See Color Plate 19.) The governor of Macao forbade the sending of goods to Japan on private ships via third-party countries, especially the Philippines. His directives were futile; Portuguese and Spanish traders with crews drawn from all over East and Southeast Asia found Manila too convenient to abandon.

Catholic missionaries seeking converts who followed the traders hoped to keep the religious wars that undermined the pope's spiritual hegemony secret from Asia. The first were Jesuits, from the order founded by Ignatius Loyola in 1534 to promote Catholic scholarship and combat the Protestant Reformation initiated by Martin Luther in 1517. Jesuits insisted that Christianizing China and Japan was not to be done with the intent to conquer, as had been the case in the Western Hemisphere. As individuals, they displayed a rare sensitivity to other cultures. They were willing to find universal principles of belief outside a European context, but they served an institution that refused to compromise with indigenous beliefs and practices. Despite the efforts of charismatic missionaries, the Catholic Church never gained the ascendancy in East Asia enjoyed by that other foreign religion, Buddhism.

The Jesuit priest Francis Xavier had worked in India and the Indies before China and Japan attracted his attention. After many misadventures, he landed on Sat-

suma in 1549. The Satsuma lord hoped that by treating Xavier well, he would attract the official Portuguese trading ships the next year. When the ships went instead to the island of Hirado, the lord expelled Xavier's party. Xavier traveled throughout western Japan as far as Kyoto, proselytizing wherever warlords gave permission. Asked why the Chinese knew nothing of Christianity if it was indeed an ancient and true religion, Xavier decided that Japan would become Christian only if China led the way. His efforts to enter China ended when he died on an island off the China coast in December 1552.

Jesuits and Dominicans soon joined the missionaries and converts Xavier left behind in Japan. In 1565, Louis Frois met Oda Nobunaga, who befriended the Jesuits to discomfort his Buddhist enemies. In 1580, Jesuits acquired Nagasaki from a warlord interested in promoting trade with Portuguese ships. In 1582, four young Kyushu samurai left Nagasaki for Lisbon and Rome, where they helped Jesuits get a papal bull that put Japan off limits to other orders. It proved to be ineffective, and quarrels between the Catholic orders over how best to present Christianity to East Asia damaged the missionaries' credibility in the eyes of Asian rulers.

Warlords trying to unite Japan under secular authority became increasingly suspicious of Christianity. If an absolute god demanded absolute loyalty, where did that leave the bonds between lord and retainer? Repression began in 1587 and intensified nine years later when the pilot of a ship wrecked on the Japanese coast allegedly pointed out that soldiers had followed Spanish missionaries to the Philippines. In 1614, Tokugawa Ieyasu decided that missionaries undermined the social order and were not essential to foreign trade. He ordered them expelled under threat of execution. He also tortured and killed Christian converts who refused to apostatize. Among the martyrs were Koreans who had been brought to Japan as slaves during Toyotomi Hideyoshi's invasions in the 1590s. The shogunate broke off relations with Catholic countries in 1624. The remaining Christians practiced their religion in secret by crafting statues of the Virgin Mary in the guise of Kannon, the Buddhist goddess of mercy.

Christianity arrived later in China. Not until 1583 did the Jesuit Matteo Ricci receive permission to move farther inland than Macao. Once he had educated himself in the style of Chinese literati, he set himself up in Nanjing. In 1601, he received tacit imperial permission to reside in Beijing. From him the Chi-

Map C5.1   Seaborne Trading Empires in the Sixteenth and Seventeenth Centuries nese learned Western-style geography, astronomy, and Euclidean mathematics. In the years after Ricci's death in 1611, Jesuits regulated the Chinese lunar calendar. They suffered occasional harassment from xenophobic officials, but they retained their standing with Chinese literati through the collapse of the Ming Dynasty and the founding of the Qing in 1644. Catholic mendicant orders allowed into China in 1633 criticized Jesuits for aiming their efforts at the ruling class and trying to fit Christian ideas into the Chinese worldview rather than remaining European in approach and appealing to the masses.

Ricci and his Jesuit successors believed that Confucianism as a philosophy could be assimilated to monotheism. Confucianists and Christians shared similar concerns for morality and virtue. Rites of filial piety performed for the ancestors did not constitute a form of worship, which made them compatible with Christianity. Mendicant orders disagreed. In 1715, religious and political quarrels in Europe exacerbated by longstanding antagonism to the Jesuits resulted in Ricci's accommodation with Chinese practices being deemed heretical. Angry at this insult, the Kangxi emperor forbade all Christian missionary work in China, although he allowed Jesuits to remain in Beijing to assist with the calendar. A Jesuit portrait painter later proved popular at the courts of his son and grandson. The outcome of the controversy over whether converts should be allowed to maintain ancestral altars, exacerbated by accusations that missionaries had meddled in the imperial succession, led the Qing to view all Europeans with suspicion.

China's rulers also tried to limit trade for strategic reasons. Between 1655 and 1675, the Qing banned maritime trade to isolate Ming loyalists on Taiwan. In addition to official trade at the state level, the Qing permitted merchants to trade with foreigners, but only under tight control. After 1759, all maritime trade, whether with Southeast Asia or Europe, was confined to Canton (Guangzhou). Merchants put up with burdensome restrictions because in exchange for silver, China provided luxury items and tea, a bulk ware, introduced to Europe in 1607.

The profits to be made in East and Southeast Asia lured traders from Protestant countries following the religious wars of the latter half of the sixteenth century. Determined not to allow their Catholic rivals to dominate the world, Protestant nations sent explorers across the oceans. Britain's defeat of the Spanish Armada in 1588 began Spain's long decline. Early in the seventeenth century, the Dutch gained a com-

Matteo Ricci. Matteo Ricci is shown here in a French lithograph holding a map of the world to which he offers the crucified Christ. *(The Granger Collection)*

petitive advantage in the world spice trade by opening a faster sailing route in the southern Indian Ocean before turning northward to Java. Both nations established East India Companies in 1600 whose ability to capitalize trade far exceeded that of the merchants of Spain and Portugal.

Like Qing emperors, seventeenth-century Japanese shoguns tried to regulate foreign trade by confining it to specific harbors. In contrast to the sixteenth century, they also tried to prevent the increasingly short supply of precious metals from leaving the country by practicing import substitution for silk and sugar. A Dutch ship carrying a mixed crew of men from Europe and the Western Hemisphere arrived in 1600. (Of five ships with a crew of 461 men, only one ship and 25 men survived to reach Japan.) The British arrived in 1613. Both Dutch and British arrived as representatives of trading companies, not of their governments. Disappointed with scant profits, the British shut down their quarters. Unhappy with what it deemed smuggling, in 1635 the shogunate issued a maritime ban that forbade all Japanese from sailing overseas and ordered those who had migrated to Southeast Asia to return home or face permanent exile. The thriving Japanese community at Hoi An in Vietnam disappeared. In a further attempt to control unregulated trade and piracy, the shogunate later banned the building of oceangoing ships. In 1641, it ordered the Dutch to move to the artificial island called Dejima in Naga-saki bay originally constructed for the Portuguese. The annual visits by Dutch ships allowed an exchange of information, continued Japan's connections with Southeast Asia, and opened the door to Western science and medicine.

Korea proved inhospitable to merchants and missionaries alike. In the seventeenth century, British and Dutch traders made several attempts to insert their goods into the trade route between Korea and Japan that later developed into a triangular trade carrying Japanese copper, Korean ginseng, and Chinese silver. Memories of piracy, fear of unregulated trade that smacked of smuggling, and suspicion of Euro-pean intentions led the government to reject them. Korean scholars in residence at the Chinese court read the Jesuits' religious, scientific, and mathematical treatises and took them back to Korea, where they attracted a small following for Catholic Christianity. The converts soon became embroiled in the factional infighting that characterized politics in eighteenth-century Korea and suffered severe persecution starting in 1791. No European missionary or merchant tried to visit Korea until three French priests landed illegally in 1836–1837. The Korean court had them and their converts executed in 1839 for spreading the "evil teaching" that ran counter to the dictates of filial piety.

The Creation of the Manchu Empire (1600–1800)

The seventeenth and eighteenth centuries were the age of the Manchus. As the Ming Dynasty fell into disorder, the Jurchens put together an efficient state beyond Ming's northeastern border and adopted the name *Manchu* for themselves. After they were called in to help suppress peasant rebellions, the Manchus took the throne themselves, founding the Qing Dynasty (1644–1911). Many Chinese did all they could to resist the Manchus out of loyalty to the Ming, but by the eighteenth century, Chinese and Manchus had learned to accommodate each other. In many ways, the eighteenth century was the high point of traditional Chinese civilization. The Manchus created a multiethnic empire, adding Taiwan, Mongolia, Tibet, and Xinjiang to their realm, making the Qing Empire comparable to the other multinational empires of the early modern world, such as the Ottoman, Russian, and Habsburg Empires.

Many historians have been attracted to research on the seventeenth and eighteenth centuries because it provides a baseline of traditional China before the rapid changes of the modern era. Besides the usual questions of why the Ming fell and the Qing succeeded, scholars have recently been asking questions about the Manchus themselves. Who were they, and how did their history shape the way they ruled China? How did they compel the allegiance of peoples of different backgrounds? How did they manage to give traditional Chinese political forms a new lease on life? Other historians have focused more on what was going on among the Chinese during these two crucial centuries. Was population growth a sign of prosperity? Or was it beginning to cause problems? How did scholars respond to Manchu rule?

THE MANCHUS

The Manchus were descended from the Jurchens, who had ruled north China during the Jin Dynasty (1127–1234). Although they had not maintained the written language that the Jin had created, they had maintained their hairstyle. A Manchu man shaved the front of his head and wore the rest of his hair in a long braid (called a queue). The language the Manchus spoke belongs to the Tungus family, making it close to some of the languages spoken in nearby Siberia and distantly related to Korean and Japanese.

During the Ming Dynasty, the Manchus had lived in dispersed communities in what is loosely called Manchuria (the modern provinces of Liaoning, Jilin, and Heilongjiang). In the more densely populated southern part of Manchuria, Manchus lived in close contact with Mongols, Koreans, and Chinese, the latter especially in the Ming prefecture of Liaodong (see Map 16.1). The Manchus were not nomads but rather hunters, fishers, and farmers. Like the Mongols, they had a tribal social structure and were excellent horsemen and archers. Also like the Mongols, their society was strongly hierarchical, with elites and slaves. Slaves, often Korean or Chinese, were generally acquired through capture. From the Mongols, the Manchus had adopted Lamaist Buddhism, originally from Tibet, and it coexisted with their native shamanistic religion. Manchu shamans were men or women who had experienced a spiritual death and rebirth and as a consequence could travel to and influence the world of the spirits.

Both the Chosŏn Dynasty in Korea and the Ming Dynasty in China welcomed diplomatic missions from Manchu chieftains, seeing them as a counterbalance to the Mongols. Written communication was frequently in Mongolian, the lingua franca of the region. Along the border with the Ming were officially approved markets where Manchus brought horses, furs, honey, and ginseng to exchange for Chinese tea, cotton, silk, rice, salt, and tools. By the 1580s, there were five such markets that convened monthly, and unofficial trade occurred as well.

The Manchus credited their own rise to Nurhaci (1559–1626), who in 1583 at age twenty-four became the leader of one group of Manchus. Over the next few decades, he was able to expand his territories, in the process not only uniting the Manchus but also creating a social-political-military organization that brought together Manchus, Mongols, and Chinese.

When the Korean Sin Chung-il traveled to Nurhaci's headquarters in 1595–1596, he encountered many small Jurchen settlements, most no larger than twenty households, supported by fishing, hunting for pelts, collecting pine nuts or ginseng, or growing crops such as wheat, millet, and barley. Villages were often at odds with each other over resources, and men did not leave their villages without arming themselves with bows and arrows or swords. Interspersed among these Manchu settlements were groups of nomadic Mongols who lived in yurts in open areas. Sin observed that Nurhaci had in his employ men from the Ming territory of Liaodong who could speak both Chinese and Manchu and could write in Chinese. Nurhaci's knowledge of China and Chinese ways was not entirely secondhand, however. In 1590, he had led an embassy to Beijing, and the next year he offered to join the Ming effort to repel the Japanese invasion of Korea. Nurhaci and his children married Mongols as well as Manchus, and these marriages cemented alliances.

Early Manchu Rulers and Their Reign Periods	
Nurhaci (Tianming)	1616–1626
Hong Taiji (Tiancong)	1627–1635
(Chongde)	1636–1643
Fulin (Shunzhi)	1644–1661
Xuanye (Kangxi)	1662–1722
Yinzhen (Yongzheng)	1723–1735
Hongli (Qianlong)	1736–1795

Like Chinggis, who had reorganized his armies to reduce the importance of tribal affiliations, Nurhaci created a new social basis for his armies in units called *banners*. Each banner was made up of a set of military companies but included the families and slaves of the soldiers as well. Each company had a captain whose position was hereditary. Many of the commanding officers were drawn from Nurhaci's own lineage. Over time new companies and new banners were formed, and by 1644 there were twenty-four banners (eight each Manchu, Mongol, and Chinese banners). When new groups of Manchus were defeated, they were distributed among several banners to lessen their potential for subversion.

In 1616, Nurhaci declared war on the Ming Empire by calling himself khan of the revived Jin Dynasty and listing his grievances against the Ming. In 1621 his forces overran Liaodong and incorporated it into

Map 16.1   Manchu Empire at Its Height

his state. After Nurhaci died in 1626, his son Hong Taiji succeeded him. In consolidating the Jin state, then centered on Mukden, Hong Taiji grudgingly made use of Chinese bureaucrats, but his goal was to replace them with a multiethnic elite equally competent in warfare and documents. In 1636, Hong Taiji renamed his state Qing ("pure"). When he died in 1643 at age forty-six, his brother Dorgon was made regent for his five-year-old son, Fulin, the Shunzhi emperor (r. 1643–1661).

The distinguished Ming general Wu Sangui (1612–1678), a native of Liaodong, was near the eastern end of the Great Wall when he heard that the rebel Li Zicheng had captured Beijing. Dorgon proposed to Wu that they join forces and liberate Beijing. Wu opened the gates of the Great Wall to let the Manchus in, and within a couple of weeks they had occupied Beijing. When the Manchus made clear that they intended to conquer the rest of the country and take the throne themselves, Wu joined forces with them, as did many other Chinese generals.

MING LOYALISM

When word of the fall of Beijing to the Manchus reached the Yangzi valley, Ming officials selected a Ming prince to succeed to the throne and shifted the capital to Nanjing, the Ming secondary capital. They were thus following the strategy that had allowed the Song Dynasty to continue to flourish after it had lost the north in 1126. The Ming court offered to buy off the Manchus, just as the Song had bought off the Jurchens. Dorgon, however, saw no need to check his ambitions. He sent Wu Sangui and several Manchu generals to pursue the rebel forces across north China. Li Zicheng was eliminated in 1645, Zhang Xianzhong in 1647.

At the same time, Qing forces set about trying to defeat the Ming forces in the south. Quite a few able officials joined the Ming cause, but leadership was not well coordinated. Shi Kefa, a scholar-official who had risen to minister of war in Nanjing, took charge of defense and stationed his army at Yangzhou. Many other generals, however, defected to the Manchu side, and their soldiers were incorporated into the Qing armies. As the Qing forces moved south, many local officials opened the gates of their cities and surrendered. Shi Kefa refused to surrender Yangzhou, and a five-day battle ensued. The Manchu general was so angered at Shi's resistance that he unleashed his army to take revenge on the city, slaughtering hundreds of thousands. As cities in the south fell, large numbers of Ming loyalists committed suicide, their wives, mothers, and daughters frequently joining them.

In the summer of 1645, the Manchu command ordered all Chinese serving in its armies to shave the front of their heads in the Manchu fashion, presumably to make it easier to recognize which side they were on. Soon this order was extended to all Chinese men, a measure that aroused deep resentment and made it easier for the Ming loyalists to organize resistance. When those newly conquered by the Qing refused to shave their hair, Manchu commanders felt justified in ordering the slaughter of defiant cities such as Jiading, Changshu, and Jiangyin. Still, Ming loyalist resistance continued long after little hope remained. The Manchus did not defeat the two main camps until 1661–1662, and even then Zheng Chenggong (Koxinga) was able to hold out in Taiwan until 1683.

Ming loyalism also took less militant forms. Several leading thinkers of this period had time to think and write because they refused to serve the Qing. Their critiques of the Ming and its failings led to searching inquiries into China's heritage of dynastic rule. Huang Zongxi (1610–1695) served the Ming resistance court at Nanjing and followed it when it had to retreat, but after 1649 he lived in retirement at his home in Zhejiang province. The Manchu conquest was so traumatic an event that he reconsidered many of the basic tenets of Chinese political order. He came to the conclusion that the Ming's problems were not minor ones like inadequate supervision of eunuchs but much more major ones, such as the imperial institution itself.

Gu Yanwu (1613–1682) participated in the defense of his native city, then watched his mother starve herself rather than live under Manchu rule. He traveled across north China in search of a better understanding of Ming weaknesses, looking into economic topics Confucian scholars had rarely studied in depth, such as banking, mining, and farming. He had only disdain for scholars who wasted their time on empty speculation or literary elegance when there were so many practical problems awaiting solution. He thought that the Ming had suffered from overcentralization and advocated greater local autonomy.

A third example is Wang Fuzhi (1619–1692). He had passed the provincial exams under the Ming, but marauding rebels made it impossible for him to get to Beijing to take the *jinshi* exams in 1642. After Beijing fell to the Manchus two years later, Wang joined the resistance. He raised troops in his native Hunan province and held a minor post at the court of the Ming pretender for a while, but he fell victim to factional strife and in 1650 withdrew to live as a retired scholar. Wang saw an urgent need not only to return Confucianism to its roots, but also to protect Chinese civilization from the "barbarians." He insisted that it was as important to distinguish Chinese from barbarians as it was to distinguish superior men from petty men. It is natural for rulers to protect their followers from intruders: "Now even the ants have rulers who preside over the territory of their nests, and when red ants or flying white ants penetrate their gates, the ruler organizes all his own kind into troops to bite and kill the intruders, drive them far away from the anthill, and prevent foreign interference."[1] The Ming rulers had failed in this basic responsibility.

THE QING AT ITS HEIGHT

For more than a century, China was ruled by just three rulers, each of whom was hard working, talented, and committed to making the Qing Dynasty a success. The policies and institutions they put in place gave China a respite from war and disorder, and the Chinese population seems to have nearly doubled during this period, from between 150 and 175 million to between 300 and 325 million. Population growth during the course of the eighteenth century has been attributed to many factors: global warming that extended the growing season; expanded use of New World crops; slowing of the spread of new diseases that had accompanied the sixteenth-century expansion of global traffic; and the efficiency of the

---

1. W. Theodore de Bary and Richard Lufrano, *Sources of Chinese Tradition from 1600 Through the Twentieth Century* (New York: Columbia University Press, 2000), p. 35.

Dinnerware. China turned out enormous quantities of plates, cups, and other dishes for export to Western countries. This set, made in the 1780s, includes cups for both tea and coffee. The design on the dishes would have been specially ordered by the importer. *(Metropolitan Museum of Art, Bequest of James Woodward, 1910. Photograph © 2002 The Metropolitan Museum of Art.)*

Qing government in providing relief in times of famine. Some scholars have recently argued that China's overall standard of living in the mid-eighteenth century was comparable to Europe's and that the standards of China's most developed regions, such as the Jiangnan region, compared favorably to the most developed regions of Europe at the time, such as England and the Netherlands. Life expectancy, food consumption, and even facilities for transportation were at similar levels (see **Biography: Jiang Chun, Salt Merchant**).

Kangxi

After the Shunzhi emperor died of smallpox (which struck many Manchus after they settled in Beijing), one of his sons who had already survived the disease was selected to succeed him. Known as the Kangxi emperor (r. 1661–1722), he lived to see the Qing Empire firmly established.

The Kangxi emperor proved adept at meeting the expectations of both the Chinese and Manchu elites. At age fourteen, he announced that he would begin ruling on his own and had his regent imprisoned. He could speak, read, and write Chinese and appreciated the value of persuading educated Chinese that the Manchus had a legitimate claim to the Mandate of Heaven. Most of the political institutions of the Ming Dynasty had been taken over relatively unchanged, including the examination system, and the Kangxi emperor worked to attract Ming loyalists who had been unwilling to serve the Qing. He undertook a series of tours of the south, where resistance had been strongest, and held a special exam to select men to compile the official history of the Ming Dynasty.

The main military challenge the Kangxi emperor faced was the revolt of Wu Sangui and two other Chinese generals who in the early years of the conquest had been given vast tracts of land in the south as rewards for joining the Qing. Wu was made, in effect, satrap of Yunnan and Guizhou, and it was his armies that had pursued the last Ming pretender into Burma. When the Qing began to curb the power of these generals in 1673, Wu declared himself the ruler of an independent state, and the other two "feudatories" joined him. The south was not yet fully reconciled to Qing rule, but Wu, as a turncoat himself, did not attract a large following. Although it took eight years, the military structure that the Qing had put together proved strong enough to defeat this challenge. At the conclusion of these campaigns, Taiwan, where the last of the Ming loyalists had held out, was made part of Fujian province, fully incorporating it into China proper.

By annexing Mongolia, the Kangxi emperor made sure the Qing Dynasty would not have the northern border problems the Ming had faced (see Map 16.1). In 1696 he led an army of eighty thousand men into Mongolia, and within a few years Manchu supremacy was accepted there. Qing forces were equipped with cannons and muskets, giving them military superiority over the Mongols, who were armed with bows and arrows only. They thus could dominate the steppe cheaply, effectively ending two thousand years of northern border defense problems.

The Qing also asserted its presence in Tibet. This came about after a group of Western Mongols tried to find a new place for themselves in Tibet. The army the Qing sent after them occupied Lhasa in 1718. In the 1720s, the Qing presence in Tibet was made firm with the establishment of a permanent garrison of banner soldiers. By this time, the Qing Empire was coming into proximity of the expanding Russian

BIOGRAPHY Jiang Chun, Salt Merchant

Jiang Chun's (1725–1793) family originally came from Huizhou in Anhui, a place famous for its merchant families. His great-great-grandfather moved to Yangzhou to enter the salt trade centered there. Salt was a special commodity, as the government claimed a monopoly over it and licensed merchants to transport and sell it. Salt merchants could grow exceptionally rich; it has been estimated that the twenty to thirty head merchants could pocket 50,000 to 100,000 taels of silver a year from the salt business alone. Government connections made possible the great wealth of the salt merchants, and the government regularly called on them to contribute huge sums for disaster relief, repair of the waterworks, or visits of the emperor.

As the Jiang family grew rich, many of its men pursued scholarly or official careers (often gaining positions through purchase, a legal but less prestigious route). But in each generation one man, like Jiang Chun, served as one of the head salt merchants. Although there are several biographical sketches of Jiang Chun, they say little about him as a merchant. Rather they concentrate on his social life; his accomplishments in poetry, archery, and cricket-raising; and the honors he received.

A description of the great sites of Yangzhou written in 1795 provides an elaborate description of Jiang Chun's garden, naming its halls, ponds, towers, terraces, and so on. Besides discussing Jiang and his talented kinsmen, the author added notes on thirty-nine men of talent in his entourage, including scholars, painters, poets, calligraphers, physicians, musicians, connoisseurs able to authenticate antiquities, craftsmen-painters good at portraits, gardeners expert in pruning plum trees, and the architects who had designed the buildings in his garden. Some were relatives through marriage. Others had lived in different buildings of his estate for years, sometimes decades. Jiang is also said to have kept two opera troupes, one that specialized in Kunqu, the other in Huapu, which was performed in the local Yangzhou accent. His Kunqu troupe was said to be one of the "seven great troupes of Yangzhou." Jiang once organized an archery contest in his

Garden of Pure Fragrance. The prominent courtesan Su Gaosen was among the guests and scored three bull's-eyes in a row, an event other guests celebrated in poems.

The Qianlong emperor made six visits to Yangzhou on his "southern tours of inspection" (1751, 1757, 1762, 1765, 1780, and 1784). Jiang met him every time, and during the last four visits, Jiang hosted the imperial party at one or both of his famous gardens. In fact, the name "Garden of Pure Fragrance" was chosen by Qianlong. The emperor wrote out the three characters of the name, which Jiang then had carved in stone and placed in a special pavilion. On one of his visits, Qianlong put Jiang's seven-year-old son on his lap, patted his head, and took off an ornamental purse and gave it to the boy, which Jiang's biographer Yuan Mei considered an exceptional honor. In 1765, Qianlong gave Jiang Chun four sable skin pelts and two ornamental silk pouches. Jiang Chun's thank you note has been preserved in the archives. Qianlong must have had some discussions of practical matters with Jiang Chun, as he once told the new director-general handling transport of tax grain to consult the experienced and knowledgeable Jiang Chun if he needed any advice.

In 1768 the top salt administration officials were accused of gross embezzlement and cashiered. Jiang Chun, like the other salt merchants, had to go to the capital to testify during the investigation. Qianlong, Yuan Mei tells us, was impressed by Jiang Chun's demeanor and made sure that the charges against him were dismissed. Nevertheless, by 1771, Jiang was out of money. Qianlong, we are told, personally lent him 500,000 taels as working capital (to be repaid with 10 percent annual interest).

None of Jiang Chun's boys or girls lived to adulthood. He adopted his brother's son, but that boy also died young. When Chun was on his deathbed at age sixty-nine, he selected another nephew to succeed him. After Jiang Chun died, on Qianlong's suggestion, the Yangzhou salt merchants purchased his famous garden to use as a clubhouse. The 50,000 taels they paid for the garden became his adopted son's main source of income.

Empire. In 1689 the Manchu and the Russian rulers approved a treaty—written in Russian, Manchu, Chinese, and Latin—defining their borders in Manchuria and regulating trade. Another treaty in 1727 allowed a Russian ecclesiastical mission to reside in Beijing and a caravan to make a trip from Russia to Beijing once every three years. The Russians were especially interested in securing a steady supply of tea.

The Kangxi emperor took a personal interest in the European Jesuit priests who served at court as astronomers and cartographers and translated many European works into Chinese. However, when the pope sided with the Dominican and Franciscan orders in China who opposed allowing converts to maintain ancestral altars (known as the "rites controversy"), he objected strongly to the pope's issuing directives about how Chinese should behave. He outlawed Christian missionaries, though he did allow Jesuit scientists and painters to remain in Beijing.

The Kangxi emperor's heir, Yinzheng, ruled for twelve years as the Yongzheng emperor (r. 1723–1735), taking the throne when he was forty-five years old. A hard-working ruler, he tightened central control over the government. He oversaw a rationalization of the tax structure, substituting new levies for a patchwork of taxes and fees.

Qianlong

The Yongzheng emperor's heir, Hongli, the Qianlong emperor (r. 1736–1795), benefited from his father's fiscal reforms, and during his reign, the Qing government regularly ran surpluses. It was during the Qianlong reign that the Qing Empire was expanded to its maximum extent, with the addition of Chinese Turkestan (the modern province of Xinjiang). Both the Han and Tang Dynasties had stationed troops in the region, exercising a loose suzerainty, but neither Song nor Ming had tried to control the area. The Qing won the region in the 1750s through a series of campaigns against Uighur and Dzungar Mongol forces. Like Tibet, loosely annexed a few decades earlier, this region was ruled lightly. The local population kept their own religious leaders and did not have to wear the queue.

The Qianlong emperor put much of his energy into impressing his subjects with his magnificence. He understood that the Qing capacity to hold the empire together rested on their ability to speak in the political and religious idioms of those they ruled. Besides Manchu and Chinese, he learned to converse in Mongolian, Uighur, Tibetan, and Tangut and addressed envoys in their own languages. He was as much a patron of Lamaist Buddhism as of Chinese Confucianism. He initiated a massive project to translate the Tibetan Buddhist canon into Mongolian and Manchu. He also had huge multilingual dictionaries compiled. He had the child Dalai Lamas raised and educated in Beijing. He made much of the Buddhist notion of the "wheel-turning king" (cakravartin), the ruler who through his conquests moves the world toward the next stage in universal salvation (see Color Plate 20).

To demonstrate to the Chinese scholar-official elite that he was a sage emperor, Qianlong worked on affairs of state from dawn until early afternoon, when he turned to reading, painting, and calligraphy. He took credit for writing over forty-two thousand poems and ninety-two books of prose. He inscribed his own poetry on hundreds of masterpieces of Chinese painting and calligraphy that he had gathered into the palace collections. He especially liked works of fine craftsmanship, and his taste influenced artistic styles of the day. The Qianlong emperor was ostentatiously devoted to his mother, visiting her daily and tending to her comfort with all the devotion of the most filial Chinese son. He took several tours down the Grand Canal to the Jiangnan area, in part to emulate his grandfather and in part to entertain his mother. Many of his gestures were costly. His southern tours cost ten times what the Kangxi emperor's had and included the construction of temporary palaces and triumphal arches.

For all of these displays of Chinese virtues, the Qianlong emperor still was not fully confident that the Chinese supported his rule, and he was quick to act on any suspicion of anti-Manchu thoughts or actions (see **Documents: Fang Bao's "Random Notes from Prison"**). After more than thirty years on the throne, when rumors reached the Qianlong emperor that sorcerers were "stealing souls" by clipping the ends of men's queues, he suspected a seditious plot and had his officials interrogate men under torture until they found more and more evidence of a nonexistent plot. A few years after that episode, the Qianlong emperor carried out a huge literary inquisition. During the compilation of the *Complete Books of the Four Treasuries*, an effort to catalogue nearly all books in China, he began to suspect that some governors were holding back books with seditious content. He ordered full searches for books with disparaging references to the Manchus or previous alien conquerors. Sometimes passages were omitted or rewritten, but when the entire book was offensive, it was destroyed. So thorough was the proscription that no copies survive of more than two thousand titles.

The Qianlong emperor lived into his eighties, but his political judgment began to decline in his sixties when he began to favor a handsome and intelligent young imperial bodyguard named Heshen. Heshen was rapidly promoted to posts normally held by experienced civil officials, including posts with power over revenue and civil service appointments. When the emperor did nothing to stop Heshen's blatant corruption, officials began to worry that he was becoming senile. By this time, uprisings in several parts of the country were proving difficult to suppress. Heshen supplied the Qianlong emperor with rosy reports of the progress in suppressing the rebellions, all the while pocketing much of the military appropriations himself.

The Qianlong emperor abdicated in 1795 in order not to rule longer than his grandfather, the Kangxi emperor, but he continued to dominate court until he died in 1799 at age eighty-nine.

The Banner System

The Kangxi, Yongzheng, and Qianlong emperors used the banner system to maintain military control and preserve the Manchus' privileges. In the first few decades of the Qing, as the country was pacified, banner forces were settled across China in garrisons, usually within the walls of a city. All the Chinese who lived in the northern half of Beijing were forced out to clear the area for bannermen, and Beijing became very much a Manchu city. In other major cities, such as Hangzhou, Nanjing, Xi'an, and Taiyuan, large sections were cleared for the banners' use. The bannermen became in a sense a hereditary occupational caste, ranked above others in society, whose members were expected to devote themselves to service to the state. They were also expected to live apart from nonbanner Chinese and were not allowed to intermarry with them.

Outside the cities, lands were expropriated to provide support for the garrisons, some 2 million acres altogether, with the densest area in the region around Beijing. In China proper, bannermen did not cultivate the fields (as they had in Manchuria) but rather lived off stipends from the rents, paid part in silver and part in grain. The dynasty supported banner soldiers and their families from cradle to grave, with special allocations for travel, weddings, and funerals. Once the conquest was complete, the banner popu-

Imperial Bodyguard Zhanyinbao. Dated 1760, this life-size portrait was done by a court artist in the European-influenced style favored by the Qianlong emperor. *(The Metropolitan Museum of Art, The Dillon Fund, 1986 [1986.206])*

lation grew faster than the need for soldiers, so within a couple of generations, there were not enough positions in the banner armies for all adult males in the banners. Yet bannermen were not allowed to pursue occupations other than soldier or official. As a consequence, many led lives of forced idleness, surviving on stipends paid to relatives. By the time of the Qianlong emperor, this had become enough of a problem that he had most of the Chinese bannermen removed from the banner system and reclassified as commoners, increasing the Manchu dominance of the banner population.

Bannermen had facilitated entry into government service. Special quotas for Manchus allowed them to gain more than 5 percent of the *jinshi* degrees, even though they never exceeded 1 percent of the population. Advancement was also easier for bannermen, since many posts, especially in Beijing, were reserved for them, including half of all the top posts. In the

DOCUMENTS

Fang Bao's "Random Notes from Prison"

As more and more varied types of sources survive, it becomes possible to get better glimpses of the less pleasant sides of life. The ordeal of judicial confinement was hardly new to the eighteenth century, but it was not until then that we have so vivid a depiction of it as that provided by Fang Bao (1668–1749). In 1711 he and his family members were arrested because he had written a preface for the collected works of one of his friends whose works had just been condemned for language implying support for revival of the Ming Dynasty. After Fang spent two years in prison, he was pardoned and went on to hold a series of literary posts. Despite this brush with imperial censorship, Fang was willing in his account of his time in prison to point to the inhumane way people not yet found guilty of a crime were treated and the corruption of prison personnel, who demanded cash in exchange for better treatment.

In the prison there were four old cells. Each cell had five rooms. The jail guards lived in the center with a window in the front of their quarters for light. At the end of this room there was another opening for ventilation. There were no such windows for the other four rooms and yet more than two hundred prisoners were always confined there. Each day toward dusk, the cells were locked and the odor of the urine and excrement would mingle with that of the food and drink. Moreover, in the coldest months of the winter, the poor prisoners had to sleep on the ground and when the spring breezes came everyone got sick. The established rule in the prison was that the door would be unlocked only at dawn. During the night, the living and the dead slept side by side with no room to turn their bodies and this is why so many people became infected. Even more terrible was that robbers, veteran criminals and murderers who were imprisoned for serious offenses had strong constitutions and only one or two out of ten would be infected and even so they would recover immediately. Those who died from the malady were all light offenders or sequestered witnesses who would not normally be subjected to legal penalties.

I said: "In the capital there are the metropolitan prefectural prison and the censorial prisons of the five wards. How is it then that the Board of Punishment's prison has so many prisoners?" [My fellow prisoner, the

middle and lower ranks of the Beijing bureaucracy, Manchus greatly outnumbered Chinese. One study suggests that about 70 percent of the metropolitan agencies' positions were reserved for bannermen and less then 20 percent for Chinese (the rest were unspecified). In the provinces, Manchus did not dominate in the same way, except at the top level of governors and governors-general, where they held about half the posts.

Bannermen had legal privileges as well. They fell under the jurisdiction of imperial commissioners, not the local magistrate or prefect. If both a Chinese and a Manchu were brought into court to testify, the Chinese was required to kneel before the magistrate, but the Manchu could stand. If each was found guilty of the same crime, the Manchu would receive a lighter punishment—for instance, wearing the cangue (a large wooden collar) for sixty days instead of being exiled for life.

Despite the many privileges given to Manchu bannermen, impoverishment of the banner population quickly became a problem. Although the government from time to time forgave all bannermen's debts, many went bankrupt. Company commanders sometimes sold off banner land to provide stipends, which made it more difficult to provide support thereafter. The Qianlong emperor also tried resettling Manchus back in Manchuria, but those used to urban life in China rarely were willing to return to farming, and most sneaked back as soon as possible.

magistrate] Mr. Du answered: ". . . The chiefs and deputy heads of the Fourteen Bureaus like to get new prisoners; the clerks, prison officials, and guards all benefit from having so many prisoners. If there is the slightest pretext or connection they use every method to trap new prisoners. Once someone is put into the prison his guilt or innocence does not matter. The prisoner's hands and feet are shackled and he is put in one of the old cells until he can bear the suffering no more. Then he is led to obtain bail and permitted to live outside the jail. His family's property is assessed to decide the payment and the officials and clerks all split it. Middling households and those just above exhaust their wealth to get bail. Those families somewhat less wealthy seek to have the shackles removed and to obtain lodging [for the prisoner relative] in the custody sheds outside the jail. This also costs tens of silver taels. As for the poorest prisoners or those with no one to rely on, their shackles are not loosened at all and they are used as examples to warn others. Sometimes cellmates guilty of serious crimes are bailed out but those guilty of small crimes and the innocent suffer the most poisonous abuse. They store up their anger and indignation, fail to eat or sleep normally, are not treated with medicine, and when they get sick they often die.

"I have humbly witnessed our Emperor's virtuous love for all beings which is as great as that of the sages of the past ages. Whenever he examines the documents related to a case, he tries to find life for those who should die. But now it has come to this [state of affairs] for the innocent. A virtuous gentleman might save many lives if he were to speak to the Emperor saying: 'Leaving aside those prisoners sentenced to death or exiled to border regions for great crimes, should not small offenders and those involved in a case but not convicted be placed in a separate place without chaining their hands and feet?'". . .

My cellmate Old Zhu, Young Yu, and a certain government official named Seng who all died of illness in prison should not have been heavily punished. There was also a certain person who accused his own son of unfiliality. The [father's] neighbors [involved in the case only as witnesses] were all chained and imprisoned in the old cells. They cried all night long. I was moved by this and so I made inquiries. Everyone corroborated this account and so I am writing this document.

———
Source: From Pei-kai Cheng, Michael Lestz, and Jonathon D. Spence, *The Search for Modern China: A Documentary Collection* (New York: Norton, 1999), pp. 55–58, slightly modified.

Within a generation of settling in China proper, the banner population were using the Chinese dialect of the Beijing area as their common language. The Qing emperors repeatedly called on the Manchus to study both spoken and written Manchu, but it became a second language learned at school rather than a primary language. Other features of Manchu culture were more easily preserved, such as the use of personal names alone to refer to people. (Manchus had names for families and clans but did not use them as part of their personal names.)

The elements of Manchu culture most important to the state were their martial traditions and their skill as horsemen and archers. Life in the cities and long stretches of peace took a toll on these skills, despite the best efforts of the emperors to inspire martial spirit. The Qianlong emperor himself was fully literate in Chinese, but he discouraged the Manchu bannermen from developing interests in Chinese culture. He knew the history of the Jin Dynasty and the problems the Jurchens had faced with soldiers living in China taking up Chinese ways, and he did everything he could think of to prevent this. Although the Qing court was as opulent as any other in Chinese history, the emperor tried to convince the bannermen that frugality was a Manchu characteristic, to be maintained if they were not to lose their ethnic identity.

Perhaps because they were favored in so many ways, the bannermen proved a very loyal service elite. Unlike their counterparts in other large empires, the banner armies never turned on the ruling house or used the resources that had been assigned to them to challenge central authority.

CONTACTS WITH EUROPE

The Qing regulated its relations with countries beyond its borders through a diplomatic system modeled on the Ming one. Countries like Korea, Ryukyu, Japan, Vietnam, and many of the other states of Southeast Asia sent envoys to the court at Beijing. Europeans were not full players in this system, but they had a marginal presence.

Trading contacts with Europe were concentrated at Guangzhou in the far south (see **Connection: Europe Enters the Scene**). Soon after 1600, the Dutch East India Company had largely dislodged the Spanish and Portuguese from the trade with China, Japan, and the East Indies. Before long, the British East India Company began to compete with the Dutch for the spice trade. In the seventeenth century, the British and Dutch sought primarily porcelains and silk, but in the eighteenth century, tea became the commodity in most demand. By the end of the century, tea made up 80 percent of Chinese exports to Europe.

In the early eighteenth century, China enjoyed a positive reputation among the educated in Europe. China was the source of prized luxuries: tea, silk, porcelain, cloisonné, wallpaper, and folding fans. The Manchu emperors were seen as wise and benevolent rulers. Voltaire wrote of the rationalism of Confucianism and saw advantages to the Chinese political system as rulers did not put up with parasitical aristocrats or hypocritical priests.

By the end of the eighteenth century, British merchants were dissatisfied with the restrictions imposed on trade by the Qing government. The Qing, like the Ming before it, specified where merchants of particular countries could trade, and the Europeans were to trade only in Guangzhou, even though tea was grown mostly in the Yangzi valley, adding the cost of transporting it south to the price the foreign merchants had to pay. The merchants in Guangzhou who dealt with Western merchants formed their own guild, and the Qing government made them guarantee that the European merchants obeyed Qing rules. In the system as it evolved, the Europeans had to pay cash for goods purchased and were forbidden to enter the walled city of Guangzhou, ride in sedan chairs, bring women or weapons into their quarters, and learn Chinese.

As British purchases of tea escalated, the balance of trade became more lopsided, but British merchants could not find goods Chinese merchants would buy from them. The British government also was dissatisfied. It was becoming suspicious of the British East India Company, which had made great fortunes from its trade with China, and wanted to open direct diplomatic relations with China in part as a way to curb the company. To accomplish all this, King George III sent Lord George Macartney, the former ambassador to Russia and former governor of Madras, to China. Macartney was instructed to secure a place for British traders near the tea-producing areas, negotiate a commercial treaty, create a desire for British products, arrange for diplomatic representation in Beijing, and open Japan and Southeast Asia to British commerce as well. He traveled with an entourage of eighty-four and six hundred cases packed with British goods that he hoped would impress the Chinese court and attract trade: clocks, telescopes, knives, globes, plate glass, Wedgwood pottery, landscape paintings, woolen cloth, and carpets. The only member of the British party able to speak Chinese, however, was a twelve-year-old boy who had learned some Chinese by talking with Chinese on the long voyage.

After Lord Macartney arrived in Guangzhou in 1793, he requested permission to see the emperor in order to present a letter to him from George III. Although the letter had been written in Chinese, its language was not appropriate for addressing an emperor. Still, the British party was eventually allowed to proceed to Beijing. Once there, another obstacle emerged: when instructed on how to behave on seeing the emperor, Macartney objected to having to perform the kowtow (kneeling on both knees and bowing his head to the ground).

Finally Macartney was permitted to meet more informally with the Qianlong emperor at his summer retreat. No negotiations followed this meeting, however, as the Qing court saw no merit in Macartney's requests. It was as interested in maintaining its existing system of regulated trade as Britain was interested in doing away with it.

Several members of the Macartney mission wrote books about China on their return. These books, often illustrated, contained descriptions of many elements of Chinese culture and social customs, less rosy than the reports of the Jesuits a century or two earlier. The official account of the embassy, prepared by George

Staunton, depicted Chinese women as subjugated: "Women, especially in the lower walks of life, are bred with little other principle than that of implicit obedience to their fathers or their husbands." Although the wives of the peasantry worked very hard at domestic tasks and did all the weaving in the country, they were treated badly: "Not withstanding all the merit of these helpmates to their husbands, the latter arrogate an extraordinary dominion over them, and hold them at such distance, as not always to allow them to sit at table, behind which, in such case, they attend as handmaids."[2] From books like these, Europeans began to see more of the complexity of China. The Chinese, by contrast, did not learn much about Europe or Britain from this encounter.

SOCIAL AND CULTURAL CROSSCURRENTS

During the late Ming, Chinese culture had been remarkably open and fluid. Especially in the cities of Jiangnan, new books of all sorts were being published; the theater flourished; and intellectuals took an interest in ideas of Buddhist, Daoist, or even European origin and, encouraged by Wang Yangming's teachings, pursued truth in individualistic ways.

The Conservative Turn

With the collapse of the social order in the early seventeenth century and the conquest by the Manchus, many Confucian scholars concluded that the Ming fell as a result of moral laxity. Wang Yangming and his followers, by validating emotion and spontaneity, had undermined commitment to duty and respect for authority. The solution, many thought, was to return to Zhu Xi's teachings, with their emphasis on objective standards outside the individual.

This conservative turn was manifested in several ways. Laws against homosexuality were made harsher. Because literati argued that drama and fiction were socially subversive, theaters were closed and novels banned. Qian Daxian, a highly learned scholar, went so far as to argue that the vernacular novel was the main threat to Confucian orthodoxy. The cult of widow

chastity reached new heights, with local histories recording more and more widows who refused to remarry, including those who lived their entire lives as the celibate "widows" of men to whom they had been engaged but who had died before they had even met.

The conservative turn in scholarship fostered a new interest in rigorous textual analysis. Some Confucian scholars turned back to the Han commentaries on the classics, hoping that they could free their understandings of the texts from the contamination of Buddhist and Daoist ideas that had infiltrated Tang and Song commentaries. Others wanted to rely solely on the classics themselves and to concentrate on verifiable facts. Yan Ruoju compiled a guide to the place names in the Four Books and proved that the "old text" version of the *Book of Documents* could not be genuine. Research of this sort required access to large libraries, and it thrived primarily in Jiangnan, with its high densities of both books and scholars.

There are always those who resist calls for decorum and strenuous moral effort, and in the eighteenth century, both the Manchu rulers and the Chinese intellectual elite provided room for the less conventional to contribute in creative ways. Exploration of the potential of ink painting for self-expression reached a high point in the eighteenth century with a closely affiliated group of painters known as the Eight Eccentrics of Yangzhou (see **Material Culture: Jin Nong's Inscribed Portrait of a Buddhist Monk**). These painters had no difficulty finding patrons, even among social and cultural conservatives. Similarly, Yuan Mei, on familiar terms with the great classicists and philologists of his day, was willing to risk their censure by taking on women as poetry students. One of his female poetry students, Luo Qilan, wrote in 1797 to defend him from charges of impropriety, arguing that if Confucius had believed in the principle that women's words spoken inside a chamber must stay indoors, he would have removed poems by women from the *Book of Poetry*.

The Dream of Red Mansions

Women with poetic talents figure prominently in an eighteenth-century novel, *The Dream of Red Mansions* (also called *Story of the Stone*), considered by many the most successful of all works of Chinese fiction. Concerned with the grand themes of love and desire, money and power, life and death, and truth and illusion, it is at the same time a psychologically sensitive novel of manners. The author of the first eighty chapters was Cao Xueqin (1715–1764). He

---

2. George Staunton, *An Authentic Account of an Embassy from the King of Great Britain to the Emperor of China* (London: W. Bulmer, 1798), 2:109.

MATERIAL CULTURE

Jin Nong's Inscribed Portrait of a Buddhist Monk

Chinese painters often combined words and images, sometimes inscribing poems or explanations of the occasions that gave rise to the paintings on the paintings themselves. The highly individualistic painters of the eighteenth century known as the Eight Eccentrics of Yangzhou sometimes carried this practice to the extreme, filling all the space on a painting with their writing. The painting shown here, by Jin Nong (1687–1764), is dated 1760. Writing in his highly distinctive calligraphy, Jin Nong fills the space around the Buddha with a history of the painting of images of Buddhas followed by personal remarks:

> I am now a man beyond seventy years of age who has no false ideas and desires. Though physically I am in the dusty world, I earnestly try to live cleanly. I wash my ten fingers, burn incense, and hold the brush to record the dignity and seriousness of humanity. What I do is not far from the ancient tradition. I offer good wishes to all men on earth.
>
> In the second lunar month, 1760, on the date when Buddha achieved enlightenment, I painted several Buddha images, four Bodhisattvas, sixteen Lohans, and distributed these sacred materials. These works are the product of my deep conviction, not in the style of famous masters of the Jin and Tang. My inspiration came from the Longmen caves that were carved a thousand years ago. When my priest friend, Defeng commented, "These paintings found [a new school] and will be followed by the coming generations," I roared with laughter.[3]

Portrait of a Monk. This hanging scroll, painted by Jin Nong in 1760 in ink and colors on paper, measures 133 by 62.5 cm. *(Collection of the Tianjin History Museum)*

3. Tseng Yuho, trans., *A History of Chinese Calligraphy* (Hong Kong: University of Hong Kong Press, 1993), p. 94, slightly modified.

died before the novel was completed, but another writer added forty chapters to complete it before it was published in 1791. Cao Xueqin came from a Chinese family that had risen with the Manchus. As bondservants of the ruling house, his family was in a position to gain great wealth and power managing enterprises for the rulers. In the eighteenth century, however, the family lost favor and went bankrupt.

The *Dream* portrays in magnificent detail the affairs of the comparably wealthy Jia family. The central characters of the novel are three adolescents: Jia Baoyu and his two female cousins of other surnames who come to live with his family. One of the cousins, Lin Daiyu, is sickly and difficult; the other, Xue Baochai, is capable and cheerful. A magnificent garden is built in the family compound in order to receive a visit from Baoyu's sister, who had become an imperial consort. After the visit, Baoyu, his cousins, and their personal servants move into the garden, an idyllic world of youth and beauty. This magical period comes to an end when Baoyu is tricked into marrying Baochai (thinking he is marrying Daiyu). While the wedding is taking place, Daiyu is on her sickbed, dying of consumption. The novel ends with Baoyu passing the *jinshi* examinations, only to leave his wife and family to pursue religious goals.

Much of the power of *Dream* comes from the many subplots and the host of minor characters from all walks of life—officials, aristocrats, monks and nuns, pageboys, gardeners, country relatives, princes, gamblers, prostitutes, actors, and innkeepers. The seamier side of political life is portrayed through memorable cases of abuse of power. The machinations of family politics are just as vividly captured through numerous incidents in which family members compete for advantage. The maids in the family are often unable to keep the lustful men away, in the process attracting the anger of the men's wives. A concubine of Baoyu's father plots demon possession against both Baoyu and his sister-in-law, the household manager Xifeng. One of Baoyu's mother's maids commits suicide after Baoyu flirts with her. This incident, coupled with Baoyu's dalliance with an actor, provokes his father into administering a severe beating.

At one point Baochai notices that Daiyu has unconsciously quoted a line from a play. She then confesses that since she was seven or eight, she and the other children in her family had read plays:

> All of us younger people hated serious books but liked reading poetry and plays. The boys had got lots and lots of plays: The Western Chamber, The Lute-Player, A Hundred Yuan Plays—*just about everything you could think of. They used to read them behind our backs, and we girls used to read them behind theirs. Eventually the grown-ups got to know about it and then there were beatings and lectures and burnings of books—and that was the end of that.*[4]

---

4. Cao Xueqin, *The Story of the Stone*, vol. 2, trans. David Hawkes (New York: Penguin Books, 1977), p. 333.

THE LESS ADVANTAGED AND THE DISAFFECTED

The eighteenth century is considered one of the most prosperous periods in Chinese history, when the government frequently ran a surplus and the population grew rapidly. General prosperity, however, did not mean that everyone benefited equally or that conflict and strife disappeared.

Qing China was both huge and economically diverse. Regions varied in density of population, types of crops grown, extent of trade, and so on. The most advanced area, with the highest level of wealth and commercial development, is generally referred to as the Jiangnan ("south of the Yangzi River") region or sometimes just as "the south." In that region, cultivation was intensive, and farmers often sold much of what they grew. It was common for cultivators to rent land from absentee landlords for fixed cash amounts, agreed to in written contracts. In north China, in most places a majority of the farmers owned their own land, but their farms were often tiny, and they might well be no richer than tenant farmers in the south. There were also differences within regions between core areas centered on major cities and more peripheral areas, where population density was much lower because the land was harder to farm. During the course of the eighteenth century, as population grew, people pushed into these peripheral areas, clearing upland areas and moving to the frontiers, in the process often pushing out aboriginal peoples who had lived in the area for centuries. New World crops, such as sweet potatoes, white potatoes, peanuts, and tobacco, made possible exploitation of land previously rejected as too hilly or infertile.

Villages all across China were "open," not closed corporate villages like in Japan (see Chapter 17). That is, villages held no land in common and had little say in who could buy or sell land or houses there. Because small farmers could easily fall into debt and sell or mortgage all or part of their land, village families could vary markedly in wealth. Families whose land was not adequate for their support often put effort into sideline work—their women and children weaving mats and baskets, for instance. During the winter, when there was little work to be done in the fields, the men might go into nearby towns to look for temporary jobs.

In some parts of the country, single-surname villages were common, with all males descended from a common patrilineal ancestor who had settled in the area centuries earlier. In those cases, village organization and lineage organization would overlap, with the lineage ancestral hall serving as the center of village life. In villages or clusters of villages where families with several surnames lived, the temple to a local god often served as the focus for communal activities.

Villages were connected to each other through marriages and marketing. Villagers normally married people from another village, so their mother's brothers and sisters and their father's sisters would reside in other local villages. Men and boys made regular trips to market towns, sometimes several hours away by foot, in order to sell agricultural surplus and buy needed tools or foodstuffs such as salt and oil. Farmers also needed to cooperate across village lines in order to maintain water-control systems, whether the diking of rivers prone to flooding or the diverting of water into irrigation canals or reservoirs. For projects of this sort, the local village heads might get together, or each village might be represented by several of its larger landowners. Written agreements would be drawn up recording what the different parties had pledged to do. When one party thought another was diverting more water than agreed, a complaint could be taken to the county magistrate to adjudicate.

By Qing times, there was relatively little in the way of legal status distinctions among the rural population. Slavery was insignificant (a contrast with Korea), and there were no nationwide outcast groups (a contrast with Japan). But that does not mean that there was no discrimination. In certain localities, particular groups might be treated as lower than commoners—such as the so-called Boat People in Guangdong and the Duomin in Zhejiang who worked as musicians, funeral managers, and yamen runners. In addition, ethnic differences were a common basis for discrimination. Throughout the south, local indigenous peoples—called Miao, Yao, Zhuang, and many other names—were often exploited and treated with contempt.

The routine of village life was from time to time disrupted by calamity, most often in the form of too little or too much water—flooding or drought. North China was particularly subject to drought, though occasionally heavy rains led to breaks in the dikes along the Yellow River, leading to devastating floods. In the drainage area of the Yangzi River, floods were more common than droughts.

When lack of rain ruined a harvest, better-off farmers might be able to hold out till the next harvest, but those without much in the way of reserves would

have to try other strategies—ranging from pawning their clothes, tools, and land, to foraging for edible plants in forests, to sending out able-bodied men to look for work in nearby towns, to the entire family's taking to the roads in search of food. When a drought lasted through two harvests or covered a large geographical areas, the numbers of refugees on the road would swell. Bands of hungry men might well seize the grain stores of the rich or crops in the field. Starving peasants would also descend on cities, expecting local officials to open soup kitchens and refugee camps. The lack of sanitation in these camps, coupled with the weakened condition of the refugees, made it all too easy for epidemics to spread, adding to the famine's death toll.

Bad harvests hurt townsfolk as well because they led to rapid escalation in the price of food. Understanding the law of supply and demand, townspeople would gather to prevent merchants from sending their grain to areas with severe shortages, fearing price rises. They would also protest officials who did not keep government granaries open long enough to bring down prices. Sometimes officials called on troops to quell food riots of these sorts.

The Qing government was remarkably successful in curbing the death toll of major famines by careful administration of granaries and provision of direct relief. Its success contributed to the rapid rise in population in the eighteenth century.

This population growth, coupled with the practice of partible inheritance, led to the proliferation of farms too small to support a family. In addition, many men could not marry because of a shortage of marriageable women—caused not only by the rich taking extra women as concubines but also by sex-selective infanticide practiced by poor families unwilling to rear another daughter. Men with little or no land and unable to marry commonly would leave their villages in search of work. Some would travel with their tools to do carpentry or farm work. Others found jobs pulling the boats that carried grain up the Grand Canal or working in cities as dock hands, sedan chair carriers, or night-soil collectors. When copper mines were opened in the southwest, unemployed men traveled long distances to get work as miners. Both the government and settled villagers were wary of these rootless men. They were quick to suspect strangers when crimes occurred.

Single men often found support in groups called brotherhoods or secret societies. The best known of these brotherhoods was called the Heaven and Earth

Society, but other names were also used, such as the Three Harmonies Society or the Three Dots Society. (In English they are often called the Triads.) To marginalized men, the attraction was security, mutual aid, and empowerment. Drawing on ideas from Daoism and popular religion, the groups promised access to supernatural powers through rituals and cultivation. Appearing first in the 1760s, the Heaven and Earth Society spread quickly through Taiwan, Fujian, Jiangxi, Guangdong, and Guangxi. Government functionaries and urban workers were among their members. The societies were explicitly antiestablishment in that they espoused a rhetoric of "overthrow the Qing and restore the Ming." Members away from home could get in touch with members elsewhere through secret signals or passwords. Lodge brothers helped each other with loans, funeral costs, and lawsuits. Lodges would arbitrate disputes between members and mete out punishments for cheating at gambling and other offenses. But their morality was not Confucian. Many lodges controlled gambling, narcotics, prostitution, and smuggling in their region. The first uprising led by the Heaven and Earth Society occurred in the 1780s in Taiwan, after which the Qing government tried without much success to suppress the society.

The Qing government was also wary of the White Lotus Society, which drew on folk Buddhist teachings that dated back to the Song period. This society had been an important element in the rebellions at the end of the Yuan Dynasty. It was not approved by regular Buddhist clergy because of its syncretic teachings, married clergy, and noncanonical scriptures. It incorporated millenarian doctrines derived from both Manichaeism and the Buddhist idea of the future Maitreya Buddha who would usher in an era of peace. Its central deity was the Eternal Mother, the original progenitor of all humankind. Grieving that her earthly children had lost their way, she wanted to bring them back to the Original Home, identified with nirvana. She sent Buddhas to earth to teach people the true way to salvation. When the end was near, floods, fires, and winds would destroy everyone who lacked faith in the Eternal Mother. Adherents were taught that repeating the mantra "Eternal Progenitor in Our Original Home in the World of True Emptiness" would bring blessings and protection from calamities. Martial arts exercises and breathing techniques that circulated *qi* were also taught as other ways to cure illnesses and promote health.

White Lotus teachings had particular appeal to women, who were welcomed as members on the same terms as men. When leaders were arrested or executed, often their wives took over. A Qing official whose city was seized by White Lotus forces described the woman who led the local group:

> When she emerges in a home, five or six young women will hold tobacco bags and towels for her, and she will be seated at the center of the hall. Both men and women make obeisance: the man puts the palm of his right hand on the back of his left hand and the woman, the palm of her left hand on the back of her right hand. They kowtow in reverence.[5]

The White Lotus sect survived repeated attempts by the government to suppress it, probably because local congregations did not depend on a central establishment. The sect was especially strong in the central provinces, from Sichuan and Shaanxi to Shandong. Itinerant prophets and teachers carried the message to new places. Leaders of these sects often combined talk of salvation with martial arts and herbal healing. In 1774 a White Lotus leader in Shandong convinced his followers that he was the Future Buddha and that his techniques would make them invulnerable, even though they were armed only with spears. They were able to capture several small towns before the Qing sent in massive armies to quell them.

Many White Lotus adherents were pious vegetarians who tried to live good lives. An offshoot of the White Lotus called the Luo sect established a mission to help canal boatmen far from their homes who normally had no means of support for several months in the winter. The sect set up hostels in Suzhou and Hangzhou where the boatmen could stay for free and could get meals on credit, to be repaid when they were paid in advance for the next year's work. Since many of these men were never able to marry, the hostels also served as retirement homes for elderly boatmen. The Qing government, however, was deeply suspicious and had all the hostels destroyed.

In 1793 the Qing government initiated a major investigation of White Lotus congregations, which soon had to take up arms to protect themselves from predatory elements in the local government. In 1796 open revolt began in Hubei and soon spread to Sichuan and Shaanxi. White Lotus forces held fortified

---

5. Cited in Kwang-ching Liu, "Religion and Politics in the White Lotus Rebellion of 1796 in Hubei," in *Heterodoxy in Late Imperial China*, ed. K. Liu and R. Shek (Honolulu: University of Hawaii Press, 2004), pp. 295–296.

villages and towns, and they used those bases to raid larger cities. Armed bands often joined them—martial arts groups and bandits alike. It took the government more than eight years to fully annihilate White Lotus forces.

Another segment of society that often felt aggrieved were non-Han ethnic groups. As the Han Chinese population swelled, more and settlers moved into Miao territories, often expropriating Miao land. The Miao aborigines put up fierce resistance beginning in the 1720s, and officials repeatedly tried to find ways to separate the Miao and the Han settlers, but with little progress. In 1795 there was a great revolt of Miao along the Hunan-Guizhou border, where a Han ethnic group called the Hakka had recently been moving in. The Qing government found the Miao uprisings to be as difficult to suppress as the concurrent White Lotus ones.

SUMMARY

How different was China in 1800 than it had been in 1600? China was part of a much larger empire—the largest since the Mongol Empire. For the first time, China was administered as part of the same polity as Tibet and Xinjiang. China was the most populous and economically dominant part of the empire, but politically the Manchus were in control. The Manchus depended on Chinese officials and soldiers to help administer their empire, but they perfected ways to ensure that the Manchus would maintain their dominance. The Manchu rulers were highly sensitive to ethnic slights, however, which may have made Chinese in high office especially cautious.

Although a large segment of the educated elite alive during the conquest did everything in its power to resist the Manchus in deep dread of another "barbarian" dynasty, the Manchus proved to be very different sorts of rulers than the Mongols had been, and by 1800, Chinese of all social levels had gotten used to Manchu rule. The Manchu rulers made a point to patronize Chinese culture, and many facets of Chinese culture thrived during this period, ranging from historical research to manufacturing technology. The standard of living in the mid-eighteenth century was high, and the population was growing. Benefits were not spread evenly, of course, and as in prior periods, those who were marginalized often also became disaffected.

CHAPTER SEVENTEEN

Edo Japan
(1603–1800)

Tokugawa Settlement
(Seventeenth Century)

Material Culture: Night Soil

Documents: Ihara Saikaku's
"Sensible Advice on Domestic
Economy"

Biography: Tadano Makuzu

Maturation and Decay
(Eighteenth Century)

Making Comparisons:
Neo-Confucianism

The social and political order imposed under the Tokugawa shoguns consolidated trends long in the making. The demarcation of villages as corporate communities, the separation of samurai from commoners, the creation of bounded domains, and the growth of and restrictions on commerce all had antecedents in the late sixteenth century. The structure of family life, in particular the emphasis on primogeniture and the custom of brides serving their husbands' families, continued practices already apparent in the fourteenth century. Yet peace also made possible economic developments that some historians deem proto-industrialization, unprecedented urbanization, and a flourishing of theater, fiction, poetry, and intellectual life.

What distinguished the Tokugawa shogunate from previous military regimes? What were the consequences of the political settlement for economic and demographic growth? To what extent did shogunal efforts to restrict foreign contact isolate Japan? What did samurai do without battles to fight? How did urban and rural commoners make their presence felt?

TOKUGAWA SETTLEMENT (SEVENTEENTH CENTURY)

Cadastral surveys and separation of warriors from the land were aimed at ordering society according to fixed criteria. The Tokugawa brought an end to the conflicts caused by sibling rivalry by insisting on primogeniture for the military ruling class and confiscating domains rived by succession disputes. As a result, a ruler's personality and level of competence mattered less than his office, and the retainers' loyalty focused on the position, not the individual. The monarch and his court lived, according to popular parlance, "above the clouds" in Kyoto. Samurai stood at the top of the official status order, followed by commoners in order of their contributions to society. In principle no one was to change residence or status, nor was marriage permitted across status lines. In reality, status boundaries were fluid. Since changing names changed identity, a commoner woman took an aristocratic name when serving a military household. Individual actors and prostitutes became celebrities, and the exclusive right to work with animal skins made some outcasts wealthy.

Tokugawa Social Hierarchy		
Core Social Statuses	Other Social Groups (Between Statuses)	Outcasts
Samurai	Priests	Blind Female
Cultivators	Doctors	Entertainers
Artisans	Monks	Beggars
Merchants		Prostitutes
		Actors
		Non-Humans *(Hinin)*
		Polluted Ones *(Kawata)*

This status order restricted rural communities to cultivators. In the seventeenth century, most villages had at least one dominant family, often descended from a rusticated warrior, which monopolized the position of headman. A council of elders comprising landholding cultivators known as *honbyakushō* provided a sounding board for matters pertaining to village affairs. The *honbyakushō* households included family members, house servants, and field workers. In central and eastern Japan, complex lineage systems with multiple branches defined relations within villages. Across Japan, social, economic, and political inequality structured village life. The men who claimed descent from village founders expected to be treated with deference; they claimed the largest and best fields, and they dominated village politics. Their wives shared their prestige; a male of lesser standing had to treat such women with respect.

Villages divided up the countryside. A village contained residential plots, rice paddies, and dry fields, each assigned to households. In some regions agricultural lands periodically rotated from family to family. These households cooperated in doing the heavy work of leveling rice paddies and building dikes, managing irrigation networks, and transplanting rice seedlings into the paddies. Women performed this last backbreaking task in a carryover of medieval religious beliefs that sanctified it as a fertility ritual (see Color Plate 17). Beyond this basic level, each household was on its own to prosper or to fail. Village boundaries also enclosed wastelands and forests, with access to their products carefully regulated by the village council. As a corporate entity embodied by the headman, the village was collectively responsible for paying taxes, both the yearly tribute measured in units of rice (*koku*—1 *koku* equals 5.1 bushels of rice, the amount needed to feed one man for a year) and various ancillary exactions—for example, fees for the privilege of exploiting forest resources.

Contiguous villages with definable boundaries constituted the building blocks of domains ruled by daimyo. The shogun had the largest domain concentrated chiefly in eastern and central Japan totaling approximately one-fourth of the total agricultural base. Vassal daimyo (*fudai*) were hereditary retainers. They governed domains; they also served as the shogun's chief advisers and his first line of defense against potential foes. According to a decree of 1634, only vassals whose domains contained over 10,000 *koku* enjoyed the status of daimyo. The shogun's retainers with smaller fiefs, often made up of parcels in several villages, were called *hatamoto* ("beneath the banner"). In addition, the shogun commanded the services of thousands of housemen who received stipends from the shogun's warehouses. Daimyo who had been shogun Tokugawa Ieyasu's rivals or peers were deemed outside lords (*tozama*). Fewer in number than the vassal daimyo, the mightiest controlled large domains that functioned almost as nations. Some of the shogun's collateral relatives also numbered among the daimyo. They were neither wealthy nor politically powerful, but they enjoyed great prestige. All daimyo, who numbered between 250 and 280, had retainer bands to be supported and employed.

Government

The government pieced together by the Tokugawa shoguns developed an elaborate bureaucratic structure (later called a *bakufu*—tent government). The senior councilors—four to five men who rotated on a monthly basis, each of them a vassal daimyo worth at least 30,000 *koku*—took responsibility for policy decisions, personnel matters, and supervising the daimyo. Their assistants, also vassal daimyo, handled matters relating to the shogun's retainers. The *hatamoto* staffed the administrative positions, beginning with the magistrates in charge of finances, cities, and temples and shrines. Finance magistrates supervised the intendants responsible for seeing that the villagers paid their taxes and general agrarian affairs. They also managed the increasingly futile task of balancing expenditures with income. Their staff, and those of the other magistrates, included an array of functionaries, guards, and servants. Although the shogun tried to reduce the size of his army in the seventeenth century, he was never able to provide more than part-time employment to his retainers; 42 percent of *hatamoto* (1,676 in 1829) served in the fatigue regiment, the default category for men without office. Each daimyo likewise had an overly abundant staff of advisers, accountants, liaison officers, attendants, tax collectors, doctors, teachers, guards, servants, and placeholders.

The shogunal and domainal governments developed the most complex, sophisticated, and coherent bureaucracies Japan had ever seen. Retainers learned to wield a brush as well as a sword, understand high finance, and accustom themselves to routinized office jobs. Administrative systems also retained non-modern elements. The shogun bestowed his former family name of Matsudaira on important *fudai* and *tozama* daimyo, both as an honor and as a reminder that rulers were kin. Opportunities for promotion depended on hereditary rank; men born of guards stayed guards. The senior councilors may have been policy experts, but they were also the shogun's vassals. Their duties included watching him perform ancestral rites, lecture on the Chinese classics, and dance in Nō. When he left the castle to go hawking or to visit one of their number, they and their subordinates had to attend him. The shogun maintained a large staff of palace women ordered in a female bureaucracy to serve him, his wife, and his mother in the great interior (*ōoku*). Their responsibilities included a yearly round of ceremonies and managing gift exchanges with the Kyoto court and daimyo families.

Although the daimyo ran their domains as they saw fit, the shogunate started to issue decrees to regulate their behavior in 1615. It limited the number of guns allowed per castle and restricted castle repairs. The daimyo were not to harbor criminals, collude against the shogun, or marry without the shogun's permission. All daimyo had the responsibility of contributing men and money to the shogun's building projects, and they could be relocated from one domain to another at the shogun's pleasure. Most important, the shogunate issued increasingly stringent guidelines governing the daimyo's attendance on the shogun. Known as *sankin kōtai* and formalized in 1635, this system stipulated that each daimyo spend half of his time in his domain and half in the shogun's capital at Edo. Each daimyo's wife and heir had to reside in Edo as hostages. Designed to keep the daimyo both loyal to the shogun and effective in local administration, the system bal-

anced the centrifugal forces that had weakened the Kamakura regime and the centripetal tendencies that had destroyed the Ashikaga. *Sankin kōtai* also had the inadvertent consequence of stimulating trade, encouraging travel, and fostering cultural exchange.

The shogunate appropriated certain national responsibilities to itself. It refurbished the highway system with post stations and checkpoints to keep guns out of Edo and female hostages in. For its own defense, it forbade the building of bridges over major rivers. It oversaw the development of coastal shipping routes, took over the mines for precious metals, and minted copper, silver, and gold coins. It initiated an official handwriting style for documents. It forbade the practice of Christianity and set up a nationwide system of temple registration to ensure compliance. In 1635 it forbade Japanese to travel overseas and banned foreign books. In 1639 it regulated relations with the West by allowing only the Dutch to trade at Nagasaki. It delegated the oversight of trade and diplomacy with neighboring countries to three domains: Satsuma for the Ryukyus, Tsushima for Korea, and Matsumae for the Ainu and the north. The shogunate supervised trade with China that took place at Nagasaki; it had less control over Chinese goods that arrived indirectly through the Ryukyus and Hokkaido.

Under the Tokugawa regime, people inhabiting the Ryukyu Islands found themselves forced into much closer proximity to Japan. An independent kingdom with tributary ties to China as well as Japan in the sixteenth century, the Ryukyus suffered invasion by Satsuma in 1609. Although the king survived and trade with China continued, he had to surrender control over his islands' diplomatic and economic affairs, to the detriment of the islanders' well-being. Intellectuals in the Ryukyus tried to craft a new identity by claiming that although they were politically subservient to Japan, they achieved moral parity with both Japan and China by cultivating the way of the Confucian sage.

Relations with the Ainu in Hokkaido evolved differently. There the shogunate had the Matsumae family with long-standing ties to the region establish a domain on the island's southern tip. The Matsumae received the privilege of monopolizing trade with the Ainu in exchange for a pledge of loyalty. In 1669 conflict between Ainu tribes over access to game and fish escalated into a war to rid Hokkaido of the Japanese.

Following its vicious suppression, the Ainu and the Japanese solidified distinct ethnic identities that incorporated elements of the other—eagle feathers and otter pelts for the Japanese ruling class and ironware,

Ainu Feeding a Hawk. This mid-nineteenth-century drawing of an Ainu feeding a hawk depicts the bird as being almost as large as its captor. The Ainu is stereotypically hairy with full beard and heavy eyebrows. *(Brett Walker/Collection for Northern Studies, Hokkaido University Library)*

rice, and sake for the Ainu. Between 1590 and 1800, the Ainu became increasingly dependent on trade with Japan for their subsistence, while periodic epidemics brought by traders ravaged their population. Many ended up working as contract laborers in fisheries that shipped food and fertilizer to Japan.

The Tokugawa shogunate survived for over 250 years not simply because it dominated Japan militarily but because, like Oda Nobunaga and Toyotomi Hideyoshi, Ieyasu and his heirs recognized the importance of ideology in transforming power into authority. Nobunaga claimed that he acted on behalf of the realm (*tenka*), not his private, selfish interests. Governance of his domain became public administration (*kōgi*). He also built a shrine to himself. Hideyoshi actively promoted a cult to his own divinity.

Ieyasu's posthumous title apotheosized him as *Tōshō daigongen*—the Buddha incarnate as the sun god of the east. Enshrined at Nikkō, he protected the shogunate from malignant spirits and worked for the good of all people. (See Map 17.1.) The third shogun Iemitsu claimed that the shogunate manifested a just social order that followed the way of heaven (*tendō*). This way is natural, unchanging, eternal, and hierarchical. The ruler displays the benevolence of the Buddha, the warrior preserves the peace, and the

commoners are obedient. The fifth shogun, Tsunayoshi, tried to domesticate the warriors by codifying mourning rituals, lecturing on Confucian classics, and forbidding the killing of animals, especially dogs (used for target practice). His successor reversed the last stricture, and the eighth shogun, Yoshimune, sought to revive the martial arts. One aim of later reforms between 1787 and 1793 was to redress the balance between brush and sword, suggesting that, for samurai, how to follow the way of heaven was not self-evident.

Agricultural Transformations and the Commercial Revolution

Cultivators, merchants, artisans, and rulers quickly exploited the peace dividend. Large- and small-scale reclamation projects, often funded by merchants at a daimyo's behest, opened rice paddies and expanded arable land by 45 percent. Rivers were diked and new channels dug to bring irrigation water to fields. Countless building projects, partly to repair the ravages of war in Kyoto but mainly to build the plethora of daimyo mansions, shogunal palaces, and merchant quarters in the new capital at Edo and the castle towns, seriously depleted forests. By the end of the seventeenth century, floods sweeping down denuded mountains threatened hard-won fields. The shogunate tried to regulate the use of forestry products, but the agricultural base continued to press against ecological limits. (See **Material Culture: Night Soil.**)

The introduction of better seeds and new crops intensified the use of land and labor. The accumulation of small innovations based on observations of soil types and climatic conditions led to the development of rice varieties suited for specific local conditions. Fast-ripening rice spread cultivation into the marginal lands of the northeast. Farther south, it allowed the sowing of a second crop, often wheat, although some paddies in Kyushu supported two rice crops a year. As in China and Korea, corn, tobacco, and sweet potato, products of the Western Hemisphere, became dry field staples along with barley and millet. In a trend that continued throughout the Tokugawa period, seventeenth-century agronomy experts traveled Japan building social networks of like-minded experimenters, seeking the most advanced methods for increasing crop yields, and disseminating their findings in books.

Cultivators also grew cash crops and developed products based on Chinese technology. The spread of cotton growing in western Japan beginning in the

Map **17.1**   Tokugawa Japan, 1600–1868

sixteenth century reduced the hours women had to spend preparing cloth for their families while revolutionizing clothing and bedding. During the seventeenth century, Japan imported Chinese silk and sugar. By the 1730s for silk and the 1830s for sugar, domestic production provided substitutes. The daimyo competed in developing products for export to fund their mandated trips to Edo. They hired teachers to show cultivators how to harvest lacquer, make paper, and raise silkworms. They promoted distinctive styles of wooden combs, paper hair ties, and ceramics. Merchants supplied the capital, and cultivators supplied the labor, although a few rural entrepreneurs managed to profit from the distribution of raw materials and the transportation of goods. Lights fueled by rapeseed oil enabled work to continue after dark. Increases in agricultural productivity spurred demand for nonagricultural goods produced by rural households. The growth of cottage industries diversified income sources

and led to a virtuous cycle of interaction between agriculture and manufacturing. Neither entrepreneurs nor domains tried to set up large-scale production units. Instead they emphasized quality and variety, trying to beat the competition by producing regional specialties found nowhere else.

The agricultural and commercial revolutions meant higher per capita productivity and a trend toward smaller families. After almost a threefold increase in the seventeenth century, Japan's population remained surprisingly stagnant in contrast to the populations of China and Korea at the same time. In villages the extended families characteristic of earlier times broke down into main families and branches or landlords and tenants. Most households cultivated parcels just big enough to support a stem family of grandparents, parents, and children. There was not enough to bestow on more than one heir. Historians have supposed that cultivators practiced abortion and infanticide lest they

Artisans. Cottage industries relied on families. Both the pattern dyers depicted on the screen to the right and the weavers shown on the screen to the left employed men and women, children and grandparents. (*LEFT: Werner Forman/Corbis. RIGHT: Sakamoto Photo Research Laboratory/Corbis*)

have more children than they could afford. Even if the heir died, the ease of adoption meant that a family could usually find someone to carry on the family line. Other factors were also at work. Men often left their homes for months at a time to work in towns and cities, especially during the winter. The female age at marriage went up in central Japan because women increasingly worked to gain experience before settling down. Disease mattered: Smallpox can reduce male fertility by 50 percent. Syphilis struck urban populations. Periodic famines hit some regions harder than others. In the early nineteenth century, population decline in the impoverished northeast offset growth in the more commercially developed and prosperous west.

One characteristic of Japan's early modern growth was that while labor remained in the countryside, capital largely concentrated in cities. Not until the late eighteenth century did rural entrepreneurs amass significant amounts of capital, and they often depended on urban merchants for financial backing. Daimyo traveling on *sankin kōtai* marketed rice they collected in taxes to merchants in Osaka who advanced them

currency and letters of credit. These promissory notes, redeemable at the merchant's branch in Edo, served as Japan's first paper money. Domains later printed their own currency, modeled on religious talismans to gain users' trust. Merchants either advanced the money to make specialty products or bought them at a discount to sell to urban consumers. Some merchants acted as purveyors to daimyo and their women, stimulating the desire for high-quality labor-intensive goods. Others catered to the broader market by selling cotton cloth, lamp oil, and soy sauce. At the end of the seventeenth century, a few Osaka and Edo merchants had become extremely wealthy, and a number of daimyo found themselves deeply in debt.

Urban Life and Culture

Edo's spatial layout mirrored the shogun's strategic concerns. Taking advantage of technological advances in fortifications, the shogun's castle was enclosed behind multiple stone walls surrounded by moats. The shogunate drained the swamp on which the city was built through canals that provided transportation for

MATERIAL CULTURE

Night Soil

The Edo city government left waste disposal in the hands of individual landlords. Daimyo and *hatamoto* contracted with nearby villages to bring vegetables to their compounds and remove waste. Communal toilet facilities in each commoner ward also had to be cleaned.

In the eighteenth century, cultivators planted crops where they had once foraged for green fertilizer. The more intensive use of land forced them to look outside their communities for soil amendments. Vegetable farmers near Edo carted away night soil and other organic wastes to supplement the manure they produced themselves. Separated into solids and liquid and cooked in its own heat to kill harmful organisms, night soil became a valuable commodity.

In the late eighteenth century, townspeople expected cultivators to pay for the privilege of collecting night soil. Landlords insisted that tenants use their toilet facilities and tried to sell their product to the highest bidder. Transactions between subcontractors, wholesalers, and middlemen raised costs. Regional alliances of cultivators petitioned the shogunate to keep prices down.

The price placed on night soil reflected status inequality. Landlords segregated toilets by sex because men's excrement was valued more highly than women's. Samurai received more for their waste than did commoners. An eighteenth-century farmhouse had a toilet for samurai made of polished wood. The tenant farmers and family members used an open pit.

Toilets. The photo on the left depicts a toilet for the use of samurai officials next to the formal reception room at a village headman's house. On the opposite side behind the stable is the pit for family and servants (right). *(Photos courtesy of Anne Walthall)*

goods and people. Bridges over moats were faced with guardhouses, forcing the traveler to make a sharp turn, and no roads led directly to the castle. Vassal daimyo and the shogun's retainers lived in its immediate vicinity, providing another ring of protection. The wealthy *tozama* daimyo had large compounds containing barracks for their retainers, storehouses, mansions, and gardens. None was allowed moats and stone walls, and quarters for the vassal daimyo surrounded them. Each daimyo maintained multiple compounds; the total number was over one thousand. The ruling class took the salubrious highlands for itself, leaving the lowlands directly east and south of the castle for commoners. Scattered throughout the city were shrines and temples. Daimyo castle towns followed a similar pattern of segregating people according to status and occupation.

The seventeenth century saw an unprecedented increase in urban growth, from little more than 1 percent of Japan's population to almost 15 percent after 1700. In addition to the castle towns were three metropolises: Kyoto became a manufacturing center of luxury goods, Osaka served as Japan's chief market, and Edo's swollen population of daimyo and bureaucrats made it a consumption center. Urbanization stimulated the growth of commercial publishing

DOCUMENTS

Ihara Saikaku's "Sensible Advice on Domestic Economy"

Ihara Saikaku (1642–1693) is often considered Japan's first professional author because he lived by his pen, writing haiku, short stories, novels, and essays that described life in Osaka during the townspeople's heyday. Here he feeds the merchants' obsession with the making and saving of money by focusing on the details of daily life and the qualities desired in a wife.

"The immutable rule in regard to the division of family property at the time of marriage," said the experienced go-between from Kyoto, "is as follows: Let us suppose that a certain man is worth a thousand *kan*. To the eldest son at his marriage will go four hundred *kan*, together with the family residence. The second son's share will be three hundred *kan*, and he too is entitled to a house of his own. The third son will be adopted into another family, requiring a portion of one hundred *kan*. If there is a daughter, her dowry will be thirty *kan*, in addition to a bridal trousseau worth twenty *kan*. It is advisable to marry her off to the son of a family of lower financial status. Formerly it was not unusual to spend forty *kan* on the trousseau and allot ten *kan* for the dowry, but because people today are more interested in cash, it is now customary to give the daughter silver in the lacquered chest and copper in the extra one. Even if the girl is so ugly that she can't afford to sit near the candle at night, that dowry of thirty *kan* will make her bloom into a very flowery bride!"

"In matchmaking, money is a very important consideration. If thirty *kan* of silver is deposited with a trustworthy merchant at six-tenths percent interest per month, the income will total one hundred and eighty *momme* monthly, which will more than suffice to support four women: the bride, her personal maid, a second maid, and a seamstress. How unselfish must be the disposition of a bride who will not only look after the household faithfully, meantime taking care never to displease her husband's family, but also at the same time will actually pay for the food she eats! If you are looking merely for beauty, then go where women are made up solely to that end, to the licensed quarters. You are free to visit them any time of night you may wish, and thoroughly enjoy it, but next morning you will have to pay out seventy-one *momme*—which is not in the least enjoyable!"

"It is better on the whole to give up dissipation in good time, for a roué is seldom happy in later life. So even if life at home seems dry and tasteless, you'd better have patience with a supper of cold rice, potluck

that created and fed a reading public hungry for knowledge and entertainment. It provided space for exhibitions from religious icons to botanical specimens and for private salons where scholars, artists, and writers met patrons. Urban residents paid for services—hairdressing, amusements—that had once been provided by servants. They bought processed food and cloth that their ancestors had made themselves. Labor and leisure were oriented toward the market, and purchasing finished products saved time. This transformation stimulated a consumption revolution—the increased demand for a greater variety of goods, from durable luxury items such as elaborately carved transoms to drug foods such as sake and tobacco.

Unprecedented urban prosperity culminated in the Genroku era (1688–1704), the heyday of townsman (*chōnin*) culture, justly celebrated in art and literature. Ihara Saikaku wrote stories about the samurai passion for boys, but most of his works focused on the foibles of the townspeople in books such as *Five Women Who Loved Love* and *The Life of an Amorous Man*. He also wrote books on how to make and keep money. (See **Documents: Ihara Saikaku's "Sensible Advice on Domestic Economy."**) Matsuo Bashō raised the seventeen-syllable verse form known as bean curd, and dried fish. You may lie down whenever you like, at perfect ease, and have a maid massage you down to the very tips of your toes. If you want tea, you may sip it while your wife holds the cup for you. A man in his own household is the commander supreme, whose authority none will dare to question, and there is none to condemn you. There's no need to seek further for genuine pleasure."

"Then, too, there are certain business advantages to staying home. Your clerks will stop their imprudent visits to the Yasaka quarters and their clandestine meetings at that rendezvous in Oike. And when in the shop, since they can't appear to be completely idle, maybe they'll look over those reports from the Edo branch office, or do some other work that they have been putting off doing—all to the profit of you, the master! The apprentice boys will diligently twist wastepaper into string, and in order to impress you, the master, sitting in the inner room, they will practice penmanship to their profit. Kyushichi, whose habit it is to retire early, will take the straw packing from around the yellowtail and make rope on which to string coins; while Take, in order to make things go more smoothly tomorrow, will prepare the vegetables for breakfast. The seamstress during the time you're at home will take off as many knots of Hino silk as she ordinarily does in a whole day. Even the cat keeps a wary watch in the kitchen and when she hears the least sound

in the vicinity of the fish hanger she will mew to scare away the rats. If such unmeasured profit as this results from the master's remaining at home just one night, think how vast will be the benefits that will accrue within the space of a whole year! So even if you are not entirely satisfied with your wife, you have to exercise discretion and realize that in the gay quarters all is but vanity. For a young master to be well aware of this is the secret of the successful running of his household."

Such was the counsel offered by the veteran go-between.

Be that as it may, let me say that the women of today, under the influence of the styles of the gay quarters, dress exactly like professional entertainers. Prominent drapers' wives, who in public are addressed as mesdames, are so attired as to be mistaken for high-class courtesans; while the wives of small shopkeepers, who once served as clerks of the drapers, look exactly like courtesans one grade lower. Again, the kimono worn by wives of tailors and embroiderers who live on the side streets bear a startling resemblance to those of the women employed in teahouses. It is fun to spot them in a crowd dressed in conformity with their respective degrees of fortune.

Source: Saikaku Ihara, *This Scheming World*, trans. Masanori Takatsuka and David C. Stubbs (Rutland, Vt.: Charles E. Tuttle Company, 1965), pp. 54–57 (modified).

haiku to a fine art, in the process making poetry accessible to commoners in town and country. Passing by a battlefield, he wrote: "A thicket of summer grass, all that remains of warriors' dreams."[1] Chikamatsu Monzaemon wrote librettos for the puppet theater that explored the complex interplay between social obligations and human feeling, as when a young man in love with a prostitute wants to buy the contract that indentures her to the brothel owner but lacks the resources to do so without causing irrepara-

ble harm to his family's business. Caught between love and duty, the couple resolves the dilemma by committing double suicide. Although Chikamatsu wrote for puppets, the literary artistry of his scripts endeared them to amateur performers and raised the quality of theatrical performances.

Two pleasure zones are associated with the Genroku era: the brothel district and the theaters, often located in proximity to each other on the margins of respectable society. These constituted the "floating world" (*ukiyo*) celebrated in woodblock prints of courtesans and actors along with pornography. In the early seventeenth century, entrepreneurs in the

---

1. Translated by Anne Walthall from *Oku no hosomichi* (*The Narrow Road to the Deep North*).

three metropolises petitioned the shogunate to establish districts for prostitution where it could be regulated and controlled. A moat and walls surrounded Edo's Yoshiwara with a main gate where guards noted the men who entered and prevented women from leaving. The earliest customers were daimyo and samurai. Merchants whose lavish spending brought them great renown soon eclipsed them. In this status-conscious society, courtesans too were ranked.

Kabuki began in the early seventeenth century on a riverbank in Kyoto where a prostitute erected a stage on which to sing and dance to attract customers. Fights over her charms led the shogunate to forbid women from appearing on stage in 1629. Boys then replaced them as actors and prostitutes. Again the shogunate stepped in to quell disorder, banning all but mature men from performing in public. To make up for a lack of sex appeal, actors developed the techniques of acting, singing, and dancing performed on elaborate and frequently changing sets that made kabuki the spectacle known today. It became enormously popular, with the highest acclaim reserved for the men who specialized in playing women. It staged reenactments of the scandals arising in townspeople's society, but it became best known for swashbuckling melodramas set in the past, for the shogunate forbade any discussion of its own affairs or those of contemporary samurai society.

Intellectual Trends

The Edo period saw an explosion in intellectual pursuits. Deprived of the opportunity to gain fame in battle, some samurai turned to scholarship and made serious efforts to understand society. In the seventeenth century, Hayashi Razan formulated the Tokugawa ideology in neo-Confucian terms that saw the social order as a reflection of the visible natural order in that both realized an underlying metaphysical principle. Among his students was Yamaga Sokō, famous for defining a way for samurai to survive during a time of peace: "The business of the samurai consists in reflecting on his own station in life, in discharging loyal service to his master, . . . in deepening his fidelity in associations with friends, and . . . in devoting himself to duty above all."[2] Kyoto scholar Itō Jinsai likewise began as a neo-Confucianist, only to reject the notion of metaphysical principle in favor of studying Confucius himself. For him, the purpose of

scholarship was to show how to put morality based on benevolence and love into practice, a goal achievable by commoners as well as samurai. Such was the cachet of Chinese philosophy that any man who had pretensions of becoming learned had to employ Chinese categories of thought. Women were not subject to this restriction, but for that reason, they had little access to scholarship beyond the study of Japanese poetry. (See **Biography: Tadano Makuzu**.)

Ogyū Sorai gained influence by attacking the neo-Confucian Hayashi school and Itō Jinsai. He argued that only the most ancient Chinese texts, those that predated Confucius, were worthy of study because they contained the teachings of the sage kings, the creators of civilization. The social order did not reflect the natural order of beasts; instead it was an artificial construct, made in history, and that was good. Men needed rules lest their passions run away with them. Japan was fortunate that its own sage king Ieyasu had created the shogunate, and his deeds were not for mere mortals to challenge. Sorai's rational bureaucratic view of government called on samurai to devote themselves to public duty. In 1703 forty-seven retainers from the Akō domain assassinated their dead lord's enemy (an incident dramatized as "The Treasury of Loyal Retainers," *Chūshingura*) because, they claimed, their honor as samurai left them no choice. Sorai applauded the deed but acceded to the official position that since they had broken the law against private vendettas, they had to atone by committing suicide. As long as people obeyed the law, government had no business interfering in their private lives.

The eighteenth century saw a proliferation of schools and thinkers. Dazai Shundai explored the ramifications of political economy. He urged daimyo to supplement flat revenues derived from an agrarian tax base by promoting the production of goods for export. Kaiho Seiryō took Shundai's ideas a step farther by arguing that all social relationships are predicated on the measured exchange of goods and services, a principle understood by merchants but not, unfortunately, by samurai. Andō Shōeki claimed that Sorai's sage kings were thieves and liars who created governments to deceive and cheat the cultivators. In his eyes, the samurai were no better than parasites.

Merchants pondered business ethics. Troubled by the excesses of the Genroku period when some financiers had gone bankrupt through lavish spending and making bad loans to daimyo, Ishida Baigan founded the Shingaku school (literally, study of the heart). He argued that merchants deserved to make a just profit

---

2. Ryusaku Tsunoda et al., eds., *Sources of the Japanese Tradition* (New York: Columbia University Press, 1959), 1:390.

Color Plate 17
Rice Planting. This sixteenth-century painting of *Rice Planting* depicts it as a fertility festival with men providing the music while women work.

Color Plate 18
The Garden of the Master of Nets. A large pond is the central feature of the *Garden of the Master of Nets* in Suzhou. Notice the use of plants, rocks, and walkways.

Color Plate 19
Arrival of the Portuguese. This six-panel folding screen
depicts the *Arrival of the Portuguese*—soldiers in short
pants, merchants in balloon pants, and priests in black
robes accompanied by African servants.

(Musee des Arts Asiatiques-Guimet, Paris, France/RMN/Art Resource, NY)

Color Plate 20
The Qianlong Emperor Receiving Tribute Horses. This detail from
a 1757 painting by the Italian court painter Giuseppe Castiglione
(1688–1768) shows the reception of envoys from the Kazakhs.
Note how the envoy, presenting a pure white horse, is kneeling to
the ground (performing the kowtow).

(Musee Guimet, Paris/The Art Archive)

Color Plate 21
Dry Goods Store in Surugacho. In this painting entitled *Dry Goods Store in Surugacho, Edo,* customers take off their shoes to enter the shop. Male clerks serve female customers while others gather around the manager. The owner is at the back of the store.

(Corbis)

Color Plate 22
Women at the Tano Festival, by Sin Yunbok (1758–?), Chosŏn Dynasty. This painting captures the eroticism that is frequently associated with Sin Yunbok's depiction of women. Notice the two boy monks stealing a glance at the women from behind the rocks.

(Kansong Museum of Fine Arts, Seoul)

Color Plate 24
Noh Robe. Fabric and design signaled age, status, and gender as well as the presence of demons and other spirits. Featuring silk embroidery and gold leaf on satin, this eighteenth-century role signified the aristocracy.

(Photograph © 1981 The Metropolitan Museum of Art/Art Resource, NY)

Color Plate 23
Procession for Crown Prince Sado. Procession returning from a visit to Hwasŏng (modern Suwŏn) to Seoul in 1795 led by King Chóngjo with his mother, Lady Hyegyŏng, to honor the 60th birthday of his father, Crown Prince Sado, who had been murdered by his own father, King Yŏngjo, in 1762.

(Han Yong'u, *Tasi ch'annuin uri yoksa [Our History, Rediscovered],* p. 11 left)

BIOGRAPHY Tadano Makuzu

Male intellectuals focused on morality, politics, and economics. Tadano Makuzu (1763–1825) drew on her observations and experience as a daughter of the samurai to analyze human relations.

Born Kudō Ayako, she grew up in a lively family of parents, her father's mother, and seven siblings. At age nine she insisted that her mother teach her classical Japanese poetry. Ayako enjoyed her grandmother's company because she was a cheerful and attractive woman who loved kabuki. To complete her education, at fifteen Ayako became an attendant to the lord of Sendai's daughter, a position she held for ten years.

Ayako's father, Heisuke, had many friends who shared his interests in medicine, botany, foreign trade, and Western countries. He hoped to arrange a good marriage for Ayako should his proposal for the colonization of Hokkaido and trade with Russia lead to a position with the shogunate. The fall of his patron in 1786 stymied his career and his plans for his daughter.

When Ayako left service, she was too old to make a good match. In 1789 she was married to a man so decrepit that she cried until she was returned to her parents. In 1797 her father found her a husband in a widower with three sons, Tadano Iga Tsurayoshi, a high-ranking Sendai retainer with an income four times that of the Kudō family. Marrying Iga meant that Ayako had to leave the city of her birth for Sendai, a move she likened to "the journey to hell." There she spent the remainder of her life, visited only occasionally by her husband, who remained on duty in Edo.

Signed with the pen name Makuzu, "Solitary Thoughts" (*Hitori kangae*) encapsulates Ayako's views on her society distilled during her years of isolation in Sendai. She bemoans her ignorance of Confucianism because her father thought it inappropriate knowledge for a woman. It was of little use even for men, she believed, because it was too clumsy to regulate the niceties of Japanese behavior. Like other intellectuals of her day, she pitied the samurai for not understanding the principle of money. Instead of a well-ordered harmonious society, she saw competition, hatred, and strife: "Each person in our country strives to enrich him or herself alone without thinking of the foreign threat or begrudging the cost to the country." Townspeople despised warriors: "They take secret delight in the warriors' descent into poverty, hating them like sworn enemies." Antagonism governed even relations between the sexes: "When men and women make love, they battle for superiority by rubbing their genitals together."

Source: Bettina Gramlich-Oka, *Thinking Like a Man: Tadano Makuzu* (1763–1825) (Leiden: Brill Academic Publishers, 2006).

---

because their profit was equivalent to the samurai's stipend. They should devote themselves to their enterprises with the same devotion a samurai owed his lord, and like the samurai they should strive for moral perfection. Texts and teachers could guide this quest, but it could be completed only through meditation and the practice of diligence, thrift, and fortitude. Baigan and his followers had no political agenda; the idea that merchants might have something to say to samurai was left to the merchant academy in Osaka, the Kaitokudō, founded in 1724. Its teachers denied that merchants caused famine and indebtedness through their pursuit of profit. Merchants, they argued, played a crucial role in society by facilitating the circulation of goods based on objective and accurate calculations. When they applied this principle to domain finances, their advice regarding fiscal policy ought to be followed. A number of them gained coveted positions as advisers to daimyo and shogun.

Other thinkers found inspiration in the Japanese past. The greatest was Motoori Norinaga, whose prodigious memory enabled him to decipher the patterns of Chinese characters used to write *Kojiki*, Japan's most ancient history. Through the study of history and literary classics, he affirmed Japan's unique position in the world as the sole country ruled by descendants of the sun goddess, and he celebrated the private world of the individual. Based as they were on the spontaneity of human feeling, Japanese values were superior to those of other peoples. "In foreign countries, they place logic first, even when it comes to revering the gods . . . all this is but shallow human reasoning." The Chinese had introduced rules that, while they might be necessary in China where people were naturally inclined toward error, were entirely unsuited to Japan, where people were intrinsically perfect in their possession of the "true heart" (*magokoro*).[3] Even when he was asked by a daimyo to comment on the conditions of his day, Norinaga remained apolitical, claiming that rulers should live in accordance with the way of the gods discernible in the study of history and poetry.

Official interest in Western studies began in 1720 when Shogun Yoshimune lifted the ban on Western books so long as they did not promote Christianity. Japanese doctors and scientists, attracted to what was called "Dutch studies," paid little attention to Western philosophy; their enthusiasm was for practical matters, in particular the study of human anatomy, astronomy, geography, and military science. Sugita Genpaku discovered that a Dutch human anatomy book provided names for body parts not found in Chinese medical texts. In 1771 he watched the dissection of a criminal's corpse, a fifty-year-old woman, performed by an outcast. Although this was not the first dissection performed in Japan, the evidence of his own eyes plus the Dutch text led him to invent Japanese terms for pancreas, nerve, and other body parts; these terms were later exported to China. The belief in empirical reason and the efficacy of experiment promoted by the Chinese "practical learning" school already constituted one strand of Japanese intellectual life; the opportunity to engage with Western scientific texts developed it further. Sugita spread his ideas through his writing and salons, whose members ranged from merchants to daimyo. Western instruments such as the telescope and microscope fascinated intellectuals. The insights they gained into the natural world percolated into popular culture when Utagawa Kunisada drew pictures of greatly magnified insects to illustrate a story about monsters.

MATURATION AND DECAY (EIGHTEENTH CENTURY)

Following the excesses of the Genroku period, shogunal and domainal officials fretted over the state of government finances and their retainers' morale. The miserly

Ieyasu had left stores of gold bullion, but his heirs spent them so freely that by the 1690s, the shogunate had to devalue the currency. Creeping inflation eroded the value of tax revenues and samurai stipends, while the growing availability of consumer products stimulated demand. Shogun Yoshimune responded by instituting reforms in the 1720s. To aid the samurai who received their stipends in rice, he supported rice prices even though urban consumers complained. He assessed a "voluntary contribution" from all daimyo of a rice donation in proportion to their domain's size in return for spending less time in Edo on *sankin kōtai*. Instead of basing taxes on each year's harvest, he tried to eliminate fluctuations in revenues by establishing a fixed tax rate. He allowed villages to open new fields in regions previously set aside to provide forage and fertilizer and encouraged the cultivation of cash crops. To reduce expenditures, he issued sumptuary legislation and cut the staff of palace women. He inaugurated a petition box, already tried in some domains, to allow commoners' suggestions to reach his ear. A famine caused by a plague of locusts in western Japan in 1732 brought the reform period to an end.

Popular Culture

In contrast to the ruling class, urban commoners generally enjoyed the benefits of the consumption revolution. By 1750, Edo's population had reached well over 1 million inhabitants, making it perhaps the largest city in the world at the time. A fish market dominated the hub of the city at Nihonbashi; the surrounding streets were lined with shops selling goods of every sort. Restaurants catered to people for whom dining out had become a pleasure. Innkeepers who specialized in accommodating plaintiffs became proto-lawyers in an increasingly litigious society. The draper Echigoya innovated a fixed price system for cash (see Color Plate 21). The world's first commodity futures market opened in Osaka. Kabuki actors incorporated advertisements into their routines starting in 1715. In 1774 a popular actor affixed his name to cosmetics sold in his store, mentioned his products on stage, and placed them in woodblock prints. Best-selling authors accepted money to praise products such as toothpaste and pipes.

The spread of commerce made education both possible and necessary. In thousands of villages across Japan, priests, village officials, and rural entrepreneurs opened schools to provide the rudiments of reading and mathematics. Coupled with private academies in castle towns and cities for samurai and merchants, their

---

3. Sey Nakamura, "The Way of the Gods: Motoori Norinaga's *Naobi no Mitama*," *Monumenta Nipponica* 46 (Spring 1991): 39.

Schoolchildren and Teacher. In this early-nineteenth-century cartoon by Hokusai, the teacher listens to three boys recite. Another student counts on his toes; roughhousing turns into a fight. *(Corbis)*

efforts led to impressive rates of literacy by the mid-nineteenth century: approximately 40 percent for men and between 10 and 15 percent for women. Students studied didactic texts; texts for women emphasized docility, modesty, and self-restraint lest the young working woman slip from seamstress to prostitute. Publishers printed one-page almanacs and Buddhist mandalas as well as pamphlets giving advice on agriculture and etiquette. Some students read well enough to enjoy multivolume works of historical fiction, but for many, the aim was more practical: to learn when to plant crops and how to calculate profit and loss.

The national road system designed to bring daimyo to Edo began to attract increasing numbers of commoners in the eighteenth century. Although the shogunate prohibited travel in the interests of preserving order, it allowed pilgrimages, visits to relatives, and trips to medicinal hot springs. With a passport issued by a local official giving name, physical description, and destination, travelers set off, usually on foot, always in groups, accompanied by neighbors to see them to the community border. Many traveled in confraternities that raised money to send a few members on pilgrimage each year. The most popular destination was Ise, with its outer shrine to the god of agriculture. Since few travelers were likely to repeat the pilgrimage experience, they were determined to see as much

as possible. They took enormous detours through temple circuits and stopped in Edo and Osaka for sightseeing and theater. Men traveled in the prime of life; women traveled either before they were married or after they had a daughter-in-law to raise the children and run the household. Rather than suffer the invasive inspection procedures required at checkpoints, women hired guides to show them byways. Men and women bought souvenirs to ship back home and distribute to those who had given them money before they left. They kept diaries of their trips; some were little more than expense accounts, and others were lengthy descriptions of things seen and heard.

Not every pilgrim was literate or had the permission of a local official. Fired, they said, with the imperative to make a pilgrimage to Ise or some other sacred spot, they escaped from parents or employers with nothing but the clothes on their backs. They depended on the charity of strangers who hoped to accrue some of the merit of making the pilgrimage by giving alms. They also fell prey to bandits and procurers. At approximately sixty-year intervals, thousands of people left towns and villages to make a thanksgiving pilgrimage (*okage mairi*) to the inner shrine of the sun goddess at Ise. Many never returned home. Instead they found their way to cities, where they joined a floating population of day laborers and prostitutes.

MAKING COMPARISONS

Neo-Confucianism

As a philosophical system and set of practices, what historians today call neo-Confucianism had a lasting impact on China, Korea, and Japan. It was distinguished by a search for a unifying explanation for the universe, the physical world, and human nature. Philosophers found this explanation in *li* (principle or pattern), an invisible metaphysical principle that informs everything. Plants, mountains, and people are what they are because of *li*, and *li* provides the link between them. Thus all things are fundamentally one, a view of the world with strong Buddhist overtones. At the same time, *li* is different in different objects—the principle in men is different from the principle in women. What gives things their physicality is *qi*—often translated as "ether," "physical force," or "matter." According to the great Song philosopher Zhu Xi (1130–1200), neither *li* nor *qi* could exist without the other.

Some philosophers believed that since human beings encapsulated *li* and *qi*, knowledge should be sought through meditation; others believed that it should be attained through studying books and examining the external world. What mediates between *li* and *qi* in human beings is *xin*—mind or heart. In its metaphysical form, *xin* is pure and flawless; in its physical form, it is clouded by desires (*yu*) and feelings (*qing*). Because desires and feelings can lead to evil, they have to be regulated.

Zhu Xi used precepts and rites centered on the virtues promoted in the Chinese classics to regulate individual behavior and family life in accordance with *li*. He warned that while food and procreation are necessary to sustain life, tasty food and too much contact with women stimulate desire. Men and women should lead separate lives, and the wife's position should differ from that of the concubines. To train people in the key virtue of filial piety, Zhu Xi detailed the appropriate rites for paying homage to ancestors. The household head and his wife played the central role, and the wife knew that, unlike concubines, she would join the ancestors on the family altar.

In Yuan, Ming, and Qing China, Zhu Xi's commentaries on the Confucian classics became required reading for all who hoped to pass the civil service examinations. The effects of this government-imposed orthodoxy were not as stultifying as one might expect, and in both Ming and Qing times it was not uncommon for neo-Confucian thinkers to reject Zhu Xi's understandings and propose radically different ideas.

In Korea, Chôson period *yangban* opposed to Buddhism seized on neo-Confucianism to order social relations and explore the nature of the universe. In the sixteenth century, scholars delved deeply into the relationship between *li* and *qi*, disputing which came first and trying to quantify their relative importance. In the eighteenth century, the positions staked out in this debate became aligned with different factions and justified purges.

Yangban incorporated separation of the sexes and filial piety into their daily lives. They reformed gender relations in the fifteenth century by diminishing women's status and property rights. As in China, they emphasized integrity, which for a widow meant that she must never remarry. The spatial arrangements for their houses separated male quarters at the front from female quarters at the back by walls and courtyard. Only sons by the primary wife could participate fully in *yangban* society, especially in taking civil service exams. The king had to venerate his father's wife in public rituals; if his mother had been a concubine, she received only private rites. When a man died, his eldest son moved to a grass hut beside the tomb where he performed elaborate rituals to feed and honor the departed.

In Tokugawa Japan, neo-Confucianism served the ideology of rule. The social hierarchy was deemed to reflect the natural order; by a sleight of hand, warriors turned into gentlemen. Even shoguns expounded on the classics praised by Zhu Xi and hired scholars to lecture on similarly suitable topics. While recognizing the centrality of filial piety and compiling records of filial children, samurai turned loyalty into an abstract, all-encompassing dictum for behavior. While some scholars investigated the external world, others evaluated desire and human feeling. A merchant philosopher taught meditation to clear the cloudy heart.

Living the neo-Confucian way was more problematic. Only wealthy members of the warrior class had the wherewithal to segregate their living space. They distinguished between wife and concubines as much for political as for moral reasons, although birth mothers received greater public acknowledgment than in Korea. Rather than waste a political asset, they forced their sisters and daughters to marry repeatedly. At the turn of the eighteenth century, the shogun codified mourning rituals that took into consideration the complex family relationships created by adoption, but Buddhist ritual specialists continued to mediate between the dead and the living. Even the most devoted follower of Zhu Xi's teachings could not bring himself to wail at his father's grave.

Hard Times and Peasant Uprisings

The underside to prosperity, continuing inequities, and injustice gave rise to thousands of incidents of rural protest. The corporate structure of the village meant that protest was organized collectively. When cultivators lodged complaints against unjust officials or pleas that the tax burden be reduced following a crop failure, they petitioned the lord to show compassion to the honorable cultivators because their hardships threatened their survival. As the village's representative, the headman was supposed to take the responsibility for seeking redress from samurai officials dealing with rural affairs. If officials deemed the matter worthy of consideration, they passed it up the chain of command. If at any point an official decided not to trouble his superiors, those below had no legal recourse. According to rural lore, in the seventeenth century a few brave headmen, epitomized by Sakura Sōgorō, made a direct appeal to the daimyo, or, in Sōgorō's case, to the shogun. Sōgorō paid for his audacity by suffering crucifixion along with his wife and saw his sons executed before his eyes. Although historians doubt his existence, he became Japan's most famous peasant martyr.

Few headmen in the eighteenth century were willing to risk their families to help their neighbors. Instead of an individual groveling before his superiors, cultivators marched together to assert their grievances en masse. They called their deeds *ikki*, harking back to the leagues that had bedeviled political authorities in the sixteenth century. In 1764, approximately two hundred thousand cultivators marched toward Edo to protest new demands for forced labor to transport officials and their goods on the national roads. Smaller outbursts roiled domains, peaking at times of economic hardship. Seldom did any district erupt more than once, and protestors wanted redress, not revolution. Yet fear that rural protest would expose such weaknesses in domainal administration that the shogun would transfer the daimyo or simply dispossess him limited efforts to expropriate the products of cultivators' labor.

The 1780s brought hard times to Japan. Mount Asama erupted in 1783, spewing ash that blocked sunlight all summer. Crop failures exacerbated by misguided governmental policies led to famine, a catastrophe repeated in 1787. It is said that the population declined by 920,000. In the eyes of many sufferers, the cause of their plight was not so much natural disaster as human failing. Unlike earlier rural protests that had demanded tax relief and government aid, the majority of incidents in the 1780s focused on commercial issues and the perfidy of merchants accused of hoarding grain while people starved. Commoners rioted for five days in Edo, punishing merchants by smashing their stores, trampling rice in the mud, and pouring sake in the street.

The famine exposed problems at all levels of society. The shogunate had struggled for years with an inadequate tax base and the increasing competition among daimyo, merchants, and cultivators for access to commercial income. Under the aegis of senior councilor Tanuma Okitsugu, it had proposed schemes to force merchants to buy shares in guilds granted a monopoly over trade in a specified item. The guild then paid regular fees in "thank you" money to the shogun. These monopolies angered those excluded, manufacturers forced to accept lower prices for their products, and daimyo who had their own schemes for profiting from trade. Following the Edo riot, the shogunate launched a second reform led by essayist, novelist, and staunch neo-Confucian Matsudaira Sadanobu to rectify finances and morals. He established new standards for bureaucratic conduct that endured to modern times. His "Edo first" policy ensured that the city remained quiescent for almost eighty years.

Sadanobu's reforms also had a darker side. A floating population of men without families or property worked as day laborers in fields and cities. Sadanobu had those in Edo rounded up and confined to an island in the bay. From there they were transported to the gold mine on Sado in the Japan Sea, where most of them died within two or three years. The harshness of this measure brought universal condemnation, and it was not repeated. Instead governments encouraged urban wards and rural villages to police themselves.

SUMMARY

What difference did two hundred years of peace make to Japan? Because the shogunate restricted foreign trade, historians once assumed that Japan stagnated. Such was not the case. Governments developed bureaucratic procedures that taught military men expertise in handling routine paperwork. Ideologues preached the virtue of the public performance of duty. Loyalty to one's lord became abstracted from individuals, a one-sided affair, and was no longer tied to reward. In economic terms, peace made possible an agricultural revolution based on a larger arable, better quality seeds, double cropping, and cash crops that forced people to work harder. Commerce boomed, and people let their pocketbooks regulate their behavior. To be sure, cultivators suffered under heavy taxes. Merchants had to accept arbitrary restrictions on commerce and pay ad hoc forced loans to meet the governments' endemic financial crises. *Sankin kōtai* kept the daimyo coming to Edo to pay homage to the shogun and scheming to enhance their domain's prosperity. Many samurai could not afford the pleasure districts, nor did their offices keep them occupied. They retreated to the private world of intellectual stimulation and the pursuit of pleasure, where they joined townspeople and rural entrepreneurs in fostering a vibrant popular culture.

PART FOUR

The Age of Western Imperialism (1800–1900)

Western Imperialism (1800–1900)

IN CONTRAST TO THE FRAIL WOODEN-hulled sailing ships that carried Europeans to the Pacific Ocean in the sixteenth century, nineteenth-century vessels were increasingly powered by coal-fueled steam engines. The industrial revolution that rescued Europe from the ecological trap of reliance on agrarian products propelled technological innovations in weaponry and an expansion in the state's ability to command men and resources. Following in the wake of trading companies, government officials regulated and taxed commerce, then administered territories, and finally recruited natives into disciplined, drilled, uniformed battalions capable of projecting force thousands of miles from European homelands. No longer mere participants in previously existing maritime trade, Europeans transformed their trading posts from India to Indonesia into colonies.

During the eighteenth century, European states had established trading posts throughout the Indian Ocean and the Pacific, the only colony there being Spain's in the Philippines. Under Catherine the Great, Russia extended its reach across Siberia to Alaska and sent teams of explorers down the Kamchatka peninsula, along the coast of Sakhalin, and into Hokkaido. Confrontations with Japanese officials led to sporadic efforts to open diplomatic relations. Having defeated French efforts to challenge its forays into India in the middle of the eighteenth century, the British East India Company spearheaded the battle for markets that brought administrators and troops to protect mercantile interests and made Britain the greatest of the European powers. While France was embroiled in revolution, Britain sent an official mission to China in 1793. Headed by Lord George Macartney, its aim was to eliminate what the British saw as frivolous restrictions on trade that limited the number, destination, and schedules of their ships. Since controlling trade helped stabilize the social order, reduced smuggling, and reaffirmed the Qing emperor's superiority over all other monarchs, the mission failed.

The Napoleonic Wars following the French Revolution remade the map of Europe and contributed to a new sense of nationalism. In Asia, Britain took over the Dutch colony at Batavia because Napoleon had tried to make his brother king of the Netherlands. The Dutch never told Japan that the only place flying the Dutch flag was Dejima in Nagasaki harbor. The Napoleonic Wars spilled over into European colonial possessions in Latin America. There, wars of liberation starting in 1809 resulted in the establishment of independent nations in the 1820s. The heightened focus on nationhood required a clear demarcation of sovereignty and a clear delineation of boundaries. No longer would small states such as Vietnam, the Ryukyus, and Korea be permitted to claim quasi-autonomy under China's mantle, and every inch of land had to belong to someone. Regardless of whether peasants saw themselves as Frenchmen, their rulers and the educated classes imagined communities in which everyone spoke the same language, professed similar beliefs, and despised foreigners. The cosmopolitan Enlightenment admiration for Chinese civilization and Confucian rationality gave way to disdain for godless heathens who failed to appreciate the superiority of Western technology. In contrast to older empires that allowed natives the opportunity to participate in running their affairs, new empires discriminated between the white man and everyone else.

By bringing decades of peace to Europe, Napoleon's defeat at Waterloo in 1815 freed nations to compete for Great Power status. Great Power status required colonies, and competition with other nations spurred imperialism. France reestablished its preeminence in North Africa, contended with Britain for ports in Burma, and tried to force a commercial treaty on Vietnam. In 1816, Britain was at war with Nepal when it dispatched a second mission to the Qing court. Because the envoy refused to participate in the customary rituals that regulated relations between tribute nations and the Son of Heaven, including the

Timeline: Western Advances in Asia

1793: Earl of Macartney travels to Beijing seeking diplomatic recognition; Russians seek same in Japan.

1797: Broughton, a British captain, surveys east coast of Korea.

1804: Russian advances in Siberia and Sea of Okhotsk culminate in emissary to Japan.

1805–1812: Russia builds forts in Alaska and northern California.

1808: British warship enters Nagasaki harbor.

1811: Britain captures Java from the Dutch; returned in 1816.

1816: Anglo-Nepalese War.

1819: Raffles, a British official, occupies Singapore for Britain.

1820: Vietnam bans Christianity and expels missionaries.

1824–1826: First Anglo-Burmese War.

1837: U.S. ship *Morrison* tries and fails to establish relations with Japan.

1839–1840: Opium War and First Anglo-Afghan War.

1842: Treaty of Nanjing.

1846: U.S. Commodore Biddle seeks trade with Japan; refused.

1852: Second Anglo-Burmese War.

1853–1854: U.S. Commodore Perry forces unequal treaty on Japan.

1856–1857: Arrow War between Britain, France, and China.

1858: Treaties of Tianjin; Japan signs commercial treaty with United States.

1857–1858: Great "Indian Mutiny"; British East India Company abolished.

1860: British and French troops occupy Beijing.

1862: Treaty of Saigon: France occupies three provinces in south Vietnam.

1863: France gains protectorate over Cambodia.

1866: France sends punitive expedition to Korea.

1871: United States sends ships to open Korea to foreign trade by force; repulsed.

1874: France acquires control over all of south Vietnam; Japan sends expeditionary force to Taiwan.

1876: Japan signs unequal treaty with Korea.

1877: Queen Victoria proclaimed empress of India.

1882: Korea signs unequal treaties with United States and other Great Powers.

1884–1885: France makes Vietnam a colony.

1885–1886: Third Anglo-Burmese War.

1893: France gains protectorate over Laos.

1894–1895: Sino-Japanese War.

1898: Scramble for concessions in China by European powers.

1898: United States seizes the Philippines from Spain; annexes Hawai'i.

1900: Boxer Rebellion.

---

kowtow, the emperor refused to see him. Britain had already established ports on the Malay Peninsula; adding Singapore gave it a harbor to protect and provision British ships sailing between India and China. British ships started appearing off the coast of Japan, sometimes threatening the natives in their quest for food and fuel. After Burmese troops, abetted by the French, threatened Bengal, the first Anglo-Burmese War ended in victory for Britain, a large indemnity extracted from the Burmese, a British diplomat sta-tioned at the Burmese court, and British hegemony over the Bay of Bengal.

Bengal supplied the opium that Britain used to buy tea. By 1750, Britain was importing well over 2 million pounds of tea from China a year, and demand was rising. Having little that China found of value, the British at first had to pay for tea with silver, thus leading to a negative trade balance. After 1761 the balance began to shift in Britain's favor. The East India Company allowed the illegal export of Bengali opium into China, bought tea for homeland consumption, and used the silver accruing as a result of the trade surplus to finance its operation and the British administration of Bengal. From the British point of view, that drug addicts multiplied as the price went down and the supply increased and that bribes to allow drug trafficking corrupted local officials simply demonstrated Chinese racial inferiority.

British merchants remained unhappy with trading conditions in China. Textile manufacturers wanted to sell machine-made cloth, and private traders resented the East India Company monopoly. When the monopoly was abolished in 1834, the government named Lord Napier to be superintendent of trade in Guangzhou. He tried to bypass the Cohong, the merchant guild responsible to the Qing court for managing foreign trade, and to negotiate directly with the provincial governor-general, who saw no reason to sully his dignity by dealing with barbarians. Diplomatic incident led to a confrontation between British warships and Chinese defenses. Napier was forced to withdraw. Trade continued, albeit with British merchants calling for warships to enforce their demands for the elimination of the Cohong monopoly over foreign trade and the opening of ports farther north.

The Opium War tested Chinese morality against British technology. In 1839, Imperial Commissioner Lin Zexu arrived in Guangzhou with orders to suppress the drug trade. He moved swiftly against dealers and users and demanded that opium under foreign control be turned over. When the British merchants proved recalcitrant, he stopped trade altogether. He appealed to Queen Victoria to allow him the same right to regulate trade and suppress drugs that administrators enjoyed in Britain. When the traders reluctantly relinquished their stocks, he allowed them to flee to the Portuguese city of Macao and thence to Hong Kong while he washed twenty thousand chests of opium out to sea. Indignant at the expropriation of their property without compensation, the traders appealed to Parliament. A fleet that included four armed steamships carrying Indian troops under British officers refused to contest the defenses Lin had built upstream to protect Guangzhou. Four ships blockaded the river mouth while the rest of the fleet sailed north to harass Chinese shipping along the coast. By the time the fleet reached Tianjin, the closest port to Beijing, the Qing court realized that it had to negotiate. In the first round of negotiations, China agreed to pay an indemnity to compensate British merchants for their destroyed property and to allow expanded trade in Guangzhou, direct access to Qing officials, and British possession of Hong Kong. When these terms proved unsatisfactory to the British home government, another round of fighting forced additional concessions.

China's defeat in the Opium War forced it to open to the West and inaugurated a new era in Western imperialism. (See Color Plate 31.) It marked the first time a Western power had emerged victorious in battle in East Asia, a debacle that sent shock waves through Japan, though not through Korea, which received its information only through official channels in Beijing. The Treaty of Nanjing opened five ports to British residency and trade, abolished the Cohong, and ceded Hong Kong to Britain. A supplementary treaty signed a year later fixed low tariffs on British imports and included the most favored nation clause whereby any privilege granted any Western power automatically accrued to Britain. In 1844, Americans signed a treaty with China that gave the United States the right to build churches and hospitals and to protect American nationals from the Chinese judicial system. "Extraterritoriality" meant that with the exception of opium traders, Americans in China were subject to American laws, judges, courts, and prisons. The British automatically participated in this infringement on Chinese sovereignty, as did other Western powers that signed treaties with China. Historian Akira Iriye has termed this "multilateral imperialism."[1] Because China and its subjects did not enjoy the same privileges abroad, most favored nation status and extraterritoriality became the hallmarks of the unequal treaty system.

Following in the British wake, American traders, whalers, and missionaries lured their government into engagement across the Pacific. During the 1840s, swift clipper ships with clouds of sail dominated trade routes. In 1846 an American ship shelled what is now Danang in central Vietnam to win the release of an American missionary who had ignored proscriptions on proselytizing. That same year, Commodore James Biddle tried to open negotiations with Japan, only to suffer a humiliating rejection. The United States completed its westward continental expansion in 1848 when it wrested California from Mexico. (It acquired Alaska by purchase from Russia in 1867.) In developing steamer routes across the Pacific to Shanghai,

---

1. A. Iriye, "Imperialism in East Asia," in *Modern East Asia: Essays in Interpretation*, ed. J. B. Crowley (New York: Harcourt, Brace & World, 1970), p. 129.

it saw Japan's coalfields as playing an important role. Whalers, too, needed access to fuel and fresh water. In 1853, Commodore Matthew Perry sailed into Uraga Bay near Edo. He forced shogunal authorities to accept a letter proposing a friendship treaty and promised to return the next year for their response. Despite Japanese efforts to fend him off, Perry obtained the Kanagawa treaty of friendship that opened two small ports to American ships, allowed an American consul to reside on Japanese soil, and provided for most favored nation treatment.

The Americans led in imposing modern diplomatic relations on Japan because Britain was busy elsewhere. Angry at what it considered unwarranted obstruction of trade and the exploitation of Burma's magnificent teak forests, Britain launched two more wars against Burma that resulted in Burma's becoming a British colony. Allied with France, Austria, Prussia, and the Ottoman Empire, Britain also fought the Crimean War of 1853–1856 against Russia for control over the mouth of the Danube and the Black Sea. Britain's rule in India suffered a temporary setback with the 1857 revolt, but the result was to strengthen Britain's hand in dealing with the remaining principalities, many of which had to accept British advisers and the protection of British troops.

Determined to open markets, Western powers soon imposed fresh demands on East Asia. After suppressing the 1857 revolt, Britain joined with France to attack Guangzhou and capture its governor-general, who had refused to pass their demands on to Beijing. Again the menace of foreign ships at Tianjin compelled the emperor to sign new treaties. Eleven new treaty ports, foreign vessels on the Yangzi, freedom of travel for foreigners in the interior, tolerance for missionaries and their converts, low tariffs, foreign ambassadors resident in Beijing, and the legalization of opium imports accrued to Britain, France, the United States, and Russia. When the Qing court tried to postpone the ambassadors' arrival and had the temerity to fire on British ships from new fortifications at Tianjin, the British and French retaliated by marching twenty thousand troops, many from India, to Beijing, where they destroyed the summer palace outside the city. In 1858, Townsend Harris, the American consul resident in Japan, pointed to what the European powers had achieved with their gunboats in China to convince the shogun's government to sign a commercial treaty with the United States. In addition to setting low tariffs on American goods, it extended the principle of extraterritoriality to Westerners in Japan. Angry at the murder of missionaries, a combined French and Spanish fleet attacked Vietnam in 1858. France went on to acquire most of southern Vietnam, a large indemnity, and a commercial treaty.

Western encroachment on East Asia waxed and waned in consort with conflicts elsewhere. In 1861, Russian sailors occupied Tsushima, an island in the strait between Japan and Korea, in part to forestall a similar action by the British and in part to gain a warm-water port. Unable to win official backing for this maneuver, they withdrew. During the American Civil War, 1861–1865, the United States managed only one military initiative: support for reopening the straits of Shimonoseki after Japan tried to close them. France, by contrast, made considerable gains. In 1863 it forced the Cambodian king to accept its protection. Two years later, it annexed two more provinces in south Vietnam and attacked Korea in retaliation for the execution of Catholic priests who had entered the country illegally. France's defeat in the Franco-Prussian War in 1871 put a temporary halt to its ambitions in Asia. In the meantime, a small American squadron tried to replicate Perry's success in Korea. When Korea refused to negotiate, it raided Korean forts guarding the entrance to Seoul and withdrew.

In contrast to priests who first spread Catholicism around the globe, nineteenth-century missionaries who likewise took the world as their stage were often nondenominational and as likely to be female as male. Unlike the Jesuits, who had tried to conciliate power holders and adjust to local practices, missionaries from Britain and the United States had a vision of Christianity that admitted no compromise with what they deemed heathen practices and beliefs. Impatient at restrictions on their activities imposed by treaties, they caused more than one international incident. Yet they also built hospitals, schools, and orphanages where none had existed before. They educated women and promoted some degree of gender equality. In Japan they opposed concubinage, and in China, foot-binding. They taught Western science and political philosophy, opening a window on the West used to advantage by East Asian reformers and revolutionaries.

Western imperialism demanded new countermeasures from China and Japan. Both nations started sending diplomatic missions abroad in the 1860s, in part to try to revise the unequal treaties or at least mitigate their effects and in part to study their opponents. Korea too sent study missions to China, Japan,

A Factory at Guangzhou. Supervised by a merchant, Chinese workers prepare tea and porcelain for export. *(Bridgeman Art Library)*

and the United States in the early 1880s. To the north, China resolved its boundary disputes with Russia. Trade increased, especially after the completion of the Suez Canal in 1869 halved travel time. The laying of telegraphic cables made communication between East and West practically instantaneous.

Western imperialism led directly and indirectly to increased migration within Asia and between Asia and the rest of the world. British plantation owners on the Malay peninsula imported Indian workers. Disruptions in local economies sent Indian merchants into Central Asia, Burma, and the South Pacific. Chinese seafarers, merchants, and laborers established overseas communities across Southeast Asia, notably in Java and Singapore. They also migrated to the United States, Hawaii, Cuba, and Peru, where they were brutally exploited because their government was perceived as too weak to protect them. The nineteenth century thus witnessed an Asian diaspora, led primarily by Indians and Chinese, that followed trade networks and filtered into colonies established by the Great Powers.

Japan soon began to mimic the Western claim that imperialism was necessary to civilize the savages by acquainting them with the material and spiritual benefits of modern technology and mechanisms of social control. In 1871 it proposed an unequal treaty with China, only to be rejected. Three years later, it dispatched a military expedition to Taiwan to retaliate for the murder of Ryukyuan fishermen. After the Qing court agreed to pay an indemnity, Japan withdrew. A similar plan to invade Korea did not materialize only because Japan's leaders did not think they were ready. Instead, Japan imposed a treaty on Korea that gave it the same privileges of most favored nation status and extraterritoriality that Westerners enjoyed in Japan. It also solidified its northern boundary by agreeing with Russia that while Sakhalin would become part of Russia, the Kuril Islands belonged to Japan.

Rivalries soon between the Great Powers brought fresh waves of Western imperialism across Asia and Africa. In 1882 the United States became the first Western power to sign a commercial treaty with Korea. Thanks to the most favored nation clause, the European powers and Japan immediately gained the same privileges. Following Vietnam's appeals for help from China, its nominal overlord, the French attacked a new naval base in China. China had to grant that Vietnam existed as a separate country and watch it be combined with Cambodia and, later, Laos into a French colony. Sandwiched between British Burma and French Indochina, Thailand remained independent by acquiescing to a series of unequal treaties. Russia and Britain tried to outbid each other for influence in Korea, while one faction at the Korean court sought American intervention to preserve Korean independence. Following decades of European exploratory trips through Africa, King Leopold II of Belgium in 1876 fostered the founding of the International Association for the Exploration and Civilization of Africa, while the British and French took over Egyptian finances to manage that country's debt to its European creditors. Britain performed a similar role in China when it undertook to collect customs duties for the Qing court. Belgium, Germany, Italy, Portugal, and Spain joined Britain and France in carving Africa into protectorates and colonies notable in varying degrees for the exploitation of natural resources and the brutal treatment of natives. (See Map C6.1.)

Imperialism in Asia entered a new phase when China and Japan fought over Korea in 1894–1895. When the Korean king requested help from China in suppressing rebellion, Japan responded first, lest China gain what it saw as unacceptable influence over the Korean court. Japan's victories on land and sea enabled it to claim Taiwan, the Pescadores islands, the Liaodong peninsula in Manchuria, forts on the Shandong peninsula, commercial concessions, and the usual bank-breaking indemnity. Russia opposed the Japanese land grab because of its own designs on Manchuria and Korea. Germany had growing commercial interests in China and wanted to divert Russia away from central Europe. France had an alliance with Russia. The three nations launched the Triple Intervention to make Japan restore the Liaodong and Shandong peninsulas to China. In a move that the Japanese public saw as blatant hypocrisy, the French then gained concessions in southern China for railroads and mines, and Russia got an eighty-year lease over the Liaodong peninsula from China that was later expanded to include Port Arthur. When the Germans built forts on portions of the Shandong peninsula, Britain took a naval base across from Port Arthur. Competition between the European powers precluded any of them from making China its colony. Instead they scrambled for concessions by carving out spheres of influence dominated by officials and traders, primarily along the coast and up the Yangzi River. Uneasy at the prospect of being shut out of the market for Chinese goods and souls, American merchants and missionaries called on their government to act. Secretary of State John Hay urged the European powers and Japan to adopt an "open door" policy that would preclude the spheres of influence from excluding Americans. The other powers agreed, albeit with reservations that protected their interests.

Even beyond the spheres of influence, missionaries brought change to northern and eastern China. Their letters to parishes back home heightened awareness of and interest in Chinese affairs. Missionaries also proved disruptive. When they forbade the rituals associated with ancestor worship, they seemingly threatened the fabric of family life. Since converts often came from the lower rungs of society, missionary efforts to protect them against the gentry or to rescue them from district magistrates' courts provoked outrage by entrenched local interests. When the missionary presence provoked violence, the Western powers dispatched gunboats and troops to intimidate local officials.

Although attacks on missionaries often roiled relations between the Western powers and China, none matched the consequences of the so-called Boxer Rebellion. It began in Shandong in 1898 as an antiforeign movement that combined martial arts with rituals promising invulnerability to weapons, somewhat similar to the Ghost Dance that rallied the Sioux against American encroachment in the Dakotas in the late 1880s. Boxers attacked converts and missionaries, sometimes with the quiet approbation of Qing officials. They routed Western troops sent to reinforce the defenses for the diplomatic community in Beijing and tore up railroad tracks between Tianjin and the capital. The Qing court ordered the massacre of all foreigners on Chinese soil and declared war on the foreign powers.

Faced with a common threat, the Western powers and Japan united against China. Efforts by Chinese generals in central and south China to suppress antiforeign elements in their areas helped Americans convince the other powers not to expand the scale of conflict beyond an expeditionary force sent to liberate the diplomatic community besieged in Beijing. When the expeditionary force reached the city in August 1900, the Qing court fled to Xi'an. Japanese soldiers watched with amazement as Western troops ran amok for three days in an orgy of looting, rape, and murder. Negotiations over the size of the indemnity to be extracted from China and its distribution among the powers dragged on for a year. The indemnity

The colonial powers and their possessions

Map C6.1   Western Imperialism in the Late Nineteenth Century imposed a crushing financial burden on the Chinese government and absorbed funds needed for economic development. Only rivalry among the powers, and particularly distrust of Russia, precluded proposals for China's dismemberment.

The nineteenth century marked the heyday of Western imperialism as practice and ideology. Following the spread of Darwin's revolutionary ideas on evolution and the survival of the fittest, Herbert Spencer and others developed the notion of Social Darwinism. They thought that not just species but also nations stood in danger of extinction unless they emerged victorious in the ceaseless competition between them. States that did not understand this principle or found themselves too weak to resist modern military technology naturally fell prey to conquerors from afar. Social Darwinism provided new justification for the Westerners' sense of racial superiority. Some used this notion to justify brutal exploitation of native populations. Others felt it their duty to bring civilization to the heathens. After the American colonization of the Philippines and annexation of Hawaii, Rudyard Kipling wrote:

> Take up the White Man's burden—
> Send forth the best ye breed—
> Go bind your sons to exile
> To serve your captives' need;
> To wait in heavy harness,
> On fluttered folk and wild—
> Your new-caught, sullen peoples,
> Half-devil and half-child."

. . . .

> Take up the White Man's burden—
> The savage wars of peace
> Fill full the mouth of Famine
> And bid the sickness cease;
> And when your goal is nearest
> The end for others sought,
> Watch sloth and heathen Folly
> Bring all your hopes to nought.[2]

Western imperialism in East Asia took a different form than in the rest of the world. Rather than establish colonies (Hong Kong and Macao being the exception), the Western powers imposed unequal treaties. Although they sought Asian labor for difficult, dangerous jobs such as building the transcontinental railroad, they issued various discriminatory exclusion laws to prevent first Chinese and then Japanese from residing permanently in their countries or becoming citizens. By dint of a Westernization project that included the enactment of Western-style commercial, civil, and criminal legal codes plus the creation of a modern army, Japan gained abolition of most favored nation treatment and extraterritoriality in 1899. Its victory in war with Russia to win control of the Liaodong peninsula in 1904–1905 gave hope to people all over Asia that Western dominance might pass.

---

2. R. Kipling, "The White Man's Burden," *McChary's Magazine* 12:4 (February 1899): 0-004.

China in Decline (1800–1900)

During the early nineteenth century, the Qing Dynasty seemed to be slipping into dynastic decline. Revenues were no longer adequate to cover the costs of administration. Rural poverty was worsening. Then in midcentury, some of the bloodiest rebellions in Chinese history broke out. On top of this, a new enemy had appeared on China's shores, one able to land its ships where it liked and destroy Chinese defenses with its cannons.

Yet the Qing Dynasty did not fall. The generals who suppressed the rebellions did not take to fighting among themselves to see which of them could found the next dynasty, as had happened so many times before in Chinese history. Some credit should go to the Qing elite, who in the 1860s and 1870s took on the task of self-strengthening. Yet progress, though real, was never rapid enough, and late in the century China suffered further blows to its pride: first its defeat by Japan in 1894–1895 and then the allied occupation of Beijing in 1900.

These internal and external threats and the way the Qing responded to them have preoccupied most historians who study nineteenth-century China. What made China's encounter with the West so different in the nineteenth century than in the eighteenth? How many of China's problems came from within and how many from outside forces? Does putting stress on the new challenges of Western imperialism distort understanding of this period, making the West into the actor and China merely a reactor? How did the Chinese elite understand the challenges they faced? Did it matter that China's rulers in this period were Manchu? Could the Qing have fared better if they had adopted different policies? Or were the forces of global capitalism and imperialism so skewed against China that different policies would have made little difference?

ECONOMIC AND FISCAL PROBLEMS

The peace that the Qing Dynasty brought to China allowed the population to grow rapidly. Although scholars have not come to a consensus on the details of China's population growth, there is wide agreement that by the beginning of the nineteenth century, China had a population in the vicinity of 300 million and was continuing to grow, reaching about 400 million by 1850. The traditional Chinese view of population increase was positive: growth was a sign of peace and prosperity. Through the eighteenth century, most still accepted that view. As developed areas became more crowded, farmers tried cultivating more intensively, making more use of irrigation and fertilizer and weeding more regularly, techniques that made possible denser population in the richest areas. Others moved to less crowded regions, both at the peripheries of the long-settled areas and the thinly populated southwest, previously occupied largely by minority peoples. The only lands suited to agriculture that were out of bounds were those in Manchuria, which the Qing maintained as a preserve for the Manchus.

In the early nineteenth century, China's standard of living fell behind Europe's. As farms grew smaller and surplus labor depressed wages, the average standard of living suffered. When the best lands were all occupied, conflicts over rights to water or tenancy increased. Hard times also led to increased female infanticide, as families felt they could not afford to raise more than two or three children and saw sons as necessities. A shortage of marriageable women resulted, reducing the incentive for young men to stay near home and do as their elders told them. Many young men who took to the road in hope of finding better opportunities never found permanent homes; instead they became part of a floating population of the unemployed, moving around in search of work. They would take seasonal farm work or work as boatmen, charcoal burners, night soil collectors, and the like. In cities they might become sedan chair carriers, beggars, or thieves. Women, even poor ones, had an easier time finding a place in a home because of the demand for maids and concubines. But poverty fed the traffic in women; poor families sold their daughters for cash, perhaps expecting them to become rich men's concubines, though many ended up as prostitutes. Population growth also added to the burdens placed on local governments. Although the population doubled and tripled, the number of counties and county officials stayed the same. Magistrates often found that they had to turn to the local elite for help, even turning tax collection over to them.

During the Qianlong reign, the government had resources to try to improve the lot of the poor. But in the nineteenth century, even determined emperors like the Daoguang emperor (r. 1821–1850) were chronically short of revenue for crucial public works and relief measures. The Daoguang emperor set an example of frugality at court and encouraged his officials to cut every possible cost, but the fiscal situation steadily worsened. He ordered repairs to the Grand Canal (see **Material Culture: The Grand Canal**), yet the years of neglect meant that more and more tax grain had to be sent by sea, exacerbating unemployment in north China.

Another problem the emperor faced was supporting the hereditary military force, the banners, which in a manner reminiscent of the decline of the Ming hereditary soldiers was no longer effective in war. To suppress the rebellions of the late eighteenth century, the government was forced to turn to local militias and the professional (as opposed to hereditary) army of Chinese recruits called the Army of the Green Standard. Because the banners were so tied to Manchu identity and privileges, the emperor could not simply disband them, as the Ming had its hereditary military households. The best the Daoguang emperor could hope for was to keep bannermen from becoming beggars, bandits, opium smugglers, or opium addicts.

MIDCENTURY CRISES

The decline of the Qing military forces was made evident to all in the 1840s and 1850s when the dynasty had to cope with military crises along its coastlines and throughout its interior.

The Opium War

As discussed in Chapter 16, the Qing Dynasty dealt with foreign countries according to a set of rules it had largely taken over from the Ming Dynasty. Europeans were permitted to trade only at the port of Guangzhou and only through licensed Chinese merchants. In the eighteenth century, the balance of trade was in China's favor, as Great Britain and other Western nations used silver to pay for steadily increasing purchases of tea. British traders found few buyers when they brought British and Indian goods to Guangzhou to sell. When Macartney asked the Qianlong emperor to alter the way trade was conducted, the emperor saw no reason to approve his request.

As discussed in **Connections: Western Imperialism (1800–1900)**, all this soon changed. By the late eighteenth century, the British had found something the Chinese would buy: opium. Made from poppy plants,

MATERIAL CULTURE

The Grand Canal

Transport canals were dug in China from ancient times. The first Grand Canal connecting Luoyang to the Yangzi River was completed during the Sui Dynasty. During Song times the canal extended south to Hangzhou, and in Yuan times it reached north to Beijing. During the Ming period the government invested a lot of effort in maintaining the Grand Canal as it carried a large share of the tax grain.

The canal that the Qing inherited was 1,747 kilometers long and crossed five major rivers. It had to rise to 138 feet above sea level to get over the mountains of western Shandong. This necessitated an elaborate system of locks, dams, sluice gates, and slipways. Pulleys driven by animal or human labor pulled boats through sluice gates and skips. Because the canal crossed the Yellow River, maintaining the dikes on the river was crucial to keep floods with their heavy deposits of silt from clogging the canal.

By the early nineteenth century, more than fifty thousand hereditary boatmen and migrant laborers worked moving the tax grain up the canal from the southeast to the capital. In 1824 the grain ships en route to Beijing became mired in silt because the canal had not been properly maintained. Boatmen were put to work making repairs, but more and more grain tax had to be sent by the sea route. By 1850 the canal was largely abandoned. Unemployed boatmen were prominent among those who joined the Nian rebellion in the 1850s.

Map **18.1**   **Grand Canal During the Ming and Qing Dynasties**

opium had been used in China for medicinal purposes for several centuries. Once a way was found to smoke pure opium sap in pipes, opium became a recreational drug that people took to relieve pain and boredom and to make tedious or taxing work more bearable. The drawback was that it was addictive; those who stopped taking it suffered chills, nausea, and muscle cramps. The Daoguang emperor was outraged when an 1831 investigation showed that members of the imperial clan, high officials, and bannermen were among those addicted to opium. Once addicted, people would do almost anything to keep up the

supply of the drug, even pawning their clothing and selling their children. To fight addiction, the Chinese government banned both the production and the importation of opium in 1800. In 1813 it went further and outlawed the smoking of opium, punishing it with a beating of a hundred blows.

The opium that the British brought to China was grown in India. Following the British acquisition of large parts of India, the East India Company invested heavily in planting and processing opium, over which it had a profitable monopoly. Once China made trade in opium illegal, the company did not dis-

Physic Street, Guangzhou. The English photographer who took this picture in the 1860s described the street as one of the finest in the city, not nearly as narrow as others nearby. The shop signs announce the sale of such things as drugs, cushions, seals, and ink. *(Photo by John Thomson/George Eastman House/Getty Images)*

tribute opium itself; rather, licensed private traders, Americans as well as British, carried the drug to China. Chinese smugglers bought opium from British and American traders anchored off the coast, then distributed it through a series of middlemen, making it difficult for the Qing government to catch the major dealers.

By 1831 there were between one hundred and two hundred Chinese smugglers' boats plying the Guangdong coastal waters. The competition among private traders led to a price war in China that drove the price of opium down and thus spread addiction. Imports increased rapidly, from forty-five hundred chests smuggled into China in 1810 to forty thousand chests in 1838, enough to supply 2 million addicts. By this point, it was China that suffered a drain of silver. The outflow increased from about 2 million ounces of silver per year in the 1820s to about 9 million in the 1830s. This silver drain hurt farmers because their taxes were assessed in silver. A tax obligation of 1 ounce of silver took about 1,500 cash to pay in 1800, but 2,700 cash in 1830.

The Daoguang emperor called for debate on how to deal with this crisis. Some court officials advocated legalizing the sale of opium and taxing it, which would help alleviate the government revenue shortfalls and perhaps make the drug expensive enough to deter some people from trying it. Other officials strongly disagreed, believing that an evil like opium had to be stopped. The governor-general, Lin Zexu, argued that rather than concentrate on the users, the government should go after those who imported or sold the drug. Unless trade in the drug was suppressed, he argued, the Qing would have no soldiers to fight the enemy and no funds to support an army. Lin's impassioned stand and his reputation as incorruptible led the Daoguang emperor in late 1838 to assign him the task of suppressing the opium trade. Once Lin arrived at Guangzhou, he made rapid progress, arresting some seventeen hundred Chinese dealers and seizing seventy thousand opium pipes. He demanded that foreign firms turn over their opium stores as well, offering tea in exchange. When his appeals failed, Lin stopped all trade and placed a siege on the Western merchants' enclave. After six weeks, the merchants relented and turned over their opium, some 2.6 million pounds. Lin set five hundred laborers to work for twenty-two days to destroy the opium by mixing it with salt and lime and washing it into the sea. He pressured the Portuguese to expel the uncooperative British from Macao, as a consequence of which they settled on the barren island of Hong Kong.

To the British superintendent of trade, Lin's act was an affront to British dignity and cause enough for war. The British saw China as out of step with the modern world in which all "civilized" nations practiced free trade and maintained "normal" international relations through envoys and treaties. With the encouragement of their merchants in China, the British sent from India a small, mobile expeditionary force of forty-two ships, many of them leased from the major opium trader Jardine, Matheson, and Company. Because Lin had strengthened defenses at Guangzhou, the British sailed north and shut down the major ports of Ningbo and Tianjin, forcing the Qing to negotiate (see Map 18.1). A preliminary agreement called for ceding Hong Kong, repaying the British the cost of their expedition, and allowing direct diplomatic intercourse between the new countries.

In both countries, the response was outrage. The Daoguang emperor had withdrawn his support for Lin as soon as the war broke out and had sent him into exile in the far northwest; now the official who negotiated the treaty was also treated like a criminal. The English sent a second, larger force, which attacked Guangzhou, occupied other ports, including Shanghai, as it proceeded up the coast, and finally sailed up the Yangzi River to Nanjing. Dozens of Qing officers, both Manchu and Chinese, committed suicide when they saw that they could not repel the British (see **Biography: Manchu Bannerman Guancheng**).

At this point, the Qing government had no choice but to capitulate, and its representatives signed a treaty on board a British naval vessel. The 1842 Treaty of Nanjing, which settled the Opium War, was concluded at gunpoint and provided benefits for Britain but not for China, making it "unequal." It was soon followed by an amended agreement and treaties with the United States and France. This set of treaties mandated ambassadors in Beijing, opened five ports to international trade, fixed the tariff on imported goods at 5 percent, imposed an indemnity of 21 million silver dollars on China to cover Britain's war costs, and ceded the island of Hong Kong to Britain. Through the clause on extraterritoriality, British subjects in China were answerable only to British law, even in disputes with Chinese. The most favored nation clause meant that whenever one nation extracted a new privilege from China, it was extended automatically to Britain. Western imperialism had its first victory in China.

At the Daoguang court, the aftermath of this debacle was a bitter struggle between war and peace factions reminiscent of the similar disputes during the Song Dynasty. Those who had favored compromising with the "sea barbarians" to avoid further hostilities included the Manchu chancellor Mujangga; those opposed were mostly Chinese degree holders who had supported Lin Zexu and believed the Qing should have put up stronger resistance. After the Daoguang emperor died in 1850, his successor announced his determination to make no more concessions by dismissing Mujangga and bringing back Lin Zexu. The court kept finding excuses not to accept foreign diplomats at its capital in Beijing, and its compliance with the commercial clauses fell far short of Western expectations.

The Opium War exposed the fact that Qing military technology was hopelessly obsolete. The Qing had no navy. Britain had not only large men-of-war but also new shallow-draft steamships that could sail up rivers. Thus, the British could land troops wherever they liked. Troops would pillage, then return to their ships to attack a new target. On a single day in 1841, a British steam-powered warship with long-distance artillery destroyed nine war junks, five forts, two military stations, and a shore battery. Even when Qing forces fought on land, they were no match for the British troops. To fight British soldiers armed with rifles, the Chinese and Manchu soldiers used swords, spears, clubs, and arrows. The minority with firearms had only matchlock muskets that required soldiers to ignite each load of gunpowder by hand.

Taiping Rebellion

Beginning less than a decade after the Opium War, the Qing Dynasty faced some of the most destructive rebellions in world history. The bloodiest was the Taiping Rebellion (1851–1864), in which some 20 to 30 million people lost their lives.

Like many of China's earlier insurrections, this one had its organizational base in an unorthodox religious sect. The founder of this sect was Hong Xiuquan (1814–1864). Hong was a Hakka (the Hakkas were a large Han Chinese ethnic group that spoke a distinct dialect and lived predominantly in the far south). Although from a humble background, Hong had spent years attempting the civil service examinations. His career as a religious leader began with visions of a golden-bearded old man and a middle-aged man who addressed him as younger brother and told him to annihilate devils. After reading a Christian tract that a missionary in Guangzhou had given to him, Hong interpreted his visions to mean that he was Jesus's younger brother. He began preaching, calling on people to destroy idols and ancestral temples, give up opium and alcohol, and renounce foot binding and prostitution. Hong spent two months studying with a Christian preacher and adopted the Ten Commandments, monotheism, and the practice of communal prayer and hymns. He called his group the God Worshipping Society and soon attracted many followers, especially among the Hakkas.

Hong was a visionary, not an organizer, and other leaders emerged who learned how to manipulate him. In 1848, while Hong and his closest associate were away from their headquarters, an illiterate charcoal maker and local bully named Yang Xiuqing elevated himself and three others to top posts within the God Worshippers. To claim superiority over Hong, Yang announced that when he spoke, it was the voice of God the Father, putting him above Hong, the mere younger brother.

In 1850 the Taiping leaders told all God Worshippers to leave their homes, pool their money into a

BIOGRAPHY Manchu Bannerman Guancheng

Guancheng (ca. 1790–1843) was born the son of a Manchu bannerman of the Hangzhou garrisons, stationed at the nearby port of Zhapu. Although he would be considered Manchu through descent on the male line, both his mother and his father's mother were daughters of Chinese bannermen in the same garrisons. His father died when he was an infant, and he was raised by his mother and his deceased elder brother's widow. In his youth the banner garrisons were chronically short of funds for bannerman stipends and payments for widows and orphans; therefore, he most likely grew up in straitened circumstances. Still, he attended banner schools, where he studied both Chinese and Manchu. By the age of twenty he was working as a tutor himself, and at age twenty-seven he attained the *juren* degree, availing himself of the special quota for Manchu bannermen. By then he also had a Chinese name, Guan Weitong, which used part of his personal name as a Chinese family name. (In Manchu, his clan name was Gūwalgiya, but Manchu clan names were not used as terms of address.) To supplement his family's income, in this period Guancheng took on some publishing jobs.

In the late 1820s, Guancheng traveled to Beijing to take the *jinshi* examinations. Beijing was the great center of Manchu life, home to perhaps 150,000 Manchus. Opium addiction had already become a major problem among the underemployed bannermen, something Guancheng would undoubtedly have noticed. But it was also home to Manchu nobles who lived a highly cultivated life. The highest-ranking member of his clan had a mansion in the city and welcomed Guancheng to his social circle. There he met descendants of Qing emperors and heard much lore about Manchu court life. The language in which they discussed these subjects was, however, Chinese.

Although Guancheng did not pass the *jinshi* exam, he was given an honorary degree and in

1833 was appointed a probationary magistrate of a county in Sichuan. He took two of his sons, ages nine and eleven, with him to Sichuan but sent his wife and two youngest sons back to Zhapu. At first he was rapidly transferred from one county to another, then from 1834 to 1842 had a long stint as magistrate of Nanchuan county, a tea-producing region 39 miles south of the Yangzi River. Local non-Chinese rebelled during his tenure, adding to hardships caused by locusts. Still, his son remembered the time in Sichuan as very enjoyable.

When Guancheng returned to Zhapu in 1842 at age fifty-three, he was something of a celebrity—a local bannerman who had succeeded in the outside world. His home community, meanwhile, had suffered a devastating blow. In 1840, at the start of the Opium War, British ships had shelled the Zhapu ports. Despite attempts to reinforce the garrisons for a possible return of the British, when they did in fact return in the spring of 1842, Zhapu's defenses proved sorely lacking. Many of those who did not die defending Zhapu took their own lives afterward, often first killing their wives and children. On his return, Guancheng, though ill himself, took on the task of writing and printing an account of the heroism of the bannermen in the defense of Zhapu. He wanted help for those who had survived and honor for those who had died. "The officers, soldiers, men and women of our garrison were ill-prepared for this, the corpses having been found piled against buildings and even suspended from the battlements. In mourning our nation's dead, how could we bear to allow these loyal clansmen to be buried without benefit of ceremony?"[1] After Guancheng died in early 1843, his son issued a revised "Record of Martyrs."

---

1. Translated in Pamela Kyle Crossley, *Orphan Warriors: Three Manchu Generations and the End of the Qing World* (Princeton, N.J.: Princeton University Press, 1990), p. 115.

Map 18.2   Internal and External Conflicts During the Nineteenth Century

common treasury, and move to Thistle Mountain in Guangxi province, a site that soon became a huge military camp. In 1851, Hong declared himself king of the Heavenly Kingdom of Great Peace (Taiping), an act of open insurrection. Men were to abandon the Manchu queue and let their hair grow long. Hong's true believers were brave in battle, maintained strict discipline, and seized large stores of government weapons as they campaigned. Their religious zeal propelled them to destroy local temples, even though this alienated many commoners. They regularly forced those whose villages they captured to join their movement, enrolling men and women into separate work and military teams. Some brigades of women soldiers fought Qing forces.

Once news of the progress of the rebellion reached the court, Qing troops were dispatched to disperse

the Taipings and arrest their leaders (see Map 18.1). To the shock of the court, the Qing troops were soundly defeated. A rebel proclamation of 1852 made use of resentment of the Manchus who, it said, "stole China's empire, appropriated China's food and clothing, and ravished China's sons and daughters."[3] Manchu bannermen and their families were often slaughtered after Taiping forces took a city.

After making Nanjing their capital, the Taipings announced plans for a utopian society based on the equalization of landholdings and the equality of men and women. Women could take the civil service examinations, which were based on Hong Xiuquan's

---

3. Franz Michael, *The Taiping Rebellion: History and Documents* (Seattle: University of Washington Press, 1971), 2:145–147.

teachings and translations of the Bible. Christian missionaries at first were excited about the prospect of revolutionaries spreading Christianity, but quickly concluded that the Christian elements in Taiping doctrines were heretical and did nothing to help them. In fact, when the Taipings tried to take Shanghai in 1860 and 1862, the Western residents organized counterattacks.

In time the Taipings were weakened by internal dissension. The group of leaders called Kings gave themselves all sorts of privileges, including well-stocked harems, while they made their followers live in sex-segregated housing. Hong and Yang turned on each other. When Yang claimed that God the Father insisted that Hong should be beaten for kicking one of Yang's concubines, Hong arranged to have Yang executed. The king entrusted with this task killed not only Yang and his family but twenty thousand followers, leading to another round of revenge killings.

The Chinese elite were horrified by the Taiping movement with its bizarre foreign gods and women soldiers. In many places, local officials and landlords organized their own defense, repairing city walls, gathering food to withstand a siege, and arming and drilling recruits. The Qing government soon realized that it would have to turn to such locally raised armies if it wished to make progress against the Taipings.

The man they turned to, Zeng Guofan (1811–1872), was back at home in Hunan province to mourn his mother. Since passing the *jinshi* exam in 1838, Zeng had risen in the government and had served in Beijing in high positions in the ministries of justice and personnel. Although a man devoted to his family, he was persuaded that his duty to his country superseded his duty as a filial son to mourn his mother.

Zeng knew the failings of the Qing armies and organized his army in a new way. He recruited officers from among the Confucian-educated elite and had them recruit their own soldiers from among farmers in their region. Zeng was given permission to draw on local tax receipts and so could pay the soldiers and officers well. Soldiers were loyal to their officers and the officers to Zeng, creating an essentially private army. After Zeng constructed 240 war junks so that he could attack by river and gathered some modern Western weapons such as artillery, he set about recovering Hunan province bit by bit. The Taipings, however, also made advances, and Zeng needed twelve years and 120,000 troops before he fully defeated the Taipings. Generals under him, including close relatives and his protégés Li Hongzhang and Zuo Zongtang, played major roles in the slow stranglehold placed over the Taiping capital at

Nanjing. When Nanjing fell, none of the Taipings survived. Elsewhere in south China, the Taipings held out longer, with some armies relocating to Taiwan and Vietnam. In Vietnam, where they were known as the Black Flags, they took an active part in resistance to French colonial expansion.

The devastation wreaked both by the Taipings' campaigns and the Qing campaigns to suppress them was horrendous. One Western observer wrote in 1865 that China's plains were "strewn with human skeletons," its rivers "polluted with floating carcasses."[4] Much of the productive power of the lower Yangzi region was ruined for a generation.

Other Rebellions

The Taipings were turned back when they took their campaign into north China, but that region soon found itself torn apart by homegrown insurrections. Along the route of the Grand Canal, poverty and unemployment had driven many villagers into banditry. These groups of the disaffected, called Nian gangs, engaged in a variety of predatory practices. Riding horseback, they would seize villagers' crops, rob traveling merchants, and kidnap the wealthy to hold them for ransom. Severe flooding in 1851 weakened the dikes of the Yellow River, which gave way in 1855, leading to a devastating shift in the Yellow River from south of the Shandong peninsula to north of it. Those made homeless by the floods joined the Nian bands simply to survive. Many joined on a seasonal basis, staying home in the summer and winter but raiding and plundering in the autumn and spring. After the Taipings fell in 1864, some of their soldiers joined the Nian rebellion. In 1865, when it was clear that the Qing regular armies had failed to suppress the Nian, Zeng Guofan and Li Hongzhang were assigned the long and difficult task.

With the transfer of armies to the interior to fight the Taipings and Nian rebels, uprisings also got out of hand in the northwest and southwest. These rebellions drew from and also exacerbated ethnic tensions and hatreds. In Yunnan, the large Muslim population had grievances based on Han Chinese settlers' moving into their territory and seizing resources such as copper, gold, and silver mines. As tensions escalated, so did feuds and violence. Han Chinese formed militias

---

4. Cited in R. Keith Schoppa, *Revolution and Its Past: Identities and Change in Modern Chinese History* (Upper Saddle River, N.J.: Prentice Hall, 2002), p. 64.

to kill Muslims, who in retaliation assassinated Chinese officials. Rebels captured the city of Dali and announced the sultanate of Panthay. The remote location of Yunnan and its mountainous topography made it difficult for the Qing to send troops there. The Qing was able to regain control in 1873 only because it learned to play opposing factions of Muslims against each other.

The Muslim rebellion in the northwest was rooted in the spread of a mystical school of Islam known as Sufism, but much of the violence came from long-standing antagonism between the Han Chinese and the Muslims. By 1867 all of Gansu was in Muslim hands. Preoccupied with its problems elsewhere, the Qing did not send Zuo Zongtang (1812–1885) to retake the region until 1866. Zuo classed Sufis as heterodox, like White Lotus or Taiping sectarians, and ordered their slaughter. The campaign took five years and consisted largely of sieges during which the population slowly starved. Zuo Zongtang marched his troops into Xinjiang, which might well have broken away from Qing control otherwise.

The Second Opium War

While the Qing court was struggling to suppress the Taiping, Nian, and Muslim rebellions, it had to face demands from foreign powers as well. Russia, seeing China's weakness, penetrated the Amur River valley, violating the borders agreed to in 1689. In new treaties of 1858–1860, Russia gained the maritime provinces of eastern Manchuria down to Vladivostok. A large part of the reason the Qing decided to march an army into Xinjiang was fear of Russian expansion there.

Britain and France were pressing China as well. Both sides wanted the trade agreement reached after the Opium War renegotiated, though for different reasons. On the grounds that China had failed to implement all the provisions agreed to a decade earlier, the British and French decided to make swift, brutal coastal attacks, a repeat of the Opium War. (They called it the Arrow War, from the name of a ship that gave the British a pretext for war.) Guangzhou was easily captured at the end of 1857 and held for three years. By mid-1858, the French and British ships were in the north and took the forts at Tianjin. At this point, the Qing court in Beijing sent senior officials to negotiate. When the British threatened to march on Beijing unless they were allowed permanent diplomatic representation in Beijing, the

hard-pressed Manchu negotiator conceded. Also secured in these treaties were the opening of ten new ports; permission for Westerners, including missionaries, to travel through China; a fixed transit tariff for foreign goods within China of no more than 2.5 percent; and an indemnity of 4 million ounces of silver for the British and 2 million for the French. Each side was to have its rulers ratify the treaties and return in a year for the signing.

The Qing emperor was strongly opposed to allowing ambassadors to reside in Beijing, viewing them as little better than spies. When the British returned and insisted on taking their ships up the Beihe River toward Beijing instead of going overland, as the Qing wanted them to, Qing forces withstood them. A new expedition was then dispatched with eleven thousand British soldiers and sixty-seven hundred French ones. When Qing authorities did not let them have their way on all matters, they charged into Beijing. The Russian ambassador, already in residence in Beijing, talked the British out of burning the palace in retaliation. The British and French then marched to the summer palace located northwest of the city, a complex of two hundred or so buildings. They looted the buildings of furniture, porcelains, robes, and whatever else attracted them and then torched the entire 10-square-mile complex. The Russian ambassador this time approached the Qing court and talked them into accepting the offered terms, which included having to pay a larger indemnity of 16 million ounces of silver and transfer of the Kowloon peninsula opposite Hong Kong island to Britain.

Because the Western powers gained many advantages through these unequal treaties, after 1860 they increasingly saw propping up the faltering Qing Dynasty as in their interest.

SELF-STRENGTHENING

In 1861 the Xianfeng emperor died and was succeeded by a young son. The child's uncle, Prince Gong, and his mother, Empress Dowager Cixi, served as regents. A change in emperor normally meant a change in chancellors and other high officials, making it easier for the court to take new directions. Certainly, new policies were needed; much of the most productive parts of the country had been laid waste by the rebellions, none of which was yet suppressed, and the British and French had only recently left Beijing after extracting new concessions.

In that same year, a scholar named Feng Guifen (1809–1874) wrote a set of essays presenting the case for wide-ranging reforms. He had taken refuge in Shanghai during the Taiping War and there had seen how the Westerners defended the city. In his essays he pointed out that China was a hundred times bigger than France and two hundred times bigger than Great Britain. "Why are Western nations small and yet strong? Why are we large and yet weak?" He called for hiring a few "barbarians" to help set up shipyards and arsenals in each major port. To get ambitious men to take on the task of managing these enterprises, he proposed rewarding them with examination degrees if the ships and weapons produced were as good as the foreigners'. He also proposed setting up translation bureaus to translate Western books on mathematics and the sciences. Westerners should be hired to teach groups of boys Western languages. "China has many brilliant people. There must be some who can learn from the barbarians and surpass them."[5] He pointed out that many Westerners had learned the Chinese language and much about the country; surely there should be Chinese people just as capable. To improve the morale of officials, he proposed subjecting high officials to election by lower-ranking officials. Local elites would be given the power to nominate local officials, thus broadening political participation considerably. Undoubtedly influenced by what he had learned of foreign election practices, he specified that the votes were to be counted.

An important minority of officials, including Zeng Guofan and Li Hongzhang, were more and more persuaded by these sorts of arguments. Prince Gong sided with them, and changes were made not only in how soldiers were trained and weapons produced, but also in the conduct of foreign affairs. Arsenals and dockyards were established, schools opened to teach European languages and international law, and a foreign office established to manage diplomatic affairs, with Prince Gong in charge. By 1880, China had embassies in London, Paris, Berlin, Madrid, Washington, Tokyo, and St. Petersburg.

5. W. Theodore de Bary and Richard Lufrano, *Sources of Chinese Tradition: From 1600 Through the Twentieth Century* (New York: Columbia University Press, 2000), pp. 236, 237.

Li Hongzhang's Self-Strengthening Projects, 1862–1893

1862 Created gun factories at Shanghai with British and German instructors
1863 Established a foreign language school in Shanghai
1864 Created a gun factory at Suzhou
1865 Established Jiangnan Arsenal at Shanghai with a translation bureau attached, jointly with Zeng Guofan
1867 Established Nanjing Arsenal
1870 Expanded machine factory in Tianjin
1872 Sent officers to study in Germany. Made request to open coal and iron mines. Jointly with Zeng recommended sending teenagers to study in the U.S. Supported China Merchants' Steam Navigation Company as a "government-supervised merchant enterprise"
1876 Sent seven officers to Germany
1877 Created the Bureau for the Kaiping Coal Mines in Tianjin
1878 Established the Shanghai Cotton Mill
1880 Established a naval academy in Tianjin. Requested permission to build a railroad.
1882 Began construction of a harbor and shipyard at Port Arthur
1884 Sent naval students and apprentices to Europe to learn shipbuilding and navigation
1885 Established a military academy in Tianjin with German teachers
1887 Established a mint at Tianjin. Began gold mining operation in Heilongjiang
1888 Established the Beiyang fleet
1891 Established a paper mill in Shanghai
1893 Set up a general office for mechanized textile manufacturing

---

After Zeng Guofan's death in 1872, Li Hongzhang emerged as the leading Chinese political figure. From 1872 to 1901 he served as the governor-general of Zhili province (modern Hebei) and headed one of the most important of the new armies. As the Chinese learned more about Western ways, Li and other modernizers came to recognize that guns and ships were merely the surface manifestation of the Western powers' economic strength. To catch up with the West, they argued, China would have to initiate new industries, which in the 1870s and 1880s included railway lines, steam navigation companies, coal mines, telegraph lines, and cotton-spinning and weaving factories. By the 1890s knowledge of the West had improved considerably. Newspapers covering world affairs had begun publication in Shanghai and Hong Kong, and more and more Western works were being translated.

For a while, China seemed to be taking the same direction as Meiji Japan (see Chapter 20), but resistance in China proved much stronger. Conservatives thought that copying Western practices compounded defeat. The high official Woren objected to the establishment of an interpreters' college on the grounds that "from ancient down to modern times" there had never been "anyone who could use mathematics to raise a nation from a state of decline or to strengthen it in times of weakness."[6] Even men like Zeng Guofan, who saw the need to modernize the military, had little respect for merchants and profit seeking.

Although to the Qing court new policies were being introduced at a rapid rate, the court never became enthusiastic about the prospect of fundamental change. Most of those in power were apprehensive about the ways changes in education or military organization would undermine inherited values and the existing power structure. Repeated humiliations by foreigners from the 1840s on fostered political rancor and denunciations of men in power. Both the court and much of the population remained opposed to doing anything that smacked of giving in to the arrogant and uncouth foreigners. As a consequence, the reforms were never fundamental enough to solve China's problems. Guo Song-tao, China's first ambassador to Britain (1877–1879), sent letters from London to Li Hongzhang praising both the British parliamentary government and its industries. On his return he became a persona non grata, and the court ordered that the printing blocks carved to publish his diary be destroyed.

Empress Dowager Cixi

During the self-strengthening period, the most powerful person at court was Empress Dowager Cixi. In 1875, when her son, the Tongzhi emperor, was nineteen, he died of smallpox, barely having had a chance to rule on his own. Cixi chose his cousin to succeed him, who is known as the Guangxu emperor (r. 1875–1908). By selecting a boy of four, Cixi could continue in power as regent for many years to come.

Empress Dowager Cixi. Cixi spent more than half a century in the palace. She entered in 1852, became Empress Dowager in 1861, and had her nephew, the Guangxu emperor, put under house arrest in 1898. *(Free Gallery of Art and Arthur M. Sackler Gallery Archives, Smithsonian Institution, Washington, D.C. Purchase. Photographer: Xunling.)*

Cixi was a skillful political operator. She recognized the fears of the Manchu establishment that they were being sidelined and presented herself to them as a staunch defender of Manchu privileges. She needed modernizers like Li Hongzhang and cajoled them with titles and honors, but she kept them in check by also encouraging their conservative critics.

It was under Cixi's watch that the old tribute system was finally dismantled. Three neighboring countries—Korea, the Ryukyu Islands, and Vietnam—had been regular, loyal tributaries, making them seem to Westerners not fully independent countries. Japan forced the Ryukyus away from China in the 1870s. In the 1880s, France forced Vietnam away.

Although no part of Vietnam had been under direct Chinese rule since Tang times, Chinese influence

---

6. Ssu-yü Teng and John K. Fairbank, *China's Response to the West* (Cambridge: Harvard University Press, 1979), p. 76, modified.

there had remained strong. The Vietnamese government was closely modeled on the Chinese, supported Zhu Xi's Confucian teachings, and used examinations to recruit officials. Official documents and histories were written in Chinese. By the mid-nineteenth century, France was eyeing "Indochina" as the best target for imperialist expansion, given Britain's strength in India. This brought France into conflict with the Qing, which viewed Vietnam as one of its most loyal vassal states, next only to Korea. In 1874, France gained privileges in Vietnam through treaties and in 1882 seized Hanoi. When the Vietnamese ruler requested Chinese help, realists like Prince Gong and Li Hongzhang urged avoiding war, but a shrill group of conservative critics insisted that China had to stop giving in, since appeasement only encouraged the bullying of the powers. Cixi hesitated, called on Li Hongzhang to negotiate, and then scuttled the draft treaty when she was flooded with protests about its terms. When the French issued an ultimatum that China withdraw its forces from Vietnam or they would attack China, Cixi sided with the conservative critics. Skirmishes between the Qing and the French quickly escalated into war. The French sailed their fleet 20 miles up the Min River to Fuzhou, home port of a

quarter of the new Chinese navy and the site of the main shipyard. In just fifteen minutes on August 23, the French fleet destroyed the shipyard and all but two of the twenty-three Chinese warships. About three thousand Chinese were killed in the action. Cixi had adopted the conservative position and stood firm; the result was not only humiliating but also a fiscal disaster. The only consolation, a bittersweet one, was that Li Hongzhang had disobeyed her order to send his northern fleet to Fuzhou to help.

Cixi officially retired in 1889 when the Guangxu emperor was nineteen *sui* and she was fifty-five. She insisted, however, on reading all memorials and approving key appointments. Since the court was filled with her supporters, the emperor had little room to go his own way, even after he began to form his own views about reform.

FOREIGNERS IN CHINA

After 1860 the number of Westerners in China grew steadily, and a distinct treaty port culture evolved. The foreign concessions at treaty ports were areas carved out of existing Chinese cities. They had foreign police and foreign law courts and collected their own taxes, a situation the Qing accepted with little protest, even though most of the population within the concessions continued to be Chinese. At the treaty ports, the presence of the British and Indians was especially strong, and the habits of the British Empire tended to spill over into these cities. Foreign warships anchored at the docks of the treaty ports, ready to make a show of force. Although missionaries and merchants often had little love for each other, they had similar tendencies to turn to their consuls for support when they got into conflicts with Chinese. When missionaries or their converts were attacked or killed, gunboats were often sent to the nearest port to threaten retaliation, a practice termed *gunboat diplomacy*.

When the disorder of the Taiping Rebellion disrupted tariff collection in Shanghai and Amoy, the British and American consuls there collected the tariffs themselves, a practice later regularized into a permanent Imperial Maritime Customs staffed at its higher level by Westerners. In addition to recording and collecting tariffs, the customs published annual reports on the outlook for trade at each port and undertook projects to improve communications, such as telegraph and postal systems.

Reparations Imposed on China (or, the Loser Pays)	
1842	21 million ounces of silver to Great Britain at conclusion of the Opium War
1858	4 million ounces of silver to Britain and 2 million to France at conclusion of the Second Opium War
1860	16 million ounces of silver, divided evenly between Britain and France after attack on Beijing
1862–1869	400,000 ounces of silver to compensate for violence against missionaries
1870	490,000 ounces of silver to France after the Tianjin massacre
1873	500,000 ounces of silver to Japan after the Japanese incursion into Taiwan
1881	5 million ounces to Russia for Qing reoccupation of the Ili valley in Xinjiang
1895	200 million ounces of silver to Japan after the Sino-Japanese War
1897	30 million ounces of silver to Japan for its withdrawal of troops from Liaodong
1901	450 million silver dollars to the countries that invaded to relieve the legation quarters

By 1900 there were a hundred treaty ports, but only Shanghai, Tianjin, Hankou, Guangzhou, and Dalian (at the southern tip of Manchuria) became major centers of foreign residence. (Hong Kong was counted not as a treaty port but as a colony.) The streetlights and tall buildings in the Western-dominated parts of these cities showed Chinese what Western "progress" was all about. The Chinese in these cities also felt the disdain of the Westerners toward China and the Chinese. To Westerners, the Chinese educated class seemed too obtuse to understand progress. Couldn't they see that the world outside China had changed drastically in the last century and that China's response to it was disastrously out-of-date?

Away from the treaty ports, missionaries were the Westerners the Chinese were most likely to encounter. Once China agreed in the treaty of 1860 to allow missionaries to travel through China, they came in large numbers. Unlike merchants in the treaty ports, missionaries had no choice but to mix with the local population, and they spent much of their time with ordinary, poor Chinese, finding the best opportunities for conversion among them.

Missionaries often ran orphanages, a "good work" that also helped produce converts, but the Chinese suspected that they were buying babies for nefarious purposes. Widely circulated antimissionary tracts were often filled with inflammatory charges of this sort. The volatility of relations between Chinese and foreign missionaries led to tragedy in Tianjin on a June day in 1870. French troops had been based there from 1860 to 1863; the French had taken over a former palace for their consulate; and they had built a cathedral at the site of a former Chinese temple—all reasons for the local population to resent them. At the cathedral, nuns ran an orphanage. They welcomed (and even paid small sums to receive) sick and dying children, wanting to baptize them before they died. When an epidemic swept through the orphanage in June 1870, so many orphans died that rumors spread that they were being killed for their body parts. Scandalous purposes seemed confirmed when the nuns would not let parents retrieve their children. When a local official came to search the premises, a fight broke out between converts and onlookers. The official ordered soldiers to put a stop to the disturbance. Meanwhile, the French consul, carrying two pistols, charged into the official's office and shot at him. After the consul was restrained, the official, unhurt, advised him not to go back on the street, where an angry crowd had

formed. Claiming he was afraid of no Chinese, the consul went out anyway. On the street, he recognized the city magistrate, whom he shot at, again missing. The crowd then killed the consul and the officer with him, as well as twelve priests and nuns, seven other foreigners, and several dozen Chinese converts. The French victims were mutilated and the cathedral and four American and British churches burned. Although the French consul had incited the violence, it was the Chinese who had to pay reparations as well as punish members of the mob and send a mission of apology to France.

By 1900 there were 886 Catholic and about 3,000 Protestant missionaries in China, more than half of them women. Although the majority of missionaries devoted themselves to preaching, over the course of the nineteenth century, more and more concentrated on medicine or education, which were better received by the Chinese. By 1905 there were about three hundred fully qualified physicians doing medical missionary work, and the 250 mission hospitals and dispensaries treated about 2 million patients. Missionary hospitals in Hong Kong also ran a medical school that trained hundreds of Chinese as physicians. At their schools, missionaries helped spread Western learning. For their elementary schools, missionaries produced textbooks in Chinese on a full range of subjects. They translated dozens of standard works into Chinese, especially in the natural sciences, mathematics, history, and international law. By 1906 there were nearly sixty thousand students attending twenty-four hundred Christian schools. Most of this activity was supported by contributions sent from the United States and Britain. Missionaries in China had more success in spreading Western learning than in gaining converts: by 1900 fewer than 1 million Chinese were Christians.

THE FAILURES OF REFORM

Despite the enormous efforts it put into trying to catch up, the end of the nineteenth century brought China more humiliation. First came the discovery that Japan had so successfully modernized that it posed a threat to China. Japan had not been much of a concern to China since Hideoyoshi's invasion of Korea in the late Ming period. In the 1870s, Japan began making demands on China and in the 1890s seemed to be looking for a pretext for war.

As discussed in Chapter 20, Korea provided the pretext. When an insurrection broke out in Korea in 1894, both China and Japan rushed to send troops. After Japan sank a steamship carrying Chinese troops, both countries declared war. The results proved that the past decade of accelerated efforts to upgrade the military were still not enough. In the climactic naval battle off the Yalu River, four of the twelve Chinese ships involved were sunk, four were seriously damaged, and the others fled. By contrast, none of the twelve Japanese ships was seriously damaged. An even worse loss came when the Japanese went overland to take the Chinese port city of Weihaiwei in Shandong province, then turned the Chinese guns on the Chinese fleet in the bay. This was a defeat not of Chinese weapons but of Chinese organization and strategy.

China sued for peace and sent Li Hongzhang to Japan to negotiate a settlement. Besides a huge indemnity, China agreed to cede Taiwan and Liaodong (the southern tip of Manchuria) to Japan and to allow Japan to open factories in China. (Liaodong was returned to the Qing for an additional indemnity after pressure from the European powers.) China had to borrow from consortiums of banks in Russia, France, Britain, and Germany to pay the indemnity, securing the loans with future customs revenue. From this point until 1949, China was continually in debt to foreign banks, which made reform all the more difficult.

European imperialism was at a high point in the 1890s, with countries scrambling to get territories in Africa and Southeast Asia. China's helplessness in the face of aggression led to a scramble among the European powers for concessions and protectorates in China. At the high point of this rush in 1898, it appeared that the European powers might divide China among themselves the way they had recently divided Africa. Russia obtained permission to extend the Trans-Siberian railway across Manchuria to Vladivostok and secured a leasehold over the Liaodong Peninsula. Germany seized the port of Qingdao in Shandong province, and the British stepped in to keep Russia and Germany in check by taking a port (Weihaiwei) that lay between their concessions. France concentrated on concessions in the south and southwest, near its colonies in Southeast Asia.

The mixture of fear and outrage that many of the educated class felt as China suffered blow after blow began to give rise to attitudes that can be labeled nationalism. The two most important intellectual leaders to give shape to these feelings were Kang Youwei (1858–1927) and Liang Qichao (1873–1929), both from Guangdong province. Kang was a committed Confucian, dedicated to the ideals of personal virtue and service to society. He reinterpreted the classics to justify reform, arguing that Confucius had been a reformer, not a mere transmitter as he had portrayed himself in the *Analects*. Liang, fifteen years younger, was Kang's most brilliant follower and went even farther than Kang in advocating political change. Liang contended that self-strengthening efforts had focused too narrowly on technology and ignored the need for cultural and political change. The examination system should be scrapped and a national school system instituted. China needed a stronger sense of national solidarity and a new type of state in which the people participated in rule. Kang, Liang, and likeminded men began setting up study societies in 1895 in several large cities. In Hunan province, for instance, fourteen study societies were founded in 1897 and 1898, the largest with over twelve hundred members. Some of these societies started publishing newspapers (see **Documents: Comparing the Power of China and Western Nations**). Worrisome to the court was that some of these societies expressed anti-Manchu sentiments, seeming to imply that many of China's problems could be solved if only the Chinese were ruling China.

The bannermen had been a hereditary military caste, in some ways comparable to the samurai in Edo Japan. In Japan, when the special status of the samurai was abolished, samurai had not only joined the new armies in large numbers as officers, but many had successfully switched to other occupations requiring skill or learning. The hereditary military caste of the Qing did not fare as well. Many bannermen became alarmed, not seeing how the banner population could survive without government handouts. Although banner garrisons had schools for banner children, many were illiterate and unprepared to step forward as the country modernized.

In the spring of 1895, provincial graduates in Beijing for the triennial *jinshi* examinations submitted petitions on how to respond to the crisis caused by the war with Japan. Some twelve hundred signed the "ten-thousand word petition" written by Kang Youwei. Kang called for an assembly elected by the general populace. Such an assembly would solve China's most pressing problems:

Above, they are to broaden His Majesty's sagelike understanding, so that he can sit in one hall and

DOCUMENTS

Comparing the Power of China and Western Nations

This essay was written in 1898 by Mai Menghua (1874–1915), a twenty-four-year-old follower of Kang Youwei. It responds to conservative critics who saw Kang's program as weakening the ruler's hand. Mai argues that modern Western governments are in fact much stronger than the Chinese government.

Nowadays, men of broad learning all say China is weak because the power of the ruler is mighty while the power of the people is slight. Those who like to map out plans for the nation say that the Western nations are strong because their way is exactly the opposite of this. Mai Menghua says: This is not so. China's misfortunes arise not because the people have no power but because the ruler has no power. Hence, over all five continents and throughout all past ages, no ruler has had less power than in present-day China, and no rulers have had more power than in present-day European nations. There are far too many points for me to compare them all here, but permit me to say something about a few.

In Western countries, the age, birth, and death of every person in every household is reported to the officials, who record and investigate it. An omission in a report is punished as a criminal offense. In China, birth, death, and taking care of oneself are all personal matters, beyond state interven-

tion. In Western countries, when property is inherited by descendants, the amount of the property and its location must be reported and registered with the authorities. An inheritance tax must be paid before the property is transmitted to the inheritors. In China, people give and take as they please, and the state is unable to investigate. In western countries, when children reach the age of eight [*sui*], they all go to elementary school. Doting parents who neglect their children's studies are punished. In China, 70 to 80 percent of the population is indolent, worthless, uncouth and illiterate, and the state can do nothing to encourage them to improve themselves. In Western countries, one must go through school to become an official, and unless one does adequately, one cannot make his own way. In China, one can be a slave in the marketplace in the morning, and bedecked in the robes of high office by evening, and this is beyond the capacity of the state to control. In Western countries, the currency system is fixed by the court;

know the four seas. Below, they are to bring together the minds and wills of the empire, so that all can share cares and pleasures, forgetting the distinction between public and private. . . . Sovereign and people will be of one body, and China will be as one family. . . . So when funds are to be raised, what sums cannot be raised? When soldiers are to be trained, what numbers cannot be trained? With 400 million minds as one mind: how could the empire be stronger?[7]

In January 1898 the emperor invited Kang Youwei to discuss his ideas with the high officials at court. Afterward Kang sent the emperor three memorials on constitutions, national assemblies, and political reform. Kang even implied that the Qing rulers should abandon the queue, noting that Western dress had been adopted in Japan and the Japanese emperor had cut his hair short. In June the emperor gave Kang a five-hour audience. Over the next hundred days, the emperor issued over a hundred decrees on everything from revamping the examination system to setting up national school, banking, postal, and patent systems. He was redesigning the Qing as a constitutional monarchy with modern financial and educational infrastructures.

---

7. Translated in Philip A. Kuhn, *Origins of the Modern Chinese State* (Stanford, Calif.: Stanford University Press, 2002), p. 123.

one country has the pound, another the ruble, and another the franc, but each currency is uniform throughout the entire country, and no one dares to differ. In China, each of the 80 provinces has a different currency, and the shape of the money is different. The people are satisfied with what they are accustomed to, and the state is unable to enforce uniformity.

In Western countries, only the government may print and distribute paper money within its borders. In China, banks in every province and money changers in every port make and circulate their own money, and the state is unable to audit and prohibit them. In Western countries, all new buildings are inspected by officials, who examine the quality of the construction materials as a precaution against collapse causing injuries. Older houses are periodically inspected, and ordered demolished or repaired. In China, one can construct as one pleases. Even if there are cracks and flaws, the state cannot supervise and reprove the builder. In Western countries, roads and highways must be broad and spacious, neat and clean. There are legal penalties for discarding trash [on the roads]. Broad roads in Chinese cities are swamped in urine and litter, filled with beggars and corpses, and the state is unable to clean them up. In Western countries, all doctors must be graduates of medical schools and be certified before they can practice medicine. In China, those who fail to do well academically switch to the medical profession; quack doctors, who casually kill patients, are everywhere, and the state is unable to punish them. In Western countries, the postal service is controlled by the government. In China, post offices run by private persons are everywhere, and the government is unable to unify them.

In Western countries, there is an official for commerce. Inferior goods cannot be sold in the market. New inventions are patented, and other merchants are forbidden to manufacture imitations. In China, dishonest merchants are everywhere, devising illicit means to make imitation products, and everything is of inferior quality, and yet the state has no control. In Western countries, wherever railroads pass, homes, temples, huts, or gravestones must be demolished. No one dares obstruct the opening up of new mineral resources in mountains. In China, conservatives raise an outcry and block every major project, and the state is unable to punish them.

Source: From J. Mason Gentzler, ed., *Changing China: Readings in the History of China from the Opium War to the Present* (New York: Praeger, 1977), pp. 90–91, slightly modified.

After three months, Empress Dowager Cixi had had enough and staged a coup with the help of Yuan Shikai's army. She had the Guangxu emperor locked up and executed those of the reformers she could capture. All the reform edicts were revoked. Kang and Liang, safely out of Beijing at the time, managed to flee to Japan, where each lived for years.

THE BOXER REBELLION

In the summer of 1898, while the Guangxu emperor was issuing reform edicts, Shandong province was suffering from a break in the dikes on the Yellow River, which flooded some two thousand villages and made millions of people refugees. Not only was that year's crop ruined, but in many places the land could not be planted even the next spring. When the government failed to provide effective relief, antigovernment resentment began to stir. Another local grievance concerned the high-handed behavior of Christian missionaries, especially a group of German missionaries who actively interfered in their converts' lawsuits, claiming the privileges of extraterritoriality for the converts. They also irritated people by forbidding their converts to contribute to traditional village festivals that involved parading statues of the local gods.

Not surprisingly, this region soon exploded into violence. Small groups began pillaging the property

Captured Boxers. Most of the men who joined the Boxers had previously worked as laborers, porters, field hands, or the like, and suffered from the deteriorating economic situation. *(Bettmann/Corbis)*

of missionaries and their converts. They were dubbed "Boxers" by foreigners because of their martial arts practices. The Boxers also practiced spirit possession, which allowed individuals to achieve direct communication with their gods and gain a sense of personal power. After the governor of Shandong suppressed them in 1899, they began drifting into other provinces, even into the capital, where they recruited new members with placards urging the Chinese to kill all foreigners as well as Chinese contaminated by their influence. They blamed the drought on the anger of the gods at the foreign intrusion.

The foreign powers demanded that the Qing government suppress the attacks on foreigners. Cixi, ap-

parently hoping that the Chinese people, if aroused, could solve her foreign problem for her, did little to stop the Boxers. Eight foreign powers announced that they would send troops to protect missionaries. Then, on June 20, 1900, the German minister was shot dead in the street. Cixi, having been told by pro-Boxer Manchus that the European powers wanted her to retire and restore the emperor to the throne, declared war on the eight powers. Although she had repeatedly seen China defeated when it was fighting only one of these powers, she deluded herself into thinking that if the people became sufficiently enraged, they could drive all eight out and solve the foreign problem once and for all. (See Color Plate 25.)

Foreigners in the capital, including missionaries who had recently moved there for safety, barricaded themselves in the Northern Cathedral and two miles away in the legation quarter. After the Boxers laid siege to the legation quarter, an eight-nation force (including Japan) sent twenty thousand troops to lift the siege. Cixi and the emperor fled by cart to Xi'an hundreds of miles away. By the end of the year, there were forty-five thousand foreign troops in north China. Most of the Boxers tried to disappear into the north China countryside, but the foreign troops spent six months hunting them down, making raids on Chinese towns and villages.

Antiforeign violence also occurred elsewhere in the country, especially in Shanxi, where the governor sided with the Boxers and had missionaries and their converts executed. Most of the governors-general, however, including Li Hongzhang and Yuan Shikai, simply ignored the empress dowager's declaration of war.

In the negotiations that led to the Boxer Protocol, China had to accept a long list of penalties, including cancellation of the examinations for five years (punishment for gentry collaboration), execution of the officials involved, destruction of forts and railway posts, and payment of a staggering indemnity of 450 million silver dollars.

THE DECLINE OF THE QING EMPIRE IN COMPARATIVE PERSPECTIVE

Late Qing reformers often urged the court to follow in the footsteps of Japan, which had adopted not merely Western technology but also Western ideas about political organization and even Western dress. Ever since, it has been common to compare the fates of Qing China and Edo Japan and ask why Japan was so much more successful at modernizing its government and economy.

The main arguments for lumping China and Japan together are that they were geographically close (both were "the Far East" to Europeans), and some significant features of Japanese culture had been derived from China, such as Confucianism and the use of Chinese characters in writing. The differences, however, should not be minimized. China in the nineteenth century was not an independent country but rather part of the multiethnic empire of the Manchus, making it more similar to other large multiethnic empires, like the Mughals in India, the Ottomans in the

Middle East, the Romanovs in Russia, and even the Hapsburgs in eastern Europe. Even if only the China proper part of the Qing is considered, it was a much larger country than Japan in both territory and population, with all that that implied in terms of political structure.

Another common way to frame the experiences of China in this period is to compare it to other countries where Western imperialism was felt. Those Chinese who urged the court to follow Japan's example also warned of being carved up like Africa or taken over like India. But only small pieces of the Qing Empire were directly ruled by foreign powers in China, giving its history a different trajectory.

Better comparisons for the Qing Dynasty in this period are probably the Ottoman and Russian Empires. All three were multiethnic, land-based Eurasian empires, with long experience with mounted horsemen of the steppe—and in the case of both the Ottomans and the Qing, currently ruled by groups that claimed this tradition themselves. All three knew how to deal with problems of defending long land borders but were not naval powers. During the eighteenth century, all had experienced rapid population growth that was reducing the standard of living for much of the population by the mid-nineteenth century. By then the military pressure put on each of them both by internal unrest and foreign pressure forced them to spend more on military preparedness at the cost of deficit financing. As the importance of cavalry declined in warfare, each lost its military advantages. In this period Western sea powers sought to profit from trade with them, forcing both empires to accept their terms, but not trying to take over management of the empires. The sea powers gained more by making loans to them that kept them in a type of debt bondage, securing their advantage through treaties without any of the responsibilities of direct rule.

In each of these empires during the mid- and late nineteenth centuries, the elites were divided between westernizers and traditionalists, each looking for ways to strengthen the government. Urban merchants were usually more willing to see changes made than were the imperial elite, who had the most stake in the existing power structure. Even when modernizers won out, improvements were generally too little or too late to make much difference when the next confrontation with Western powers came. Reform programs could not outpace the destructive effect of economic decline, social turmoil, and the intrusion of the West. Foreign powers did not encourage domestic challenges

MAKING COMPARISONS   Monarchical Institutions

Through the nineteenth century, China, Japan, and Korea all had hereditary monarchies. Rulers were viewed as divinely sanctioned; ritual prescribed how others interacted with them; and powers behind the throne often controlled them, all features of premodern monarchies around the world. Beyond that, however, the monarchical systems of China, Japan, and Korea were not especially alike.

First, consider the number of royal houses. In historical times, Japan has claimed to have had a single royal family. Since Korea was unified by the state of Silla in the seventh century, the royal house changed only twice (the Koryŏ and Chosŏn Dynasties). In China, however, there were ten major royal families (Shang, Zhou, Qin, Han, Sui, Tang, Song, Yuan, Ming, and Qing) and more than a dozen minor ones. The frequent changes in Chinese ruling houses owes much to the concept of the Mandate of Heaven, which required a new ruling house when the existing dynasty lost Heaven's favor. In Japan, the myth of the descent of the royal family from the sun goddess Amaterasu had just the opposite effect on people's conceptions of kingship: not selecting someone descended from the royal line became unthinkable.

In all three countries, the office of monarch carried with it obligations to perform sacred rituals. In China, the key rituals—sacrifices to Heaven and the royal ancestors—were described in the Confucian classics and thus were always considered part of Confucianism. In Japan, the ruler's ritual responsibilities grew from the complex of early religious rites generally termed Shinto. In both China and Korea, Confucianism was also strongly associated with the authority of officials as critics of monarchs and their exercise of power. In China, this strain of Confucianism was countered by Legalist ideas that validated firm control from the center by the ruler, ideas that played a much smaller role in Korea and Japan.

Because succession to the throne follows principles of the family system, differences in the original family systems of the three countries also can be seen in their systems of monarchy. In both Korea and Japan in the years before 1000 (and in Japan a couple of times later as well), women from time to time succeeded to the throne as daughters of the royal family. In China, this never happened. In China, there was a strong preference for selecting an heir from among a ruler's sons and, if he had none, from among patrilineal kinsmen of the same generation as sons. This not infrequently led to the succession of young boys. In Japan and Korea, younger brothers more frequently succeeded to the throne even when there were sons, which sometimes led to contentious succession disputes. When a boy became ruler in China, the normal practice was to have his mother or grandmother serve as regent, perhaps a reflection of the great weight placed on filial piety to both parents. In Japan, boys most often became rulers because the previous ruler had abdicated, and for several centuries the most likely person to serve as regent was the father of the monarch's mother or wife (normally from the Fujiwara family). In nineteenth-century Korea, when a series of boys succeeded to the Chosŏn throne, men from consort families served as regents.

Several times in Chinese history, the eunuchs who were supposed to be the ruler's servants came to control the palace and access to him. In late Tang, eunuchs even installed and deposed rulers. Eunuchs played a much smaller role in Korea and none at all in Japan.

As adhering to Confucian norms became more important in Korea in the Chosŏn period, principles of succession came to resemble China's (women no longer succeeded as queens, and succession consistently went to sons rather than brothers). The rituals the king performed also were modeled on the Confucian classics. Convergence only went so far, however. The power of the aristocratic *yangban* class kept the king in check more effectively than Chinese scholars did. *Yangban* aristocrats even dethroned two kings in the Chosŏn Dynasty.

to the dynastic rulers, perhaps fearing that they would lose the privileges they had gained through treaties. Thus, many of those who sought radical change came to oppose both the foreign powers and the ruling dynasty, giving rise to modern nationalism.

SUMMARY

How different was China in 1900 than it had been in 1800? At the beginning of the nineteenth century, most Chinese had no reason to question the long-held belief that China was the central kingdom: no other country had so many people, Chinese products were in great demand in foreign countries, and the borders had recently been expanded. True, an alien dynasty occupied the throne, but the Manchus administered the country through institutions much like those earlier Chinese dynasties had employed, and even proved generous patrons of strictly Chinese forms of culture, such as publications in Chinese. Chinese civilization thus seemed in no danger. By 1900 this confidence was gone. Besides traditional evidence of dynastic decline—peasant poverty, social unrest, government bankruptcy—new foreign adversaries had emerged. China had been humiliated repeatedly in military encounters with Western nations and more recently with Japan and was deeply in debt to these countries because of imposed indemnities. Most of the educated class had come to feel that drastic measures needed to be taken. Chinese civilization—not just the Qing Dynasty—was at stake.

Japan in Turmoil (1800–1867)

Many commoners in Japan's cities and villages prospered during the first three decades of the nineteenth century, but the same could not be said for the laboring poor, the low-status samurai, or the daimyo wrestling with shortfalls in domainal finances. Belying prosperity were problems such as vagrancy, gambling, and prostitution that threatened the social order propped up by administrators and wealthy entrepreneurs. Added to these signs of domestic distress was an increasing fear of threats from abroad. The shogunate's ineffectual attempts to deal with these problems weakened it in the eyes of the military ruling class. Its decision to seek approval for foreign treaties from the monarch opened the door for wide-ranging debate that enabled commoners as well as officials to participate in a new political public realm. Beset on all sides, the shogunate collapsed at the end of 1867, ushering in a regime headed by the newly named emperor.

Historians have long searched the early nineteenth century for clues as to what brought about the Meiji Restoration. Those who emphasize domestic factors point to the way the social and political order came unglued in the early nineteenth century. But that begs the question of whether the fall of the Tokugawa shogunate should be seen as a coup d'état or a revolution. Was it primarily the effect of domestic changes or a reaction to foreign pressure?

DOMESTIC SECESSIONS (1800–1842)

Early-nineteenth-century villages had to deal with internal conflict. Outcasts deemed polluted by their association with dead animals protested discrimination and the indignities they had to suffer. Accustomed to apportioning the village tax assessment, headmen tended to treat expenses for family business and village administration as one and the same. The walls around their houses had gates; the roofs had eaves that marked their superior status. Complaints against headmen perceived to be unjust in dividing the tax burden, efforts to clarify the costs of village administration, and demands that the headman cease to lord it over his neighbors led to lawsuits that sometimes dragged on for decades. A recalcitrant headman might be subjected to ostracism. Sometimes disputes resulted in the village council's being expanded to include a cultivator's representative to verify the tax assessment. In villages where the position of headman had once been hereditary, it might instead rotate among a group of families. Some villages started having heads of household elect the headman. When a woman was the house head, she too voted.

In eastern Japan, village leaders agonized over fields gone to waste because of population decline. Gamblers and bandits disrupted the social order. Village officials organized regional leagues, inserting a new level of administration between the village and ruling authority. In the 1780s in the region around Osaka, these leagues launched province-wide appeals to eliminate restrictions on commerce and to regulate the price of herring meal fertilizer from Hokkaido. In 1805 the shogunate started sending security patrols through the Edo hinterland, where villages might be fragmented among several domains. Some headmen organized militia; others hired unemployed swordsmen, some running protection rackets, to keep the peace. Longer-term solutions came in the teachings of the peasant sage Ninomiya Sontoku. Sontoku revitalized villages, increasing their population and bringing fields back into production by preaching an ethic of diligence, fortitude, and frugality to repay the bounty of the gods while instituting mutual aid associations to give villagers who had fallen into debt access to low-interest loans. His emphasis on rational planning to wring the most from land and labor demanded steady work habits instilled in men and women alike.

Hirata Atsutane and his followers offered a vision of a just social order that largely ignored existing political arrangements. Although they acknowledged shogunal authority and the Confucian principles of social inequality, they sought the wellspring of human virtue in Japan's ancient past and looked to the monarch as a manifest god who linked the divine and human worlds. Atsutane claimed to be a disciple of Motoori Norinaga, thus putting him in the mainstream of nativist thought. Unlike his teacher, he did not envision the afterlife as a filthy, polluted realm but rather as an invisible world that parallels the visible world. From that vantage, the deceased watch over and protect their descendants. Atsutane's teachings placed primacy on agricultural practices that brought people into communion with the gods and each other. Village officials and rural

entrepreneurs were his most numerous disciples because they believed his message to contain the secret for revitalizing the village community without threatening their role either socially or economically (see **Biography: Kitahara Inao**).

Domainal Reforms

Faced with challenges from below, rural entrepreneurs sought new ways to bolster their prestige. Rather than marry within the village, they sought marriage partners of similar background a day's walk or more away. They educated themselves; they also educated their daughters to standards beyond what could be achieved by an ordinary cultivator. They studied Chinese philosophy and classical poetry as well as Western science and geography. They took up swordsmanship. In the 1830s and 1840s, their quest to enhance their dignity meshed with the ruling authorities' need for funds. In return for loans, wealthy commoners received permission to wear swords on official business and to use surnames, privileges supposedly reserved for the samurai.

The willingness of daimyo to sell markers of prestige to commoners was but one sign that their governments verged on bankruptcy. Owing to rural opposition, tax revenues had long since ceased to cover the expenses of carrying redundant personnel on the books, supporting the daimyo's women and children in the style to which life in Edo had accustomed them, and paying for trips made by the daimyo and his retinue back and forth to Edo. Daimyo borrowed money from merchants with the promise of repayment out of future tax receipts. In the 1830s, domains across Japan launched administrative and financial reforms. Those that tried to increase exports and restrict imports disrupted markets and created shortages. Some instituted monopolies by strengthening existing controls: Satsuma doubled its profits in sugar. Most domains sought to reduce expenditures by cutting costs. Concerned that luxury-loving commoners both threatened samurai privilege and encouraged samurai extravagance, governments issued sumptuary legislation forbidding socially inferior people to wear silk garments, ornamental hairpins, and other products of the commercial revolution.

The samurai, especially those in the lower ranks, saw themselves beset on all sides. Wealthy commoners in crested kimono and carrying swords challenged their sense of status superiority. Educated, capable samurai were frustrated by the system of hereditary ranks

BIOGRAPHY   Kitahara Inao

In the early nineteenth century, rural entrepreneurs dominated their villages politically, socially, and economically. A representative figure was Kitahara Inao (1825–1881), who had an abiding concern with national affairs.

Based in the mountains of central Japan, Inao's family claimed warrior connections through an ancestor who died in battle in 1575 and through him to the Minamoto lineage. His father received permission to wear swords and use a surname for his work on water control projects; he also served as one of the village's headmen, managed the family's land, and sold the silk produced by Inao's mother. He educated himself, his children, and his neighbors in Western geography and Japanese poetry. When his eldest son wished to learn a musical instrument called the *samisen*, he sent him to Kyoto. The boy was murdered en route. Thus did Inao become his father's heir.

The short-tempered Inao had a brief career as village headman. In 1852 cultivators from the village's upper elevations complained that they had to pay for flood control that benefited only their wealthier neighbors on the plain. Four years later, they questioned the way costs had been assessed. A meeting with Inao turned into a shouting match. One man called Inao a liar, and Inao slugged him.

The cultivators announced that to strike one was to strike them all. Inao had to resign his office and concentrate his efforts on teaching village boys and girls.

Inao helped found the Hirata school in the Ina valley by hosting study groups, proselytizing, and publishing Atsutane's works. He paid to publish a chronology composed by Atsutane that traced the monarchy back to the creator gods and raised money to publish Atsutane's magnum opus, the multivolume *Koshiden (Lectures on Ancient History)*. In 1867 he helped build a shrine to the four great nativist teachers, ending with Atsutane. Through these efforts, his valley acquired the largest population of Hirata disciples outside Edo.

Following the Meiji Restoration, Inao organized a development fund to promote new agricultural products and bring mechanized filatures to the Ina valley. Conditions for loans were so strict and interest rates so high that only landlord families could benefit, to the resentment of poor folk who had contributed to the fund. Despite his promotion of industrialization, Inao continued to castigate westernizers who did not understand the fundamental principle of respecting Japanese ways and despising the foreign. At the end of his life, he wrote a set of precepts for his descendants that emphasized harmony, diligence, and frugality. He urged them to be modest in dress, eat simple food, and marry plain but intelligent women.

---

that relegated them to dead-end menial tasks. During domainal reforms, low-ranking samurai proposed that men of talent and ability be promoted to decision-making positions. Satsuma heeded this call, allowing Saigō Takamori to rise from rural administrator to the daimyo's adviser in 1854. Efforts to promote men from below often led to factional disputes when upper-status samurai fought to preserve their hereditary privileges. "Borrowing" stipends posed the most ubiquitous threat to samurai welfare. While some domains tried to confine the practice to samurai without regular bureaucratic appointments and pretended that the cuts were temporary, others insisted that everyone must make sacrifices. In one case, guards assigned to escort a daimyo to his regular audience with the shogun protested arrears in their salary by going on strike.

Conditions reached a crisis when poor harvests in the 1830s recalled the famines of the 1780s. Commoners assumed that food shortages owed more to greedy merchants than to crop failures. They turned on village leaders for not offering relief, and they called on the gods of world renewal (*yonaoshi*) for salvation from economic hardship and political ineptitude. Women played an active role, marching with men to protest arbitrary government policies and complaining to rice merchants that hoarding grain threatened the poor with starvation. A retired shogunal policeman named Ōshio Heihachirō decided that government and merchants had become morally bankrupt. Raised in the Confucian tradition that deemed bureaucratic work a service to the people, Ōshio had also studied Wang Yangming, who argued that at time of crisis, a man had to use his intuition, not institutional norms, to guide his behavior (see Chapter 14). In 1836, Ōshio petitioned the Osaka city magistrate to save the starving. When the magistrate refused, Ōshio sold his books to buy food. In a last desperate effort, he issued a manifesto that charged shogunal officials with corruption and led a rural army against the city. A quarter of Osaka burned before shogunal troops caught up with him, and he committed suicide.

Religion and Play

One secessionist response to economic dislocation and political ineptitude came in the form of new religions. In 1838 a long-suffering rural woman named Nakayama Miki was possessed by a spirit who deemed her to be the "shogun of heaven" and the mouthpiece for the true and original god of salvation. She insisted that her family sell all their property, the proceeds of which were used to succor the poor. According to the god's divine wisdom (*tenri*), the shogun and daimyo were far too removed from daily life to aid the people; instead, the people should trust in the god of world renewal and work together, offering mutual assistance in time of need. Like other new religions of the time, Tenri-kyō envisioned a world opposed to the hierarchical and socially stratified system of the past and present. In a renewed world saturated with divine goodness, the poor would receive relief, and everyone, men and women, would be equal.

An alternative to the secessionist impulse found in the new religions came in the form of play. Dominated by the theater, urban culture celebrated bodily pleasures. Townspeople employed the possibilities presented by multiple identities—merchant, poet, sword-wearing samurai—to escape from the rigidities of the status system (see **Documents: Kohei's Lawsuit**). Readers of popular literature in the 1830s had alternatives to didactic tracts that bolstered the official status order. They indulged in novels that depicted the immediate world of human feelings, such as Jippensha Ikku's travelogues featuring an irreverent pair, Kita and Yaji, who poked fun at self-important samurai, stole when they could, seduced serving maids, and laughed at farts. Woodblock prints and kabuki, in particular ghost stories staged by Tsuruya Namboku and his successors, portrayed bloodshed and gruesome murders. In 1850 the story of Sakura Sogoro appeared on stage with scenes of his crucifixion and reincarnation as an angry spirit. Although these dramas went to extraordinary lengths to rivet the audi-

ence's attention, they remained linked to social mores. Dramas might be set in the daimyo's domestic quarters, but the subjects of action were commoners who acted according to the logic of everyday life.

Japanese commoners played hard. Festivals in town and country became increasingly elaborate, and laborers demanded more of them. Kabuki troupes discovered the money to be made in touring the countryside. In prosperous regions, villages built kabuki stages and competed in presenting plays to their neighbors. City folk flocked to entertainment districts. The shops with female clerks, theaters, and variety shows surrounding Asakusa temple in Edo combined appeals to prayer and play. Play constituted one way to appeal to the gods, and the pursuit of pleasure had a spiritual dimension.

Another sign that the practices of everyday life had escaped governmental control can be seen in prostitution. Unlicensed prostitutes plied their trade in informal entertainment districts that had sprung up across Edo and in castle towns. Post stations employed maids to lure customers to inns and teahouses, where singers, dancers, and servants often sold themselves. The development of a commercial economy contributed to the spread of prostitution in two ways: it put more money in the pockets of potential customers, and it stimulated the monetization of female labor. When women lacked opportunities to supplement the family income by raising silkworms or working for wages, prostitution became the logical alternative.

As part of a reform effort in 1841, the shogunate tried to curtail what it saw as the excesses of urban culture. It clamped down on unlicensed prostitution by closing teahouses and other venues where women sold their bodies. It forbade women to dress men's hair, teach them music, serve as attendants at archery ranges, or perform onstage in public. In an effort to promote public morality, it even outlawed men and women sharing public baths. Gambling, lotteries, and full-body tattoos were forbidden. The shogunate tightened censorship over the publishing industry, refusing to permit romantic novels or erotica, including the serial best-seller, *The False Murasaki and the Rustic Genji*, produced by Ryŭtei Tanehiko between 1829 and 1842. Theaters and entertainment districts received undesired attention. The shogunate condemned extravagance and ordered commoners not to dress, eat, or house themselves above their station. It tried to enforce these strictures by making examples of egregious violators in hopes of intimidating the rest. These measures had but a temporary effect.

DOCUMENTS

Kohei's Lawsuit

In a litigious society, people turned to the shogun's court to decide disputes. The summation of a conflict over inheritance that follows, titled "Action by Kohei of Haruki-chō, Hongō, against Heisuke of Sugamo-chō and Kurōbei of Fujimae-chō, Komagome as to the succession and division of personality of Sawamura Gisaburō, Master Carpenter," exposes a particularly complex set of family relations and the permeability of supposedly strict occupational and status boundaries. Note that the people involved in the suit, including the deceased, took different names depending on the occupation of the moment. Why is the conflict over Gisaburō's personality, not simply his possessions?

5th month, 1849, Inquiry by the city magistrate to the engineering magistrates:

Kohei demanded succession and division of personality of Sawamura Gisaburō, master-carpenter, subject to your lordships' authority, producing for evidence Gisaburō's will written by a person other than the testator; the defendants, on the other hand, deny the validity of the will, and the parties are at issue.

Kohei alleges that his sister's husband Sawamura Gisaburō made a will so that his personality may be divided according to the will, and that Gisaburō's adopted son Kosuke may be made to succeed Gisaburō.

Rubric: This Kosuke was one who, calling himself Utazō, tenanted the land of Ichibei in Yanaka, and was engaged in the management of a public bath-house. Four years ago, in 1845, he was adopted by Gisaburō, and in the 11th month of the same year, his petition to be a master-carpenter on probation was granted. It has been found that he is still living in a separate house on Ichibei's land and is working as a master-carpenter on probation.

What Heisuke alleges is as follows: His adoptive father Sawamura Gisaburō was a master carpenter in service of the shogunate.

Gisaburō was formerly called Heisuke and was engaged in the management of a tavern at Sugamo-chō. About that time this person [Heisuke] was adopted by Gisaburō and in 1835 he succeeded to Gisaburō's family name. Gisaburō served as a master-carpenter from 1810, and from 1812 to 1834 he was also registered in the census book of Sugamo-chō under the name of Heisuke. Therefore it seems that he was entered in two different census registers.

Gisaburō bought two years ago in 1846 a piece of land at the market in front of Yushima Tenjin Shrine, and on this occasion Heisuke advanced part of the purchase money. On the deed of sale, the land was entered as the property of Sei, daughter of Saku, Gisaburō's concubine. Gisaburō had a house on this land repaired for Saku to occupy. Lately he himself moved into this concubine's house, and because of old age, he called in one Kosuke, who is more in the relation of a servant to him, to wait on him, and had this Kosuke, by nominally adopting him, serve as a master carpenter on probation. Besides the above piece of land, some other lots in Gisaburō's possession have been nominally the property of Gisaburō's grandson Chōsuke, for whom Heisuke has

FOREIGN AFFAIRS (1793–1858)

The Russians were the first foreigners to encroach on Japan. During the eighteenth century, they started to trade with the Ainu in the Kuril Islands and Kamchatka. In 1793, Adam Laxman, a delegate to Catherine II, tried to open relations between Russia and Japan. He got as far as Nagasaki, only to be rebuffed by Matsudaira Sadanobu, who insisted that respect for his ancestors prohibited him from initiating new foreign relations. In 1798 the shogunate sent an exacted as guardian. The deeds of sale of these lands were kept by Gisaburō, as they were often used, by agreement of Gisaburō and Heisuke, for financing the business when Gisaburō engaged in various contracts, government and otherwise. When in 1847 Gisaburō married Sei, Saku's daughter [by her former husband] to one Mohachi and had Mohachi inherit the family name of Yoshikawa, palanquin-maker for the Shogunate, Heisuke on Gisaburō's request, advanced 500 *ryō* to Gisaburō to cover the expenses. Since Heisuke had advanced Gisaburō great sums of money for the latter's contract business, government, and otherwise, Heisuke should be given the right to decide on the succession and other matters.

Yasuda Chōsuke is son to Hanzaemon and grandson to Gisaburō and was formerly called Toraichirō. He is registered as a houseowner of Fujimae-chō. He has served, under the guardianship of the defendant Heisuke, as purveyor and contractor of commodities and laborers for the Fukiage Garden [in the shogun's palace] and is living with his father.

Nakamura Hanzaemon is adopted husband to Hisa born to Gisaburō by Gin, his former wife, since divorced. He was formerly called Shōgorō, and while tenant of a shop belonging to Kanbei, Fujimae-chō, Komagome, was engaged in dealing in socks. He is said to have become a guard in service of the Banner Magistrates for the Shogunate.

The defendant Kurōbei is nephew to Sawamura Gisaburō and head of Gisaburō's original family. Because of this relationship, Gisaburō, repairing a house on his land, had Kurōbei and his wife Chiyo, whose other name is Shige, live there. Even now Gisaburō's domicile is registered at the office of the Engineering Department as at this house on Kurōbei's land. So it was rumored that the boxes containing Gisaburō's papers and books etc. are kept in the above Kurōbei's godown [storehouse], including the instruments pertaining to the various money transactions which Gisaburō mentioned in his will.

The plaintiff says that when, during this autumn, he went to negotiate with Heisuke and Kurōbei, Kurōbei together with the ward officers admitted plainly that he had in his care the papers in question. The plaintiff continues that it seems possible, however, that Heisuke, taking advantage of his having access to the household of the Lord of Kaga through his business in contracting for transport horses, may have here done something tricky; that there is no box containing instruments kept now at Kurōbei's house in Fujimae-chō. It is suspected that it has since been taken to Heisuke's house. Heisuke has for several years past been in the habit of advancing loans to the household of the Lord of Kaga out of money belonging to Sawamura Gisaburō.

Instrument of Settlement to be filed: Both parties have agreed that we should petition for Gisaburō's adopted son Sawamura Kosuke to succeed Gisaburō, and should agree that neither party has grounds on which to dispute further about the deposit instruments said to be entrusted by Gisaburō with Heisuke and Kurōbei and about the money which Heisuke claims to have advanced Gisaburō, since the issue utterly lacks proof. Therefore we have come to a compromise, and will never in future resort to action or dispute.

Source: John Henry Wigmore, ed., *Law and Justice in Tokugawa Japan, Pt. VIII-A: Persons: Legal Precedents* (Tokyo: University of Tokyo Press, 1982), pp. 214–242 (modified).

pedition to Hokkaido to assess the Russian threat. Based on its report, the shogunate decided to annex Hokkaido and Sakhalin. Its reach exceeded its grasp; it did not have the forces to defend either. Russians again asked for permission to trade at Nagasaki in 1804. When that was not forthcoming, officers attacked trading posts on Sakhalin and the Kurils in 1806 and 1807. In 1811, Japan captured Vasilii Golovnin, the captain of a Russian surveying crew, and held him at Hakodate for two years before Russia secured his release. His captivity narrative intrigued readers across Europe.

The Closing of Japan

The British posed a more serious threat. In 1808 their warship *Phaeton* barged into Nagasaki bay in search of Dutch ships. Despite orders from the Nagasaki city magistrate to destroy it, the *Phaeton* left with food and supplies. In two separate incidents in 1824, British whaling ships raided villages on the coast north of Edo and southern Kyushu. The first village belonged to the Mito domain, home to one of the shogun's relatives, the xenophobic Tokugawa Nariaki. The second was located in Satsuma, the powerful outside (*tozama*) domain that dominated the Ryukyus. The next year, the shogunate issued new instructions for dealing with Westerners. With the exception of Dutch ships allowed at Nagasaki, all foreign ships, regardless of the circumstances, were to be driven off without hesitation. This order announced that the shogunate was closing the country (*sakoku*) to the West, its first truly isolationist policy.

The decision to close the country came as a result not only of foreign intimidation but also of information gathered by scholars and officials. The head of the shogunate's translation bureau established in 1811 argued that foreigners must be kept away from Japan lest they subvert the credulous masses with Christian teachings. In 1825 an adviser to Tokugawa Nariaki named Aizawa Seishisai wrote his "New Theses" (*Shinron*). Mito scholars believed that loyalty to their lord had to be predicated on his loyalty to the monarch. Although they based their arguments on neo-Confucian principles, their ideas were assimilated to the nativist belief that Japan was superior to all other countries, including China, because the monarch was descended from the sun goddess. Aizawa had studied writings about the West, and he interrogated the British sailors who had landed on the Mito coast in 1824. *Shinron* argued that Japan had to beware of foreigners, even if they said they came only to trade. Trade would weaken Japan because Japan would lose precious metals, and the pursuit of novelty and luxury items would erode the people's moral fiber. But traders brought something more pernicious than goods: Christianity. They hoped to beguile the foolish commoners with their religion, turn them against their rightful leaders, and "conquer from within by recruiting the local inhabitants into their ranks." To counter the threat of "barbarian teachings," Aizawa urged his lord to convince the shogunate to launch educational, religious, and military initiatives that would reform the armed forces by allowing daimyo to recruit cultivators as soldiers and educate the masses in Japan's

unique spiritual essence (*kokutai*).[1] *Shinron* had a lasting impact on nationalist thought.

Despite domainal penury, the Mito reform movement of the 1830s largely involved strengthening coastal defenses, a policy followed by a handful of other domains. Domains ignored shogunal restrictions on the number of guns permitted each castle. Mito and Saga in Kyushu built reverberatory furnaces to cast cannon. *Tozama* domains in southwestern Japan—Satsuma, Fukuoka, Kumamoto, and Chōshū—bought mortars, howitzers, and field guns from weapons dealers in Nagasaki and manufactured their own. Fear of foreigners spurred a renewed emphasis on military training. Domains also mobilized militia to man coastal lookout points and serve as a first line of defense. They competed for access to military technology, and they refused to cooperate in developing systems to warn of approaching foreign ships. They saw themselves as defending not an entity known as Japan but rather their own territory. Building coastal fortifications increased their isolation from each other while weakening the shogun's authority in matters of defense.

The shogunate too tried to bolster its military preparedness, spurred by reports of the British victory over China in the Opium War. (See **Connections: Western Imperialism [1800–1900]**.) In the 1841–1842 reform, it began to adopt Western military technology and trained a small contingent of foot soldiers in the use of guns. It also tried to reassert its dominance by ordering an end to domain monopolies that interfered in commerce, seeking to transfer daimyo from one domain to another and threatening to suppress copper coins and paper money minted in the domains. In 1843 the shogun went to Nikkō to worship at the shrine for his ancestors, escorted by 150,000 men commanded by the daimyo, in an affirmation of Tokugawa supremacy. At the same time, the shogunate announced a more conciliatory policy toward foreigners: shipwrecked sailors succored, Japanese castaways allowed to return home, and ships in need to receive supplies before being sent on their way.

Unequal Treaties with the United States

When Commodore Matthew C. Perry sailed four ships into Edo Bay on July 8, 1853, he had been preceded by the 1846 expedition under Commodore James Biddle, and the Dutch had warned of his arrival. Perry

---

1. Bob Tadashi Wakabayashi, *Anti-Foreignism and Western Learning in Early Modern Japan* (Cambridge, Mass.: Harvard University Press, 1986), p. 211.

treated the shogunate's exclusion order with disdain, and he refused to shift anchorage until he had handed over a letter from President Millard Fillmore addressed to the monarch. He paraded his men, opened his gunports to expose his cannons, and announced that he would return the next year for a reply. This time he had six ships under his command, having commandeered two more in Hong Kong. Intimidated by this display of force, the shogunate signed a friendship treaty with the United States. Japan made all the concessions: American ships were to be allowed to call at Shimoda and Hakodate and to obtain coal and other supplies. Shipwrecked sailors were to be treated fairly, and the United States had the right to station a consul at Shimoda.

Perry brought gifts that displayed the wonders of the Industrial Revolution—a telegraph using Morse code and a quarter-size steam locomotive with carriages and track. Sailors in blackface put on a minstrel show. Men and women flocked to see the strange black ships with their steam stacks and guns.

The shogunate soon found itself making further concessions. In 1856, Townsend Harris arrived as the first U.S. consul at Shimoda, to the consternation of shogunal officials, who had never expected a barbarian to live on Japan's sacred soil. A failed businessman in the China trade, Harris was determined to sign a commercial treaty with Japan. Realizing Shimoda's isolation, he bullied Japanese officials to allow him to negotiate in Edo. Fearing that delay might bring the same gunboats to Japan that had devastated China's coast, shogunal officials signed the treaty Harris wanted on July 29, 1858. According to its provisions, the two countries were to exchange diplomatic representatives. Japan was to open six cities—Edo, Osaka, Kanagawa (later Yokohama), Hyōgo (Kōbe), Nagasaki, and Niigata—to foreign residence and trade just as the Chinese treaty ports had earlier been opened. Japan had to accept low tariffs on imported goods, whereas its own exports faced steep tariffs in the United States. Finally, Japan had to allow foreign residents and visitors the privilege of extraterritoriality. Japan soon signed similar treaties with the Netherlands, Britain, France, and Russia.

Debates on the Foreign Threat

Unnerved by the unprecedented responsibility of signing treaties with Western powers, the shogunate revoked its 250-year-old monopoly over foreign policy. In 1854 it asked leading daimyo for their opinions; in 1858 it asked the monarch Kōmei to endorse the

Portrait of American Official. This image depicts an American official who landed with Perry at Uraga bay. This woodblock print emphasizes facial features most like those of demons—large nose and red mouth with gaping teeth. *(Peabody Essex Museum, Salem, MA/Bridgeman Art Library)*

Harris commercial treaty. In neither case did it achieve a consensus. Worse, Kōmei rejected the treaty, urged the shogun to consult the leading daimyo, and demanded the foreigners' expulsion. When the shogunate signed the treaty against Kōmei's wishes, it was considered treasonous. People from many walks of life began to collect and debate information on political affairs. By ignoring prohibitions on discussion of contemporary events and creating a new public political realm, they helped bring about what hindsight has deemed as the last days of the shogunate.

Some voices supported engagement with the West. Sakuma Shōzan argued for a proactive policy of seeking advanced Western military technology in order to strengthen Japan and of fusing Western science to Japan's Confucian ethical base. Only by opening Japan to trade could it achieve the knowledge and tools needed to compete in the emerging world order. His ideas found supporters among advisers to important daimyo such as Yokoi Shōnan, who popularized the slogan *fukoku kyōhei* (rich country, strong army), taken from a line in the Chinese classics. Both Sakuma and Yokoi died at the hands of xenophobic assassins.

The men who opposed signing treaties with the West had a rational basis for their stance. Tokugawa Nariaki believed that allowing trade with the West would weaken Japan both materially, in that Japan would lose precious metals in exchange for fripperies, and spiritually, because it would be infected by Christianity. The only way to revive Japan's martial spirit was to fight, even though fighting meant certain defeat. Yoshida Shōin had studied military science in Chōshū. In 1854 he opened a small school where he taught public policy under the rubric *sonnō jōi* (revere the monarch and expel the barbarian). By this he meant that the monarch should participate in policy decisions and the foreigners must be driven off. He was furious that by spinelessly signing the treaties, the shogunate had made Japan look weak in the eyes of the world.

The social networks that had previously transmitted information on agricultural innovation and the rice market now disseminated news of current events. Doctors, merchants, and samurai in Edo told friends and relatives in the countryside about Perry's arrival and the shogun's response. Their letters circulated widely, and the recipients copied their contents into diaries to discuss with like-minded neighbors. Proselytizers for the Hirata school and experts in swordsmanship linked people across domainal boundaries. Broadsheets (*kawaraban*) reported gossip on the treaty negotiations. They circulated primarily in urban areas, where they could be easily and anonymously sold, but travelers also took them back to villages. A few commoners presented plans for coastal defense to their daimyo for forwarding to the shogun. They traveled to Edo and Kyoto to see for themselves the changes taking place (see **Material Culture: From Palanquin to Rickshaw**).

POLITICAL TURMOIL (1858–1864)

The shogunate found itself stymied by Kōmei's disapproval of the Harris treaty and a dispute over shogunal succession. Prodded by Satsuma, Mito, and other activist daimyo, Kōmei urged shogunal officials to appoint Nariaki's son, Hitotsubashi Yoshinobu, perceived as more capable than the man who had the strongest claim by blood, Tokugawa Iemochi. The senior councilors rejected interference in the decision that was theirs alone to make. They appointed a vassal daimyo, Ii Naosuke, regent for Iemochi and chief senior councilor. Ii purged his daimyo opponents and arrested, exiled, or executed over one hundred men employed as agents by daimyo and court nobles. In 1859 the shogunate executed Yoshida Shōin for plotting to assassinate the shogun's emissary to Kyoto. The daimyo cowed and opponents silenced, Ii asserted that the shogunate had sole responsibility for foreign affairs.

On a snowy morning in the third month of 1860, young samurai from Mito and Satsuma assassinated Ii outside Edo castle. Angry at the execution of men they revered, they committed their lives to the politics of direct action. Their deed galvanized public opinion against Ii by deeming him a traitor for having executed men of high purpose (*shishi*) whose only aim was to serve the monarch. Equally alarming, the assassins had overcome the antipathy that distanced *tozama* domains such as Satsuma from Mito, home to the shogun's relative. The shogunate abandoned its authoritarian stance for a more conciliatory posture. It proposed a union of court and military (*kōbu gattai*) that would give important *tozama* and collateral daimyo advisory positions on foreign affairs and reinstated daimyo purged by Ii. It sealed the deal by having Shogun Iemochi wed Kōmei's younger half-sister, Kazunomiya, in return for a promise to expel the barbarians.

Within this framework of cooperation, self-styled able daimyo called for national reforms to match the military reforms they had carried out at home. They urged the shogunate to employ men of talent and ability, regardless of their domainal affiliation, promote the study of Western technology, and strengthen the nation's defenses. To fund these goals, the shogunate agreed to cut its expenses, reduce the daimyo's attendance in Edo to one hundred days every three years, and permit the daimyo to take families held hostage in Edo to their domains. Women and servants had to abandon the only city they had ever known for life in provincial backwaters.

The *shishi* demanded expulsion of the barbarians in accordance with Kōmei's wishes. Young and reckless, they absconded from their domains to study swordsmanship in Edo and Kyoto and imbibe the ideas of Aizawa Seishisai and Yoshida Shōin. Filled with the Japanese spirit (*Yamato damashii*), they swaggered through the streets, less concerned with personal grooming than with purity of purpose. As soon as Yokohama opened as a treaty port in 1859, they launched a reign of terror against foreign merchants, sailors, and officials. (See Color Plate 26.) Following

MATERIAL CULTURE

From Palanquin to Rickshaw

Before the coming of the railroad, feet provided the means of locomotion for most Japanese travelers. Arising at 4:00 A.M. and moving briskly on straw sandals, they generally covered thirty miles a day before seeking an inn for the night. Occasionally a traveler rented a horse for a day's journey, but most horses carried merchandise. Boats plied the Inland Sea and Lake Biwa, carrying travelers as well as goods. Given the boats' reputation for capsizing, many travelers preferred to walk.

The chief alternative to feet was the palanquin. These came in several sizes and styles, depending on their function and the status of the user. Most travelers rode in a wicker basket seated on a cushion, grasping a strap to keep their balance. Rural entrepreneurs transported their brides in enclosed palanquins; in cities these were reserved for the daimyo and high-ranking samurai. Most palanquins were carried by two men, with relays running in front and back.

The rickshaw superseded the palanquin. Invented in 1869 by Izumi Yōsuke, a restaurateur in Tokyo (formerly Edo), it substituted human-powered carriages for horse-drawn coaches. Built in various sizes to carry up to four people and various designs, depending on whether strength or speed was the object, rickshaws spread from Japan to China and the rest of Asia. They made unmerciful demands on human labor, but they were cheap, simple to make and repair, and nonpolluting. Nothing could beat them for short distances until the taxi arrived in 1912.

Fifty-Three Stations on the Tōkaidō. At Kusatsu, one of the fifty-three stations on the Tōkaidō depicted in woodblock prints by Hiroshige, travelers rest their weary feet. Three types of palanquins are featured in this scene. *(Tokyo National Museum/TNM Image Archives/DNPArchives.com)*

Kazunomiya's marriage, *shishi* in Kyoto assassinated advisers to the daimyo and nobles they held responsible.

Monarch, shogun, and daimyo feared that the *shishi*'s antics would so weaken the established political order as to invite foreign invasion. Satsuma forced its radicals to return home in disgrace. When *shishi* tried to capture the palace in the eighth month of 1863, planning to place Kōmei at the head of an army to unite western Japan under the slogan of "Restore monarchical rule," Satsuma allied with shogunal forces to drive them from Kyoto. Many fled to Chōshū. The daimyo of Tosa forced *shishi* in his domain to leave or commit suicide. *Shishi*-led uprisings in the foothills of Yamato and at Ikuno near the Japan Sea were brutally suppressed. Conflict between radical expulsionists and conservatives in Mito erupted in civil war. In the seventh month of 1864, Chōshū *shishi* returned to Kyoto with supporters from other domains and rural militia in tow. Once again, the shogunate routed them.

The exploits performed by *shishi* had less impact on policy than on public opinion. They dramatized the monarchy's cause and ruptured the alliance between shogun and court. But how significant was the expansion of a public political sphere based on the discussion and exchange of information given that 60 percent of the population was illiterate? Most commoners remained bystanders. Historians who emphasize that commoners remained quiescent during the years leading to the Meiji Restoration and that therefore it cannot be deemed a revolution from below overlook a similar inertia in the ruling class. Most daimyo did nothing, either because they sided with the shogun out of loyalty and self-interest, he being the ultimate guarantor of their office, or because opposing factions had gridlocked domainal administration. Most samurai remained embedded in the vertical hierarchy predicated on loyalty and obedience to their lord. They had less to do with the eventual outcome than did rural entrepreneurs who provided supplies to traveling *shishi*, enlisted their tenants in rural militia, and supported the monarchical cause or the shogunate with their pocketbooks.

THE FALL OF THE SHOGUNATE (1864–1867)

The *shishi*'s attacks on foreigners and shogunal forces had unforeseen consequences. The British demanded that the men from Satsuma responsible for killing a British merchant be handed over to them and an indemnity paid. When Satsuma refused, British ships bombarded Kagoshima in the seventh month of 1863. Despite its military reforms, Satsuma was still no match for foreign gunboats. In the eleventh month, it signed a peace treaty acceding to British demands. In compliance with Kōmei's decree that the barbarians be expelled in the fifth month of 1863, Chōshū gunners fired on French and American ships in the straits of Shimonoseki. In the eighth month of 1864, the foreigners retaliated. These salutary lessons were not lost on their victims. Just days before foreign ships attacked Chōshū, the shogunate had it branded an enemy of the court for harboring *shishi* and sent a coalition of daimyo troops to its borders. Chōshū backed down. It apologized for its misdeeds, expelled radical court nobles who had sought refuge there in 1863, and executed three high-ranking officials. The shogunate declared victory and withdrew its forces.

The shogunate had less success controlling the consequences of foreign trade. Beginning in 1859, foreign merchants in the treaty ports at Nagasaki and Yokohama discovered that the silver-to-gold ratio in Japan was one-third what it was in the West, meaning that any man with silver in his pockets could buy gold at ludicrously low prices. The gold rush ended only when the shogunate recoined and devalued gold, silver, and copper. When it granted daimyo permission to mint money, counterfeiters flooded the market, and inflation soared. Foreign merchants bought tea and silk in exchange for weapons, making gunrunning a lucrative enterprise, but also leading to a sudden expansion in cash crops on rice paddies. Weavers lost work because they could not compete with foreigners for silk thread. In the summer of 1866, rising unemployment, crop failures, inflation, and shogunal efforts to tax trade created the conditions for the most widespread riots in Edo history, particularly in the shogun's stronghold of eastern Japan.

The shogunate hoped to use new taxes levied on foreign trade to subsidize its military modernization program. It imported thousands of weapons through Yokohama and drilled its retainer band in rifle companies supplemented by rural recruits. It sent missions abroad. The first in 1860 signed a friendship treaty with the United States; subsequent envoys emphasized the study of foreign technology. In 1861 it opened a naval training school at Hyōgo. In 1865 it started an ironworks at Yokohama and a shipyard at Yokosuka. It also received Kōmei's sanction for signing foreign treaties, and it marginalized the *to-*

Ee ja nai ka. As amulets fall from the sky, men, women, and children, some in costume, dance in thanksgiving, shouting, "Ain't it great?" (*Ee ja nai ka?*). *(National Diet Library, Tokyo, Japan)*

zama daimyo by excluding them from policymaking circles.

The shogunate's revitalization campaign destabilized the balance of power with the daimyo. When it announced a second punitive campaign against Chōshū because *shishi* had returned to positions of power, it pushed former enemies together. Chōshū and Satsuma formed an alliance in the first month of 1866. Both had launched self-strengthening programs, using emergency funds to buy arms through Nagasaki, sending retainers on fact-finding missions abroad, and organizing Western-style armies. Now they argued that the shogunate ought not move against Chōshū when pressing domestic and foreign problems remained to be solved. Few domains responded to the shogun's call; riots in Edo and Osaka tied down garrisons; and the attack on Chōshū ended in ignominious defeat. Iemochi's death at just that juncture provided the shogunate with a face-saving out. But when Kōmei died unexpectedly just five months later, the shogunate lost its strongest supporter at court. Unlike the shogun's opponents, who had come to believe that Japan should have but a single monarch, Kōmei supported the division of power that left administrative and foreign affairs in the shogun's hands.

Hitotsubashi Yoshinobu reigned as shogun for less than a year. At first he tried to reassert shogunal authority and continue military reforms. His efforts stirred up turmoil and strengthened the alliance against him. In the eighth month of 1867, a new popular movement swept the coast from the inland sea to Edo. Claiming that amulets inscribed with the name of the sun goddess that portended a prosperous future had fallen from heaven, men and women danced in the streets chanting, "Ain't it great?" (*Ee ja nai ka?*). When the movement reached eastern Japan, dancers threw stones at foreigners to drive out barbarian demons and rehearsed a mock funeral for the shogunate. In the tenth month, the court issued a secret decree to Satsuma and Chōshū to overthrow the Tokugawa. Realizing he could no longer fulfill the duties of shogun, Yoshinobu returned his patent of office to the monarch. The restoration of monarchical rule was at hand.

In the name of the Meiji emperor, Kōmei's fifteen-year-old son, leaders of the Sat-chō forces abolished the offices of shogun and regent and replaced them with new advisory positions open to daimyo, court nobles, and "men of talent." They declared Yoshinobu a traitor to the emperor, revoked his court rank, and confiscated his family lands. When the shogunate fought back, it was defeated after four days of fighting outside Kyoto in the first days of 1868. The imperial armies moved slowly north, hamstrung for lack of cash, which they tried to ameliorate by demanding loans from wealthy commoners. The long-standing animosity between eastern and western Japan prolonged the fighting until Aizu fell in the ninth month after suffering heavy casualties of men and women. The last stronghold of shogunal support at Hakodate did not surrender until the middle of 1869, supported to the last by the American envoy. Both official and popular opinion feared that prolonged civil war might give foreign troops an excuse to invade Japan. A better alternative was to unite around the new emperor. Although retainers died, Yoshinobu and the daimyo of Aizu survived to take their places in the new imperial peerage and join their efforts to the task of strengthening state and economy to compete in the new world order. Hirata disciples and other imperial loyalists rushed to offer their services to the new government; people in Edo watched warily as their old masters were replaced with new.

SUMMARY

What changed between 1800 and 1868? Long before the Meiji Restoration, the social and political order crafted in the seventeenth century had ceased to fit everyday practice. The commercial economy, opportunities for travel, and information networks eroded the status and geographical divisions that kept people in their place. Reforms by shogun and daimyo to shore up their authority and fill government coffers could not rectify the gap between reality and their ideal of the proper relations between rulers and commoners. Debates over how to deal with the foreign threat added further strain to the system at the same time that they drew more people into the public political sphere. When the shogunate collapsed in 1867, it left behind a dynamic economy, a pool of able administrators, and a population well educated for its time. Also bequeathed to the fledgling government was a set of treaties with the Great Powers that recast Japan's relations with the outside world and opened the country to foreign trade, though not on terms favorable to Japan.

Meiji Transformation (1868–1900)

The restoration of the Meiji emperor as head of state marked the beginning of profound changes in Japanese politics, culture, and society. A small group of self-selected men, who had led the drive to overthrow the shogun, implemented programs to abolish status distinctions that had compartmentalized social groups and to centralize government. Fearful of the West, they acknowledged the necessity of importing Western military technology, industry, legal norms, constitutional thought, science, dress, and food. (See **Material Culture: New Food for a New Nation.**) They built railroads, shipyards, and schools. They propounded a new ideology to rally the citizens. They colonized the Ryukyu Islands and Hokkaido. They projected Japan's power abroad in Taiwan and Korea and renegotiated treaties. They faced considerable opposition, often from within their own ranks. Farmers rioted against new state policies that threatened their livelihood; samurai rebelled at the loss of their traditional identity. Local notables promoted democracy. Intellectuals, novelists, and essayists hammered out new identities that refused to fit a single pattern. By the end of the century, modernity had arrived.

To what extent did changes in the latter half of the nineteenth century build on what had gone before? Did the Meiji Restoration herald a revolution in politics and society, or simply a transition? Did modernization mean Westernization?

THE MEIJI STATE (1868–1900)

Oligarchs who created the institutions for a centralized government had little idea of what they hoped to accomplish and disagreed on what to do. An amorphous group of samurai from Satsuma and Chōshū, plus a few activist Kyoto aristocrats and imperial loyalists from other domains, they had diverse interests and goals. Their first pronouncement came in the Oath of 1868, offered by the emperor in the company of court nobles

MATERIAL CULTURE

New Food for a New Nation

Although rice had been grown in Japan since the eighth century B.C.E., it did not become a staple of the average Japanese diet until imported from Korea and China starting in 1873. Before that, most people ate wheat, barley, and millet. Between 1869 and 1900, the per capita consumption of rice went from 3.5 bushels a year to 5 bushels a year. Rice balls became ubiquitous in lunch boxes, and except for the poor, steamed rice replaced rice gruel for breakfast.

The Meiji government officially promoted the eating of meat because it was thought to produce stronger workers and soldiers. In 1869 it established the Tsukiji beef company. In 1871 a butcher shop in Tokyo's Asakusa district became popular selling beef for sukiyaki, a Meiji period invention, as well as milk, cheese, and butter. In the 1880s butcher shops started selling horse meat. It was cheaper than beef or pork and redder than chicken.

Vegetables, fruits, and breads had a harder sell. Asparagus, cabbage, cauliflower, and tomatoes did not blend easily into Japanese cuisine. Importing apples and grapes stimulated the cultivation and spread of indigenous fruits such as persimmon, Satsuma tangerine, and Asian pear. Bread and cakes became popular only after they were modified to suit Japanese taste.

By selectively adapting Western foods, Japanese people developed a much more varied diet than they had had in the past. They ate more, and what they ate was more nutritious, although overly refined rice caused beriberi in soldiers. An improved diet made most people stronger and healthier. It increased life expectancy and child-bearing rates. A population of approximately 33 million at midcentury had grown to 45 million by the end of the nineteenth century.

Aguranabe. This flyer advertising Aguranabe, a butcher shop, linked eating beef to "civilization and enlightenment." *(Tokyo Metropolitan Foundation for History and Culture DNPArchives.com)*

and daimyo to the gods of heaven and earth. In it he promised that everyone was to unite in promoting the nation's well-being, government policy was to be decided through public discussion, all would be allowed to fulfill their just aspirations, "the uncivilized customs of former times shall be broken through," and "intellect and learning shall be sought throughout the world in order to establish the foundations of the Empire."[1] The Five Injunctions issued to commoners the next day had a different message. It ordered them to practice the Confucian virtues of loyalty, filial piety, chastity, obedience, and harmony; to desist from demonstrations and protests; to abjure Christianity; to conform to international public law; and to stay in Japan. Emigration to Hawaii began shortly thereafter.

Ambiguities in the oath speak to the lack of agreement on national goals. The nation's well-being could justify a national land tax and universal military conscription; it could require promoting entrepreneurship and compulsory education. None of the men present envisioned public discussion of national affairs to include anyone but themselves. In the context of the past, when each daimyo had set policy for his domain, it meant that decisions and power were to be centralized. It did not mean parliamentary democracy, although it was later interpreted that way. The third clause implied that hereditary status distinctions would be abolished and held out the promise of social mobility. Abolishing old customs acknowledged the reality of cultural imperialism inherent in international law and unequal treaties. The purpose of gaining knowledge was to serve the state.

At first, oligarchs looked to eighth-century models for a new government. The Council of State became the highest deliberative body. It was assisted by a board of 106 advisers, the activists in the Meiji Restoration, who made the real decisions. The Council of Shinto Affairs enjoyed a brief existence equal to the Council of State. This structure was reorganized four times in the next four months. Most daimyo remained in control of their domains, leaving the oligarchs who spoke in the emperor's name only the former shogun's lands. Monetary proof of support for the emperor from daimyo, former shogunal retainers, merchants, and rural entrepreneurs staved off fiscal crisis in the short run. The necessity of finding sufficient tax revenues to fund the government forced the oligarchs to take hesitant steps toward centralization.

Centralization required convincing the daimyo to give up their domains. Some daimyo hoped to play a larger role in national affairs; some concentrated their efforts on self-strengthening. Most stayed aloof from government and isolated from each other. In 1869, the daimyo of Satsuma and Chōshū agreed to make a formal declaration of returning their land and population registers to the emperor, with the understanding that he would then confirm their holdings as governors. The government put all domainal retainers above the level of foot soldiers into one general category called former samurai (*shizoku*). To eliminate the redundancies of 270 domain administrations and centralize tax collection, the oligarchs in 1871 abolished the domains and established prefectures (see Map 20.1). They started the process of consolidating 170,000 towns and villages into larger administrative units with a new hierarchy of local officials and inaugurated a household registration system whereby each household head had to establish a place of legal residence and inform the government of births, deaths, marriages, and divorces in his family.

Daimyo accepted the loss of their hereditary lands with equanimity. The most important became prefectural governors. Since the number of prefectures was seventy-two, later reduced to fifty, the area under their control expanded. All daimyo benefited by no longer having responsibility for their domains' debts and being guaranteed a substantial income for their personal use. They did not have to support standing armies of retainers. In place of their former titles, they received court rank. In return for giving up their already circumscribed autonomy, they received wealth and prestige.

Abolishing domains disinherited roughly 2 million *shizoku*. All they received were small stipends later commuted to government bonds. Oligarchs urged them to find another line of work, in agriculture, forestry, business, and the colonization of Hokkaido. Some succeeded; many did not. Former shogunal bureaucrats staffed the new government offices, but most domain samurai remained in castle towns. Political power had become sufficiently bureaucratized over the course of the Edo period that neither samurai nor daimyo became landed gentry.

Having taken the first steps toward a more centralized state, in 1871, one faction of oligarchs left for the United States and Europe. Forty-nine officials and fifty-eight students, including five girls, made up the delegation. Headed by Iwakura Tomomi, a former court noble, their goal was to convince the Western

---

1. Donald L. Keene, *Emperor of Japan: Meiji and His World, 1852–1912* (New York: Columbia University Press, 2002), p. 139.

Map 20.1   **Modern Japan**

powers to revise the unequal treaties that infringed on Japanese sovereignty. Informed by President Ulysses S. Grant that Western powers would never consent to treaty revision unless Japan reformed its laws and institutions along Western lines, the diplomatic mission became a study mission. Wealth and power that the West had created through industrialization and centralized political institutions came as a shock. Officials inspected prisons, schools, factories, and government agencies. They expected their absence to preclude any initiatives by the leaders left behind; in 1873, when Saigō Takamori proposed to invade Korea for having insulted the emperor in the first diplomatic exchange following the restoration, they rushed home to stop him. They opposed not the use of force but

its timing. Domestic reform had to precede military engagements abroad.

Reforms and Opposition

Abolition of domains took place in the context of social reforms that did not suit everyone. For many farmers, the emperor's progress from Kyoto to Edo (renamed Tokyo in 1869) in 1868 symbolized the Meiji Restoration. This, they felt, would usher in new prosperity and social justice. Instead, village officials continued to collect taxes, rents remained the same, and moneylenders charged exorbitant interest. Disappointment fueled the rage with which rural and urban people punished what they saw as wrongdoing. When the new government replaced familiar faces in domain administrations with men from foreign parts, this too led to protest, as did the official end to discrimination against outcasts when status distinctions were erased and the outcasts became "new commoners." The first ten years of the Meiji period saw more protest and more violence than had any time during the Edo period.

Bureaucrats initiated reforms and technological innovations to strengthen the state against its domestic and foreign enemies. They hired Western experts to transform government, economy, infrastructure, and education. Drawing on Western models, they issued civil and criminal codes that replaced different regulations for different statuses with rule by law that considered only the nature of the crime. They built telegraph lines and railroads to improve communications and foster unity. On January 1, 1873, they replaced the lunar calendar that farmers had used as a guide to planting and harvesting with the Western calendar. They outlawed traditional hairstyles for men and suppressed village festivals. They issued these directives without warning or explanation. In defense of time-honored custom, farmers rioted.

Religious practices also provoked controversy. In the third month of 1868, the oligarchs ordered the separation of Shinto and Buddhism and the conversion of what had been shrine-temple complexes into shrines by eliminating Buddhist icons, rituals, and priests. In some regions, officials infected with Hirata Atsutane's doctrines destroyed Buddhist temples where the farmers' ancestral tablets were kept. The establishment of Yasukuni shrine to the war dead in 1869 used Shinto to promote national goals. The development of State Shinto in the 1870s consolidated local shrines and brought them into a hierarchy with the Ise shrine to the sun goddess at the top. Rather than shrines containing only deities particular to their region, people had to accept deities of national significance in addition. New religions founded in the Edo period received official recognition as Sect Shinto. Meiji period new religions were viewed with suspicion, if not proscribed outright. (See **Biography: Deguchi Nao.**) Farmers protested the destruction of their familiar temples, and Buddhist priests fought back by associating Buddhism with anti-Christian sentiment, recalling ties to the imperial house, and helping immigrants in Hokkaido.

Directives that had immediate effects and aroused the strongest opposition dealt with education, the military, and taxes. In 1872, the government decreed eight years of compulsory education for all children (shortened to four in 1879 and then increased to six in 1907) to fit them for their responsibilities as productive citizens in a modern nation. Communities had to pay for schools themselves. Enraged at the cost, farmers destroyed or damaged nearly two hundred schools between 1873 and 1877. Pre-Meiji teachers continued their unlicensed schools and dissuaded parents from sending their children to new ones. Needing their children's labor or unable to afford tuition, many parents never enrolled daughters or even sons or allowed them to attend only a few months. Over time, compliance increased until it reached 90 percent in the twentieth century.

The slogan of the day was "Rich Country, Strong Army." In January 1873, the government issued the conscription ordinance that summoned all males over the age of twenty to serve on active duty in the armed forces for three years, followed by four years in the reserves. In accord with the French system, heads and heirs of family farms and businesses received exemptions, and exemptions could be purchased. The policy's architect was Yamagata Aritomo from Chōshū, who had spent 1869–1870 in Europe studying French and German conscript armies. The conscription ordinance put Japan's defense on the shoulders of the masses. It provided a way to educate conscripts and their families in the goals of government leaders. By revoking the samurai's monopoly of force, it did more than any other reform to eliminate status distinctions and create equality of opportunity.

Both farmers and *shizoku* opposed conscription. The ordinance used the term "blood tax," meaning that all citizens should willingly sacrifice themselves for their country. Farmers who took it literally assumed that the government wanted their blood. Even those who understood the message believed that farmers could best contribute to the nation by growing crops. Commoners opposed to conscription rose up in sixteen localities in the months after the ordinance's promulgation. Samurai opposition took longer to develop but cost more lives. Conservative oligarchs such as Saigō Takamori had already insisted that the national army be composed of the men bred to military service. When Iwakura and his faction outvoted Saigō on whether to invade Korea, he left the government. In 1876, the government ordered *shizoku* to stop wearing the two swords that distinguished them from the rest of the population. Between 1874 and 1877, over thirty rebellions erupted in defense of samurai privilege. The largest and last, in Satsuma and led by

BIOGRAPHY   Deguchi Nao

Women played a major role in the founding of Japan's new religions. Deguchi Nao (1836–1918), an illiterate commoner, became a prophet.

Nao was born in a castle town near Kyoto to a family in declining circumstances. Her grandfather had the privilege of wearing a sword and using a surname as an official carpenter. Her father squandered his life on drink; he died when Nao was nine. Nao went to work for a merchant who provided her with room and board. Her earnings went to her mother. Nao helped with the cooking and cleaning; she spun thread and strung coins, thereby gaining a reputation for diligence and hard work. In her third year of service, the domain awarded her a prize for being a filial daughter.

Nao hoped to marry the man she loved, but her widowed aunt Yuri insisted that she accept an arranged marriage and be adopted into the Deguchi family as Yuri herself had done. Yuri drowned herself after Nao repeatedly rejected her offer. A few days later, Nao developed a high fever and lost consciousness. Upon her recovery, she attributed her illness to Yuri's vengeful spirit. To placate it and care for the Deguchi ancestral tablets, Nao agreed to marry the man Yuri had selected for her and continue the Deguchi house.

Nao's husband was no better than her father. By 1872 she had borne five children and was living in a rented house in Ayabe. She opened a small restaurant, and when it failed, she sold sweet-bean buns. She continued to have children—eleven in all, three of whom died in infancy. When her husband became paralyzed from a fall off a roof in 1885, Nao collected rags to support her family. His death in 1887 freed her to work in a filature as well.

One winter morning in 1892 as she was out collecting rags, Nao became possessed by a god. The experience transformed her personality and her outlook on the world. Instead of being gentle and deferential, she became dignified, filled with divinely inspired authority. She rejected the social order because it rewarded vice and valued money. Since the oligarchs and the emperor were responsible for these conditions, they exemplified absolute evil. They would soon be destroyed and replaced by a divine order of harmony and equality. Under the spell of her god, this formerly illiterate woman wrote hundreds of texts that spelled out what was wrong with the world and what was to come. She also became a faith healer. In 1899, her adopted son Deguchi Onisaburō organized a sect called Ōmoto-kyō based on her revelations. Under his leadership, the group grew rapidly and suffered repeated government persecutions. Nao quarreled with him over his interpretation of her writings and his refusal to reject all that was modern. She died frustrated that she had not been able to reconstruct the world in accordance with her beliefs.

Source: Emily Groszos Ooms, *Women and Millenarian Protest in Meiji Japan: Deguchi Nao and Ōmoto-kyō* (Ithaca, N.Y.: East Asia Program, Cornell University, 1993).

Saigō, required the mobilization of sixty-five thousand troops and took eight months to suppress. Saigō committed suicide. In 1878, samurai counterrevolution ended with the assassination of the oligarch Ōkubo Toshimichi, also from Satsuma, because he had opposed invading Korea and arbitrarily initiated reforms.

Satsuma rebels also had reason to oppose the 1873 tax law. Applied nationwide to agricultural land, its aim was to provide a steady flow of income for the government by replacing the old hodgepodge of domain taxes on fluctuating harvests with a single, uniform property tax. In most regions of Japan, land surveys that accompanied the new tax simply confirmed de facto proprietary rights farmers already enjoyed. Satsuma domain had allowed *gōshi* (rustic warriors) to assign land to cultivators and treat them like tenant farmers. Faced with loss of income as well as hereditary status and privilege, *gōshi* became the shock troops for the Satsuma rebellion.

Even though Meiji oligarchs tried to promote industry and demanded loans from merchants, they had an agrarian mindset. Nearly 80 percent of the government's revenues came from tax on agricultural land through the 1880s. Farmers with market access for their products benefited; those who misjudged the market or suffered a crop failure had to sell their land to pay taxes. In some areas, officials imposed the new tax while requiring farmers to con-

Composition of Tax Revenues, 1872–1940 (%)									
Fiscal Year	Land Tax	Liquor Tax	Customs Duties	Income Tax	Corporation Tax	Business Tax	Sugar Excise	Inheritance Tax	Other
1872	90.1	1.5	3.3	—	—	—	—	—	5.1
1880	72.3	14.9	4.4	—	—	—	—	—	8.4
1890	58.1	22.9	6.9	1.6	—	—	—	—	10.5
1900	34.6	38.0	10.9	4.3	1.2	3.9	1.3	—	5.8
1910	23.8	26.2	15.3	10.0	2.9	7.0	5.1	0.9	8.8
1920	10.2	22.6	11.1	23.5	11.8	6.6	6.8	1.1	6.3
1930	7.9	26.4	15.1	22.1	6.6	6.2	9.6	3.5	2.6
1940	0.9	8.9	2.9	34.0	11.7	2.6	3.2	1.6	33.9

Source: Based on Minami Ryōshin, *The Economic Development of Japan: A Quantitative Study,* trans. Ralph Thompson and Minami with assistance from David Merriman (New York: St. Martin's Press, 1986), p. 340.

tinue to pay the ancillary taxes it was supposed to replace. Farmers petitioned for redress; they killed officials suspected of being corrupt. In 1876, widespread, if uncoordinated, opposition to the tax forced the government to reduce it from 3 percent of assessed value to 2.5 percent.

While dealing with opposition from outside the government, oligarchs also quarreled among themselves. They created and abolished ministries to consolidate their power or deny rivals and disputed what kind of government Japan was to have. In the early 1870s, Kido Takayoshi and Ōkubo advocated some measure of popular representation in government lest arbitrary rule generate unrest. Their proposal contained a veiled attack on Itō Hirobumi and Yamagata. Disgruntled at having been shut out of power, Itagaki Taisuke left the government in 1874, joined with disaffected *shizoku* from his home domain of Tosa to form the Patriotic Party, and petitioned the government to establish an elected national assembly. He disbanded the party when he was invited back into the government in 1875 at the Osaka Conference. There, the oligarchs agreed to establish prefectural assemblies (done in 1878) and plan for a national assembly. Four months later, the emperor announced that he would promulgate a constitution after due deliberation.

Constitution and National Assembly

Publicity generated by the promise of a national assembly and constitution stimulated responses that coalesced into the Popular Rights Movement. *Shizoku*, village officials, rural entrepreneurs, journalists, intellectuals, and prefectural assemblymen held meetings and circulated petitions for an immediate national assembly that collected hundreds of thousands of signatures. Radicals and impoverished farmers rioted and planned attacks on the government in the name of human rights. A woman who held property demanded to be allowed to vote in prefectural elections (she was denied). Kishida Toshiko and Fukuda Hideko gave public lectures at which they demanded rights, liberty, education, and equality for women. Baba Tatsui drew on Social Darwinism to argue that since democracy based on an egalitarian society was the most advanced form of government, it should be established forthwith. Local notables drafted model constitutions. Activists criticized the oligarchs for blocking communication between emperor and people. They argued that a representative government would harmonize imperial and popular will by providing a forum for the free expression of popular opinion, thereby strengthening the nation. Drawing on natural rights theories propounded by French and British philosophers, Ueki Emori propounded a theory of popular sovereignty and right of revolution.

Oligarchs responded to the Popular Rights Movement by issuing increasingly draconian peace preservation laws. Press censorship began in 1875; the 1880 Ordinance on Public Meetings stationed policemen at assemblies to ensure that the speakers did not deviate from texts that had been approved beforehand. Excluded from audiences were soldiers, off-duty police, teachers, and students. Demonstrations in Fukushima opposed to a particularly arbitrary governor in 1882, the Chichibu uprising of 1884 that mobilized tenant farmers in demanding debt relief, and other violent incidents met with mass arrests and executions. Having learned the cost of direct action, local notables turned to organizing political parties in anticipation of the first election for the national assembly promised in 1890.

The Meiji Constitution defined institutions established before its promulgation. In 1878 the military General Staff was made directly responsible to the emperor, bypassing the War Ministry run by bureaucrats. A new peerage destined to fill the upper house of the bicameral national assembly, known as the Diet, was announced in 1884. It included oligarchs, former daimyo, and Kyoto nobility. Over time it expanded to include entrepreneurs and academics. The lower house was to be elected by commoners. The highest policymaking institution, the cabinet, replaced the Council of State in 1885. It was composed of ministers in charge of education, finance, foreign affairs, and other bureaucracies under the prime minister appointed by the emperor.

Itō Hirobumi drafted the constitution in great secrecy. He traveled to Europe in 1882 where for nine months he studied in Berlin under the most respected constitutional theorists of his day. Itō and his brain trust then created a document that defined the emperor in terms of his descent from the gods and employed Western notions of the rights and obligations of citizens. Once the constitution was finished, the Privy Council, a new institution headed by Itō, met to discuss it. On February 11, 1889, the date chosen to be the anniversary of Jimmu's accession 2,349 years earlier, the Meiji emperor bestowed the constitution on the prime minister. Three days of festivities announced to people across the nation that they were now citizens of a state founded on principles enshrined in a constitution.

Oligarchs wanted a constitution that secured the governing bodies and protected the imperial house through which they exercised power, and they mistrusted "ignorant" masses. After its promulgation, they designated themselves *genrō*, elder statesmen, charged with picking cabinet ministers for the emperor. The constitution defined the emperor as sovereign and sacred. The emperor:

- exercises executive power through the cabinet
- exercises legislative power with the consent of the Imperial Diet
- has supreme command of the army and navy
- declares war, makes peace, and concludes treaties
- determines the organization of the government
- convokes the Diet and dissolves the lower house

Subjects had rights and duties to:

- present petitions, provided that they observe the proper form of respect
- enjoy freedom of religious belief within limits not prejudicial to peace and order, and not antagonistic to their duties as subjects
- enjoy freedom of speech, within the limits set by law[2]

Subjects had to serve in the military, a clause that excluded women from the category of "subject."

Japan's first experiment with parliamentary democracy nearly did not work. Although Itō and Yamagata had assumed that party politics had no place in an institution directly responsible to the emperor, they had to deal with opposition parties headed by Itagaki and other men who had been ejected from the oligarch's inner circle. Suffrage was limited to men paying at least fifteen yen a year in property taxes, a qualification met by only 1.1 percent of the population, most of them in rural areas. Once elected, members discovered that the Diet had more power than the oligarchs had intended. Diet members could criticize the cabinet in memorials to the emperor; they could make speeches, published in newspapers, that outside the Diet might have landed them in jail. They had the power to approve the budget. If they refused, the previous year's budget remained in effect, but it seldom sufficed for the government's needs. When the Diet stood up to the cabinet, the prime minister dissolved it, forcing members into costly re-election campaigns. Campaign finance scandals and vote buying tarnished the reputations of politicians and oligarchs alike. Twenty-five men died during the 1892 election, most at the hands of the police.

Divided by personality, political preference, and self-interest, oligarchs had to seek political support outside their narrow circle. In so doing, they enlarged the realm of political actors to include bureaucrats, military officers, and politicians. In 1898, Itō had the quasi-oligarchs Ōkuma Shigenobu, head of the Progressive Party, and Itagaki Taisuke, leader of the Liberal Party, participate in a coalition cabinet as prime minister and home minister, respectively. Aghast at this concession to politicians, Yamagata Aritomo sabotaged their cabinet by having the army minister refuse to accept cuts in the military budget. A few months

---

2. Hugh Borton, *Japan's Modern Century* (New York: Ronald Press Co., 1955), pp. 490–507.

Triptych Showing Inauguration of the First Diet. Members of the upper house dressed in uniform are in the foreground; lower house members sit farther back. The emperor is in the box at upper left. *(Museum of Fine Arts, Boston. Jean S. and Frederic A. Sharf Collection, 2000.535)*

later, Yamagata became prime minister for the second time. To increase military autonomy, he made it a requirement that all army and navy ministers be active-duty officers. To dilute the power of political parties and their resistance to higher taxes, he expanded the suffrage to 2.2 percent of the population and gave more representation to urban districts. In 1900, Itō responded by forming and becoming president of a new political party, the Friends of Government (*Seiyūkai*). His compromise with politicians dramatized the oligarchs' difficulty in controlling the institutions they had created.

Industrialization

Oligarchs promoted economic reform and industrialization. They appropriated the arms-related industries already established by the domains and the shogunate. Some of the industries came under state control to supply the military; others were sold to cronies at favorable terms. Iwasaki Yatarō founded Mitsubishi enterprises on the maritime shipping line he acquired from Tosa and expanded it with low-interest government loans. The oligarchs had foreign experts write banking laws; they set up banks and issued paper currency. Their initial investments were in advanced and expensive technologies, the kind needed to build railroads and shipyards. Although building support industries for the military consti-

tuted their first priority, they also worried about the effects of unequal treaties on the balance of payments and unemployment. To maintain social stability and to compete with foreign products, they built cotton spinning and weaving factories to make cloth for domestic consumption and imported French silk spinning technology to produce thread for export. They founded a sugar refinery to help growers market their crop and compete with Chinese sugar. By bringing the state's resources to bear on industry, oligarchs squeezed out private capital.

Agriculture supported industrial growth. Agricultural development groups, seed exchange societies, journals, and lecture circuits taught farmers about new seed varieties, commercial fertilizers, and equipment. Without more arable land, annual agricultural productivity rose between 1.5 and 1.7 percent in the late nineteenth century. Since the land tax remained fixed, the increase put more income in the hands of rural entrepreneurs for use in promoting small-scale industry. Farmers were already accustomed to producing handicrafts; the elimination of internal restrictions on trade made it easier for them to market their goods.

Entrepreneurs and artisans developed intermediate technologies that adapted Western machines to Japanese circumstances. They modified the manufacture of new daily necessities such as matches to suit the domestic and Asian markets and undersold

Steam Engine. The steam engine epitomized the industrial age. Its use on the railroad that paralleled the Tōkaidō eliminated palanquins and long distance foot traffic. *(Yokohama Archives of History)*

Western brands. The metric system, the new calendar, and Western timepieces brought the standardization and regularization modeled by military organization to ordinary work practices. Local clubs tried to preserve handicrafts in the face of foreign imports and sought national and international markets for specialty products. They pooled capital to upgrade indigenous skills, brought in foreign technology when it fit their needs, and hosted industrial exhibitions to diffuse technological knowledge and stimulate competition. In the mid-1870s, small water-powered filatures spread throughout the mountain valleys of central Japan, close to the silk-producing regions and a work force of young women. By 1900, silk thread accounted for one-third of the value of Japan's commodity exports, and textiles totaled over half.

Another model for private enterprise was Shibusawa Eiichi. Son of a rural entrepreneur, he used his connections with oligarchs to become president of First National Bank. In that capacity he provided capital for the construction of a privately owned shipyard at the mouth of Tokyo Bay. In 1880 he started the Osaka Spinning Mill and went on to found more than one hundred companies. By the beginning of the twentieth century, thanks to investments like his, Japan's imports were of raw materials; it exported manufactured goods. Other entrepreneurs built equipment for railroads, mines, and factories. Many thrived with the government as their biggest customer. They justified their immense wealth by insisting that they worked for the good of the nation.

In 1880 the government faced financial disaster. It had printed money recklessly during the 1870s to finance its projects, and private banks issued their own notes. It spent heavily suppressing *shizoku* rebellions and other police actions; most of the industries it built operated at a loss. Inflation that doubled the price of rice in Tokyo between 1877 and 1880 reduced the value of property tax revenues, and taxes did not cover expenditures. The negative balance of payments sucked gold and silver out of the country. From an economic point of view, Japan faced the most serious crisis of the Meiji period.

After acrimonious debate, the oligarchs decided on a deflationary policy of retrenchment. Finance Minister Matsukata Masayoshi balanced the budget, reduced government expenditures until they fell within revenues, and established a sound currency backed by gold and silver. Except for railroad, telegraph, and military-related industries, he sold at a loss all industries that the government had tried to develop. He recalled students sent abroad on government scholarships, fired foreign experts, enacted sin taxes on tobacco and sake, and increased old taxes. Between 1881 and 1885, he reduced the quantity of currency by 20 percent and stifled commerce. Farmers who saw the price of rice fall 50 percent while taxes remained the same worked longer hours to increase production. Bad loans bankrupted banks started with samurai capital. Small businesses collapsed. The ranks of tenant farmers and factory workers swelled. By 1886 key industries had become concentrated in the hands of a few wealthy capitalists with excellent government connections. The government had rid itself of drains on its income, the budget was balanced, and prices were stable.

By the 1890s Japan had a substantial work force in light and heavy industry. Filatures employed single farmwomen who worked eighteen-hour days when demand was high. When they contracted tuberculosis, as many did, they were returned to their families. The disease's spread made it modern Japan's most severe epidemic. The women who worked twelve-hour shifts in cotton mills were often married. Factory owners assumed that since women did not maintain households independent of fathers or husbands, they had no need to pay a living wage. The first strike in Japan's industrial history occurred at a filature in Kōfu in 1885 where women protested a proposed increase in hours and decrease in pay. Women unable to find factory work turned to prostitution. Poor women from Kyushu were lured to brothels in Southeast Asia. Money remitted to their families helped Japan's balance of payments.

Male factory workers in heavy industry earned up to five times the wages of women. They worked under bosses called *oyakata* who contracted for specific jobs. Because workers ran the factory floor, they were able to retain a measure of autonomy that gave them pride in their work. They moved at will from one factory to another because they possessed skills in high demand. Despite these advantages, wages barely covered the rent for a shack in the slums and a dismal diet of rice and vegetables. In 1898 railroad workers launched the largest strike of the nineteenth century. They demanded respect, higher status, and an increase in overtime pay.

Conditions for miners were worse. The low wages, dangerous work, and prison-like barracks made it so difficult to attract workers that the owner of the Ashio copper mine contracted for convict labor. By the end of the nineteenth century, the mine's demand for timber had stripped surrounding hills, leading to deadly floods. Effluent from the mine had killed marine life in the Watarase River, devastated farmland, and caused premature deaths. Reactions to environmental damage pitted proponents of "Rich Country, Strong Army" against the well-being of ordinary citizens in a con-flict that was to play out repeatedly in Japan's modern history.

Civilization and Enlightenment

Local notables who had responded enthusiastically to the Popular Rights Movement wanted to bring a cultural revolution to their villages. In place of past hidebound customs, they wanted "Civilization and Enlightenment," a slogan promoted by urban intellectuals and by oligarchs bent on modernizing communications, hairstyles, and education. The Meiji 6 Society founded in Tokyo in 1873 published a journal in which the members debated representative government, foreign affairs, modernizing the Japanese language, ethics, and religion and roles for women. That same year, local notable Ida Bunzō bought a copy of Samuel Smiles's *Self Help*. In a local magazine, he explained the virtues of perseverance and frugality, competition and progress, moral responsibility and the national interest. Other local notables used informal discussion groups to promote better hygiene and social improvement through hospitals, new foods, better roads, and technological innovation based on Western models. They tried to overcome their neighbors' antipathy to the government-mandated schools that they saw as the best hope for improving conditions for rural people and for raising Japan's standing in the world.

The man who coined the phrase "Civilization and Enlightenment" was Fukuzawa Yukichi, a leading member of the Meiji 6 Society. In 1868 he founded Keiō University for the study of Western science and business. His multivolume *Seiyō jijō* (*Western Matters*) described modern institutions—schools, hospitals, newspapers, libraries, and museums—and Western ideas regarding the importance of entrepreneurship and achievement. In the best-seller *Encouragement of Learning*, he indicted Japan for its backwardness and urged citizens to seek learning for its practical value in the modern world. He also served as adviser to Mitsubishi and Mitsui, destined to become the largest conglomerates in Japan. Although he advocated equality, freedom, and education for women, he kept his daughters ignorant and arranged their marriages.

Civilization and enlightenment also pertained to personal appearance. To use Western technology, it was more efficient to wear Western-style clothes. Replacing distinctive styles of samurai armor with standardized military uniforms submerged the individual in the ranks. Uniforms distinguished policemen from civilians. Changing appearances might help Japan gain the respect of foreigners who flaunted their cultural superiority. The government issued directives to men to stop shaving their pates and to women to stop blackening their teeth and shaving their eyebrows. Emperor and empress led the way. At his first public performance, the Meiji emperor had dressed in the court robes of his ancestors. He wore cosmetics and powder and had false eyebrows smudged on his forehead. Within two years he had changed to Western-style uniforms, had cut his hair, and had grown a beard. The empress too appeared in Western-style clothing and hairstyles.

The new nobility and educated elite followed the imperial family's example. In 1883 the foreign minister built a modern two-story brick building called *Rokumeikan* (Deer-Cry Pavilion) that contained a restaurant, billiard room, and ballroom. Invitations to garden parties, charity balls, and receptions included Japanese and foreigners, husbands and wives, a startling innovation because samurai women had not previously socialized with their husbands. Western-style dancing by couples was de rigueur, even at parties far from Tokyo sponsored by prefectural governments. The late 1880s government became known as the "dancing cabinet."

Newspapers, journals, and other mass media exemplified and promoted civilization and enlightenment. Woodblock prints used chemical dyes to depict the marvels of westernization. Prints of horse-drawn carriages, steam locomotives, imposing new schools, and red brick buildings illuminated by gaslight in Tokyo's downtown Ginza district inspired progressive youths to seek modernity. (See Color Plate 27.) Magazines for women urged them to become educated in modern modes of thought to help them fulfill their roles as "good wives and wise mothers" (*ryōsai kenbo*). Fukuchi Gen'ichirō epitomized the professional journalist. He covered Saigō's rebellion in 1877 and later became chief editor of the influential *Tōkyō nichinichi shinbun* (Tokyo Daily Newspaper). It was a so-called big paper written in a style only the highly educated could read, with a focus on politics and serious editorials. Founded in 1874, the *Yomiuri Newspaper* aimed at the barely literate. Like other "small papers," it covered scandals and titillating stories of sex and murder. Hawked on street corners, it exploited the growing market for information and entertainment.

Modern newspapers serialized modern novels. In 1885 the aficionado of kabuki and student of English literature Tsubouchi Shōyō wrote *Essence of the Novel*, which tried to define a new realistic literature. *Floating Clouds* (1887–1889) by Futabatei Shimei is deemed Japan's first modern novel, because it tried to get inside the protagonist's head and used language close to the colloquial. Perhaps the most subtle and gifted writer was Higuchi Ichiyō, who garnered recognition in the male world of letters only at the end of her short life. Dominated at the end of the century by the medical doctor Mori Ōgai who had studied in Germany, and Natsume Sōseki who had studied in Britain, this world embraced modernity while questioning the superiority of Western civilization.

CONSERVATIVE RESURGENCE (1880S–1900)

By the middle of the 1880s, many people thought that aping Western customs had gone too far. They tried to retain traditional values while accepting the need for Western rationalism in scientific inquiry and Western technology. In 1882 Kanō Jigorō began the transformation of martial arts into judo and other forms through the scientific selection of techniques from earlier jujitsu schools. He emphasized that judo built character in a way that complemented developments in the study of ethics by religious figures and Western-trained philosophers. By establishing an absolute standard for "the good," they sought to promote community suppression of socially disruptive thought. The head of the Hygiene Bureau, Gotō Shimpei, claimed that the only way to get people to respond to public health initiatives was to work through established community structures and appeal to community values. Bureaucrats argued the need for the state to promote social welfare and a collectivist ethic through factory laws, tenancy laws, and agricultural cooperatives lest a social revolution undo their efforts to build a strong state. In 1890 the revised Police Security Regulations forbade women to participate in politics. The intent was to eliminate the need for selfish and unpatriotic competition and conflict.

The educational system bore the brunt of the conservative resurgence. In the 1870s it imparted strictly utilitarian and materialistic knowledge; in the mid-1880s it included Confucian ethics, Shinto mythology, and civic rituals. For the few who could afford to go beyond compulsory schooling, the Educational

Code of 1872 had specified that a rigorous examination system would qualify students for middle schools, and the best would then take examinations for university. Founded in 1877, Tokyo University remained the only public institution at that level until 1897. Private universities such as Keiō and missionary schools provided lesser avenues for educational advancement. In 1886 the Ministry of Education established specialized higher schools above the middle schools. The First Higher School funneled students into Tokyo University for positions in the most prestigious ministries. Some higher schools offered degrees in liberal arts for students going on to universities and then to careers in the bureaucracy or business world. Others were vocational schools, military schools, teachers colleges, and women's colleges. Each socialized the students by crafting character suitable to their station in life.

Education prepared citizens to serve the nation; it also provided the opportunity for personal advancement. Oligarchs opened the ranks of government service to men who had demonstrated talent and ability. These qualifications were measured through academic achievement, but only men from families affluent enough to support them through years of schooling had any chance of success. Women were to serve the state as wives and mothers. Class and gender thus placed limits on equality, and the promise of social mobility concealed an economically stratified society.

Education trained citizens in civic virtues personified by the emperor. In the 1870s and 1880s he toured Japan to unite the people under his gaze. Newspaper reports of his diligent work habits and concern for his subjects' welfare made him into a symbol of national unity and progress. He moved his headquarters to Hiroshima during the Sino-Japanese War (1894–1895), celebrated war victories, and appeared at imperial funerals, weddings, and wedding anniversaries. Hung in every school and public building, his portrait had to be treated with utmost respect. In 1890 he issued the Imperial Rescript on Education. It urged students to practice filial piety, harmony, sincerity, and benevolence; to respect the constitution; to obey the laws; and to be loyal to the *kokutai* (national polity).

The 1898 Civil Code adjusted the norms of Western jurisprudence to the conservative concern for civic morality. Unless the primacy of the house and the patriarchal authority of the household head were maintained in law, the legal scholar Hozumi Yatsuka warned, reverence for the ancestors, loyalty, and filial piety would perish. The Civil Code affirmed legal equality, individual choice, and personal ownership of property for all men and single women, regardless of their former social status. Succession was to follow the male line, with all assets to go to the eldest son. A husband had authority to dispose of his wife's real property, though not her personal property (her trousseau); he decided when and whether to register a marriage and their children. Divorce by mutual consent freed both partners for remarriage in a continuation of Edo period practice. The Civil Code thus balanced a concern for social stability and modern Western norms with an understanding of customary mores.

IMPERIALISM AND MODERNITY (1870s–1895)

When Japan appropriated and adapted Western industrial technology, juridical institutions, constitutional theory, and culture, it also imbibed Western imperialism. Gaining colonies compensated for the humiliation suffered in accepting unequal treaties, put Japan on the side of the civilized world by exporting enlightenment to the backward peoples of Asia, and demonstrated Great Power status. A sense of national identity that could unite factory owners with factory workers demanded imperialist enterprises to divert attention from their differences. Social Darwinism taught that nations had to conquer or be conquered. Seeing what had happened to China and India, Fukuzawa Yukichi urged Japan to "leave Asia" lest it too be conquered. (See **Documents: Fukuzawa Yukichi's "Leaving Asia."**)

The connection between modernity and imperialism appeared early in the Meiji period. Japan's overtures to China in 1870 included an effort to extract an unequal treaty because having taken steps toward a modern centralized state made it the more civilized. A treaty negotiated in 1871 granted mutual extraterritoriality. In 1874 Japan used the murder of Ryukyuan fishermen by Taiwanese three years earlier as an excuse to send an expeditionary force to Taiwan. The ostensible purpose was to punish the Taiwanese; a covert aim was to bring civilization to the natives by establishing a colony. The war dragged on for five months before a settlement reached in Beijing acknowledged China's claims to Taiwan and Japan's claims to the Ryukyus. The expeditionary force withdrew, though not before Japanese newspapers had celebrated its victory over barbarism.

DOCUMENTS

Fukuzawa Yukichi's "Leaving Asia"

The most prominent intellectual and promoter of westernization of Meiji Japan, whose views on domestic policy were decidedly liberal, Fukuzawa here takes a hard-line approach to foreign affairs. His ruthless criticism of Korea and China, published on March 16, 1885, can be read as justifying colonialism, while at the same time he urges his readers to reject the civilization they had to offer. In 1895, ten years after writing this call to action, he rejoiced at Japan's victory over China.

Though our land of Japan is situated on the Eastern edge of Asia, the spirit of its people has already shaken off the backwardness of Asia to accept the civilization of the West. Unfortunately, however, we have two neighboring countries, one being called China, the other called Korea. The people of these two countries are no different from us Japanese people in having been brought up since olden times in the Asian culture and customs, and yet, whether because they are of another racial origin, or because, while similar in culture and customs, differ from us in the main lines of their traditional education, a comparison of the three countries, Japan, China, and Korea, reveals that the latter two resemble each other more closely than they do Japan. The people of those two countries do not know how to go about reforming and making progress, whether individually or as a country. It is not that they have not seen or heard of civilized things in the present world of facile communication; yet what their eyes and ears perceive have failed to stimulate their minds, and their emotional attachment to ancient manners and customs has changed little for the past hundreds and thousands of years. In this lively theater of civilization, where things change daily, they still speak of education in terms of Confucianism, cite humanity, justice, civility, and wisdom as their principles of school education, are completely obsessed only with outward appearance, are in reality not only ignorant of truths and principles but so extreme in their cruelty and shamelessness that for them morality is completely non-existent, and yet are as arrogant as if they never gave a thought to self-examination.

In our view, these countries have no likelihood of maintaining their independence in

---

The Ryukyus and Hokkaido became internal colonies. In 1871 the Ryukyus were incorporated into Kagoshima prefecture. In 1879 the king was invited to reside in Tokyo and become a member of the new Japanese nobility while a Japanese governor took his place. Japanese fishermen and settlers had already spread as far north as Sakhalin and the Kuril Islands, territory that Russia claimed. In 1874 Japan evacuated Sakhalin and negotiated a treaty ceding it to Russia in exchange for Japanese control of the Kurils. It turned Hokkaido into a Japanese prefecture and established a modern definition of property ownership under which it sold off land Ainu had customarily used for hunting and fishing to Japanese developers. Without material support, Ainu culture lost its meaning.

Japan's relations with Korea also illustrate the relationship between modernity and imperialism. Oligarchs sent a diplomatic mission to "open" Korea in 1875–1876 that mimicked Perry's tactics in 1853–1854. The treaty forced on Korea replicated the unequal treaties Japan had signed in the 1850s. The following years saw successive incidents as factions at the Korean court abetted by Japan and China collided over the country's future course. In Japanese eyes, Korea was a weak, backward nation, easy prey for aggressive Western powers. A German military adviser warned that were Korea to be controlled by any other power, it would become a dagger pointing at the heart of Japan. In 1890 Yamagata Aritomo linked parliamentary political participation with a the current tide of civilization's eastward advance. Let there not be the slightest doubt that, unless they are fortunate enough to have motivated men appear in their lands who, as a first step to improve the condition of their countries will plan such a great enterprise of overall reform of their governments as our Restoration was, and succeed in altering their people's minds through political reforms, those countries will meet their doom in but a few years, with their territories divided among the civilized countries of the world.

Civilized western man is not without a tendency to regard all three countries as identical because of their geographic proximity and to apply his evaluation of China and Korea to Japan also. For example, when he finds that the governments of China and Korea are old-fashioned autocracies without abiding laws, the western man will suppose Japan too to be a lawless country. When he finds that the gentlemen of China and Korea are too deeply infatuated to know what science is, the western scholar will think that Japan too is a land of Yin-Yang and the Five Elements. When the Chinese display their servility and shamelessness, they obscure the chivalrous spirit of the Japanese. When the Koreans employ cruel means of physical punishment, the Japanese too are surmised to be just as inhuman. Such examples are too numerous to count. This may be compared to the case in which most of those in a string of houses within a village or town are foolish, lawless, cruel, and inhuman; an occasional family that heeds what is just and right will be eclipsed by the other's evil and its virtue will never be noticed. It is indeed not infrequent that something similar happens in our foreign relations and indirectly interferes with them. This should be regarded a great misfortune for our country of Japan.

To plan our course now, therefore, our country cannot afford to wait for the enlightenment of our neighbors and to cooperate in building Asia up. Rather, we should leave their ranks to join the camp of the civilized countries of the West. Even when dealing with China and Korea, we need not have special scruples simply because they are our neighbors, but should behave toward them as the westerners do. One who befriends an evil person cannot avoid being involved in his notoriety. In spirit, then, we break with our evil friends of Eastern Asia.

Source: Centre for East Asian Cultural Studies, comp., *Meiji Japan Through Contemporary Sources, Vol. 3, 1869–1894* (Tokyo: Centre for East Asian Cultural Studies, 1972), pp. 129–133, modified.

militant international stance by telling the first Diet that for Japan to maintain its independence, it had to protect its territorial boundary, the line of sovereignty, and an outer perimeter of neighboring territory, a line of interest. Korea fell within Japan's line of interest.

Pressure brought by domestic public opinion to revise the unequal treaties affected Japan's diplomatic relations with its Asian neighbors. When negotiations for revision stalled in the face of Western intransigence, clamor intensified for an aggressive stance toward China and Korea on the part of patriotic Popular Rights advocates as much as conservatives. In 1886 Britain and Germany proposed the partial abolition of extraterritoriality in exchange for allowing unrestricted travel by foreigners. The strength of domestic opposition to this compromise was so strong that the foreign minister had to resign. Finally, in 1894 Western powers promised to abolish extraterritoriality and to give Japan tariff autonomy in 1899.

Treaty negotiations took place in the context of the first Sino-Japanese War of 1894–1895. (See Chapter 18.) Fought over Korea, it lasted nine months. Japanese troops expelled the Chinese army from Korea, defeated the north Chinese navy, captured Port Arthur and the Liaodong peninsula in south Manchuria, and seized a port on the Shandong peninsula. The Treaty of Shimonoseki in April 1895 gave Japan Taiwan and the Pescadores, Port Arthur and the Liaodong peninsula, an indemnity, and a promise by China to respect

Korea's autonomy. Japan's victory took Western powers by surprise. In their eyes, it threatened peace and stability in East Asia. A week after the treaty was signed, Russia (with its own designs on Manchuria), France (Russia's ally), and Germany (hoping to steer Russian expansion toward what was now referred to as the Far East) collectively advised Japan to surrender its claim to territories in China. Despite popular outcry at the "Triple Intervention," the government had no choice but to obey. Russia then grabbed control of Port Arthur and the Liaodong peninsula.

SUMMARY

How should we assess the changes that Japan experienced in the latter part of the nineteenth century? Historians who note that ordinary people's lives changed only gradually if at all prefer to speak of a Meiji "transition." Others who point to the official abolition of status distinctions and restrictions on mobility as well as new opportunities for political engagement talk about revolution. Comparing 1868 with the end of the nineteenth century makes it hard to deny that Japan had been transformed from a decentralized, largely agrarian regime into a centralized industrializing nation. Molded by schools and the military, informed by newspapers and journals, the peoples of Japan had become citizens. They had learned to ride on trains, wear Western-style clothes, work in factories, and be self-reliant in striving for success. In dealing with the outside world, they had discovered that economic development and national defense required expansion abroad. Adaptation of Western models to local circumstances meant that Japan did not simply undergo a process of westernization. After all, the constituents of modernity, especially its effects on community and family relations and definitions of individual identity, required wrenching changes in Western nations as well.

CHAPTER TWENTY-ONE

Korea in the Turbulent Nineteenth Century (1800–1895)

Korea's nineteenth-century vicissitudes were marked by three rebellions caused primarily by the failure of the state to solve long-standing institutional and economic problems, intermittent persecution of Catholics, domination of government by consort relatives of mostly minor kings, and the threat to national survival by foreign imperialism. The last half of the century saw the birth of Korea's first new religion, abortive attempts at reform followed by conservative Confucian anti-foreignism, and unprecedented Chinese interference in Korean affairs. Domestic rebellion and a strengthened Japan brought Chinese influence to an end in the Sino-Japanese War of 1894–1895 and seemingly opened a path for serious reform.

What were the reasons behind the rebellions and the state's inertia in response to rebellion and foreign aggression? What changed in the lives of people outside of government? What capacity existed for reform and independent action from 1876 to 1895? And finally, what were the causes of the Sino-Japanese War?

POLITICS AND SOCIETY UNDER CONSORT RULE (1800–1864)

The death of King Chŏngjo in 1800, leaving an heir of only eleven years old, marked the beginning of consort clan domination of the royal house, which lasted to the end of the century. One reason was that all four nineteenth-century kings came to the throne as minors under regencies established by the eldest living dowager queen or were selected by such dowager regents when there was no crown prince. The dowager regent retained power until she resigned voluntarily or the king decided that it was time for him to rule on his own. Male relatives of dowager regents and queens benefited from this situation because they received appointment to high office.

Conflict between clans for control of the king turned on which had ties to the eldest living dowager and which supplied the king's wife. When King Ch'ŏlchong died without an heir in 1863, Queen Sinjŏng of the P'ungyang Cho clan was now the eldest living queen. She selected the twelve-year-old second son of King Ch'ŏlchong's second cousin as the new king, King Kojong. His father received the title of Taewongun, or grand prince, a title reserved for the father of a king who had never been king himself. The dowager became regent and held the position for only two years, to 1866, but the young King Kojong was kept unaware of his right to rule. Instead, the Taewongun continued as de facto regent from 1863 to 1874 even though he had no formal title or position. He and his supporters clashed repeatedly with his son's wife, Queen Min, and her clan, causing his political fortunes to rise and fall with startling frequency until his death in 1898.

New Social Policies

The early nineteenth century found the government grappling with the consequences of social change. It took positive measures to improve the lot of slaves; it persecuted Christian converts. At the same time, it had to deal with a series of rebellions caused in part by maladministration. Social dislocations, new diseases such as cholera, flood exacerbated by deforestation, and drought brought an end to the eighteenth-century population increase. Instead the population dropped to 12.4 million by 1816 and then fluctuated between 12.2 and 12.7 million until 1876, in contrast to the population increases seen during the same period in China and Japan.

In 1801, the dowager regent manumitted most of the sixty-seven thousand official slaves, while retaining those slaves working in local offices. This measure recognized what had already happened; many government slaves had already gained their freedom either through military service or purchase, and the remainder no longer worked for the government. Some slaves owned slaves; some slaves owned land. The 1801 decree constituted an important liberalization of the slave system, but hereditary slavery of several million private slaves remained until 1886. Slavery itself was abolished in 1894, but the mostly *yangban* slave masters retained their power until the dynasty itself was near its end.

The same year, the dowager regent authorized renewed persecution of Catholics and other minority factions. Supported by the Patriarch faction and the

Party of Principle (*pyŏkp'a*), she ordered the institution of a five-family mutual surveillance system to ferret out Christians in the southerner faction. Sent into exile for his beliefs, Chŏng Tasan wrote several treatises proposing reforms in local administration and the penal system. Also banished were a Chinese missionary and the previous king's half-brother, wife, and daughter-in-law. The situation for Christians worsened when officials intercepted a letter from the Christian Hwang Sayŏng to the papal court in Rome requesting a military expedition from France to protect Korean Christians from persecution. Outraged by this act of treason, the dowager executed over three hundred Christians that year alone and persecuted members of the southerner faction and Party of Expediency (*sip'a*). These factions were kept out of office for another half-century.

The Christian issue emerged once again in 1839 when the government executed three French missionaries and scores of converts. Six years later it martyred Korea's first priest, Kim Taegŏn, trained in Macao, who had proselytized in secret. Between waves of persecution, the number of converts continued to grow. Their composition changed from primarily *yangban* to commoners, including a remarkable number of women.

Social Ferment and Popular Culture

The nineteenth century saw important developments in intellectual activity and popular culture. No longer dominated by men of *yangban* origin, new ideas that tried to make sense of society and promote reform were propagated by men of intermediate statuses. Many elements associated with Korea's traditional culture today either arose in this period or took on the form by which they are now known.

The practical learning tradition blossomed in the early nineteenth century. Based on empirical observation and the careful comparison of texts, it produced scholars who challenged the Confucian orthodoxy promoted at court. Sŏ Yu-gu's *Sixteen Treatises Written in Retirement* contained a distillation of his thoughts on agricultural practices, economic developments, and *yangban* leisure pursuits. *Observations on Examining Two Stone Inscriptions* by Kim Chŏng-Hŭi, also a famous poet and calligrapher, recorded his meticulous comparisons of sixth-century stele. Men whose social backgrounds prevented them from attaining bureaucratic office compiled biographies of superior men who had likewise suffered from discrimination.

"Wrestling" by Kim Hongdo. The first painter to depict daily life in Korea, Kim Hongdo here illustrates an informal match before an audience of men and women. Note the peddler waiting for a sale. *(National Museum of Korea, Seoul, Korea)*

Written by a man from a fallen *yangban* family, Ch'oe Han-gi's *Personnel Administration* (1860) proposed that the government select its officials from men of talent and ability regardless of their status background. He also urged openness to foreigners. The *chung'in* Ch'oe Sŏng-hwan took a similar stance in urging reform of the tax and forced labor systems, arguing that taxes should be collected in cash and that the government should pay workers rather than commandeer them.

Commoners composed in a range of genres. They wrote poetry, compiled in 1857 into *Third Selection of Poems of the People*; they wrote historical novels that celebrated the glories of Korea's martial past and, like Sin Chae-hyo, they composed lyrics for *p'ansori*. Music, painting, and dance crossed the social divide, with anonymous artists imitating subjects admired by *yangban* and producing genre paintings to brighten the walls of temples. Comprised of dance, song, and narrative, masked drama flourished. One famous passage from *Festival at Naval Headquarters* mocked the *yangban* by using a food image that must have been highly satisfying for a commoner audience:

> I'll eat them raw at low tide, cram my maw at high tide,
> Devour my *yangban* masters nine and ninety.
> Then I'll eat one more and lo!
> A dragon now become, mount the throne of Heaven.[1]

---

1. Ki-baik Lee, *A New History of Korea*, translated by Edward W. Wagner with Edward J. Shultz (Cambridge Mass.: Harvard University Press, 1984), p. 260.

Men practiced a range of martial arts, some derived from Chinese traditions. Kim Hongdo (pen name, Tanwôn) sketched wrestlers performing as they had since the Koguryŏ era in a style akin to Japanese sumo.

Economic Developments and Rebellion

Historians disagree over the extent of economic development in the decades before foreigners made their presence felt. Many of the positive indications seen in the eighteenth century—the spread of markets and signs of commercialization—did not lead to greater output. Peasants adopted a number of strategies for survival; when these failed or when officials proved rapacious, they rebelled.

One of the most enduring survival strategies was the *kye*, a voluntary organization that promoted mutual assistance. Like similar credit associations that arose in Japan, the *kye* provided a mechanism for people to pool funds and then take turns using the capital. Early *kye* had specific functions: to give members access to support groups and the large sums needed to pay for funerals and weddings. Even *yangban* and wealthy households joined them. Later *kye* emphasized the pooling of resources to overcome hardship. Some had specific community-wide goals, such as repairing an irrigation system, whereas others allowed individual members to use the money for diverse purposes. The *kye* still function in modern Korea, where they provide a means for women to gain access to credit, and in overseas communities where immigrants lack access to banks.

Other survival strategies included planting New World crops and opening marginal fields. The sweet potato arrived via Japan in 1763; the white potato arrived via China around 1840. Both were cultivated as insurance against famine. Another nineteenth-century addition to the diet was cabbage (see **Material Culture: Kimchi**). Despite these dietary supplements, tenant farmers and farmers of small plots led a precarious existence. After a year or two of poor harvests, they abandoned their fields, wandered the country, and died of starvation by the thousands. In desperation they practiced slash-and-burn agriculture on hillsides that denuded the uplands and increased the frequency of floods. Some peasants joined bands of brigands that coalesced into small armies and ravaged the countryside. When all else failed, they migrated into Manchuria and the Russian Maritime Province.

Rebellions constitute the chief indicators of social unrest in the nineteenth century. A major rebellion led by fallen *yangban* and professional geomancer Hong Kyŏngnae broke out in the northwest P'yŏng'an province in 1811. One cause was perceived injustice in the taxation and service systems. General discontent with the prejudicial policies of the central administration and resentment against blocking promotion to high office among its examination passers led men of intermediate statuses to organize a army of rebels. Although it was quickly suppressed, small-scale outbreaks continued.

In 1862 the government's failure to solve the problems of maladministration in the land tax, military cloth tax, and grain relief and loan systems provided the main cause for a series of rebellions throughout the country, primarily in the three southern provinces. Although taxes had earlier been combined into a single land tax, corruption by clerks and magistrates more than offset the reductions gained from distributing taxes equally among all residents. More massive and widespread than earlier outbreaks of social unrest, the rebellion of 1862 lacked central organization. Despite a few attacks against *yangban* landlords, it was aimed mainly at government officials. The largest uprising occurred in Chinju on the southern coast and spread from there. Although *yangban* participated in the planning of some protests, they usually withdrew when the protests became violent. Armed with bamboo spears, commoners provided the leadership in dozens of spontaneous uprisings that killed government functionaries and burned official buildings. Once the rebels' thirst for vengeance had been slaked, the uprisings died down.

Ch'oe Cheu and the Tonghak Religion

A more lasting response to social dislocation came in the form of a new religion. Discontented with his life as a déclassé *yangban* (his mother had remarried, thus barring him from the civil service examination) and the sorry situation of his country, Ch'oe Cheu experienced a vision in which he believed Hanŭnim (the Lord of Heaven) entrusted him with the task of spreading a new faith to the Korean people and saving mankind on earth. Ch'oe also created a potion for curing illness. He called the faith Tonghak (Eastern Learning, or "Korean National Teaching"). It combined Confucian ethics with Buddhist faith, Taoist naturalism and longevity, geomancy, and the use of talismans, imprecations, and shamanistic appeals to spirits in an amalgam that was supposed to represent Korean thought as a counterpoise to Western learning or Christianity (see **Documents: Tonghak Beliefs**).

MATERIAL CULTURE

Kimchi

The food most associated with Korean cuisine is kimchi, but it developed into its current form only in the nineteenth century.

Koreans began pickling vegetables, especially long radishes, in salt to preserve them through long winter months around the seventh century. In the twelfth century, spices and seasonings such as soy sauce came to be added, and people started eating kimchi year-round. Although hot red peppers originating in the Americas arrived in Korea from Japan following Hideyoshi's invasion of 1592, it took two hundred years for them to be used to flavor kimchi. The peppers give kimchi its distinctive red color. The final, essential ingredient is Chinese cabbage (*baechu*), introduced in the nineteenth century. Although other vegetables continue to be pickled, cabbage became the favorite. A Chosŏn cookbook explains how to make kimchi for the royal court:

> First, cut well-washed cabbages and radishes into small chunks and salt them. Second, mix them with chopped hot red pepper, garlic, dropwort (minari), leaf mustards (gat), and seaweed. Third, boil fermented fish in water and cool it. Fourth, add the fish sauce to the blended vegetables. Fifth, store the mixture in a pot and wait till it is fermented.[1]

Today pickled cabbage is eaten across northern Eurasia, but the spiciest is kimchi, prepared not only in Korea but also in eastern Siberia.

----

1. http://www.koreanrestaurantguide.com/kimch/kimch_o.htm

Kimchi. Making kimchi requires cabbage, spices, salt, and other seasonings that can stain and damage the skin—hence the gloves. *(Chung Sung-Jun/AsiaPac/Getty Images)*

DOCUMENTS
Tonghak Beliefs

What are the circumstances under which men achieve revelation? Here Ch'oe Cheu describes how external pressure and domestic turmoil so afflicted his spirit that he became ill. In that state, he had conversations with the Supreme Being, who offered him solutions to his problems and those of Korea as a whole. This conversion narrative, a testimony to faith, illustrates the path to belief.

CH'OE CHEU ON PROPAGATING VIRTUE

From the distant past up to the present day, every year without fail spring has eventually turned into autumn, and all four seasons have come and gone in the proper sequence. This is a display for the entire world to see of how the Lord of Heaven regulates the changes and transformations in the universe. Yet ignorant folk know only that rain and dew are natural phenomena and do not know how it is that they are able to benefit from them.

Recently people have tended to do whatever they feel like doing instead of acting in accordance with heavenly principles. They no longer pay any attention to the decrees of heaven. I have worried about this night and day, but did not know what to do about it.

It got worse in 1860. That is when I learned that Westerners, claiming that they were only doing what the Lord of Heaven wanted them to do and were not trying to be rich or to lord it over others, began using military force to seize territory all over the world. Everywhere they went they set up churches and promoted their way of doing things. I asked myself if this really could be happening, and if so, how could such things happen?

Then a totally unexpected event occurred one day in the fourth month of that year. All of a sudden a chill came over my heart and my whole body shivered. It was as if I had abruptly fallen ill, but I couldn't tell what sort of illness had attacked me. Then my ears seemed to pick up a strange voice. It is difficult to describe. The closest I can come to describing it is to say that it sounded like the voice of one of those immortals who lives deep in the mountains. I was frightened and asked, "Who are you?" An answer came back, "You don't have to be afraid. I am the one whom human beings call the Lord Above. Don't you know who the Lord Above is?" Startled, I asked why he was talking to me. He replied, "So far I haven't been able to accomplish all that I have wanted to accomplish. Therefore I have sent you into this world so that you can teach human beings the right way to do things. So cast all fear and doubt aside and listen to me."

I then asked, "Do you want me to teach people the Western way of doing things?" He replied, "No, not at all. I have a talisman that is called the 'medicine of the mountain immortals.' It resembles the Great Ultimate [the name neo-Confucians give to the wellspring of all existence]. Take this talisman and use it to heal people of the various diseases that afflict them. Also, I am giving you an incantation that I want you to use to teach human beings on my behalf. If you do this, you will live a long life and will propagate virtue all over the world."

This all happened at a time when terrible diseases were sweeping across our country. Everyone was worried day and night that they or someone dear to them might be the next victim. It was our bad luck that this was happening at the same time that Westerners were on a rampage. I wondered if there wasn't some way to help our country and put the minds of the people at ease.

Unfortunately people these days don't understand what a precarious situation we are in. If they happen to hear what I have to say, it goes in one ear and out the other. Even worse, some of them criticize me publicly. They are ignorant of the way and don't follow it. This is really a pitiful situation.

Source: Don Baker, "The Great Transformation: Religious Practice in Ch'ŏndogyo" in Robert E. Buswell, Jr., ed., *Religions of Korea in Practice* (Princeton: Princeton University Press, 2007), pp. 455–457, modified.

Cheu's followers were mostly commoners and slaves because the *yangban* regarded his departure from Confucian orthodoxy as unacceptable. They also rejected his teaching that all men were equal in their duty to serve the Lord of Heaven with whom they were intrinsically united. His ideas thus constituted a threat to both the stability of the dynasty and the purity of Confucian belief. Although he was not involved in the many local rebellions that began in the south in 1862, he was arrested by the authorities the next year for fomenting dissent by his heterodox teaching. In 1864 they decapitated him. The movement went underground and did not reemerge (except for one minor rising in 1879) until 1893. Even in 1864 it signaled that popular discontent was calling into question the power of Confucian orthodoxy to solve the problems Korea faced.

ATTEMPTS AT REFORM AND EXTERNAL PRESSURE (1864–1894)

The year 1864 marks a divide in Korea's nineteenth century. Although Korean diplomats at the Qing court had received news of China's defeat in the Opium War, its magnitude had remained concealed from them. (See **Connections: Western Imperialism.**) Wei Yuan's *An Illustrated Essay of the Maritime Nations* had reached Korea in 1845, but its recommendations for improving defenses against Westerners had been ignored. Succeeding encroachments on China and Japan also had little effect on policy until China gave Russia a lease on the Liaodong peninsula contiguous to Korea in 1860. Official responses to the foreign threat had to wait until King Kojong took the throne at the age of twelve with his father, the Taewongun, behind him.

The Taewongun tried to revive dynastic power and the Korean state by pursuing a course of domestic reform and foreign isolationism. He addressed the causes of the 1862 rebellions; he rebuilt the Kyŏngbok Palace left in ruins after Hideyoshi's invasion of 1592 to elevate the prestige and power of the king; he abolished the majority of private academies in the provinces (they had become centers of *yangban* factional interest); he persecuted Korean Catholics for suspected treasonous collaboration with foreigners; he minted the first multiple-denomination coin in Korean history, the 100-cash, to pay for expenses; and he resisted Western and foreign demands for treaties and trade. The reform program resulted in a partial land survey to register land hidden from tax collectors, the imposi-

tion of the military cloth tax on *yangban* households for the first time (but in the names of their slaves to save them embarrassment), and the cancellation of past unrecoverable loans in the official grain loan program administered by district magistrates. Peasants escaped from permanent indebtedness, and the Taewongun shifted the administration of grain loans from corrupt district magistrates and their clerks to local elders.

These reforms were less radical than they seemed because the land survey did not cover the whole country, and village *yangban* had already been included among villagers to pay the combined tax. Nonetheless, *yangban* found imposition of the military cloth tax particularly galling because it was a direct affront to their status. The abolition of all but forty-seven private academies dedicated to Confucian worthies of the dominant factions was an insult to both hereditary factions and past titans of Confucian scholarship. Government spending and the inflation that resulted from the 100-cash were a violation of conservative Confucian attitudes toward profligacy.

Reaction to Reforms

The Taewongun received more criticism for his domestic reforms than for his xenophobia. Conservative Confucians opposed institutional tinkering and believed that good government required only frugality, the reduction of taxes, and the cultivation of Confucian virtue. Almost all Confucian scholars supported his foreign policy. Their favorite slogan was "Defend Confucian correctness against foreign perversity." The Taewongun rejected all requests from foreigners for treaties because he was determined to avoid the unequal treaty system imposed on China and Japan.

In 1866, when Korean Catholics offered to mediate with the Russians in their demands for trade, the Taewongun suspected a plot to undermine Korean security. He ordered a nationwide persecution of Korean Catholics that lasted to 1871 and reduced their ranks from twenty thousand to eight thousand. The French landed troops on Kanghwa Island to chastise the Koreans for their refusal to tolerate Christianity, but Korean troops were able to force the small French force to withdraw.

Military Pressure from the West

Western powers tried to change the Taewongun's isolationist stance. In 1866, a ship of U.S. registration, the *General Sherman*, with an English captain and a

Map **21.1**   Military Pressure from the West, 1866 and 1871

crew of Malays and Chinese, ran aground in the Taedong River near Pyongyang and demanded trade. Irate local residents attacked the ship, burned it to ashes, and killed its crew. The governor of P'yŏng'an Province submitted a plan for strengthening coastal defenses by building new forts along the coast, particularly one at the mouth of the Taedong River, recruiting more soldiers skilled in the use of firearms,

and instituting a special examination for them. The Taewongun approved this.

Another memorial aimed at self-strengthening was based on Wei Yuan's *Illustrated Essay of the Maritime Nations*. Since Wei had written that the secret of Western strength was the domination of the seas by a small number of skilled troops with superior cannon, not superior numbers, the memorial recommended that Korea concentrate on building advanced cannon and sea mines and distribute them to coastal garrisons. The Taewongun ordered the construction of three new warships and a cannon for laying mines. He even ordered construction of Korea's first steamboat in 1867, although it failed its trial on water and had to be broken up for scrap metal.

In the bizarre foreign incident of 1868, the German adventurer Ernst Oppert tried to disinter the bones of the Taewongun's father to hold them as ransom before Korean troops forced his withdrawal. In 1871, the United States landed marines on Kanghwa Island to teach the Koreans a lesson for the *General Sherman* incident and to force a treaty of trade and amity. The marines did this by killing dozens of Korean defenders. There is no evidence that new warships, cannon, and mine-laying cannon played any role in either of these two incidents. The Taewongun declared victories for Korean arms when the foreigners withdrew. He issued a manifesto that anyone who advocated peace with the foreigner was a traitor to the state.

Frustration caused by ambiguity over who was responsible for the conduct of Korean foreign relations under the tributary system constituted one reason for the foreigners' use of violence. They wanted to know whether Korea was a sovereign nation with a king who had the authority to sign treaties. If not, they would negotiate with China as the suzerain power. Not only did the Taewongun refuse to negotiate with them, but the Qing government also evaded responsibility because it knew that if Koreans violated any codicil in a treaty with a foreign power, that power would demand reparations from China.

In 1868, Japan added to the pressure on Korea from abroad. When the new government sent a note in the Meiji emperor's name to the king of Korea asking for a treaty of trade and amity, the Taewongun refused even to accept the note on the grounds that there was only one legitimate emperor, the emperor of the Qing Dynasty in China. Japanese resentment over what radical samurai perceived as an insult to the Meiji emperor almost resulted in Japan's invasion of Korea in 1873 before cooler heads prevailed. (See Chapter 20.)

The Kanghwa Treaty of 1876

Korea's isolationist stance began to change once Queen Min and her faction convinced King Kojong that he, not his father, should rule (see **Biography: Queen Min**).

Queen Min. Queen Min of the Yŏhung Min family, 1851–1895, was assassinated by Japanese thugs and soldiers in the palace in 1895. This picture commemorates her posthumous title of Empress Myŏngsŏng. *(5,000 Years of Korean Art, p. 183)*

She had considerable influence over her husband, and her male relatives remained in power to 1894. King Kojong adopted the advice of officials who advocated accepting communications from the Meiji emperor on the grounds that his title was a domestic issue irrelevant to Korea and that eliminating animosity and restoring friendship with Japan would result in a continuation of trade relations and friendship that had prevailed from 1609 to 1868. Learning of this new attitude, Japan created an excuse for hostile action by sending a survey ship up the Korean coast in 1875 in the expectation that Korean shore batteries would fire on it. When the Koreans obliged by doing so, Japan landed a battalion of troops on Kanghwa Island and threatened military action unless King Kojong signed the Kanghwa Treaty with Japan in 1876.

BIOGRAPHY   Queen Min

Born in 1851, Queen Min maneuvered to preserve Korea's independence at a desperate time in its history. Selected for King Kojong by his father, the Taewongun, because her branch of the Yŏhŭng Min had little power, Min entered the palace when Kojong was thirteen and she was fourteen. The marriage took place a year later. On seeing this teenage bride, the Taewongun is said to have commented that "she was a woman of great determination and much poise of manner." After their differences became apparent, he remarked sarcastically, "She evidently aspires to be a doctor of letters; look out for her."

Animosity between the wife and the father of King Kojong had political consequences. Queen Min had only one son, born five years after her marriage, who died within three days. She found it all too easy to believe rumors that the Taewongun had poisoned the boy. After he was forced into retirement in 1874, she moved her relatives into positions of power. Her first brush with death came in 1882 when members of the old capital guard units, angry about arrears in salary, invaded the palace to murder her and her relatives. For the next thirteen years, her faction maneuvered between China and Japan, favoring whichever side promised the least interference in Korea's affairs but always opposed to the Taewongun. In 1895, she chose Russia. The Japanese minister to Seoul decided that to eliminate the Min family from politics, it was essential to assassinate her. In October he sent Japanese police disguised as Korean guards into the palace, where they killed her and burned her body on the spot. Once again the Taewongun took charge of government.

When King Kojong was declared emperor of the great Han dynasty in 1897, Queen Min received the posthumous title of Empress Myŏngsŏng.

As Korea's first modern treaty, the Kanghwa Treaty had most of the provisions of the unequal treaty system. King Kojong agreed to open three ports to trade with Japan—Tongnae near Pusan and two more to be selected in the future—and limited Japanese traders under the treaty to a small radius around them. Imposing extraterritoriality on Korea gave Japanese in the treaty ports the right to run their own affairs. King Kojong assumed that Japan would be content to trade without invading Korean space elsewhere or making further demands. In fact, he had opened the door not only to trade but also to foreign interference.

First Attempts at Modern Diplomacy

King Kojong accepted the Kanghwa Treaty's provisions on China's recommendation. At first he had opposed the opening of two new ports and the demands for a Japanese legation in Seoul until a recommendation entitled "Strategy for Korea" sent to him in 1880 by Huang Zunxian, a Chinese legation official in Tokyo, persuaded him to reconsider his position. Huang argued that Korea should negotiate treaties with all the Western powers as a means of self-protection.

Huang Zunxian's recommendation was in line with Li Hongzhang's policy for Korea. Advocate of self-strengthening and chief of Qing Dynasty relations with Chosŏn, Li sought to capitalize on the rivalries among the imperialist powers to check any attempt by Russia and Japan to strip China of its suzerainty over Korea. He realized that China was militarily too weak to maintain its tributary control over Korea by force, and his policy depended on the willingness of foreign powers with little interest in trade with Korea to check their imperialist rivals. It allowed China to maintain control until the Sino-Japanese War of 1894, but only by changing the nature of the tributary system itself.

During the next five years, King Kojong took a number of steps to promote reform and self-strengthening, always shadowed by conservative opposition. He dispatched a secret investigative mission to Japan to report on developments there, followed by a second study mission in 1881. Another training mission went to China to study military science. King Kojong agreed to open two additional ports to Japan at Inch'ŏn and Wŏnsan and to allow the first Japanese minister to Korea to establish a legation in Seoul. In 1881, he set up the Office for Management of State Affairs (*T'ong-nigimu amun*) to handle diplomacy, trade with foreign states, and reform, and he welcomed the first Japanese ambassador. He also hired a Japanese officer to train a small unit of troops in the capital in Western military tactics and weapons. These initiatives aroused a conservative protest movement. In the fall of 1881, a plot by the Taewongun to overthrow the king and abolish the *T'ongnigimu amun* was uncovered. His subordinates were arrested and executed.

In charting the treacherous territory of modern diplomacy, Korea relied heavily on China. King Kojong consulted with China on how to make modern weapons and conduct negotiations with the United States and other Western powers. In 1881, Li Hongzhang negotiated with Commodore Robert W. Shufeldt of the U.S. Navy to conclude a treaty of amity and trade between the United States and Korea. It contained several elements of the unequal treaty system such as extraterritoriality and the most favored nation clause, which guaranteed the United States any advantages obtained by other foreign powers in future treaties with Korea. During negotiations, Li Hongzhang tried to insert a clause indicating that Korea was a tributary of China. Shufeldt refused to accept it because the United States would never agree to sign a treaty with a dependency. He compromised by allowing King Kojong to send a letter to President Chester A. Arthur declaring that Korea was both "self-governing" and a Chinese tributary, a description that fit the reality, since the Qing regime had never interfered with either Korea's domestic problems or its relations with Japan. The United States ignored the contradiction and acted as if Korea was a sovereign state. Signed by King Kojong and Shufeldt in May 1882 and soon followed by similar arrangements with other nations, the treaty did not change the fact that both Korea and China regarded the tributary relationship as undamaged.

China's policy of noninterference in Korea's domestic affairs soon changed. Incensed at favorable treatment afforded the new Japanese-trained unit in the capital and delay in the payment of their salaries, members of the old capital guard units killed a Japanese training officer, burned the Japanese legation, and drove the ambassador and his party from Korea. They even invaded the palace to murder the queen and her relatives, but she was able to escape. The rebels forced King Kojong to recall his father, the Taewongun, to the capital and appoint him chief of administration. Fearing that the Taewongun's hostility to Japan might provoke a Japanese invasion of Korea, China dispatched forty-five hundred troops to Seoul. Invited to what was supposed to be an amicable meeting, the Taewongun found himself hustled onto a Chinese ship, transported to China, and kept under close surveillance for three years. After his departure, Chinese troops wiped out the rebels.

Kidnapping the de facto head of state and the king's father was unprecedented. It marked a departure from the tradition of noninterference in Korean affairs and transformed China's relations with Korea to that enjoyed by Western imperialists. For the first time, China negotiated a commercial treaty with Korea that provided privileges to Chinese merchants trading in Korea that were denied other states. China also instructed King Kojong to pay reparations to Japan to prevent any hostilities. The Chinese restored the king, queen, and her relatives to power and allowed them to repress the Taewongun's supporters.

Late in 1882, King Kojong called on Koreans to submit memorials recommending policy to fit the times. He received one hundred private memorials, of which one-fifth advocated reform. Many cited *Iyan* (*Simple Talk*) by Zheng Guanying, a Chinese comprador merchant for a Western company. Zheng had written the book in 1862 to alert China to the need to manufacture Western-style weapons by hiring Western experts. Many Korean reformers traveled to China to meet Zheng, and his book exerted greater influence in Korea than in China. His main theme was the need to adopt Western technology while still maintaining fundamental Confucian values. Kojong republished the book in *han'gŭl* in 1883 and urged everyone to read it. This formula was to prove as inadequate for meaningful reform in Korea as it had in China because Western culture included more than machines and tools.

Abortive Reform and the 1884 *Kapsin* Coup

In contrast to xenophobic conservatives associated with the Taewongun and gradualists around Queen Min who took a pro-China stance, a more radical faction believed that Korea had to follow Japan's lead. Calling for social equality, the appointment of men with talent and ability, centralized administration, and enlightenment, it convinced King Kojong to institute a number of reforms in 1883: a modern post office, the Ministry of Culture and Information, and publication of the first newspaper, the *Hansŏng sunbo* (*Seoul Weekly*). The government also sponsored some forty students to study military and technical subjects in Japan. Fearing that if they did not act first they would be killed and hoping that conflict with France over Vietnam would keep China too busy to interfere, the radical faction under the leadership of Kim Okkyun organized a coup to seize power. Because the conspirators had no support inside Korea, Kim Okkyun convinced the head of the Japanese legation to let him use legation guards. The coup leaders seized the palace, held King Kojong captive as their symbol of legitimacy, summoned high officials to court, and decapitated them on the spot.

Before the coup leaders had time to issue any orders, China acted. Led by Yuan Shikai, Chinese legation guards and regular Korean troops attacked the palace, killed half-dozen leaders, and drove the rest of the plotters, along with the Japanese ambassador and his entourage, out of the country. Once again, China's intervention restored the political situation to the status quo ante and scotched the chance for significant reform. Following negotiations with Japan, China forced Korea to pay Japan reparations for the murder of Japanese victims and property damage. Because the Japanese ambassador had authorized the use of Japanese troops to aid the plotters without prior authorization from Tokyo, he was tried in Japanese courts but let off for lack of evidence.

Qing Control

For the years between 1884 and 1894, Japan acquiesced in China's domination of Korea's affairs. To avert conflict between the two nations, it negotiated the Convention of Tianjin with Li Hongzhang in 1885 by which both sides withdrew their troops and agreed that neither would supply officers to train Korean soldiers. If either Japan or China should feel it necessary to send an army, it would inform the other in advance. Later that year, Li Hongzhang appointed Yuan Shikai resident commissioner for Korea, the first instance of a Chinese overseer on Korean territory since the departure of the Mongols in the mid-fourteenth century. For the next decade, Yuan sat at King Kojong's side, preventing him from doing anything that might interfere with China's control over Korea and lead to national independence. King Kojong was not allowed to conduct diplomacy by dispatching ambassadors to foreign countries. When the British navy temporarily seized Komun Island (Port Hamilton) off the southern coast of Korea in 1885 as a feint to block the Russians from obtaining a leasehold at Wŏnsan and expanding their influence into Korea, China took no action to force the British to retreat. Russia, which both China and Japan

perceived as a threat to their interests, also accepted the continuation of China's traditional relationship with Korea.

Yuan Shikai also interfered in Korea's domestic affairs. When a provincial Korean official blocked the export of rice and beans to Japan in 1888 to preserve food stocks during a famine after Japanese merchants had purchased them, Yuan insisted that Korea pay the penalty demanded by Japan. He obstructed Japanese efforts to build a telegraph line from Pusan to Seoul and to reform Korean coinage at the Korean court's request. He also blocked Korean attempts to obtain foreign loans and foreign military advisers. Yuan's actions demonstrated that China's direct intervention in Korea's foreign and domestic affairs had become part of the new relationship.

Western Influences

During the 1880s, Protestant missionaries from the United States brought education and medicine to China, Japan, and Korea. In the 1890s, Japanese and other businessmen fostered interest in trade, modern transportation projects, and the exploitation of natural resources. Trains started running between Inch'ŏn and Seoul, and a railroad bridge connected Seoul and Noryangjin over the Han river in 1900. The first streetcar arrived in 1898, demonstrating to the populace its advantage over palanquins for female *yangban*, donkeys and horses for male *yangban*, and ox-drawn carts for commoners. The laying of tracks for streetcars and trains preceded cobblestones or macadamized streets, overcoming one of the most important obstacles to rapid transportation of goods and people: unpaved roads that turned to impassable mud in the rainy season.

Protestant Christianity and Efforts to Modernize

Just as Korean Catholics had found their faith in the late eighteenth century before the arrival of missionaries, so too did Koreans start practicing Protestant Christianity before guidance came from the West. Arriving from the United States in 1884, the first Protestant missionaries sweetened their message with the demonstration of good works, such as the construction of hospitals and schools. The Presbyterian Horace Allen, a twenty-six-year-old doctor, gained acceptance by King Kojong and Queen Min for saving the life of her relative during the *kapsin* coup of December 4, 1884. Kojong made him physician to the royal court and allowed him to establish the first Western hospital the next year. Allen later gave up his status as missionary, became a secretary to the Korean legation in Washington, D.C., U.S. minister to Korea and consul-general in 1890, and ambassador plenipotentiary from 1901 to 1905. As a businessman, he arranged opportunities for Americans to exploit Korea's best gold mine and to build rail and trolley lines, Seoul's waterworks, and telephone service.

In 1885 the Methodists Henry G. Appenzeller, Dr. William B. Scranton, and Scranton's wife, Mary Fitch Scranton, journeyed to Korea. William Scranton founded the first Methodist Hospital and taught Western medical techniques. Appenzeller started the *Paejae haktang* (School for Training Men of Talent), and Mary Scranton opened the first school for women, which Queen Min dubbed *Ehwa haktang* (Pear Blossom School). Ehwa University is still Korea's premier institution of higher learning for women. Little attached to Confucian norms that discriminated against them, non-*yangban* intellectuals and businessmen supported the missionaries even though propagating heterodox beliefs was still punishable by death.

The first efforts to modernize included reorganization of the bureaucracy and the establishment of a Western-style post office in 1884, followed by a customs agency overseen by the German P.G. von Moellendorff. While under house arrest in 1887, Yu Kilchun, who had studied in Japan while living with Fukuzawa Yukichi and then in the United States, wrote his famous account of conditions in Western nations, *Sŏyu kyŏnmun* (*What I Saw and Heard in the West*) that advocated adopting Western institutions. Over the next fifteen years, Protestant missionaries and Japanese businessmen introduced hospitals, schools, banks, currency, telegraph lines, electric power lines, and brick buildings for public offices. Most of these developments occurred in Seoul, Pyongyang, and a few border towns. Only a small segment of the urban population had the opportunity to gain a modern education or to read newspapers published by men trying to promote new ideas.

THE TONGHAK REBELLION AND THE SINO-JAPANESE WAR (1894–1895)

Both economic hardship and religious persecution played roles in the Tonghak Rebellion, the largest rebellion in Korean history. The treaties signed with foreign powers worsened conditions for ordinary people. Japan bought Korean rice, but the profits from the increase in prices went to middlemen, not producers. Japanese fishery companies invaded Korean coastal waters, and Japanese ships took over Korea's carrying trade. Droughts in 1876–1877 and 1880–1889 reduced tax revenues, but state expenditures had risen with the payment of indemnities to foreigners and the need to finance modern institutions such as the army. Desperate for income, the government allowed tax collectors ever greater leeway in oppressing the peasants. Under its second patriarch, Ch'oe Sihyŏng, the Tonghak had petitioned the government repeatedly for an end to persecution and for religious toleration. Furious at venal officials and determined to drive the Min faction from court, the Tonghak launched an insurrection in 1894. The rebellion was also fueled by xenophobic reaction to the presence of Japanese and other foreigners on Korean soil and a rejection of Christianity.

Having lost confidence in his army's ability to repress the Tonghak rebels, King Kojong asked China for help. Before it arrived, he reached an agreement with the Tonghak military leader, Chŏn Pongjun, to call off the rebellion in return for religious toleration and a promise to allow the Tonghak to administer their captured territory. Japan took this opportunity to force a war on China by sending more troops than had China and by making unacceptable demands. Japan attacked China without bothering to declare war, surrounded the Korean palace, and kept the king and queen under detention while the war continued. (For information on the prosecution of this war, see Chapter 18.)

Kabo Cabinet Reforms

Japan's efforts to foster reform in Korea aroused opposition. Japan sponsored Pak Yŏnghyo and Sŏ Kwangbŏm, former leaders of the 1884 coup exiled to Japan, and placed them in the Kabo cabinet. Alarmed by Japan's takeover of the Korean government and the return of men they regarded as the traitors of 1884, the Tonghak under Chŏn Pongjun rose again to drive Japan out of the country. This time, they had to fight against superior Japanese forces with advanced weapons and units of the Korean army. While this struggle was underway, King Kojong also proved obstructive. He finally agreed to exclude the queen and her relatives from decisions and to consult with ministers before making them. He then declared the end of Korea's tributary relationship with the Qing Dynasty.

Chŏn Pongjun (1854–1895). The leader of the Tonghak rebel army after his capture in 1895. *(Sajinuro ponun tongni undong: Oech ŏim kwa tŏujaeng, sang, p. 30)*

Launched by men who had studied abroad and hoped to emulate Meiji Japan, the reform program aimed at remaking government and society. It called for rationalizing the bureaucracy, abolishing sinecures, establishing a regular budget and a uniform currency, ending the king's control over the exchequer, creating a new judicial structure with professional judges and a modern police and military, initiating a modern educational system through high school for both sexes (compulsory through primary school), and expanding railroads and telegraph lines. It abolished slavery. It promised universal health care. It put an end to civil service examinations based on Confucian classics, status distinctions between *yangban* and commoners, economic controls, and the mistreatment of wives. It promoted national identity through the use of *han'gŭl* on government documents and teaching Korean, not Chinese, history in the new schools.

The reform measures had mixed results. Not all slaves were manumitted immediately, and members of the educated *yangban* elite continued to monopo-lize admission to government office under the new system of examinations run by individual ministries. Opening the door to upward mobility to members of lower-status groups allowed the educated *chung'in* clerks and specialists, northerners, military officials, secondary sons, and local functionaries (*hyangni*) to begin a trek up the bureaucratic ladder. This trend continued into the colonial period.

The reform cabinet lasted sixteen months. The Triple Intervention in April 1895 by Russia, France, and Germany to force Japan to give up its territorial gains following the Sino-Japanese War meant that Japan had to retreat from Korea as well. Pak Yŏnghyo's ambition to become prime minister was foiled when a Japanese legation official leaked his proposal to assassinate the queen. He barely escaped to Japan. One faction at court centered on Queen Min favored turning to Russia as a counterbalance to Japan. When the Japanese minister to Seoul orchestrated her assassination, it roused the ire of the Korean people and caused deep embarrassment to the Japanese govern-

MAKING COMPARISONS   Slavery

The tale of *Sanshō the Bailiff*, set in Japan's Heian period, tells of a mother and two children kidnapped and sold into slavery. The mother was forced to become a prostitute, and the children found work as field hands. In an era of labor shortages, their fate was not uncommon. People also became slaves in China and Korea, though not necessarily in the same way. Human capital now determines a nation's ability to compete in the modern world; in the days when land meant nothing without the labor to work it, slaves were human capital.

In Japan, both early and late documents regarding slavery point to its connection with war. Third-century Chinese sources mention that warriors enslaved the vanquished; sixteenth-century European accounts tell how warriors kidnapped commoners and sold them, sometimes overseas to Southeast Asia. During the late twelfth and early thirteenth centuries, famine forced the starving to sell themselves or family members for food. Debt was the third reason people became slaves. Some became personal slaves; others became field hands. A person might become a slave for a specified time period or a lifetime. The thirteenth-century law code tried to specify whether a slave's children were also slaves, suggesting that slavery could become hereditary. In transfer documents, slaves were listed alongside livestock as possessions. As the population and hence the labor supply rose after 1280, slavery apparently become less common even though traffic in children continued. After the last upswing in the 1500s, when some villages may have been as much as 20 percent slave, slavery largely disappeared.

In China, the incidence of slavery varied by region as well as era. Slaves, many captured in war, provided a substantial portion of the labor force during Shang. Slaves also figured in human sacrifices, either to propitiate the gods or to follow the king in death. Slavery declined thereafter in core regions, though the government might enslave the relatives of those who committed the most serious crimes. Han Dynasty eunuchs who served the emperor were slaves, many captured from "southern barbarians," a practice that continued into late imperial times. As in Japan, debt forced men to sell family members into slavery.

Slavery was a common practice among the tribal societies along China's borders, which often waged war to get slaves—both from other nomadic groups and from settled Chinese. Following the fall of the Han and depopulation of the north, nomads launched slave raids to acquire labor, and the southern Chinese dynasties had such a difficult time keeping men under arms that they reached farther south in search of slaves to be made into soldiers. The Mongols used captives to perform heavy labor; once they had conquered China, they sold off parts of the population. Down to the nineteenth century, families in distress had the option of selling off their women as bondservants or prostitutes. This happened in Japan as well, but whether this system of poor relief should be seen as slavery or as indentured servitude is still debated.

In the period after 1000, slave labor played a larger role in the economy of Korea than in that of China or Japan. Slavery first appears in Korean records during the Three Kingdoms era, when the rise of aristocracy brought about a concomitant lowering in the status of many farm laborers. Generals and aristocratic officials received land grants and war captives to work them. Silla kings set up separate villages for slaves. Some had been acquired through conquest; others had become slaves as punishment for crimes. Aristocrats continued to own slaves, whom they armed for internecine combat. They held onto their status and their slaves through the founding of the Koryŏ Dynasty. A decree from 1037 codified what had been customary: slavery was a hereditary status. The government owned public slaves; aristocrats and temples bought and sold private slaves. Within a century, slaves constituted a good 30 percent of the population, a situation that continued into Chosŏn. If either parent of a child was a slave, the child too became a slave. In some cases, slaves paid their owners fixed fees in the form of goods and services; anything else they produced they could keep for themselves. Some were slaves in name only. When king and officials fled Japan's invasion of 1592, slaves burned slave rosters and Ministry of Punishments offices. Slavery started to decline in the eighteenth century when the government offered manumission in return for military service. In 1801, it took the first steps in freeing government slaves, but slaves remained in private hands to 1894 and beyond.

ment. A few hundred armed Koreans loyal to the queen attacked the palace to murder members of the cabinet but were driven off by Japanese guards. The cabinet then had King Kojong issue a decree for all adult men to cut off their topknots, a traditional Korean rite of passage to adulthood. A similar measure had been adopted in Meiji Japan to mark the rejection of old customs and a commitment to modernity, but Korean men were not ready for the shock. Opponents to this decree attacked authorities all over the country. After King Kojong escaped to the Russian legation, he fired the Kabo cabinet.

SUMMARY

How did Korea change during the nineteenth century? Population decline, rebellions, and reports of famines indicate that life got harder for commoners. In contrast, festivals, popular entertainments, and tales of martial valor suggest that society was opening up to groups that fit poorly within the old social hierarchy. Wrangling by *yangban* factions and the king's relatives slowed Korea's response to foreign pressure, but by 1895 it had ended its tributary relationship with China. Its diplomacy rested on treaties, and it had started to build a modern state. Korea's most successful reforms were those that meshed with the desires of men long suppressed by *yangban* to achieve upward mobility through education and government service.

East Asia in the Modern World

Rise of Modern Japan (1900–1931)

The early 1900s found Japan deeply entangled in world affairs. Wars on the Asian continent brought it colonies and complicated notions of national identity. Contradictory impulses toward democracy and totalitarianism, modernity and atavism marked the home front. The state impinged more directly than before on the everyday lives of Japanese citizens. The same mechanisms that allowed it to do so—conscription, education, and mass media—provided channels for people to oppose state policies, create new organizations at the community level, and define individual goals. Changes in the economic structure heightened the importance of industrial labor and the fears of social unrest. A new middle class provided a ready market for popular culture. The most visible signs of modern life concentrated in the cities, to the disgust of people who located the preserve of Japanese values in pristine communities of the countryside.

The first decades of the twentieth century are often analyzed to explain what came after. To what extent was Japan's descent into fascism preordained? Why consider countervailing forces, given that they failed? What is this period's legacy for postwar Japan?

A FLUID INTERNATIONAL ORDER

Foreign affairs resonated through Japan's economy, politics, society, and culture. The imperative to challenge white supremacy by achieving great power status and rising in the hierarchy of nations shaped Japan's national identity. Colonies came to be seen as an economic necessity, both to supply raw materials for Japan's emerging industries and to provide living space for Japan's teeming population.

Japan began the drive for great power status by signing an alliance with Britain in 1902 and going to war against Russia in 1904–1905. Alliance committed each country to come to the defense of the other should a third party join the enemy in time of war. It functioned as planned against Russia. Russia's leasehold on the Liaodong peninsula and fortification of Port Arthur threatened Japan's interests in Korea. When Russia refused to make concessions, Japan's military launched a surprise attack on Port Arthur. It hoped to win a short war before Russia could mobilize its larger army and bring it to the scene of battle, but the siege dragged on longer than expected. By the time Port Arthur fell, Japan's army was exhausted. U.S. President Theodore Roosevelt offered to negotiate a peace settlement. The Treaty of Portsmouth gave Japan the southern half of Sakhalin (called Karafuto in Japanese), Russia's leasehold on the Liaodong peninsula, the South Manchurian Railway built by the Russians between Port Arthur and Mukden and its associated mining concessions, and Russian acknowledgment of Japan's paramountcy in Korea. In demonstrating that a "yellow race" could beat the "white," Japan inspired Asians with hopes that they could throw off the colonial yoke.

Japan landed troops in Korea two days before it declared war on Russia. Two weeks later, it forced the Korean king to accept a limited protectorate that made Korea Japan's ally and subject to Japan's lead in administrative matters. The Japanese army then occupied the country. Six months later, Korea had to accept Japanese financial and diplomatic advisers. They reformed the currency and drew up a government budget. They took over the communications system for reasons of national security. The army imposed martial law to prevent sabotage. The Taft-Katsura agreement of 1905 acknowledged Japan's control of Korea in return for Japan's acquiescence in U.S. colonization of the Philippines. In 1906, Korea became a Japanese protectorate with Itō Hirobumi as resident general. Government offices had to obey Japanese advisers, courts came under the jurisdiction of Japanese judges, the Korean army was disbanded, a Japanese police force maintained order, and Japan took over Korea's diplomatic relations. When the king complained to the Hague Peace Conference of 1907, Itō forced him to abdicate. In 1909, a Korean nationalist assassinated Itō. In 1910, Japan annexed Korea. At the same time, Japan formalized control over Taiwan. Both remained in the Japanese empire for the next thirty-five years, and Japan had joined the ranks of imperial powers. (See Map 22.1.)

Japan envisioned that its empire would bring not only prestige but also coal and iron for its factories, food for its people, a market for the export of finished products, and space for its expanding population. Taiwan supplied sugar financed by Japanese capital

Cartoon of Empress Jingū and Britannia. This cartoon of legendary Empress Jingū, invader of Korea, and Britannia celebrates the 1902 signing of the Anglo-Japanese alliance. These symbols representing Japan and Great Britain cast a benevolent, protective gaze over Korea. *(Saitama Municipal Cartoon Art Museum/DNPArchives.com)*

and, after 1920, rice produced on family farms that inadvertently promoted the island's economic development. The Oriental Development Company bought land in Korea to sell to Japanese settlers, channeled capital to Japanese-owned businesses, and participated in the development of Manchurian mines. The military government improved the infrastructure by building roads and railways and opening schools. It ruthlessly suppressed all dissent. Japanese who migrated to Korea enjoyed a higher standard of living than did Koreans and special privileges in education and employment.

World War I proved advantageous for Japan both economically and diplomatically. Its alliance with Britain allowed it to absorb Germany's leasehold on China's Shandong province and acquire a mandate over German-held islands in the Pacific. In 1918,

Map 22.1   **Japanese Imperial Expansion, 1868–1910**

Allied forces joined Japan in invading Siberia. Japan also tried to impose the infamous Twenty-One Demands on China. Most of them ratified and prolonged Japan's existing privileges in Manchuria and along the China coast. The last set of "requests" would have turned China into a Japanese protectorate. A public outcry in China and abroad forced Japan to back down. China complained bitterly about the Twenty-One Demands at the Versailles Peace Conference, but to no avail. Despite the open door policy promoted by the United States, no Western power was willing to challenge Japan's interests in China.

Following World War I, Japan collaborated with Western powers. It joined the League of Nations. In 1921 it participated in the multilateral Washington Conference designed to preserve the status quo in the Pacific and China and to prevent a new naval arms race. A delegation of Japanese businessmen sent abroad in 1921–1922 demonstrated Japan's commitment to participation in the developed world's economy. Japan had been unable to get a clause on racial equality in the Versailles Peace Treaty, and in 1924 the United States offended Japan by passing the Oriental Exclusion Act. Despite this insult, Japan signed the Kellogg-Briand Pact of 1928 that outlawed war in the settlement of international disputes. In 1930 civilian diplomats agreed to additional naval limitations in the London Naval Treaty over the navy's objections and without addressing the military's concerns regarding China. When the army acted on its own to take over Manchuria, it ended the era of cooperation with the West.

ECONOMIC DEVELOPMENT

In the early twentieth century, Japanese corporations took advantage of international technological and managerial innovations often called the "second industrial revolution." Japan's electrical technology became second to none. Electric streetcars appeared in Tokyo in 1904, several years after they had appeared in Seoul. Of Japanese households, 85 percent had electricity in 1935, compared to 68 percent in the United States. Techniques of mass production required both standardized equipment and scientific management or Taylorism, an American theory of rational labor practice that Japan adapted to make the work force more efficient. Localities hoping to attract businesses developed research centers to find foreign technology, channel it to the factory floor, and modify foreign

products for domestic consumption. Large enterprises developed new metallurgical and chemical technologies, often at the prompting of the Japanese military, which promoted the automobile and airplane.

A dual structure characterized Japan's modern economy. Conglomerates linked through holding and trading companies called *zaibatsu* (financial cliques) dominated the most modern sectors of the economy—mining, shipbuilding, machinery, steel, and chemicals—and produced standardized, high-volume products. Although each company within the *zaibatsu* pursued a single enterprise and remained legally distinct, access to the *zaibatsu*'s capital through its bank, a central advisory committee that set policy and long-term goals, and interlocking boards of directors tied them together. In some cases, *zaibatsu* cooperated in cartels that divided up raw materials and access to markets, as in the textile industry and maritime shipping. *Zaibatsu* chairmen enjoyed access to bureaucrats and cabinet ministers who steered public investment their way and smoothed the regulatory road. Small firms made specialty items and basic consumer goods such as processed food, housing, and clothing. They produced ceramics and toys for export by the *zaibatsu* and functioned as suppliers and subcontractors to the large enterprises.

Japan's industrial sector was well placed to take advantage of World War I. Coal fueled locomotives, factories, and generators. Steel works had capacity to spare. Mitsubishi both built ships and operated a worldwide shipping line in competition with the Sumitomo-backed OSK shipping company. These and other enterprises profited from the Allies' demand for munitions and war-related materiel. Japanese textiles and consumer goods filled the vacuum left by the departure of British exports from Asia. Business profits soared, and Japan's gross national product jumped by 40 percent between 1914 and 1918. The percentage of real national income contributed by manufacturing passed that of agriculture.

Imbalances between different sectors of the economy and cycles of contraction and expansion characterized the 1920s. Japanese companies assumed that demand would continue after World War I. When Britain took back markets in China and South Asia and when European manufacturing replaced Japanese exports, companies found themselves overextended financially and forced to lay off workers. They had just pulled out of the postwar recession when the Great Kanto Earthquake of September 1, 1923, leveled factories and workshops between Tokyo and

Real National Income Produced, 1878–1936
(million yen at 1928–1932 prices)

Year	Total	Primary Industry	Secondary Industry	Tertiary Industry
1878	1,117	691	95	331
1890	2,308	1,429	224	655
1900	3,640	1,671	818	1,151
1914	5,665	2,127	1,354	2,184
1920	6,316	2,147	1,686	2,483
1925	9,268	2,779	2,216	4,273
1929	10,962	2,740	2,911	5,311
1930	12,715	2,477	3,550	6,688
1931	13,726	2,372	3,716	7,638
1932	13,843	2,594	3,987	7,262
1936	16,133	3,149	5,096	7,888

Primary industry = agriculture, forestry, fisheries. Secondary industry = mining, manufacturing, construction, transportation, communication, and utilities. Tertiary industry = commerce and services. Source: G. C. Allen, *A Short Economic History of Modern Japan* (New York: St. Martin's Press, 1981), p. 284.

Yokohama; 140,000 people died, and 570,000 structures (70 percent of Tokyo and 60 percent of Yokohama) were destroyed. Aftershocks ruptured gas and water pipes, snapped electrical lines, and halted transportation and communications. Most companies rebuilt using generous credit provided through the government to banks, which led to a credit crisis in 1927. Trouble came to the domestic market when silk sales slipped and cotton mills in China cut into Japan's biggest Asian market. In contrast to stagnation and decline in the textile industry and agricultural sector, old *zaibatsu* grew by absorbing existing enterprises and diversifying into new areas. Founded in 1908, the Chisso chemical corporation became a new *zaibatsu* through diversification, grew to become Japan's third largest manufacturer, and industrialized northern Korea. When the Great Depression hit at the end of 1929, Japan's economy was already depressed. Japan joined other industrialized nations in imposing steep tariffs on imports, secure in the knowledge that except for oil and scrap iron used in making steel, its colonies had given it the requirements for an autarchic economy.

CONSTITUTIONAL GOVERNMENT

In the public's eyes, oligarchs' efforts to control the selection of cabinet ministers demonstrated the persistence of clique government dominated by men from Satsuma and Chōshū. To counter Itō Hirobumi's influence in the lower house, Yamagata Aritomo forged a faction of conservative bureaucrats, members of the Privy Council and the upper house, and prefectural governors. In 1907 he made it possible for the military to issue orders in the emperor's name independent of the prime minister. Itō's protégé among elected politicians, Hara Takashi, had experience in the Foreign Ministry and business world that helped him arrange compromises between oligarchs and Diet and showed him the way to manipulate the bureaucracy. During the Russo-Japanese War, Hara promised Seiyūkai (Friends of Government Party) support for the cabinet and convinced Yamagata to trust him with the powerful position of home minister.

Hara used his control over the Home Ministry to make Seiyūkai the dominant party in the Diet. The Home Ministry appointed prefectural governors and district chiefs. It ran the police, health bureau, and public works bureau. Hara worked with bureaucrats in the Tokyo office and built a following for Seiyūkai in prefectural offices. Since prefectural officials supervised elections and influenced the local economy, a prefecture with a bureaucracy that supported Seiyūkai was likely to elect Seiyūkai politicians to the Diet. Hara also perfected pork barrel politics. Unlike early parties that simply opposed government spending and tried to cut taxes, Seiyūkai followed a "positive policy" of government spending for economic development. Railroad lines spidered across the country, linking cities, towns, and centers of Seiyūkai support in remote mountain villages. Roads, schools, bridges, irrigation works, and harbors graced the districts that voted Seiyūkai.

Even before Hara became prime minister in 1918, Diet members had mastered manipulating the electorate. Businessmen provided political funds in return for favors. They also offered politicians and bureaucrats positions on their companies' boards of directors. In buying votes, some Diet members relied on election brokers. Others used prefectural assembly members, tainting them as well with the stench of corruption. Playing on Yamagata's fears of a socialist revolution following the Bolshevik takeover in Russia and nationwide rice riots in Japan in 1918, Hara convinced him that party control of an expanded electorate was the safest way to channel popular unrest. The 1919 expansion of the electorate to 5 percent of the population benefited small landlords, not urban workers. In 1921 an unemployed railroad worker assassinated Hara because of what he saw as Hara's disdain for the military.

Between 1924 and 1932, selection of the cabinet shifted back and forth between the two major parties in the lower house. Former bureaucrats and prefectural governors became politicians and ran for the Diet. Although it was not in Seiyūkai's interest to widen the electorate, the pressure of public opinion, maneuvering by other political parties, and the Privy Council's fear of social upheaval led the Diet to pass a bill for universal suffrage for males over age twenty-five in 1925. In the next election three years later, eight proletarian candidates were elected out of 450 contested seats.

The politics of compromise developed by Hara continued after party cabinets became the rule. The Privy Council, House of Peers, much of the bureaucracy, and the military remained beyond the parties' control. Despite the efforts of constitutional scholar Minobe Tatsukichi to devise a theoretical legitimization for party cabinets, they rested on neither law nor precedent but on a pragmatic balance of power.

The crises that bedeviled Japan in the late 1920s and early 1930s tested the limits of constitutionally sanctioned parliamentary democracy. Japan had to deal with the Great Depression and fears of Russian or Chinese threats to Manchuria. Right-wing ultranationalists inside the military and outside the government accused the parties of having traitorously weakened Japan by their corrupt pursuit of self-interest. In 1930 one of their number attacked Prime Minister Hamaguchi Osachi for having signed the controversial London Naval Treaty. He died of his wounds nine months later. Convinced that the party cabinet was about to sacrifice Japan's interests in Asia, colonels in the army acted unilaterally in taking over Manchuria. The early months of 1932 saw assassinations of a former finance minister and an industrialist blamed for hardships brought by the Great Depression. Prime Minister Inukai Tsuyoshi also died at the hands of a group of naval cadets, junior army officers, and civilians. The next prime minister was a military man, as were his successors up to 1945, with two exceptions, both of whom supported the military. The parties still dominated the lower house, but they received only minor cabinet appointments. Even during the fifteen-year war from 1931 to 1945, the Diet continued to function. The cabinet continued to decide policy, although the military's right of access to the emperor precluded debate over its actions. The constitution remained the law of the land.

Imperial Democracy

According to critics in Japan before World War II, liberalism's focus on the individual contradicted the notion that all Japanese were part of the same body politic, *kokutai*, also translated as "national essence." Democracy was a foreign import, antithetical to indigenous custom based on harmony, consensus, and service to the emperor. Many Japanese people proved them wrong by striving for a more open government and society. In the early twentieth century, the struggle for democracy engaged academic theorists, journalists, feminists, outcasts, and working men and women who expressed themselves in riots and in efforts to organize unions.

For Japanese intellectuals, liberalism meant representative government, constitutionalism, and rule by law. It meant individual rights and freedom from undue governmental interference in the individual's life. It distinguished between the naturalness of society and the artifice of the state. The problem for liberals was that imperial ideology defined the emperor as present at society's inception. The imperial institution was not to be analyzed as though it were an artificial construct because it united state and society. Liberals were patriots. They approved of the government's efforts to promote industrialization and make Japan the equal of the West, and they never questioned the centrality of the emperor.

Intellectuals who professed liberal views jeopardized their careers. Yoshino Sakuzō had to resign his position at Tokyo University because he had argued that people are the basis of the state and the aim of the state is to promote their well-being. The public interest, that of people as a whole, has to supersede private, partial interests of oligarchs, bureaucrats, politicians, and businessmen. Minobe Tatsukichi argued that according to the constitution, the Diet, in particular the lower house, was the organ that represented the people. Sovereignty lay not in the emperor but in the state, and the emperor was one of its organs. In 1935 he was accused of disrespect for the emperor, his writings were banned, and his membership in the upper house was revoked.

Educated women promoted democracy through their organizations and deeds. Teachers, many of them Christian or influenced by missionaries, hoped to improve and reform society. The Woman's Christian Temperance Union found adherents in Japan because men's drinking wrecked the home. In 1886 the Tokyo Women's Reform Society opposed concubinage and prostitution, both deemed trafficking in women. Since oligarchs kept concubines and the Meiji emperor fathered the crown prince on a concubine, the notion that civilized behavior included sexual fidelity was a hard sell. More acceptable was the Reform Society's work in aiding earthquake victims and providing financial support for former prostitutes. In 1901 members of the Reform Society joined the Greater Japan Women's Patriotic Association. Under its auspices they could speak in public to women, and they received government support for their activities.

The staging of Henrik Ibsen's *A Doll's House* in 1911 and the inauguration of the journal *Bluestocking* marked the arrival of the "new woman" in Japan. The play offered a scandalous alternative to the government-sponsored ideology of "good wife and wise mother" when Nora walked out on husband and children. Matsui Sumako, who played Nora, gained fame as Japan's first Western-style actress. Her tumultuous private life dramatized her rejection of domesticity. *Bluestocking* started as a literary magazine, but it soon became a forum for discussing women's roles and expectations. Feminist activist Hiratsuka Raichō and poet translator and social critic Yosano Akiko debated state support for motherhood, Hiratsuka wanting government protection and Yosano arguing that state support would be degrading and would cost women their independence. They agreed that marriage is not sacrosanct, patriarchy need not

go unchallenged, and women ought to have equal legal, educational, and social rights.

In the 1920s, feminists advocated family planning and women's suffrage. Katō Shidzue brought Margaret Sanger to Japan in 1924 to promote birth control as a way to deal with the threat to family budgets and women's health posed by too many children. The government refused Sanger permission to land until she promised to make no public speeches. The examples of Britain and the United States that granted women the vote after World War I and the growing numbers of women who followed politics in mass-circulation newspapers and magazines convinced some politicians and bureaucrats that political rights for women marked advanced societies. In 1922 the Diet revoked the law that barred women from political meetings. In 1931 a bill for local women's suffrage passed the lower house but foundered on a conservative coalition in the House of Peers. Give women the right to vote, and they will stop having children, predicted one baron. The end to party cabinets stymied proposals for women's political rights.

Mass Movements

Modern mass movements emerged in the context of Japanese imperialism. In 1905 newspapers and speechmakers informed the public that the Russo-Japanese War had concluded without the indemnity that a Great Power deserved from a defeated foe and with slight territorial gain to justify the sacrifices made by Japanese troops. Riots began at Tokyo's Hibiya Park outside the palace and continued for three days, destroying over 70 percent of police boxes that provided shelter for policemen stationed across the city and fifteen trams. (See Map 22.2.) Smaller riots erupted in Kobe and Yokohama. All but two of the forty-four prefectures reported rallies in cities, towns, and villages. Between 1905 and the rice riots of 1918, Tokyo experienced nine serious riots, many part of larger movements that swept the nation. Although rioters attacked police stations and government offices, they did so in the name of the emperor. By conflating imperial and popular will, they differentiated between evil advisers behind the throne and the throne itself.

Rice riots in 1918 protested high prices, degrading work conditions, and government ineptitude. They began with fishermen's wives who organized demonstrations along the Toyama coast and grew to include urban rioters who castigated war profiteers and asserted a right to free speech, tenant farmers who demanded

Map **22.2**   **Modern Tokyo**

lower rents and decent treatment from landlords, and coal miners who demanded higher wages and respect as human beings. Out of them grew the mass movements of the 1920s for *burakumin* (outcast) liberation and labor organization.

Outcasts found that the Meiji transformation did not improve their lot. Losing the monopoly over leather work and other lucrative, if unpleasant, tasks brought poverty. The household registration system made it well nigh impossible for outcasts to escape their past.

Women Supporters of the Suiheisha. This nationwide organization tried to end discrimination against *burakumin* in the 1920s. These women were from the Fukuoka branch in northern Kyushu. *(50 Years of History of Suiheisha by Buraku Liberation Publishing House/DNP Archives.com)*

Schools refused to admit them, employers to hire them, landlords to rent to them, public baths and barbers to serve them, and other Japanese to marry them. When conscripted into the military, they were assigned menial tasks and never promoted. In the early twentieth century, the central government set up advisory committees to deal with the issue of poverty lest socialism creep into Japan. Since *burakumin* were among the worst off, they became one focus. In 1908 the cabinet encouraged them to emigrate. In 1911 the Home Ministry started to distribute funds for improvement of *burakumin* communities, and in 1920 it started the Harmony Movement to mobilize *burakumin* to work for gradual reform. Private organizations lent support. Both assumed that the reason for discrimination lay in *burakumin* filth, ignorance, and immorality. In 1922 a group of young *burakumin* organized the Leveller's Society (*Suiheisha*) to protest discrimination and promote the equality of all Japanese subjects before the emperor.

The *burakumin* liberation movement of the 1920s blamed *burakumin* problems on prejudice and discrimination. The goal was to change social attitudes, but Leveller's Society members could not agree on tactics. Some believed in educational programs and nonviolent confrontations that aimed at greater democracy. Others wanted a social revolution to overthrow capitalism through challenging institutions known to oppose fair practices. Denunciation campaigns targeted primary schools that permitted students and staff to insult *burakumin* and public officials and individuals who uttered derogatory remarks. The offenders would have to offer an apology, sometimes publicized in newspapers. In 1926, the first year of the Shōwa emperor's reign, antimilitarism plus anger at the treatment of conscript *burakumin* led to a movement promoting noncompliance with military organizations. Despite police repression, denunciation campaigns continued into the 1930s. Only after the outbreak of the China war in 1937 did the Leveller's Society agree to support national unity and the war effort.

Tenant farmers and industrial workers tried to gain acceptance for their organizations and redress for their grievances. The 1898 Civil Code gave landlords the right to buy, sell, and lease land without any protection for tenants who might have farmed it for generations. Of Japan's farm families, 28 percent owned no land, while another 41 percent owned some and rented the rest. Tenants and tenant-owners organized unions in the 1910s to demand rent reductions and the right of cultivation, especially in the most economically advanced regions in central and western Japan, where landlords had previously been in the forefront of encouraging agricultural improvements. The tenants established a national federation in 1922 that grew to nearly seven hundred branches. In the 1920s, over eighteen thousand disputes between tenants and landlords filled police dockets.

Agricultural conditions had deteriorated even before 1930. The economic downturn in the 1920s, when synthetic fabrics replaced silk and the government allowed the import of rice from Asia, reduced the demand for agricultural products and unskilled labor. Real income for farm families declined by 30 percent. Unseasonably cold weather in the agriculturally backward northeast brought crop failures between 1931 and 1933. Landlords tried to repossess tenanted land, refused to reduce rents, or even tried to raise them. Debt-ridden farmers migrated to Japan's overseas colonies or sold their daughters into prostitution. Tenants petitioned the Agriculture Ministry for rural relief. The ministry responded by organizing cooperatives and providing funds for development. In central and western Japan, where absentee landlords no longer performed ceremonial and support functions, tenants lost their former deference. Their habit of looking on the land they cultivated as theirs led to rent refusals and conflict. With the coming of war in 1937, agricultural conditions improved when the government moved to limit rice imports and tenant unions disbanded in the drive for national unity.

Industrial development led to labor activism, though not labor solidarity. Heavy industry employed highly skilled and relatively well-paid male workers sufficiently educated to read newspapers and understand socialist theory. Textile mills continued to hire cheaper and, it was hoped, docile women and girls. Even in 1930, women constituted over 50 percent of the factory work force. Urban women found jobs as teachers, journalists, nurses, clerks, ticket sellers, bus conductors, telephone operators, actresses, and café hostesses. Small firms employed male and female workers at low wages to manufacture parts for other sectors of the economy. Below them were rickshaw pullers and delivery boys. At the bottom were the miners.

Worker grievances and the ability to organize varied across industries and within factories. The 1907 riot at the Ashio mine originated with ore diggers, the most highly paid workers, not copper refinery workers, whose wages had recently dropped and who feared being laid off. The expansion in heavy industry and the need to raise productivity prompted factory owners to reduce worker autonomy and eliminate bosses who contracted for specific jobs. Workers countered with demands that they be treated with respect. (See **Documents: Negotiations Between Strike Group Representatives and Company Directors.**) In 1912 they organized the Friendship Society (Yūaikai) to provide mutual aid, self-improvement classes, and improved relations with employers. If employees worked hard and deferred to foremen, factory owners ought to treat them with benevolence. To keep skilled workers, employers instituted a seniority system of raises and offered fringe benefits.

In many cases, implementation of paternalistic benefits came only after workers had launched work stoppages and strikes. Over one hundred labor disputes erupted between 1902 and 1917. In 1919 the Hara cabinet interpreted the Public Order and Police Act of 1900 to mean that workers might organize unions and go on strike so long as they remained nonviolent. In 1921 the Yūaikai became the Japan Federation of Labor. Union membership burgeoned in the 1920s, although it never included more than 8 percent of the industrial work force. Hundreds of strikes a year roiled both heavy and textile industries. Despite owners who resisted unionization, workers bargained collectively for higher wages, severance pay, a minimum wage, better working conditions, shorter workdays, an end to child labor, and improved housing.

Minorities

Although nationalist propaganda assured the Japanese people that they were uniquely homogeneous, the pairing of colonialism and modernity created groups perceived as different. The government defined Ainu as "formerly indigenous people" and demanded that they assimilate into the Japanese mainstream by renouncing their peripatetic lifestyle and settling in villages. Officials who supervised their transformation into tenant farmers, laborers, and welfare recipients in the course of selling off their lands and opening Hokkaido to development saw them as a dying race. Many Ainu accepted the necessity of assimilation despite discrimination at the hands of employers, teachers,

DOCUMENTS

Negotiations Between Strike Group Representatives and Company Directors

This confrontation between strike group representatives Itō, Iwasa, and Shiga and company directors for the Yokohama Dock Company Tōjō and Miyanaga on September 28, 1921, exposes conflict between workers and management over work conditions and financial issues such as wages and severance pay. The hyperbole on both sides scarcely conceals fundamentally different attitudes regarding company goals, the value of work, and the treatment of workers.

Itō: Today the three of us have come as worker representatives with this petition.

Miyanaga: Does this demand for a 20 percent daily wage increase mean an average wage increase of 20 percent for all the workers?

Iwasa: Our wages average 1 yen 60 sen. Out of 1,000 people, if there is one getting 3 yen, the rest are getting around 1 yen 40 sen. With days off, one month is 25 days and, with a wife and children, we can't make ends meet. This is why we have asked for a pay raise. With the present severance pay, if one of us is fired, he is reduced to poverty.

Miyanaga: We want you to understand the company's situation. As you are well aware, the economy, especially the shipbuilding industry, is facing a severe depression. The question of how to support the workers in this situation is one that troubles us greatly. Because of the shipbuilding depression there have been many layoffs, and aware of your anxiety about this, the other day we announced that we would not carry out any large-scale layoffs. As for ship re-pairs, which this company has been engaged in since its founding, in good times we were able to charge the shipowners a good price, but today the situation is so bad that, even if we offer a price below cost, they won't take it. Shipbuilding revived briefly after the war and we were able to make some profit, but now we are making no profit and are taking orders at a loss. In this depression, we are taking on such orders because we do not want to have to lay off you workers. We understand well your plight, but, even at present pay levels, the situation is as I have described, so we would hope to have your understanding regarding the pay raise. You also raised demands regarding severance and retirement pay. As I have already noted, our policy is to avoid layoffs at all costs in the hopes that this will reduce your anxiety, so we would like to gain your understanding on these points also.

Itō: Are you saying you will absolutely not lay off any workers?

Miyanaga: I can't promise "absolutely" but . . .

and non-Ainu neighbors. Others objected to contradictory policies that made them use the Japanese language and forgo tattooing and earrings while setting them up as tourist attractions and anthropological exhibits. During the 1920s, Ainu scholars recorded Ainu songs, legends, and customs. Ainu activists created self-help programs to cope with alcoholism and violence. Social critics drew on radical thought to counter prejudice and discrimination. Fearful lest Hokkaido go red with the Soviet Union so close to its border, government officials and assimilationist Ainu founded the Ainu Society in 1930 to improve the individual lot through education and to remind Ainu of the gratitude they owed the emperor.

The government's attitude toward the Ryukyus was more complicated. The land tax was not imposed in the Ryukyus until 1903. Ryukyuans had a social hierarchy topped by a monarch and aristocracy that made sense in the eyes of Japanese accustomed to inherent social inequality. Ryukyuan nobles used their status to gain favors from the prefectural governor's office and insisted on their right to speak for the commoners. To be placed on a par with Ainu was, they felt, an insult to their superior culture.

Miyanaga and Itō (together): Insofar as possible.

Itō: In that case wouldn't it be better to decide on severance pay and relieve our anxieties in that way?

Miyanaga: Our thinking is that is would be even kinder to take the policy of avoiding layoffs rather than getting involved in the severance pay issue.

Itō: So you mean to say that there is no necessity to decide on severance pay? If your policy is not to lay off workers, well, this is a bit of an extreme example, but in that case wouldn't it be just as well to set severance pay at 10 to 20 thousand yen?

Miyanaga: I didn't say that there was no need. We are now considering the issue of severance pay.

Itō: You say "insofar as possible," but does that mean that in the eventuality of a layoff you will handle it as in the past?

Miyanaga: We are now also considering the possibility of increasing the level in the future.

Iwasa: Isn't what you are saying merely that, if you accept our demands, your profit will be narrowed? For us this is a matter of life and death.

Miyanaga: You say "our profits are narrowed," but in fact, not only are we not expecting any profit, but the company is going so far as to operate at a loss.

Itō: We have already heard at length from Mr. Yamaguchi on this point and understand it well. In any case, we regard the fact that the company will not now announce its intention to change the present severance pay as an indication of the company's total lack of sincerity regarding this entire affair. Let's go back and report this to all the others.

Miyanaga: You say that we are insincere, but as I have already explained the company is striving to promote your welfare and guarantee your security, and we'd like you to report this to the others.

Iwasa: The other day a worker named Tsukui, who was working in one of your manufacturing shops, was fired for going to another shop and talking to a worker there. You said that this was a violation of company rules, so he was fired. But this is something which other workers are constantly doing. If you look for such little matters and fire someone every day, pretty soon you'll have fired all the workers. Therefore, all your kind words are just the attitude of a man who stands laughing after having strangled seven people. We'll go and report this situation to all the other workers.

Source: Andrew Gordon, *The Evolution of Labor Relations in Japan: Heavy Industry, 1853–1955* (Cambridge, Mass.: Council on East Asian Studies, Harvard University, 1985), pp. 116–119, modified.

Nearly three hundred thousand Koreans lived in Japan by 1930. The earliest arrivals in the late nineteenth century were students of Japan's resistance to Western imperialism. Next came workers forced from their villages by colonial policies that expropriated land and put Japan's dietary needs first. Enticed by labor contractors who promised employment in factories, mines, and construction, workers ended up in low-paying jobs and substandard housing. Excluded from skilled labor except when used to break strikes, they performed dirty and dangerous jobs shunned by Japanese at wages half those of Japanese workers.

Although the government made Koreans citizens of Japan and promoted an ideology of racial brotherhood under the emperor, Koreans in Japan were deemed inherently stupid, lazy, bellicose, and vicious. Accused of having set fires and poisoned wells following the Great Kanto Earthquake, thousands died at the hands of Japanese vigilantes.

Koreans who showed intellectual promise earned the mistrust of Japanese officials, who feared, with reason, that they harbored anti-Japanese sentiment. Korean students in Japan suffered arrest, imprisonment, and death for supporting national resistance movements and joining Japanese students who professed universal brotherhood, socialism, and communism. The Osaka Confederation of Korean Laborers earned official enmity when it called for an end to capitalism. Moderate Korean residents feared that opposition to colonialism would only invite repression. They organized mutual aid societies to help Koreans find work, adequate housing, and health care. Government officials promoted assimilation policies to bring Koreans gradually and peacefully into Japanese society, albeit with the proviso that ethnically they could never become Japanese.

Radicals

The government suppressed ideas it deemed dangerous. In 1901 the Socialist Democratic Party enjoyed mere hours of existence before being outlawed. It advocated public ownership of land, capital, and communications; abolition of the military; education funded by the state; workers' rights to unionize; universal suffrage; and abolition of the House of Peers. It did not reject the emperor system, unlike the anarcho-syndicalists Kōtoku Shūsui and Kanno Suga. Kōtoku opposed capitalists, militarists, aristocrats, and politicians on behalf of workers and farmers. Kanno advocated overthrow of the government and assassination of the emperor. In what is known as the Great Treason Trial of 1911, they were convicted and sentenced to death, although they were innocent of the charges brought against them. Ōsugi Sakae believed that society consists of two classes: the conquerors and the suppressed. It was up to workers to abolish the state and destroy capitalism. Following the Great Kanto Earthquake, he and his wife, the feminist and anarchist Itō Noe, were strangled by the police. The nihilist Kaneko Fumiko advocated Korean independence. She died in prison. In 1933, the proletarian writer Kobayashi Takiji, who had graphically depicted the brutal conditions of fishermen in *The Cannery Boat* (1929), died at the hands of the police.

During the 1920s, a few socialists enjoyed a brief opportunity to propagate their views. The Red Wave Society, founded in 1921, urged women to join the fight against capitalist society that enslaved them inside and outside the home. Sakai Toshihiko organized a study group to discuss socialist ideas in the late 1890s. In 1922, he participated in the secret founding of the Japanese Communist Party. Inuta Shigeru launched a literary movement that advocated self-rule for farmers through land reform. Kawakami Ha-

jime took a tortuous path from religious movements and nationalism to Marxism, revolutionary communism, and the study of historical materialism. Between 1927 and 1937, socialists and communists debated the nature of Japanese capitalism, seeking to find a balance between universal Marxist categories and Japanese history that determined the kinds of political action possible in the present. The Peace Preservation Law of 1925 promised punishment for attacks on the emperor system or capitalism. In the early 1930s, the police arrested over ten thousand people a year for propagating ideas disloyal to the emperor and dangerous to the *kokutai*. Their intent was to induce a repudiation of socialist thought and conversion to a belief in Japan's sacred mission. Men and women who refused to confess and convert remained in prison until after World War II.

MODERN URBAN CULTURE

Industrial growth and expansion of the government bureaucracy created a new middle class of salaried white-collar workers. (See **Material Culture: Houses for the Middle Class.**) In contrast to the old middle class of shopkeepers and landlords, these workers got their jobs through educational achievement and enjoyed the security of lifetime employment with fringe benefits such as subsidized housing and medical care. Income depended on seniority as much as on proficiency or accomplishment. In his novels *Sanshirō* (1908) and *Kokoro* (1914), Natsume Sōseki depicted socially mobile young men from the countryside. The character Sanshirō found himself torn between an academic career, the glittering world of business, and a return to his village. *Kokoro* expressed the sense that the era of great expectations passed with the death of the Meiji emperor in 1912. His son, the Taishō emperor, was universally seen as a lesser figure. In the 1920s, the opportunities for becoming extremely rich declined, but the new middle class continued to grow.

The Great Kanto Earthquake of 1923 that brought down brick buildings and wooden houses ushered in modern Japanese culture. The new Tokyo had more ferroconcrete. Even before the earthquake, the new middle class had started moving south and west of the city limits. Private railroads and the real estate developers who owned them intensified this trend. With the exception of the publishing industry, light industry moved east of the city; heavy industry moved

MATERIAL CULTURE

Houses for the Middle Class

Houses built after the Great Kanto Earthquake for the new middle class were derived from Western architectural styles. Rooms had fewer functions but greater privacy than before. They had walls and doors and were further separated from one another by corridors. Guests were received at the front of the house in the parlor, decorated with sofa, chairs, antimacassars, and carpet. In line with the changing social etiquette of the time, guests were discouraged from making unexpected calls, and the telephone gave them little excuse for doing so. The family living room overlooked the garden. Although located on the dark north side of the house, the kitchen had a floor. Bedrooms were on the second floor. A modern water supply made it possible for each house to have its own bath.

New middle-class furnishings were designed chiefly for entertainment and convenience, rather than being objects with which to impress guests. The living room ideally contained a phonograph and a radio. Appliances included the gas range for cooking, a gas heater with ceramic grill, an electric fan, and an electric rice cooker. For reasons of etiquette and security, old-style houses had required that someone always be home to greet guests and guard the premises. Western-style front doors made it easy for the housewife to lock the door and go shopping, visit friends, or see a movie.

Modern Living Room. This modern living room was photographed for the journal *Homu raifu* (*Home Life*). Chairs, tables, lamp, potted plants, a sofa, and cushions provide a Western-style backdrop for the woman wearing a kimono.

BIOGRAPHY Kobayashi Ichizō

Entrepreneur, politician, and diplomat, Kobayashi Ichizō (1873–1957) fostered consumer culture by founding a railroad, a department store, a baseball team, and the Takarazuka Girl's Theater.

Kobayashi had wanted to become a writer, but after graduating from Keiō University, he joined the Mitsui Bank in 1893. In 1906 he left the bank to become executive director for a private electrical railroad near Osaka. Through hard work and creative planning in the building of new lines and improving service, he made his company dominant in train travel between Osaka and Kobe. In 1918 he became president of the newly named Hankyū electric railroad. To attract riders, he expanded into real estate by building suburban housing developments for the new middle class.

Kobayashi's interests tended toward popular culture. One of his train lines went to Takarazuka, an old hot springs resort. To lure customers, he built a zoo and, in 1913, the Takarazuka Girl's Theater. In 1919 he founded the Takarazuka Music Academy to train young women for his productions. The first revue with chorus line and musical spectaculars was *Mon Paris*, staged in 1927. Having watched commuters surge through the Hankyū terminal in Osaka, he opened a market adjacent to the station in 1924. Five years later it became the Hankyū department store with restaurants, an art gallery, and a bookstore. Kobayashi also founded the Tōhō Cinema Company to make and distribute films. He built his movie empire with a mass audience in mind by scheduling show times and setting ticket prices for the benefit of workers. In 1936 he joined other railroad magnates and real estate developers to establish Japan's first professional baseball league to give people another reason to ride trains in search of entertainment. Loyal fans still cheer the Hankyū Braves. In 1940, Kobayashi reached the pinnacle of his career by becoming commerce and industry minister and special ambassador in charge of trade to the Netherlands.

Kobayashi insisted that the performers in the Takarazuka Girl's Theater be of unquestionable virtue; his aim was to provide entertainment for respectable women and to mold his actresses' character so that they could later perform as good wives and wise mothers on their most important stage, the home. The Music Academy provided training in etiquette, ethics, and homemaking as well as singing and dancing. On stage, women played male roles; they also played Asians from countries incorporated into the Japanese empire. Lest actresses aspire to make the theater a profession, Kobayashi insisted that they retire at the peak of their popularity while they were still considered young enough to make a good match.

Source: Jennifer E. Robertson, *Takarazuka: Sexual Politics and Popular Culture in Modern Japan* (Berkeley: University of California Press, 1998).

---

south to Kawasaki. The space left behind filled with offices, retail shops, and entertainment arcades.

Modern culture incorporated a second wave of westernization driven not by national goals but by individual inclinations. Dry goods stores had already transformed themselves into department stores at the turn of the century. After the earthquake, they added theaters, galleries, exhibition halls, and rooftop arcades. In 1926, vending machines started providing refreshment for travelers at Tokyo and Ueno stations. In 1927, the first subway in Asia connected corporate headquarters in Ginza with movie houses and cafés in Asakusa. Mass transit changed urban patterns of work, family life, leisure, and consumption. Unlike the old middle class whose members lived behind their businesses and shopped in the neighborhood, the white-collar worker commuted from his suburban home to his work downtown. Entertainment districts that grew up around train terminals enticed him to spend evenings at coffee shops and cafés.

The new middle class consumed a modern culture removed from politics. Mass literacy spurred the development of mass media. Self-help books and magazines taught the rudiments of popular science, how to be modern, how to succeed in business, and how to create the perfect home environment. (See Color

Plate 28.) By 1920, eleven hundred newspapers found 6 to 7 million buyers. Registered magazines were ten times that number. Journals for men appealed to the highbrow, the middlebrow, and the vulgar. Women's journals calibrated according to class, and girls' and boys' journals divided the market into ever more discrete segments. Retail bookstores jumped from three thousand in 1914 to over ten thousand in 1927. They sold complete editions of Western authors in translation, serious works of idealist philosophy by the Kyoto School, novels by such best-selling male authors as Tanizaki Junichirō and female authors as Uno Chiyo, and illustrated books given to escapist sensationalism. Cinemas showed films from abroad alongside domestically produced animated cartoons and historical dramas. Movie stars became celebrities. Government-operated radio stations started broadcasting in the mid-1920s. Record companies churned out patriotic songs. Popular music celebrated romantic love and the delights of Tokyo, including hanging out in Ginza. A cheap escape from the workaday world was to watch small balls bounce down a pachinko board, the vertical version of the pinball machine.

Modern mass culture promoted a privatizing world of pleasure and self-expression. Women danced in chorus lines and performed in Takarazuka Girl's Theater. (See **Biography: Kobayashi Ichizō**.) In the novel *Naomi* (1924–1925), Tanizaki depicted the transformation of a café waitress into a *modan gaaru* ("modern girl"; *moga* for short) who bobbed her hair, wore revealing dresses, and danced the Charleston. The *moga*'s less flamboyant companion was the *mobo* ("modern boy"). Together they scandalized onlookers by smoking cigarettes and holding hands in public. The late 1920s are often characterized by the words *ero*, *guro*, and *nansensu*—eroticism, grotesquerie, and nonsense, referring to both the flood of foreign words in urban vocabularies and the perceived decline in public morals. Materialism, individualism, and decadence had apparently replaced the beautiful Japanese virtues of diligence, decorum, and duty.

ALTERNATIVES TO MODERNITY

People repelled by modern culture found solace in folk traditions of rural Japan, high art of ancient Japan, and communities of the devout created by the new religions. Ethnographer Yanagita Kunio sought a cultural authenticity that had been lost in urban areas. Traveling from Tohoku to the Ryukyus, he collected folk tales and documented what he viewed as pristine customs of the folk. Industrialist and builder of the Mitsui *zaibatsu* Masuda Takashi tried to preserve Japan's artistic patrimony and supported the government's system for designating cultural artifacts as national treasures. First established in 1897, the designation applied foremost to religious objects from Kinai, declared Japan's sovereignty over its past, magnified differences between Japan and the outside world, and demonstrated that Japan possessed a world-class culture.

New religions provided alternative visions of modernity that did not please the state. Deguchi Onisaburō, organizer of Ōmoto-kyō, criticized government policies that disadvantaged the poor. In the 1920s, he proclaimed that as the Maitreya, he would establish a new order on earth, a message that found believers even among government officials and army officers. In the early 1930s, he founded a semimilitaristic youth group to restore the kingdom of God at Ōmoto-kyō headquarters. Ōmoto-kyō was suppressed in 1921 and again in 1935. New religions founded after 1905 more commonly based their teachings on Nichiren Buddhism and answered the needs of uprooted, underprivileged masses in the cities. Charismatic leaders preached a gospel of social equality and promised either a pure new world or salvation to come. They emphasized faith healing, deliverance from suffering, and a focus on this world's benefits. For recent urban migrants, new religions provided self-help groups, a sense of identity, and a community that was neither self-righteously traditional nor alienatingly modern.

Twentieth-century agrarianism exhibited more virulent antimodernism. It identified agriculture as the ethical foundation of the state when agriculture was no longer the country's main source of wealth. Its adherents professed a farm *bushidō* (way of the warrior) that assimilated the farmers' virtues of diligence, frugality, fortitude, and harmony with loyalty and self-sacrifice on behalf of the state. This agrarianism criticized city life for making people selfish and ambitious; it detested capitalism for increasing the corrupting power of money, destroying the farm family economy, and eroding harmony between city and country. It demanded a spiritual alternative to materialism and a national alternative to universal socialism. Its nostalgic search for a return to a primitive rural society that manifested the *kokutai* frequently turned violent in the 1930s.

SUMMARY

How did Japan change during the first third of the twentieth century? On the positive side, it developed a robust parliamentary democracy supported by an electorate that encompassed the entire male population. The industrialized economy and modern bureaucracy fostered the growth of a well-educated middle class. The development of mass media provided opportunities for mass movements that aimed at improving the lot of the downtrodden. Whether they liked it or not, the complexity of modern society gave people the opportunity to make choices rather than simply follow the ways of their forebears and to pursue private, individual goals. Yet historians also see darker currents. On an institutional level, the military became increasingly independent of civilian control. Although it provided employment, the industrial sector left workers in poverty. Modern Japan contained conflicting visions of what it meant to be Japanese, who should be incorporated into the nation and how, and what Japan's role in the world should be. The relatively peaceful world of the 1920s allowed space for controversy. When the Great Depression struck in 1930, plural and critical voices within Japan appeared as dangerous as threats from abroad to Japan's economic and national security.

CHAPTER TWENTY-THREE

Modernizing Korea and Colonial Rule (1896–1945)

After the Sino-Japanese War ended in 1895, Korea had a brief period to debate its future and launch modernizing projects before losing independence to Japan. The colonial period involved major social, economic, cultural, and ideological transformations that entailed both human suffering and possibilities for development. One legacy was the rise of nationalism and the introduction of communism that created the basis for political division after 1945.

Should attention focus on how people suffered under Japanese oppression or on the progress made in economic development, education, liberation of women, and introduction of modern mass culture? Who did the right thing: anti-Japanese (often communist) guerrilla fighters who patriotically resisted Japanese imperialism, cultural nationalists who acquiesced to Japanese control and tried to educate the masses to higher national consciousness over the long term, or expatriate nationalists in the United States who worked to persuade Western nations to liberate Korea? And how should collaborators—Korean landlords and businessmen who not only prospered under Japan but supported Japan's efforts in the late 1930s to eliminate Korean language and culture—be judged?

ATTEMPTS AT REFORM (1896–1910)

Competition between Japan and Russia gave Koreans the opportunity to promote reforms, nationalism, and modern modes of social interaction. Competition also meant constraints when both Russia and Japan demanded concessions. In the end, Korea's efforts to remain independent came to naught when the court of world opinion sided with Japan.

Russia's Interests

Russia's development of Siberia that started in the late nineteenth century gave it a narrow boundary with northeastern Korea below the trans-Siberian railway to Vladivostok. In 1896, Russia began construction of a second railway, the Chinese Eastern Railway, which stretched across Manchuria through Harbin to shorten the distance to Vladivostok. The next year, it obtained a twenty-five-year lease on Port Arthur (Dalian) on the Liaodong peninsula, which it had taken away from Japan in 1895, and it obtained railroad rights from there to Harbin to connect with the Chinese Eastern Railway. Japan could only watch these events in ever-growing frustration.

In 1896, King Kojong escaped from Japanese control in his palace and fled to the Russian legation. Russia and Japan signed two agreements that granted Russia equal rights with Japan to station legation guards and grant loans to the Korean government. They almost divided Korea into two spheres of influence. Korea also signed a secret agreement in which Russia promised to protect King Kojong and provide military and financial aid. Strapped for funds to pay off indemnities and finance his government, King Kojong began to lease rights to the exploitation of natural resources—lumber to the Russians, gold mines to the Americans, and railroad construction to the Japanese and others in return for loans. After he returned to his palace in 1897, he changed the title of his kingdom to The Great Empire of Korea and adopted the title of emperor to put himself on par with Chinese, Russian, and Japanese rulers.

Nationalist Movements

Popular reaction against the king's sacrifice of national resources gave rise to the first explicitly nationalist movements as Koreans struggled to find a national identity fit for the modern age. After King Kojong dismissed the reform cabinet upon his arrival at the Russian legation, a street mob killed reform ministers, and the new conservative cabinet reversed the topknot edict. The new Independence Club demanded the dismissal of corrupt officials and strove to educate people on the need to modernize the country. It organized street meetings and education sessions and established a newspaper, *The Independent*, written in the vernacular and English. Membership in the group increased as its leaders made public speeches, established branches in small towns, campaigned for

the construction of an Independence Gate as a sign of liberation from subservience to China, held mass meetings and demonstrations in Seoul, and demanded and received seats on the king's council. Its leaders included men like Sŏ Chaep'il (also called Philip Jaisohn), an American citizen who returned to Korea; Syngman Rhee, who had attended Paejae Christian missionary school; and Yun Ch'iho, who visited Japan and was educated in the United States. In thrall to American progressivism, they denigrated Korea's heritage while proclaiming the need to create a truly independent nation.

Although the Independence Club was banned after two years, it inspired elite women to debate sexual equality and education for women in the context of Korean nationalism. They organized the Ch'anyanghoe (Praise the Lord Society) in 1898 to form a school for women and the Yŏuhoe (Friends of Women) the next year to demand the abolition of concubinage. Esther Park, the first woman doctor, began practice at the Women's Hospital (Pogu yŏgwan) in 1900 and taught sanitation in addition to clinical work.

For the first time, women started taking public action. After 1900, the royal mint and private textile companies began to hire women workers. Women established organizations to pay back foreign debts incurred by the regime. Others protested administrative corruption, called for independence, and organized participatory groups. Women founded societies in 1906 and 1907 to campaign for women's education, oppose separation of the sexes, stop wearing shawls to cover their faces in public, establish a hospital, and publish a new journal, *A Guide for Women*. Two prominent leaders were Yi Okkyŏng and Helen Kim. Louise Yim wrote vividly about her struggles to achieve more independence for women (see **Documents: Louise Yim's Writings on Female Independence**).

One sign of the rise of a modern civil society is the appearance of organizations advocating political goals outside the government. Inaugurated in 1904, the Korea Preservation Society opposed attempts by Japan to turn state land into private land for sale to Japanese developers. As its name suggests, the Society for the Study of Constitutional Government advocated institutional change to deal with the challenges threatening Korea. When it was outlawed, its successor took the name of the Korea Self-Strengthening Society. It tried to promote economic development and the spread of education. Other organizations aimed at similar goals, though they often had to organize

Louise Yim's Writings on Female Independence

Louise Yim (Im Yŏngsin) was a patriot who suffered torture for participating in resistance to Japanese rule. She earned a B.A. and an M.A. from the University of Southern California and served in the Republic of Korea National Assembly after the Korean War (1950–1953). She began her career by protesting against Korean conventions, including restrictions on women's education. She opposed arranged marriages for children and advocated individual freedom.

On Grammar School

Often I stood outside the boys' school which my father had started and I would listen to the boys repeating the lessons after their teacher. One day after the boys had gone home I went inside the little, square, mud-walled building.

"May I speak?" I asked Cho Tugy, the teacher.

He was so startled that he dropped a pencil. Then he saw me and smiled.

"If I may have the honor to listen," he replied formally.

"Would it be possible for a girl to learn how to read and write?"

He said nothing for a little while. I was afraid he would laugh and send me home. Then he said:

"If the gods have given you the courage to ask, we can hope they have given you the power to learn, little one. Come to school anytime and I will teach you."

By the time I was twelve [1912], there were rumors that Korean girls were going to be forced to marry Japanese. Therefore, all parents were in a hurry to get their daughters married. My sister was to marry soon and my turn was to be next.

One day, two women came to my room. I knew right away who they were. They were matchmakers. I had never hated anybody as much as I did those two women. I felt as though they were trying to imprison me.

Instead of answering their questions, I questioned them and I lectured them. They were shocked and sometimes they put their hands to their faces and moaned as I spoke.

I told them it was a crime to force marriage on a girl too young to know what it was all about. This was almost too much for them to bear. A Korean child was not supposed to speak this way to her elders.

When they left, I heard one say to the other, "We will speak to her mother. She will come to no good, that one. Her blood is wild."

On High School, ca. 1916

I knew then that the masculine belief that females did not have a place in the national life of Korea was the belief of men who knew nothing about women and in their ignorance shut them out of the family's life too. It has always been a great mystery to me why men think that women are different from them intellectually. I wish I could go to every man and tell him that besides certain physical differences and the ability of a woman to bear children, a woman thinks of all the things a man does. Just because she allows herself to be exiled in the kitchen a woman does not give up her feelings as an individual.

———

Source: Louise Yim, *My Forty Year Fight for Korea* (Seoul: Chungang University, 1964), pp. 27, 39, 56.

in secret as Japanese pressure intensified. Newspapers, too, rallied to the cause of Korean independence, particularly after the Russo-Japanese War. They publicized acts of Japanese aggression, at least until forced to close by Japanese censorship. Even the manner of their demise contributed to heightening Korean political consciousness.

Korea's first new religion took on the trappings of a fully organized institution and supported nationalist goals. In 1905, the Tonghak movement changed its name to Religion of the Heavenly Way (Ch'ŏndogyo). Having supported an uprising against official corruption, Son Pyŏnghŭi, the third patriarch, had gone into exile in Japan. He returned to form the Progressive Party, which then linked up with the Unity and Progress Society. Both went farther than the Independence Club in seeking members among rural farmers as well as city dwellers. Under Song Pyŏngjun, the Unity and Progress Society favored Japanese leadership in achieving reform and volunteered to assist Japanese forces during the Russo-Japanese War. Its collaboration led to a split with the Progressive Party. Another new religion with nationalist overtones was the Taejonggyo (Religion of Tan'gun Believers) that worshipped the progenitor of the Korean race.

The development of modern culture was inseparable from the rise in nationalism. The demand for education in Western learning with practical application for protecting Korea from foreign aggression led to the founding of at least 2,250 private academies across the country. Although most trained men, a few, founded by Koreans, educated women. Schools also provided venues for debates and campaigns that heightened the students' patriotism. Weaned from their addiction to Chinese culture, scholars studied Korean language, history, and literature. They also published books on nation-building experiences elsewhere in the world. Outside academe, the "new novel," a precursor to modern Korean fiction, emerged. Its protagonists advocated Korean independence and a new Korea founded on principles of social equality, equality of men and women, and replacement of superstition with rationality. Sung to the melodies of Western hymns or popular music, songs glorifying Korea spread nationalist sentiment across the country.

The Russo-Japanese War (1904–1905)

For years before war broke out, Russia and Japan contended for concessions inside Korea. In 1901, Japan made plans to complete the railway between Pusan and Seoul and build a connection from Seoul to Uiju, while Russia tried to expand its leasehold around the Yalu River. Owing to its growing mistrust of Russia, Japan entered into an alliance with Great Britain in 1902. This measure prevented Germany and France from supporting Russia in a repetition of the Triple Intervention of 1895 and opened the possibility of a war by Japan against Russia alone (see Chapter 22).

Despite a last-ditch appeal by Korea for neutralization of the Korean peninsula, when the Russo-Japanese War began in February 1904, Japan sent an invasion force to occupy Seoul. During the war, Japan appointed advisers to all the Korean ministries. Russia withdrew from Korea after its defeat in 1905. Britain extended its alliance with Japan and acknowledged Japan's freedom to take any action it saw fit in Korea, as did the United States .

Following the war, in November 1905, Japan established a protectorate over Korea. When Emperor Kojong and several of his ministers refused to sign the protectorate treaty, Itō Hirobumi, who was in charge of the negotiations with the Chosŏn court, ignored him and declared that a majority of ministers had approved it. Min Yonghwan of the Yŏhung Min clan and military aide to the emperor committed suicide in protest.

Itō headed the new residency general that Japan created for Korea. His vision was to maintain an "independent" Korean government that would willingly carry out institutional reforms under Japanese guidance. To this end, he used Japanese police and regular army units to maintain order while Emperor Kojong was left on the throne as a figurehead.

Despite Korean attempts to rally foreign opinion to its side, Japan outmaneuvered it. Emperor Kojong secretly sent messages to heads of European states for help in gaining independence. In 1907 the American missionary Homer Hulbert led a mission to the Second International Conference on Peace at the Hague to present Korea's case. The mission was refused admission because Korea had ceased to exist once it became a protectorate. Japan claimed to have become a civilized nation; according to international law, only civilized nations were deemed sovereign, and as a result of Japan's public relations campaign, Korea was seen as uncivilized.

Koreans launched fierce opposition to Itō's initiatives. When he dethroned Kojong in favor of his son, riots broke out in the street. Itō ordered the dissolution of the Korean army. The discharged soldiers began a guerrilla war that lasted for four years before it was crushed by superior Japanese forces, resulting in the loss of thousands of lives. At Itō's directive, the Korean Home Ministry took charge of peace preservation, banned freedom of association, and instituted censorship of newspapers and books. Itō's plan to maintain a facade of Japanese paternalism behind a nominally independent Korea finally failed in the face of Korean opposition. When he made a trip to Harbin to gain Russian acquiescence to Japan's determination to annex Korea, he was assassinated by An Chunggǔn, a Korean patriot. The new resident general, Terauchi Masatake, clamped down on all criticism of Japanese policy. On August 22, 1910, Korea became Japan's colony, as announced to Koreans on August 29.

JAPANESE COLONIAL RULE (1910–1945)

Japan's colonial rule went through three phases. The first was the period of military rule from 1910 to 1919, during which Japan created a police state called the Government-General (GG) of Chōsen. It eliminated all Korean political participation, restricted Korean business activity, and invested heavily in the promotion of rice cultivation for export to Japan. It instituted flogging as punishment for minor offenses even though it had been banned in Japan in 1882. In addition, the GG granted extensive authority to the police to use violence on the spot, levy fines, detain suspects for long periods, and use torture in interrogation.

Despite suppression, Korean nationalist movements continued. At first they worked underground, mainly through religious groups organized by Christians, new religions, and Buddhists because Japan was reluctant to persecute Christianity and offend Western nations. They erupted on March 1, 1919, when thirty-three patriots signed a Declaration of Independence and marched peacefully to the Japanese authorities to petition for liberation. They had been inspired by Woodrow Wilson's call for self-determination for people subject to foreign rule following World War I, and they expected support from the United States and other Western powers. In contrast to earlier political clubs, the participants in the March First Movement came from all walks of life and from all over the country, marking a significant spread of national consciousness.

The March First Movement forced Japan to change its policy. At first it responded to nonviolent demon-strations with mass arrests and executions. Then it shifted to a "cultural government" policy, which allowed a certain degree of freedom of speech and association and permitted the establishment of Korean businesses. That policy marked the second phase of colonial rule and lasted until the Manchurian Incident of 1931, when the Japanese army in Manchuria launched a coup d'état against the Chinese governor and established the puppet state of Manchukuo.

The third phase lasted from the Manchurian Incident to the defeat of Japan by the United States in 1945 (see **Connections: World War II**). During this period, Japan invested huge amounts of capital in heavy industry and infrastructure in Korea in support of Japan's wars. Japan severely repressed the freedoms that had flourished in the 1920s. After 1937 it instituted military conscription, forced labor, and Korean assimilation to Japan. It forced Koreans to use the Japanese language, worship the Japanese emperor in Shinto shrines, and adopt Japanese names in an effort to eradicate Korean identity.

Scholars' views of Korea's colonial period generally divide into two broad categories. The first takes a negative view of Japan, focusing on its tyranny, its exploitation of the Korean economy, its reduction of the mass of the population to bare subsistence, its prevention of modern industrial development, and its attempt to obliterate Korean culture without granting equal citizenship rights. The second fits the colonial experience into major trends that lasted to the end of the twentieth century. These trends included abolishing inherited social status as a barrier to advancement; liberating women from male domination; introducing modern mass education for both sexes; fostering the appearance of mass media and popular culture; creating a modern economy through heavy investment in railroads, bridges, and harbors; establishing a modern financial sector in the 1920s; and industrializing the peninsula in the 1930s. A small middle class of businessmen and shopkeepers arose, and a half-million farmers were converted to factory workers and miners. In retrospect, the most important economic contribution was Japan's use of state-led industrialization involving planning and controls of all kinds in the process of late industrialization to catch up to the advanced economies of Western imperialists. This process, now known as developmentalism, was a far cry from the free-market capitalism of Britain and the United States, but it opened the eyes of some Koreans to economic development without liberal democracy.

March First Movement. Japan's initial response to the March 1 movement was repression—the mass execution of demonstrators performed in public. *(Roger-Viollet)*

The Land Survey

Colonial economic policy aimed at expanding agricultural production by investment in reclamation, irrigation, chemical fertilizer, and the introduction of new seeds to grow rice for export to Japan. To create an efficient land tax for raising revenue, the colonial government adopted a land registration program in 1911 to record the owners of all land. Korean nationalists and scholars have condemned this policy as a sham designed to transfer land from Korean owners to Japanese by force or guile. Japan justified it on the grounds that Chosŏn Dynasty law had not clearly defined landownership. Private landownership had been the economic basis of the Korean elite at least for a thousand years, but security of tenure was weak because judges in civil cases were district magistrates from *yangban* families who defended landlord inter-

ests. Written evidence of landownership existed in the form of deeds, inheritance documents, bills of sale, and state registers of land, but not every owner possessed them. Because landowners had not registered their land with the state to avoid taxes, the government lacked funds to modernize its military and fund development projects.

At first the land investigation program did not result in a major transfer of land from Korean to Japanese hands. From 1910 to 1925, Korea experienced an economic boom and a rise in the price of rice. Korean landlords, most of whom were *yangban*, fared far better than sharecroppers, and Japan succeeded in winning *yangban* landlords' compliance to colonial rule by granting them noble titles and guaranteeing their private property rights. As a result, landlords took little part in the development of active nationalist resistance to Japanese rule.

Conditions changed following the world depression of 1929. Indebted smallholders lost their land to Japanese creditors. By 1940 the price of rice had dropped to 39 percent of the 1925 price. Korean farmers who both owned and rented land earned a reasonable living, but pure tenants did not. Rice consumption declined because of exports to Japan, and although the diet was supplemented by millet from Manchuria, Koreans perceived this as a serious deprivation of their favorite staple food.

Farmers took political measures to protect their livelihood. Established in 1924, the Chosŏn Labor-Farmer General Alliance supported the many tenant disputes of the 1920s and tried to wage class struggle against the capitalist class. Farmers later left to form their own General Korean Farmer Alliance. Middling farmers, rather than the poorest sharecroppers, led the tenant disputes and demanded reduction in sharecropping fees from 50 to 40 percent or less of the crop. Most tenant disputes ended favorably before 1925. After 1929 many smallholders went bankrupt. The percentage of tenant households increased from 41 to 50 percent of the farm population in the 1930s, and the number of tenant unions increased from about 30 in 1922 to 1,301 in 1933. In the early 1930s sixty-nine radical farmer unions challenged local officials. In 1933 the Japanese government instituted the Tenancy Mediation Law to resolve tenant disputes in the courts, and many were resolved in favor of tenants. After Japan ended its policy of promoting rice production in 1934, agriculture declined steadily to 1945. Farmers took the route of passive resistance—failing to fulfill contracts or hiding crops from the authorities. After Japan attacked Pearl Harbor in 1941, the GG banned all tenant protest, exacerbating sharecropper resentment.

The colonial government encouraged Korean migration to northeastern Manchuria to ease rural distress and expand Japan's influence. Unlike Chinese farmers, Korean settlers had access to loans from Japanese banks that enabled them to invest in better tools and seeds. They obtained favorable rates for buying land and support for forming agrarian cooperatives. Southern Manchuria was different; there Koreans lacked rights to own property or even to work. Japanese officials in the northeast protected Koreans in disputes with the indigenous population, so long as Koreans retained passports issued by colonial authority and did not become naturalized Chinese citizens. Koreans accepted this arrangement because it allowed them to retain their Korean identity. By 1942 approximately 1.5 million Koreans had settled in Manchuria, where they provided shelter for anti-Japanese political movements. In Chinese eyes, they were agents of Japan.

The Growth of Korean Industry

In the 1920s, Korean businesses emerged despite limited capital resources. Large landlords launched a number of small-scale enterprises—for example, the Kyŏngbang textile corporation founded by Kim Yŏnsu and Kim Songsu, members of a landlord family from Chŏlla province in the southwest. The Kim brothers used capital accumulated from tenant rents to establish the company; when it was threatened by bankruptcy, they turned to Japanese banks for working capital that saved the company and allowed it to expand. They also received help from Japanese trading companies in marketing products. The GG provided protection by allowing the Kims' company to carve out a niche in the cheap textile sector for the Korean economy while Japanese textile companies produced more expensive goods. It also summoned the Kims to offer their opinions in economic policy councils.

Most Korean companies in dyeing, paper, leather, ceramics, milling, and brewing were undercapitalized small-scale operations that supplied goods for the domestic market. Korean-owned breweries supplied half the domestic market demand. Landlords and rich merchants from south Chŏlla province capitalized Tong'a Rubber Company with three hundred thousand yen, and a Korean merchant raised fifty thousand yen to found the Pando Rubber company. By 1930, Korean rubber plants outnumbered Japanese thirty to seventeen. The dominant industry in Korean hands other than cheap textiles was food processing. Most Korean metal factories were no more than blacksmiths' shops.

Japanese investment in Korea dwarfed the paid-in capital of Korean firms. Japan Steel had a big plant at Kyŏmip'o, and Japan Mining had a smelting plant at Chinnamp'o. The Japanese *zaibatsu* Mitsui founded the Sansei Mining Company, Mitsubishi the Chōsen Anthracite Company, and Noguchi the Chōsen Nitrogen Company to make fertilizer. Japanese firms also established chemical, electrical, textile, mining, and railroad companies. They provided hydroelectric power, railroad lines from Pusan to Sin'uiju on the Manchurian border, and cement, chemicals, and the like for export to China. Japanese businesses purchased large amounts of forest land and invested in cotton textiles, food processing, brewing, milling, paper, and printing. While some argue that Japan took an economic interest in Korea to obtain raw materials and markets for its exports, Japan invested more than it ever received in profits because it put strategic and political objectives first.

In the 1930s, Japan built up both infrastructure and industry to support its puppet state of Manchukuo and to supply essential equipment to its military stationed there. By 1941, over 90 percent of the capital invested in Korean industry came from Japan. A south-to-north railroad trunk line funneled goods from both Japan and Korea into Manchuria and, after the outbreak of the Sino-Japanese War in 1937, to China. Heavy investment in hydroelectric power plants along the Yalu River and elsewhere and power lines throughout the country provided energy for steel, chemical, machinery, metal, and machine factories to support Japan's war effort. Most weapons were manufactured in Japan, leaving the Korean machine industry repairs, vehicles, and shipbuilding. Japan subsidized the Mitsui, Mitsubishi, and Sumitomo *zaibatsu* to mine copper, zinc, manganese, tungsten, molybdenum, and other metals for military purposes. The average annual growth in Korea's industrial production in the 1930s was 15 percent, almost double the rate from 1910 to 1928.

Koreans continued to develop small-scale businesses. They owned about a fifth of metal, machine, tools, and chemical plants as well as ceramics kilns and wood and lumber mills; roughly half of pharmaceutical companies, rice mills, and printing; over 70 percent of beverages; and over 90 percent of textile firms. Kyŏngbang Textile Corporation took advantage of Japanese expansion to set up textile plants in Manchuria and buy a textile plant in Nanjing after the Nanjing massacre of 1937. When Kyŏngbang had labor problems over wages and working conditions, it summoned Japanese police to put down strikes. Other businessmen such as Min T'aesik, Min Kyusik, and Pak Hŭngsik received financing from the Japanese Development Bank. Pak established the Hwasin Department Store and became one of Korea's wealthiest businessmen. Yi Pyŏngch'ŏl started with a rice mill and then prospered in the liquor business.

After liberation in 1945, businessmen such as the Kim brothers of Kyŏngbang Corporation garnered a reputation for being "national capitalists." It was said

that they placed the welfare of the Korean nation above collaboration for profit, even though the evidence shows that they became full partners in Japanese imperialism on the continent. Korean businessmen could not have prospered or survived unless they cooperated with Japan, but recently they have been condemned for collaboration.

Although Japan did not aim to improve the welfare of the Korean population, Korea became industrialized. Korean capitalists became the core of a new bourgeoisie, and a minuscule proletariat expanded to about five hundred thousand by the time Japan was defeated in 1945, not counting factory workers, miners, and other forced laborers in Japan and Manchuria. With farmers abandoning their homes for higher-paying jobs, the expansion of industry stimulated urbanization. Korea was beginning to take on the lineaments of an advanced industrial economy, with most Koreans as the underclass.

Education and Modern Mass Culture

In the 1920s, the liberalization allowed by the colonial government came hedged with restrictions. The GG allowed the publication of newspapers, magazines, and books in Korean, but it subjected all publications to the sharp eyes of Japanese censors. It expanded primary education, but it limited the number of Korean private schools and restricted compulsory education to the first few grades. It founded a single university in Seoul as part of the imperial university system, Keijō (Kyŏngsŏng in Korean) Imperial University, but it allowed only a small minority of well-to-do students to attend it or colleges in Japan. Despite its aim to assimilate Koreans to Japanese culture, it established separate (and better) schools for Japanese students in Korea.

The coming of modernity opened opportunities for women. Urban women took the lead in promoting new standards of hygiene and sanitation in rural areas, just as they did in Japan. Women established education centers, including night schools in churches and rural areas, to educate the illiterate. Women founded Sŏngjukhae (Pine and Bamboo Society) in 1910 to foster national consciousness. Buddhist women organized the Buddhist Women's Association in 1920. Helen Kim, a Christian and the first person to receive the doctorate in Korean history (from Columbia University in 1929), and other women from Ewha

School took a tour of rural areas to enlighten the public before the police put a stop to their efforts. She and Kim Pilye organized the Korean YWCA in 1922. Many women received training in nursing either in Japan or at the Women's Medical College under the missionary nurse Margaret Edmond. The first women's medical school, the Kyŏngsŏng Medical College, was founded in 1928. The GG hired female clerical workers; private industry put women in factories.

The civil code promulgated under Japanese auspices in 1912 generally confirmed traditional practices regarding male succession to family headship, ownership of property, and the sole right of men to initiate divorce. In 1918 women were given the right to petition for divorce, provided they had approval from both their husband and parents. A 1922 ordinance elevated the minimal age of marriage for women to fifteen, banned polygamy and concubinage, and allowed a woman to divorce her husband for polygamy or adultery, commission of a crime, insult, or abandonment for three years. These provisions did not halt discriminatory practices against women.

Women found a public voice. In the 1920s two women's journals began publication: Kim Wŏnju's *The New Woman* and Na Hyesŏk's *Women's World*. Socialist women's groups appeared in 1924. They and nonsocialist women demanded abolition of early marriage, female slavery, licensed prostitution, and wage discrimination.

Korean literature in the vernacular flourished with support from the New Culture Movement launched by Korean nationalists. One founder of the Kyŏngbang Corporation, Kim Sŏngsu, established the *East Asia Daily* newspaper and Posŏng Normal School (later Koryŏ University). Influenced by Tolstoy, Yi Kwangsu published the first modern novel, *Heartless* in 1917, followed by *Rebirth*, *Earth*, and many others. Hyŏn Chin'gŏn portrayed the suffering of common men and women under traditional customs and colonial rule. His novel about a Paekche general who resisted Tang armies was banned. Kim Tongin established *Creation* magazine in 1919 and wrote about the denizens of the slums and the life of a shaman. Yi Hyosŏk joined the KAPF (Korean Art Proletarian Federation) literary movement from 1928 to 1932. Like almost all other members of KAPF, he abandoned socialism to write about itinerant peddlers and the anomie produced by urban life. In 1936, Yi Sang wrote a stream-of-consciousness story, "Wings," about

a solipsistic husband who dealt with his wife's prostitution by sealing his mind from the shame of external facts.

Korea's modern mass media began during the colonial period. For the first decade after annexation, Japan monopolized film production. With the beginning of "cultural government" policy, the first Korean films appeared: *Righteous Revenge* (1919) directed by Kim Tosan and *Plighted Love Under the Moon* (1923) directed by Yun Paengnam. There were close to 9 million moviegoers by 1935. Despite censorship, the movies *Ari-rang* (1926) and *Searching for Love* (1928), directed by Na Un'gyu, and *Wandering* (1928), by Kim Yuyŏng, produced by the KAPF told stories of oppression of farmers by landlords and the evils of Japanese imperialism. Linked to the movie by the same name, *Ari-rang* is the best known of Korean songs. It tells of partings—of lovers kept apart by a hill, of workers dragooned from their homes to rebuild the Kyŏngbok Palace, of Koreans separated from their nation. Before Japan banned Korean films in 1935, the Korean film industry had produced some 160 silent movies.

Radio broadcasting began in 1927 under the Japanese Korean Broadcasting Company. Korean-language programs expanded from one-third to one-half of airtime, and in 1933 the first all-Korean station was allowed. It devoted many programs to Korean history, science, the arts, international affairs, translations of Western plays, popular songs with a distinct Korean flavor, and instruction in the use of *han'gul* and the standardization of Korean grammar. Even after the ban on the use of Korean in public in 1938, GG tolerated Korean-language programs. In the 1930s newspapers, mass-circulation magazines, films, and radio spread the tastes in fashion and fiction of the admittedly tiny urban middle class to a wider audience and signaled the arrival of a growing consumer culture.

The Rise of Communism and Militant Nationalism

The colonial period spurred Koreans to debate different definitions of national identity. Some intellectuals looked back on Korea's past and saw only a sad history of subservience, both political and cultural, to China. Students radicalized in Japan returned to Korea to organize study groups with socialist agendas. Militant nationalists viewed the colonial period in black-and-white terms: one was either a true patriot willing to die for national liberation and independence or a collaborator who worked with the Japanese and gained riches as a landlord or businessman. They therefore expected a struggle against Japanese rule to kill two birds with one stone by overthrowing the Japanese and Korean capitalists and landlords and achieving Korean independence. In their eyes, Korea needed militancy and struggle as healthy antidotes to its long history of subjugation to Chinese power and culture. Although the colonial government moderated the harshness of its first decade of rule, it increased the number of police and intensified surveillance. It also hoped to co-opt potential militants and convert them to the harmless pursuit of educational and cultural projects.

The movement to establish a Korean Provisional Government (KPG) in exile with a provisional national assembly began in April 1919 in Shanghai. The assembly drew up a constitution for a Great Korean People's Republic. In 1922 it chose Syngman Rhee (Yi Sungman) as president. Yi Tonghwi, a guerrilla commander in 1907 who later joined the Communist party in Vladivostok, became prime minister. This KPG combined radical left-wing and conservative right-wing elements. Yi Tonghwi favored military action against Japan, while Rhee preferred diplomacy to sway the United States and other powers to intervene on behalf of Korean independence. Yi Tonghwi soon left Shanghai in disdain and returned to Manchuria to resume armed struggle. Rhee went to work in the United States.

Between 1919 and 1924, about fifty Korean anarchists formed a terrorist group, the Ŭiyŏltan (Righteous Heroes), which carried out three hundred acts of violence. After two failed assassination attempts, all three hundred members were exterminated by Japanese police. Patriot and anarchist Sin Ch'aeho founded the Anarchist Black Youth League in 1921. It dissolved in 1924.

In contrast to the anarchists, Korean nationalists such as authors Yi Kwangsu, Yun Ch'iho, and others believed that the Korean public lacked national consciousness and needed more education before forming the basis for a viable nationalist movement. Yi's slogan, "Reconstruction!", meant just that. He and the others, known as "cultural nationalists," postponed national independence into the indefinite future.

Communists and radical noncommunist nationalists claimed that cultural nationalism was tantamount to outright collaboration. Their intense nationalism was the product of a new awareness of the long history of Korea's past of supine subordination to Chinese dynasties and Chinese culture, particularly to the Confucian ethical justification of tributary relations. Writers such as Sin Ch'aeho began a new historiographical tradition of extolling examples of militancy and resistance in the Koguryŏ Dynasty and the leading military heroes of the Korean past. Soon after the Russian Revolution of 1917, Nam Man-ch'un formed the first Korean Communist party (KCP) in Irkutsk in Siberia. The early Korean communists were divided geographically between groups in Moscow, Siberia, Manchuria, Shanghai, and Korea proper. Inside Korea, communists supported strikes and succeeded in establishing a Korean Communist party in 1925. Japanese police broke it up, and the communists abandoned the attempt in 1928.

In the eyes of Korean nationalists, Marxist-Leninist theory offered a powerful interpretation of their nation's plight. They were attracted to Lenin's economic explanation of the rise of imperialism as the product of monopoly capitalism, capitalism's last stage, in which core capitalist states, having saturated their domestic markets, sought colonies around the globe to provide cheap raw materials and markets for their manufactured products. This theory thus fitted Korea into a universal system of historical development. Korean communists believed that the struggle against Japan would lead simultaneously to the overthrow of capitalism and national liberation. In practical terms, the Soviet Union was the only country offering monetary and spiritual support to Koreans and other national liberation movements.

Establishing Communist parties meant accepting direction from the Comintern in Moscow. As it had in China, the Comintern decided that Korea was still in a "feudal" stage of development without a proletariat, and it pushed the Korean communists to form a united front with bourgeois nationalists to achieve a bourgeois-democratic revolution. Although Korean communists opposed joining class enemies in a united front, they capitulated to Comintern pressure and joined the New Root Society in 1927, only a couple of months before Chiang Kaishek, the leader of the Chinese Nationalist Party, attacked his communist allies (see Chapter 24). In 1927, women organized the Friends of the Rose of Sharon, which included some socialists and cooperated with the New Root Society. It helped organize strikes and tenancy disputes. It planned a nationwide protest demonstration after an anti-Japanese student protest movement broke out in Kwangju in Chŏlla province in 1929, but police arrested the leaders before it could take place. Thereafter, New Root Society's headquarters turned more moderate, even deciding to support the Korean self-government movement and use the legal system to improve conditions. Dissatisfied with this appeasement, communist members called for the Society's dissolution in December 1930. The women's organization also closed down.

Manchuria

During the 1920s, the Government General of Korea encouraged Koreans to set up their own institutions to govern themselves in Manchuria. The Korean Association provided aid for the poor, public facilities such as cemeteries, public hygiene to control contagious diseases, instruction in farming methods, management of irrigation systems, education, and cultural activities. About 84 percent of the population joined. The Korean Association oversaw the Financial Association that made loans to rich landlords at reasonable rates. The Mutual Aid Association made small loans to tenant farmers. Although these organizations functioned for Japan's benefit as a colonial power, they also provided cover for their leaders to support anti-Japanese activities.

Koreans who resisted Japanese imperialism moved back and forth across national boundaries. They began in Manchuria in 1919, only to be chased into the Soviet Union's Maritime Province by Japanese forces. There Korean military units joined the Soviet Red Army in battles against the Japanese army dispatched to Siberia in 1918 to attack the new Soviet regime. Confrontation ended when the Soviet Union reached a peace agreement with Japan in 1921.

In 1932, the Japanese army in Manchuria established the puppet regime of Manchukuo. Later that year, Kim Il Sung (Kim Ilsŏng), the future leader of the Democratic People's Republic of Korea, organized a small guerrilla unit of eighteen men in northern Manchuria. Jiandao in south Manchuria just north of the Yalu River, where Koreans composed 76 percent of the population, became the center of anti-Japanese activity. In 1934, Chu Chin, one of four guerrilla commanders in the area, led the nine hundred men of the Second Division of the Northeast People's Revolutionary Army in hundreds of engagements against Japan.

In 1934, Korean communist guerrillas faced a series of crises. Koreans disaffected with radical reform created self-defense leagues against "bandits." Chinese communists in Manchuria had incorporated Korean communists in their ranks but insisted that they devote themselves to China's struggle against Japan and not dilute the effort by attacking Japanese in Korea. Accusing their Korean communist allies of being spies for Japan, they began a purge that killed anywhere from five hundred to two thousand Korean communists. The Korean patriot Kim San was sent to Manchuria to help smooth relations between Chinese and Korean communists but was himself arrested (see **Biography: Kim San**). Persecution continued until March 1935, when the Chinese General Wei Zhengmin called a halt. There is circumstantial evidence that Kim Il Sung, who was fluent in Chinese and close friends with Wei, played a crucial role in persuading him to stop.

Korean exiles in China and Manchuria disagreed on the best course of action to take against Japan. Allied with different factions in China's United Front, they also had to take their hosts' interests into account. In Manchuria, Kim Il Sung had a choice between forming his own unit to operate independently or keeping his unit with Chinese communist forces. Kim chose to keep his men with a Chinese unit because it afforded a better chance of survival, even though he has been criticized for subservience to Chinese interests. On June 4, 1937, he launched the most successful guerrilla raid against the Japanese in the Korean peninsula at Poch'ŏnbo, just south of the Yalu River. He occupied it for a day, retreated, defeated a pursuing Japanese police contingent, and a few days later joined another force to attack the Yokoyama timber camp. Although Japan followed the attack with a bloody reprisal against the town, Kim earned a reputation for daring heroism.

After Japan initiated war with China in 1937, it looked to Korea for support. The colonial government requisitioned Koreans for forced labor in Japanese and Manchurian mines and factories (see **Material Culture: A Colonial Gold Mine**), recruited young men into the Japanese army, and abducted or enticed thousands of Korean women with false promises of jobs and then forced them to become "comfort women" for Japanese troops in active theaters

BIOGRAPHY Kim San

Kim San (a pseudonym for Chang Chi-rak, 1905–?) was one of many Korean patriots who became a communist to fight for Korean national liberation against Japanese imperialism. He did it by moving to China and joining the Chinese communist movement because it was easier to fight Japanese imperialism there than in Korea. In 1937 he was in Mao Zedong's base in Yan'an in northwest China when Helen Foster Snow, journalist Edgar Snow's wife, interviewed him and transcribed his life story into English.

Born to a poor farmer family in 1905 just south of Pyongyang, seven-year-old Kim San was shocked in 1912 when two Japanese policemen came to his home where they slapped and bloodied his mother's face because she had delayed reporting for a vaccination. His mother brought him up as a Christian and provided personal warmth. His father's detachment and harsh discipline turned him away from Confucianism and caused him to run away to live with a married brother nearby.

In grammar school Kim San admired the anti-Japanese guerrillas. He entered a Christian middle school but left at the age of fourteen to join the March First Movement of 1919. Amazed at the passive reaction of Christians who prayed while Japanese police bloodied unarmed civilians, he abandoned Christianity, belief in God, and trust in nonviolence.

Kim San attended school in Tokyo where he met Japanese anarchists and Marxists. He left his studies there and traveled to Manchuria to attend a Korean Nationalist military school for three months. In 1920 he moved to Shanghai and then in 1921 to Beijing, where he attended the Union Medical College for over three years. He studied Marxist theory, joined the Korean Communist

Youth Organization, and then he left school to join the Chinese Nationalists when the Canton uprising occurred in 1925. After Chiang Kaishek massacred communists in Shanghai in 1927, Kim joined communists in the Canton commune. The Nationalists forced him to flee Canton to the Hailufeng Soviet nearby in 1928. He later had to escape from Hailufeng through the mountains, where his health was ruined from exposure, malaria, and tuberculosis.

Kim San returned to Beijing to become secretary of the Beijing Communist party. When he was sent to Manchuria in 1932 to smooth relations between Chinese and Korean communists, he was arrested and subjected to water torture for forty days. Released because he refused to confess membership in the Communist party, he returned to Beijing only to suffer impeachment by fellow Communists for leftist deviation in 1931 and rightist deviation the next year! In 1933, Chinese Nationalists held him under arrest for a brief period. After he recovered from a suicidal depression, he moved to Mao's headquarters in Yan'an in 1937. After that date, neither he nor his two wives and child were ever heard of again.

Kim San summarized his career as a revolutionary as follows:

My whole life has been a series of failures, and the history of my country has been a history of failure. I have had only one victory—over myself. This one small victory, however, is enough to give me confidence to go on. Fortunately, the tragedy and defeat I have experienced have not broken but strengthened me. I have few illusions left, but I have not lost faith in men and in the ability of men to create history.[1]

---

[1] Nym Wales, *Song of Ariran* (San Francisco: Rampart Press, 1941), p. 315.

of operations in China, Manchuria, the South Sea islands, and Southeast Asia. Some young Korean men took to the hills to evade forced labor and military conscription, but most were trapped. Then there was Park Chung Hee (Pak Chunghŭi), the dictator of South Korea from 1961 to 1979, who graduated

from a military academy in Japan and became an officer in the Japanese army in Manchuria to do battle against opponents of Japanese colonialism, including Korean guerrillas. Once Japan's industrial base became the target of bombs toward the end of the war, Japan started building more factories in Man-

Comfort Women. Korean comfort women photographed in China at the end of the war. Note that the woman on the right is pregnant. *(National Archives)*

churia and northern Korea. Korean manufacturers took advantage of Japan's need for supplies to earn handsome profits and the ire of their compatriots.

Koreans who continued the struggle for independence had to move outside of Japanese-controlled territories. Kim Il Sung fought skirmishes in Manchuria against Japan between 1937 and 1940 until Japan eliminated the Chinese communist armies in Manchuria and forced him to cross into Russian territory by March 1941. Kim's men joined Chinese guerrillas in a Russian training camp near Vladivostok, and Kim was appointed major in the new 88th Division of the Far Eastern Command of the Soviet army. Korean communists in China commanded the Korean Volunteer Corps. Others commanded Chinese units under Mao Zedong in Yan'an. Noncommunist nationalists such as Kim Ku fought with Chinese Nationalist forces. An Ch'angho organized the Corps for Promoting Scholars in Los Angeles in 1911 and joined the Korean Provisional Government in

Shanghai, He was arrested in 1932 and sent to jail in Korea. Syngman Rhee spent two decades in the United States to gain support for Korean liberation. In the end, neither communists nor noncommunists succeeded in obtaining Korea's independence, nor did any leaders agree on how to shape Korea's future.

SUMMARY

What were the effects of Japanese colonial rule on Korea? By allowing Korean landlords and businessmen to flourish, it established models for successful enterprises. By breaking down hereditary status barriers, it opened opportunities to people previously blocked from upward mobility. By introducing modern education, it introduced some Koreans to science, foreign languages, and social science, and it enabled the birth of modern mass culture. It also forced

MATERIAL CULTURE

A Colonial Gold Mine

In the name of industrialization, Japan opened mines in Korea and Manchuria to provide raw materials for factories. Rather than use machinery or develop new, initially more expensive techniques, Japan relied on labor intensification—pickaxes, not bulldozers; manpower, not trucks. This photograph clearly shows the labor hierarchy, with workers scraping at the soil or carrying rocks on their backs, a foreman giving directions and, standing on the bank above, a manager in Western-style hat. The only sign of mechanization is the cogwheel behind him. The Korean laborers received lower wages than those paid to Japanese, even when they did the same type of work. Treatment was so harsh that many Koreans went into hiding or took refuge in the hills to avoid it.

Korean Miners. Korean miners mobilized by Japan during the 1930s for mining alluvial gold in South Chŏlla province. *(Sajinuro ponun Choson sidae: Saenghwal kwa p'ungsok* [The Choson Period in Pictures: Life and Customs] *Seoul: Somundang, 1986, volume on* Independence Movement Through Pictures II, *p. 120)*

the migration of millions of Koreans from their village communities to Japanese factories and mines across the Japanese empire. It eliminated meaningful participation in the political process. It encouraged a growing economic gap between capitalist industrialists and wealthy landlords versus a new proletariat and a mass of sharecropping tenants. In short, Japanese colonialism produced wealth and poverty, acceptance and animosity, revolutionary potential and conservative reaction.

Remaking China (1900–1927)

The first decade of the twentieth century was a period of rapid change in China, especially in cities and among the educated. Chinese cities were being paved, lighted, and policed. The Qing court announced plans for gradual transition to a constitutional monarchy. Voluntary reform societies tackled problems like foot binding and opium smoking. Then, in 1911, the Qing Dynasty was overthrown. Although the dynasty handed over its armies to the republican government under Yuan Shikai, military unity was soon lost, and regional armies and warlords competed to secure bases. In the 1920s, the Nationalist Party under Sun Yatsen built a base in Guangdong, and in 1926 launched the Northern Expedition, which reunified the country.

Nationalism was central to much of the cultural activity of this period. Patriots wanted to reconstitute China as a nation of the Chinese people and make it strong enough to stand up to foreign threats. A new type of intellectual emerged: trained at modern universities or abroad, deeply concerned with China's fate, and attracted to Western ideas ranging from science and democracy to anarchism and communism. Young people attacked old social norms, especially filial piety and arranged marriages. The encounters between new and old and East and West stimulated a literary and scholarly renaissance.

Understanding these changes has been the central goal of most of the research on this period. Who led the way in the changes to the Chinese economy, education, and political organization? How was resistance to change overcome? What role did foreign countries play? Did the militarization of society slow down or speed up other changes? Which changes were felt even by farmers in the countryside?

Map 24.1   Northern Expedition and Warlords

THE END OF MONARCHY

As the twentieth century opened, the Qing Dynasty needed to regain the people's confidence after the debacle brought on by its support of the Boxers and the imperialists' subsequent intervention. It faced a fiscal crisis. The Boxer Protocol of 1901 imposed a staggering indemnity of 450 million silver dollars, twice as large as the one exacted by Japan a few years earlier and nearly twice the government's annual revenues. It was to be paid from customs revenue in thirty-nine annual installments, with interest. When interest on existing foreign loans was added, the debts absorbed all of the customs revenue. Little was left for the ordinary operation of the government, much less investment in modernization.

Local Activism

Forced to look after their own interests, local elites increasingly took on modernization projects. They set up new schools and started periodicals, which by one estimate increased tenfold from 1901 to 1910. Interest in Western forms of government was growing as people asked how the European powers and

Japan had gained wealth and power. Yan Fu, one of the first to study in England, published translations of books such as J. S. Mill's *On Liberty* (1903) and Montesquieu's *The Spirit of Laws* (1909). Yan Fu argued that the Western form of government freed the energy of the individual, which could then be channeled toward national goals. As he saw it, the West had achieved wealth and power through a complex package, a key part of which was a very differently conceived nation-state. Yan Fu once commented that only 30 percent of China's troubles were caused by foreigners; the rest were its own fault and could be remedied by its own actions.

Interest in Western forms of government did not translate into positive feelings toward the Western powers, which were seen as gaining a stranglehold on the Chinese economy. Activists solicited funds to buy back railroads built by foreign firms. Between 1905 and 1907, there were boycotts of the United States for its immigration restriction law and its mistreatment of Chinese at the 1904 World's Fair in Saint Louis. In treaty ports, protests were staged over Westerners' extraterritoriality. Some protesters even talked of waging their own opium war after the British refused to stop shipping opium to China on the grounds that opium cultivation in China had not been fully eradicated.

In this period, Japan served as an incubator of Chinese nationalism. By 1906, of the thirteen thousand students studying abroad, ten thousand were in Tokyo. The experience of living in a foreign country, where they felt humiliated by China's weakness and backwardness, aroused nationalistic feelings in the students, who often formed groups to discuss how Japan had modernized so rapidly and what could be done in China. One student newspaper reported, "Japanese schools are as numerous as our opium dens, Japanese students as numerous as our opium addicts."[1] The two best-known reformers, Kang Youwei and Liang Qichao, had settled in Japan. In Chinese magazines published in Japan, Liang promoted the idea that China could become strong through "democracy," which to him meant a government that drew its strength from the people, but not necessarily a representative government or one that defended individual rights. Liang had traveled in the United States for five months in 1903 and found the American

form of populist democracy unsatisfactory. He preferred the statist ideas and constitutional monarchies of Japan and Germany. When Japan defeated Russia in 1905 (see Chapter 22), some reformers drew the inference that Japan's constitutional form of government had enabled it to best autocratic Russia.

The Anti-Manchu Revolutionary Movement

Ever since the late nineteenth century, some people had argued that the root of China's problems lay in its subjugation by a different "race": the Manchus. In 1903 the nineteen-year-old Zou Rong published an inflammatory tract calling for the creation of a revolutionary army to "wipe out the five million barbarian Manchus, wash away the shame of two hundred and sixty years of cruelty and oppression, and make China clean once again."[2] He described the "sacred Han race, descendants of the Yellow Emperor," as the slaves of the Manchus and in danger of extermination. The language of Social Darwinism, with its talk of countries in desperate competition for survival, seemed to many to describe China's plight accurately.

The anti-Manchu revolutionary who would eventually be mythologized as the founding figure of the Chinese republic was Sun Yatsen (Sun Zhongshan, 1866–1925). Like Hong Xiuquan, Kang Youwei, and Liang Qichao before him, Sun came from Guangdong province. Unlike them, he was neither from a literati family nor trained in the Confucian classics. Several of his close relatives had emigrated, and in 1879 he was sent to join a brother in Hawaii. Later he went to Hong Kong to study Western medicine, completing his degree in 1892. In Hong Kong, Sun and his friends began discussing the advantages of a republic. The best way to overthrow the Manchus, they concluded, would be to ally with the secret societies so pervasive in south China. Groups like the Triads were anti-Manchu, had large mass followings, and had an organizational base reaching from one province to another, making them an ideal base for an insurrection, they thought.

Sun set up the first two chapters of the Revive China Society in Hawaii and Hong Kong. The society's efforts to instigate an uprising with secret society members as the muscle never got very far, however. In

1. Cited in Douglas R. Reynolds, *China, 1898–1912: The Xinzheng Revolution and Japan* (Cambridge, Mass.: Harvard University Press, 1993), p. 62.

2. Cited in Michael Gasster, "The Republican Revolutionary Movement," in *Cambridge History of China*, vol. 11, pt. 2 (Cambridge: Cambridge University Press, 1980), p. 482.

1896, Sun cut off his queue and began wearing Western clothes. He spent time in England, where he discovered that many Westerners saw flaws in their own institutions and were advocating a variety of socialist solutions. Sun began to think that China could skip ahead of the West by going directly to a more progressive form of government. In Japan in 1905 some Japanese helped Sun join forces with the more radical of the student revolutionaries to form the Revolutionary Alliance. Despite the difference in social background, the students from educated families were excited by Sun's promise of quick solutions to China's problems. This alliance sponsored seven or eight attempts at uprisings over the next few years. Sun himself continued to spend most of his time abroad in search of funds and foreign backers, especially overseas Chinese.

In these years Sun worked out his theory of the Three People's Principles: nationalism (which opposed both rule by Manchus and domination by foreign powers), democracy (which to Sun meant elections and a constitution), and the "people's livelihood," a vague sort of socialism with equalization of landholdings and curbs on capital. Sun admitted that the Chinese people were unaccustomed to political participation; nevertheless, he believed that they could be guided toward democracy through a period of political tutelage, during which the revolutionaries would promulgate a provisional constitution and people would begin electing local officials.

The Manchu Reform Movement

Amid all this activism and agitation, the Manchu court began to edge in the direction of parliamentary government. Empress Dowager Cixi in 1901 announced the establishment of a national school system and called for putting questions about foreign government and science on the civil service examinations. In 1905 she took the momentous step of abolishing the civil service examination system altogether, a system that had set the framework for relations between the government and the elite for a millennium. New military academies were set up and new armies formed, trained by German or Japanese instructors. With the death of Li Hongzhang in 1901, Yuan Shikai emerged as the most powerful general, serving as both commander of the Northern Army and head of the Baoding Military Academy.

In 1905, Cixi approved sending a mission abroad to study constitutional forms of government. On its return the next year, the commission recommended the

Japanese model, which retained the monarchy and had it bestow the constitution on the country (rather than a constitution that made the people sovereign). In 1907 plans for national and provincial assemblies were announced, with a full constitution to be in place by 1917. The next year, the seventy-three-year-old Cixi died (the thirty-three-year-old Guangxu emperor had died suspiciously the day before). She had arranged for a three year old to succeed her. His regents did not prove to be particularly effective leaders and soon dismissed Yuan Shikai. Hope for a Japanese-style constitutional monarchy looked less and less promising.

Still, in 1909 assemblies met in each province and sent representatives to Beijing. Although less than 1 percent of the population had been allowed to vote, the elections generated excitement about participatory government. The provincial assemblies circulated three petitions calling for the immediate convening of the national assembly, the last reportedly signed by 25 million people. In 1910 the provisional national assembly met, with one hundred members elected by the provincial assemblies and one hundred appointed by the court. Anti-Manchu feelings rose, however, when in May 1911 the court announced the formation of a cabinet with eight Manchu, one Mongol, and only four Chinese members.

The 1911 Revolution

The Manchu court's efforts to institute reform from above satisfied very few, and in October 1911 a plot by revolutionaries finally triggered the collapse of the Qing Dynasty. In the city of Wuchang on the Yangzi River, a bomb accidentally exploded in the headquarters of a revolutionary group. When the police came to investigate, they found lists of the revolutionaries, including many officers of the new army division located there. Once the police set out to arrest those listed, the army officers, facing certain execution, staged a coup. The local officials fled, and the army took over the city in less than a day. The revolutionaries then telegraphed the other provinces asking them to declare their independence. Within six weeks, fifteen provinces had seceded.

The Qing court did not immediately capitulate. In desperation it turned to Yuan Shikai, whom the court had dismissed only a few years before, and asked him to mount a military campaign against the revolutionaries. Yuan went back and forth between the court and the revolutionaries, seeing what he could get from each. The biggest fear of the revolutionaries

Cutting Off a Queue. After the success of the 1911 revolution, soldiers often forced men to cut off their queues. *(Roger Viollet)*

was foreign intervention, and to avoid that they were willing to compromise. In the end, agreement was reached to establish a republic with Yuan as president; the emperor would abdicate, but he and his entourage would be allowed to remain in the Forbidden City, receive generous allowances, and keep much of their property. Thus, unlike the Bourbons in France or the Romanovs in Russia, the Manchu royal family suffered neither executions nor humiliations when it was deposed.

In February 1912, the last Qing emperor abdicated, and in March Yuan Shikai took over as president. As a mark of solidarity with the revolutionaries, men cut off their queues, the symbol of their subordination to the Manchus.

THE PRESIDENCY OF YUAN SHIKAI AND THE EMERGENCE OF THE WARLORDS

Yuan Shikai had strong credentials as a reformer of the old, self-strengthening type. While governor, he had initiated reforms in education, commerce, and

industry, and his army not only was equipped with modern weapons but also was trained along lines established by German and Japanese advisers. He believed in careful central planning of the sort Germany and Japan had shown could be effective. He was committed to a strong China but not a republican one. If local or provincial assemblies were empowered to act as they liked, how could China move rapidly toward a modern nation-state?

Yuan did not prevent parliamentary elections from being held in 1913, but when Sun Yatsen's new Nationalist party won a plurality of the seats, Yuan was unwilling to accept the outcome. The key Nationalist organizer, Song Jiaoren, was soon assassinated, and the shocked public assumed Yuan was responsible. Then Yuan, without consulting the national assembly, negotiated a $100 million loan from a foreign consortium. By summer the Nationalist party was organizing open revolt against Yuan, and seven provincial governments declared their independence. This second revolution ended in military rout, and Sun Yatsen and other Nationalist leaders once more fled to Japan. Yuan outlawed the Nationalist party; in 1914 he abolished all assemblies down to the county level, trying to nip participatory democracy in the bud.

Yuan did undertake some progressive projects, extending elementary education, suppressing opium cultivation, and promoting judicial reform. But he was out of touch with the mood of younger people, especially when he announced that Confucianism would be made the state religion. When in August 1915 he announced that he would become emperor, the educated and politically aware elite were outraged, their protests dying down only after Yuan died unexpectedly in June 1916.

During the decade after Yuan Shikai's death, China was politically fragmented. Without a central strongman, commanders in Yuan's old army, governors of provinces, and even gangsters built their own power bases. The outer regions of the Qing Empire, such as Tibet and Mongolia, declared their independence. Tibet soon fell under British sway and Mongolia under Russian. Manchuria was more and more dominated by Japan. In the far south, Sun Yatsen and his allies tried to build a power base for the Nationalist revolutionaries. A government of sorts was maintained in Beijing under the domination of whichever warlord held the region. It was hardly stable, however, with six different presidents and twenty-five successive cabinets. For a while, the key struggle seemed to be for control of the north, as the strongest warlords waged highly destructive wars across north China.

Warlords, not surprisingly, did little to maintain infrastructure or advance modernization. They disrupted rail lines and allowed the dikes on the Yellow River to deteriorate, leading to some catastrophic floods. They caused havoc in the countryside because the armies lived off the land, looting wherever they moved. One warlord reported, "My men would surround a village before dawn and fire several shots to intimidate the people. We told them to come out and give up. This was the classic way of raiding a village. Sometimes we killed and carried away little pigs. . . . We took corn, rice, potatoes, taro."[3] Because they also needed money to buy weapons, warlords instituted all sorts of new taxes. Foreign countries were more than willing to sell modern arms to the warlords, often backing their own favorite contender. Opium cultivation had been nearly eradicated in many places until the warlords entered the scene and forced peasants to grow it as a revenue source.

TOWARD A MORE MODERN CHINA

Social, cultural, and political change was rapid in the early decades of the twentieth century, some of it flowing directly from the pens of those advocating change of many sorts, some of it the direct or indirect consequence of changes in China's economy and political situation. Even forms of entertainment changed (see **Material Culture: Shanghai's Great World Pleasure Palace**).

The New Culture Movement

Young people who received a modern education felt that they had inherited the obligation of the literati to advise those in power. Their modern education, they believed, uniquely qualified them to "save" China. They had expected much of the 1911 revolution, only to have their hopes dashed.

The newly reorganized Beijing University played a central role in this New Culture movement. Chen Duxiu, the founder of the periodical *New Youth*, was appointed dean of letters. Chen had received a traditional education and had taken the civil service examinations before studying in Japan and France. A participant in the 1911 revolution, he became a zealous advocate of individual freedom. In the first issue

of *New Youth* in 1915, Chen challenged the long-standing Confucian value of deference toward elders. Youth, he asserted, was worth celebrating: "Youth is like early spring, like the rising sun, like the trees and grass in bud, like a newly sharpened blade." He urged his readers not to waste their "fleeting time in arguing with the older generation on this and that, hoping for them to be reborn and remodeled." They should think for themselves and not let the old contaminate them. In other articles, he wrote that Confucianism had to be rejected before China could attain equality and human rights: "We must be thoroughly aware of the incompatibility between Confucianism and the new belief, the new society, and the new state."[4] To him, "loyalty, filial piety, chastity, and righteousness" were nothing but "a slavish morality."[5] Young people responded enthusiastically to his attack on filial piety and began challenging the authority of their parents to make decisions for them about school, work, and marriage. Conflict between parents and their marriage-age children became extremely common as the young insisted on choosing their own spouses.

Soon leaders of the New Culture movement proposed ending use of the classical literary language that had been the mark of the educated person for two thousand years. The leader of the movement to write in the vernacular was Hu Shi, appointed to the faculty of Beijing University by Chen Duxiu after he returned from seven years studying philosophy in the United States. "A dead language," Hu declared, "can never produce a living literature."[6] Since Chinese civilization had been so closely tied to this language, Hu's assertions came dangerously close to declaring Chinese civilization dead. Hu Shi did recognize that the old written language had allowed speakers of mutually unintelligible dialects to communicate with each other and thus had been a source of unity, but he argued that once a national literature was produced in vernacular Chinese, a standard dialect would establish itself, much as standard vernaculars had gained hold in France and Germany. Chen Duxiu concurred

3. Cited in James E. Sheridan, *China in Disintegration* (New York: Free Press, 1975), p. 91.

4. Cited in Chow Tse-tsung, *The May Fourth Movement: Intellectual Revolution in Modern China* (Stanford: Stanford University Press, 1960), p. 482.

5. Ssu-yu Teng and John K. Fairbank, *China's Response to the West: A Documentary Survey* (New York: Atheneum, 1971), p. 241.

6. Cited in Leo Ou-fan Lee, "Literary Trends I: The Quest for Modernity, 1895–1927," in *Cambridge History of China*, vol. 12, ed. John K. Fairbank (Cambridge: Cambridge University Press, 1983), p. 467.

MATERIAL CULTURE

Shanghai's Great World Pleasure Palace

Commonplaces of modern life such as malls and window shopping were once new and controversial. In China, they usually appeared first in Shanghai. In 1917 an entrepreneur who had made his fortune in medicine built the Great World, a six-story amusement park touted as the Crystal Palace and Coney Island rolled into one. At the intersection of two major roads in the International District, from the outside it seemed an agglomeration of European building motifs with columns holding up a decorative tower. Inside, it catered more to Chinese tastes, and its customers were primarily Chinese. On the first floor were gaming tables, slot machines, magicians, acrobats, sing-song girls, and fans, incense, fireworks, and other miscellaneous things for sale. On the next floor were restaurants as well as acting troupes, midwives, barbers, and earwax extractors. The third floor had photographers, jugglers, ice cream parlors, and girls in high-slit dresses. The fourth floor had masseurs, acupuncturists, and dancers. The fifth floor had storytellers, peep shows, scribes who composed love letters, and a temple. On the top floor were tightrope walkers, places to play mahjong, lottery tickets, and marriage brokers.

Great World Pleasure Palace. The building is seen here in a photo from the 1920s. *(Shanghai Historical Museum)*

with Hu, and soon *New Youth* was written entirely in vernacular Chinese.

One of the first to write well in the vernacular was Lu Xun (1881–1936). In 1902, Lu had gone to Japan to study medicine after traditional doctors had failed to cure his father of tuberculosis. He gave up medicine, however, after watching a newsreel of the Russo-Japanese War that showed a group of Chinese watching apathetically as Japanese in Manchuria executed a Chinese accused of spying for the Russians. From this Lu Xun concluded that it was more important to change the spirit of the Chinese than to protect their bodies. He began reading widely in European literature, especially Russian. The May 1918 issue of

New Youth contained his first vernacular short story, "Diary of a Madman." In it the main character goes mad (or is taken to be mad) after he discovers that what his elders saw as lofty values was nothing more than cannibalism. The protagonist of his longest story, "The True Story of Ah Q," is a man of low social standing. Always on the lookout for a way to get ahead, he is too cowardly and self-deceiving ever to succeed. No matter how he is humiliated, he claims moral superiority. His ears prick up in 1911 when he hears talk of a revolution, but soon he discovers that the old, classically educated elite and the new, foreign-educated elite are collaborating to take over the revolution for themselves and want him to stay away. In the end, he is executed by representatives of the revolution for a robbery he would have liked to have committed but actually had not managed to pull off. In stories like these, Lu Xun gave voice to those troubled by China's prospects and weary of China's old order but wary of promises of easy solutions. Lu Xun put the blame for China's plight on China's own flaws much more than on foreigners. (See **Documents: Lu Xun's "Sudden Notions."**)

By 1919 *New Youth* had been joined by many other periodicals aimed at young people aspiring for a New China. Magazines were filled with articles on Western ideas of all sorts, including socialism, anarchism, democracy, liberalism, Darwinism, pragmatism, and science. The key goals were enlightenment and national survival. The movement to write in the vernacular caught on quickly. In 1921 the Ministry of Education decided that henceforth elementary school textbooks would be written in the vernacular.

Industrial Development

Despite the political and cultural turmoil of the first two decades of the twentieth century, a modern economy began to take off in China. China had opened some modern enterprises as early as 1872, when Li Hongzhang had started the China Merchant Steamship Navigation Company, but those were government-supervised and -supported ventures, not true capitalist ones. In 1895, Japan won the right to open factories in China, and the other imperialist powers leaped at the chance to set up factories as well, since labor costs in China were very low by international standards. By the eve of World War I, China had an emerging bourgeoisie made up of merchants, bankers, industrialists, compradors working for foreign firms, and overseas Chinese engaged in import-export. Foreign investment grew rapidly, with big increases especially in Japanese investment. In the first decade of the century, more and more chambers of commerce had been established in cities large and small, giving this bourgeoisie more of a voice in politics. With the deterioration of the national government after 1915, often the chambers of commerce took over running cities, seeing to sanitation, education, and police. Many of those who returned from study abroad took jobs in modern enterprises, where their foreign degrees brought prestige and often higher salaries. (See **Biography: Sophia Chen and H. C. Zen, a Modern Couple.**)

Commercial Press Pay Scale by College, 1912–1927 (yuan per month)	
Chinese college	80
Japanese college	100–120
Japanese imperial college	150
Western college	200
Harvard, Yale, Oxford, Cambridge	250

World War I gave China's businesses and industries a chance to flourish. Britain, France, Germany, and Russia were preoccupied with what was happening in Europe and no longer had spare goods to export. Imports from the West thus dropped dramatically, giving Chinese manufacturers a chance to sell more profitably. At the same time, the demand for products from China increased, helping China's export industries. The number of Chinese textile mills increased from 22 in 1911 to 109 in 1921. Tonnage of coal produced grew from 13 to 20 million tons between 1913 and 1919. Modern banking took off: between 1912 and 1923, the number of modern banks soared from 7 to 131. Telephone and electric companies were formed not only in major cities but also in county seats and even in market towns. New fortunes were made. For instance, the Rong brothers, from a family of merchants in Wuxi, built a flour mill in 1901 and another in 1913. As opportunities opened up, they built eight new factories between 1914 and 1920, expanding into textiles.

Industrialization had its predictable costs as well. Conditions in China's factories in the 1910s were as bad as they had been a century earlier in Britain,

DOCUMENTS
Lu Xun's "Sudden Notions"

The fiction writer and essayist Lu Xun (1881–1936) disagreed with those who urged preserving China's "national character" or "national essence." When he considered China's history, he saw the recurrence of undesirable patterns rather than past glories to be remembered with pride. This essay on these topics was published in February 1925.

I used to believe the statements that the twenty-four dynastic histories were simply "records of mutual slaughter" or "family histories of rulers." Later, when I read them for myself, I realized this was a fallacy.

All these histories portray the soul of China and indicate what the country's future will be, but the truth is buried so deep in flowery phrases and nonsense it is very hard to grasp it; just as, when the moon shines through thick foliage onto moss, only checkered shadows can be seen. If we read unofficial records and anecdotes, though, we can understand more easily, for here at least the writers did not have to put on the airs of official historians.

The Qin and Han Dynasties are too far from us and too different to be worth discussing. Few records were written in the Yuan Dynasty. But most of the annals of the Tang, Song, and Ming Dynasties have come down to us. And if we compare the events recorded during the Five Dynasties period or the Southern Song Dynasty and the end of the Ming Dynasty with modern conditions, it is amazing how alike they are. It seems as if China alone is untouched by the passage of time. The Chinese Republic today is still the China of those earlier ages.

If we compare our era with the end of the Ming Dynasty, our China is not so corrupt, disrupted, cruel or despotic—we have not yet reached the limit.

But neither did the corruption and disruption of the last years of the Ming Dynasty reach the limit, for Li Zicheng and Zhang Xianzhong rebelled. And neither did their cruelty and despotism reach the limit, for the Manchu troops entered China.

Can it be that "national character" is so difficult to change? If so, we can more or less guess what our fate will be. As is so often said, "It will be the same old story."

Luckily no one can say for certain that the national character will never change. And though this uncertainty means that we face the threat of annihilation—something we have never experienced—we can also hope for a national revival, which is equally unprecedented. This may be of some comfort to reformers.

But even this slight comfort may be cancelled by the pens of those who boast of the ancient culture, drowned by the words of those who slander the modern culture, or wiped out by the deeds of those who pose as exponents of the modern culture. For "it will be the same old story."

Actually, all these men belong to one type: they are all clever people, who know that even if China collapses they will not suffer, for they can always adapt themselves to circumstances. If anybody doubts this let him read the essays in praise of the Manchus' military prowess written in the Qing Dynasty by Chinese, and filled with such terms as "our great forces" and "our army." Who could imagine that this was the army that had conquered us? One would be led to suppose that the Chinese had marched to wipe out some corrupt barbarians.

But since such men always come out on top, presumably they will never die out. In China, they are the best fitted to survive; and, so long as they survive, China will never cease having repetitions of her former fate.

"Vast territory, abundant resources, and a great population"—with such excellent material, are we able only to go round and round in circles?

Source: From *Lu Xun: Selected Works* (Peking: Foreign Languages Press, 1980), 2:125–127.

BIOGRAPHY Sophia Chen and H. C. Zen, a Modern Couple

The first generation to return to China from study abroad found many opportunities to put its new skills to work. Although many of its members returned to marry spouses their families had selected for them, others, like Sophia Chen (1890–1976) and H. C. Zen (1886–1961), found their own marriage partners while abroad.

H. C. Zen was the English name taken by Ren Hongjun. He was born into an educated family in Sichuan and in 1904 graduated from a modern middle school, then took the first stage of civil service examinations. After the exam system was abolished the next year, he left China to study at a technical college in Tokyo, where he joined Sun Yatsen's Revolutionary Alliance. When the revolution broke out in 1911, he returned to China and at age twenty-five was made secretary to the president. Disagreeing with Sun's successor, Yuan Shikai, he resigned and went to the United States to study chemistry at Cornell and Columbia (1912–1917), finishing with a master's degree. While there, he became friends with Hu Shi and courted Chen Hengzhe, who was studying at Vassar. She took the English name Sophia Chen. While still in China, Zen also helped found the Science Society of China, an organization that sponsored scientific monographs and translations, lectures, and exhibitions. He served as its president from 1914 to 1923.

Sophia Chen, from an official family in Jiangsu, had experienced more difficulty getting satisfactory schooling in China, either being tutored at home or studying in mediocre schools. In her teens, she convinced her father to withdraw from a marriage arrangement he had made for her so that she could continue her studies. In 1914 at age twenty-four, she was selected to study in the United States in the examinations held for Boxer Indemnity Fund scholarships. She studied history at Vassar, then went on for a master's degree at the University of Chicago in 1920. That year she returned to China and became the first woman to be offered a professorship at Peking University. The same year, she and H. C. Zen married.

Since he had returned to China in 1917, Zen had held posts at Peking University and the Ministry of Education. When he became editor of the Commercial Press in 1922, the family moved to Shanghai. Two years later, they moved to Nanjing, where Zen became vice chancellor of Nanjing University and Chen taught Western history. Chen did not continue teaching after 1925, however, deciding to concentrate instead on writing. Her *History of the West* went through many printings. She also edited the *Independent Critic*, a liberal journal that she cofounded and that flourished in the 1930s. Both she and her husband wrote pieces for it. Most of Zen's time, however, was taken up with a series of prominent posts. From 1935 to 1937 he was head of the National Sichuan University.

After the Japanese invasion, the family moved to Kunming, where Zen, as the secretary general of the Academic Sinica and director of its Institute of Chemistry, tried to keep scientific research going under difficult circumstances. After a few years, they moved to Chongqing, where Zen took up other posts.

Both Chen and Zen made return trips to the United States. Chen attended several international conferences and after a meeting in Canada in 1933 traveled in the United States, which she found much changed since the advent of the automobile age. Zen visited the United States after the war in 1946–1947.

After 1949, both Zen and Chen, nearing retirement age, stayed in China, living in Shanghai. Of their three children, two settled in the United States and one stayed in China.

---

with twelve-hour days, seven-day weeks, and widespread child labor, especially in textile mills. Labor contractors often recruited in the countryside and kept laborers in conditions of debt slavery, providing the most minimal housing and food. That many of the factories were foreign owned (increasingly Japanese owned) added to management–labor friction.

The May Fourth Incident

In 1914, Japan as an ally of Britain and France seized German territories in China. In 1915, when the European powers were preoccupied with their war, Japan took steps to strengthen its hand in China. It presented Yuan Shikai's government with the Twenty-One

Demonstrating at the Gate of Heavenly Peace. For months after May 4, 1919, students continued to gather at the Gate of Heavenly Peace to protest. *(The Sidney D. Gamble Foundation for China Studies)*

Demands, most of which entailed economic privileges in various regions of China. Others confirmed Japan's position in the former German leasehold in Shandong. The fifth group of demands would have made China in effect a protectorate of Japan by requiring that Japanese advisers be attached to key organs of the Chinese government, even the police. When a wave of anti-Japanese protests swept China, Japan dropped the last group but gave Yuan an ultimatum to accept the rest. The day he did, May 7, was in later years called National Humiliation Day.

In 1917, the Republic of China joined the allied war effort, and although China sent no combatants, it did send some 140,000 laborers to France, where they unloaded cargo ships, dug trenches, and otherwise provided manpower of direct use to the war effort. China was thus expecting some gain from the Allies' victory, particularly in light of the stress placed on national self-determination by the U.S. president, Woodrow Wilson. Unfortunately for China, Japan had reached secret agreements with Britain, France, and Italy to support Japan's claim to German rights in

Shandong. Japanese diplomats had also won the consent of the warlord government that held Beijing in 1918. At Versailles the Chinese representatives were not even admitted, while those from Japan were seated at the table with the Western powers.

On May 4, 1919, when word arrived that the decision had gone in favor of Japan, there was an explosion of popular protest. Some three thousand Beijing students assembled at Tiananmen Square in front of the old palace shouting patriotic slogans and trying to arouse spectators to action. After some students broke through police lines to beat up a pro-Japanese official and set fire to the home of a cabinet minister, the governor cracked down on the demonstrators and arrested their leaders. These actions set off a wave of protests around the country in support of the students and their cause. Everyone, it seemed, was on the students' side: teachers, workers, the press, the merchants, Sun Yatsen, and the warlords. Japanese goods were boycotted. Soon strikes closed schools in more than two hundred cities. The Beijing warlord government finally arrested 1,150 student protesters, turning parts of Beijing University into a jail, but patriotic sympathy strikes, especially in Shanghai, soon forced the government to release them. The cabinet fell, and China refused to sign the Versailles Treaty. The students were ebullient.

The protesters' moral victory set the tone for cultural politics through the 1920s and into the 1930s. The personal and intellectual goals of the New Culture movement were pursued along with, and sometimes in competition with, the national power goals of the May Fourth movement. Nationalism, patriotism, progress, science, democracy, and freedom were the goals; imperialism, feudalism, warlordism, autocracy, patriarchy, and blind adherence to tradition were the evils to be opposed. Intellectuals struggled with how to be strong and modern but still Chinese. Some concentrated on the creation of a new literature in the vernacular, others on the study of Western science, philosophy, and social and political thought. Among the prominent intellectuals from the West invited to visit China to lecture were Bertrand Russell (in 1920 and 1921), Albert Einstein (in 1922), and Margaret Sanger (in 1922). When the educational reformer John Dewey visited between 1919 and 1921, he was impressed. "There seems to be no country in the world," he commented, "where students are so unanimously and eagerly interested in what is modern and new in thought, especially about social and economic matters, nor where the arguments which can be brought in favor of the established order and the status quo have so little weight—indeed are so unuttered."[7]

Not all intellectuals saw salvation in modern Western culture. Some who for a while had been attracted to things Western came to feel that Western culture was too materialistic. Fear that China was in danger of losing its "national essence" was raised. Liang Qichao, by now a conservative, saw more to admire in China's humanistic culture than in the West's rationalism and hedonism and worried about the threat to China's national character.

The Women's Movement

All the major political and intellectual revolutionaries of the early twentieth century, from Kang Youwei and Liang Qichao to Sun Yatsen, Chen Duxiu, Lu Xun, and Mao Zedong, spoke out on the need to change the ways of thinking about women and their social roles. Early in the century, the key issues were foot binding and women's education. In a short period of time, women's seclusion and tiny feet went from being a source of pride in Chinese refinement to a source of embarrassment at China's backwardness. Anti–foot binding campaigners depicted the custom as standing in the way of modernization by crippling a large part of the Chinese population. The earliest anti–foot binding societies, founded in the 1890s, were composed of men who would agree both to leave their daughters feet natural and to marry their sons to women with natural feet. After 1930 it was only in remote areas that young girls still had their feet bound. (Bound feet continued to be seen on the streets into the 1970s or later, as it was difficult and painful to reverse the process once a girl had reached age ten or twelve.)

As women gained access to modern education, first in missionary schools but then also in the new government schools and abroad, they began to participate in politics. Some revolutionaries appeared, most famously Qiu Jin, a woman who became an ardent nationalist after witnessing the Boxer Rebellion and the imperialist occupation of Beijing. Unhappy in her marriage, in 1904 she left her husband and went to Japan, enrolling in a girls' vocational school. Once there, she devoted most of her time to revolutionary politics, even learning to make bombs. She also took up feminist issues. In her speeches and essays she castigated female infanticide, foot binding, arranged marriages, wife beating, and the cult of widow chastity. She told women that they were complicit in their oppression because they were willing to make pleasing men their goal. In 1906 she returned to Shanghai, where she founded the *Chinese Women's Journal* and taught at a nearby girls' school. In 1907 she died a martyr, executed for her role in an abortive uprising.

Schools for women, like the one at which Qiu Jin taught, were becoming more and more common in this period. In 1907 the Qing government mandated the opening of schools for girls. By 1910, there were over 40,000 girls' schools in the country, with 1.6 million students; by 1919, the figures had reached 134,000 schools and 4.5 million students (though schoolboys still outnumbered schoolgirls seven to one). Schools offered girls much more than literacy: they offered a respectable way for girls to interact with unrelated people. After 1920, opportunities for higher education also rapidly expanded, leading to a growing number

---

7. Cited in Chow Tse-tung, op. cit., p. 183.

Pilgrims at Taishan. Taishan, one of the sacred peaks of China, attracted many pilgrims, like these women photographed in the 1920s. Notice that some have made it up the mountain despite their bound feet. *(The Sidney D. Gamble Foundation for China Studies)*

of women working as teachers, nurses, and civil servants in the larger cities. In the countryside, change came much more slowly. A large-scale survey of rural households in the 1930s found that fewer than 2 percent of the women were literate, compared to 30 percent of the men.

Young women in middle and high schools read *New Youth* and other periodicals just as avidly as their brothers. Lu Xun wrote essays and short stories that targeted old moral standards that constrained women. In an essay on chastity, he noted how a woman who committed suicide to avoid being ravished won great glory, but no man of letters would write a biography of a woman who committed suicide after being forcibly raped. In his short story "The New Year's

Sacrifice," a poor widow who was forced by her parents-in-law to remarry was viewed by herself and others as ill omened after her second husband also died. She ended up surviving by begging, worried that she would have to be split in two after death to serve her two husbands. Foreign literature also had an impact, especially Ibsen's *A Doll's House*, which first appeared in translation in *New Youth* and soon was performed on stage many places. Women debated whether, like Ibsen's Nora, they could leave the old system and create their own identities.

Besides attempting to change people's ways of thinking, activists fought for changes in women's legal status. Efforts to get the vote were generally unsuccessful. However, in the 1920s, both the Nationalist and Communist parties organized women's departments and adopted resolutions calling for equal rights for women and freedom of marriage and divorce. Divorce proved the trickiest issue. As Song Qingling, the widow of Sun Yatsen, reported, "If we do not grant the appeals of the women, they lose faith in the union and in the women's freedom we are teaching. But if we grant the divorces, then we have trouble with the peasant's union, since it is very hard for a peasant to get a wife, and he has often paid much for his present unwilling one."[8]

REUNIFICATION BY THE NATIONALISTS

The ease with which Yuan Shikai had pushed the revolutionaries out of power demonstrated to them that they needed their own army. Sun Yatsen in 1917 went to Guangzhou, then controlled by warlords, to try to form a military government there. That year, the Bolshevik Revolution succeeded in Russia, and Sun began to think that Russia might offer a better model for political change than Japan. Russia had been a large, backward, despotic monarchy that had fallen behind the West in technology. Both China and Russia were predominantly peasant societies, with only small educated elites. Why shouldn't the sort of revolution that worked in Russia also work in China? The newly established Soviet Union wanted to help build a revolutionary China. In Marxist-Leninist theory, socialist revolution would occur by stages, and since China had not yet gone through a bourgeois, capitalist stage, a victory by the Nationalist revolutionaries who would overthrow the imperialists appeared to be the next stage for China. Besides, a weak China might invite the expansion of Japan, the Soviet Union's main worry to the east.

For help in building a stronger revolutionary party and army, in 1920, Sun turned to the Comintern (short for Communist International, the organization Lenin had founded to promote communist revolution throughout the world). The Comintern sent advisers to Sun, most notably Michael Borodin, who drafted a constitution for the Nationalist party, giving it a more hierarchical chain of command. When some party members thought it resembled the Communist model too closely, Sun countered that "the capitalist countries will never be sympathetic to our Party. Sympathy can only be expected from Russia, the oppressed nations, and the oppressed peoples."[9]

By 1925 there were about one thousand Russian military advisers in China helping the Nationalists build a party army. Chinese officers were also sent to the Soviet Union, including Chiang Kaishek, who was sent there for four months' training in 1923. On Chiang's return, Borodin helped him set up the Whampoa Military Academy near Guangzhou, and the Soviet Union made a substantial contribution to its costs. The communist Zhou Enlai, recently returned from France, became deputy head of this academy's political education department. The first class was admitted in 1924 with nearly five hundred cadets ages seventeen to twenty-four. The cadet corps was indoctrinated in Sun's Three Principles of the People and dedicated to the rebuilding of national unity. As they rose within the Nationalist army, the former cadets remained fiercely loyal to Chiang.

At the same time Comintern advisers were aiding the buildup of the Nationalists' power base, they continued to guide the development of a Chinese Communist party (discussed in Chapter 25). This party grew slowly, and at no time in the 1920s or 1930s did it have nearly as many members or supporters as the Nationalist party. In 1922, on Comintern urging, the two parties formed a united front, as a consequence of which members of the Communist party joined the Nationalist party as individuals but continued separate Communist party activities on the side. Sun Yatsen endorsed this policy, confident that the Nationalist party would not be threatened by a small number of Communists and eager to tap all possible resources for building a strong state.

Among those the Comintern sent to Guangzhou was Ho Chi Minh, a Vietnamese who had become a communist in France and had gone to Moscow to work at Comintern headquarters. Ho spent much of the next twenty years in China and Hong Kong organizing a Vietnamese communist movement among Vietnamese patriots in exile in south China.

Nationalism continued to grow during the 1920s as one incident after another served to remind people of China's subjection to the imperialist powers.

---

8. Cited in Anna Louise Strong, *China's Millions* (New York: Coward-McCann, 1928), p. 125.

9. Cited in C. Martin Wilbur and Julie Lien-ying How, *Missionaries of Revolution* (Cambridge, Mass.: Harvard University Press, 1989), p. 92.

On May 30, 1925, police in the foreign-run International Settlement of Shanghai fired on unarmed demonstrators, killing eleven. Three weeks later, a sympathy protest in Guangzhou led foreign troops to open fire, killing fifty-two demonstrators. A fifteen-month boycott of British goods and trade with Hong Kong followed. The time seemed ripe to mobilize patriots across the country to fight the twin evils of warlordism and imperialism.

In 1925, before the planned Northern Expedition to reunify the country could be mounted, Sun Yatsen died of cancer. The recently reorganized Nationalist party soon suffered strain between the leftists, who shared many of the goals of the communists, and the rightists, who thought that Borodin had too much power and the communists were acting like a party within the party. Nevertheless, in July 1926, the two-pronged Northern Expedition was finally launched with Chiang Kaishek as military commander and Russian advisers helping with strategy. Communists and members of the left wing of the Nationalist party formed an advanced guard, organizing peasants and workers along the way to support the revolution. Many warlords joined the cause; others were defeated. By the end of 1926, the Nationalist government was moved from Guangzhou to Wuhan, where the left wing of the party became dominant. By early 1927, the army was ready to attack Shanghai. This would mark the end of the United Front, a topic taken up in Chapter 25.

SUMMARY

How different was China in 1927 compared to 1900? Two thousand years of monarchical government had come to an end. Nationalism had become a powerful force. Political parties had come into existence. Through the spread of modern schools, the outpouring of new publications, and much more extensive study abroad, a much larger proportion of the population knew something of Western countries and Western ideas. Confucianism was no longer taken to be an obvious good. Radically new ideas such as individualism and democracy were widely discussed and advocated. Young people with modern educations had become important political actors as protesters and agitators. Women had come to play much more public roles in society. An urban proletariat had come into existence with the growth of factories in the major cities. China was changing very rapidly.

World War II

IN BOTH WESTERN AND EASTERN THEATERS, World War II was characterized by indiscriminate bombing of civilian populations and death tolls in the millions. The aggressors were the Axis: Japan, Germany, and to a lesser extent, Italy. Allied against them were the British Commonwealth (including India and Australia), the United States, and the Soviet Union, along with the Chinese government under Chiang Kai-shek. What is known as the fifteen-year war began with Japan's invasion of Manchuria in 1931. In 1937, Japan launched all-out war against China. The war in Europe began in 1939 when Hitler provoked a declaration of war from Britain and France by invading Poland. The United States joined when Japan bombed Pearl Harbor on December 7, 1941, and Hitler declared war on the United States.

The belligerents each had reasons for fighting. Still angry at the punitive terms that included a loss of territory imposed on it by the armistice that ended World War I, Germany insisted that it needed living space for its growing population. Hitler's Nazi party believed that Aryans were superior to all other races and were destined to rule the world. Many people in Japan believed that their country was superior to the rest of Asia. Nazis, Fascists in Italy, and Japan's ultranationalists agreed that social dislocations in the early twentieth century had been caused by individualistic liberalism expressed in hedonistic urban culture and the compromises and corruption of politicians. They opposed capitalism and the capitalist powers—England, France, and the United States—that dominated the world economically and militarily. They also feared universal so-

Timeline: The Greater East Asia War	
1931–1932	Japan's Kwantung army takes over Manchuria
1932	January 28: Japan bombs Shanghai
1933	May 27: Japan withdraws from the League of Nations
1935	November 24: Puppet government established in Beijing
1936	January 25: United Front against Japan
1937	July 7: Marco Polo Bridge Incident; Japan invades China
	November 20: Chinese capital established at Chongqing
	December 13: Rape of Nanjing begins
1938	United States embargoes war materiel to Japan
1939	May through August: Japanese and Soviet troops fight at Nomonhan
1940	Spring: U.S. Pacific Fleet moves to Pearl Harbor in Hawai'i
	September 26: Japan invades North Vietnam
	September 27: Japan, Italy, and Germany sign Tripartite Mutual Defense Pact
	October 15: United States embargoes scrap iron and steel to Japan
1941	April 13: Japan signs neutrality pact with Soviet Union
	July 26: Britain and United States cut off trade with Japan
	December 7: Japan attacks Pearl Harbor
	December 8: Japan attacks the Philippines, Wake, Guam, Hong Kong, and Malaya
	December 23: Japan bombs Rangoon, Burma

1942	January 23: Japan takes Rabaul north of New Guinea
	January 26: Japan lands on Solomon Islands
	February 15: Japan captures Singapore
	February 27–March 1: Battle of Java Sea
	March 9: Japan conquers Java
	April 9: U.S. Army on Bataan peninsula in the Philippines surrenders
	May 2: Japan captures Mandalay in Burma
	May 7: Battle of Coral Sea
	June 4–7: Battle of Midway
	June 12: Japan occupies Attu in Aleutian Islands
	July 9: Chinese Nationalist forces win a major battle in Jiangxi province
	July 21: Japan captures Buna, New Guinea; drives toward Port Moresby
1943	February 9: Japan retreats from Guadalcanal in Solomons
	July 1: Allied offensive in South Pacific
	July 29: United States drives Japan from Aleutian Islands
	November 22: U.S. troops land on Tarawa in Gilbert Islands
1944	February 2: Invasion of Marshall Islands
	February 17: Battle of Truk lagoon
	June 15–July 7: U.S. forces take Saipan
	August 11: U.S. forces take Guam
	August: Britain retakes Burma
	October 23–25: Battle of Leyte Gulf
1945	March 10: Firebombing of Tokyo
	March 17: United States captures Iwo Jima
	April 1: Invasion of Okinawa begins
	June 22: Okinawa falls
	July 26: Potsdam Declaration
	August 6: Atomic bomb dropped on Hiroshima
	August 8: Soviet Union declares war on Japan
	August 9: Plutonium bomb dropped on Nagasaki
	August 15: Japan surrenders

cialism emanating from the Bolshevik revolution that threatened the national polity. Germany expanded eastward; Italy conquered Ethiopia; Japan believed that it needed colonies for national security and self-respect. Despite a common ideology, the Axis never coordinated strategy, especially in comparison with the more ideologically diverse Allies.

Fear that Soviet expansion threatened Japan's interests in Asia led Japan to take over Manchuria. The army installed a puppet government in what it called Manchukuo headed by Puyi, the last Qing emperor. Treating Manchukuo as a new frontier, it encouraged settlers from Japan and Korea to displace indigenous people in farming what then became wide-open spaces. By 1945, Manchuria had absorbed approximately 270,000 Japanese immigrants.

Japan's conquest of Manchuria sparked a wave of anti-Japanese demonstrations and a boycott of Japanese goods in China's major cities. The Japanese navy retaliated by bombarding civilian quarters in Shanghai before the eyes of the largest international community in China. An explosion of outrage filled foreign newspapers, but foreign governments did little. The League of Nations sent a fact-finding team to China, and when the League Assembly accepted the team's report that castigated Japan's aggression in Manchuria, Japan withdrew from the League.

Japan's attempts to establish a buffer zone in north China fed growing anti-Japanese nationalist sentiment among Chinese people. A national salvation movement led by student demonstrations demanding national unity and resistance to Japan erupted in Beijing

Crying Baby. This photograph of a crying baby, which appeared in *Life* magazine following the Nanjing Massacre, garnered America's sympathy for China in its struggle against Japan. *(Getty Images)*

and spread to other cities. The communists in Yan'an issued a call for all to resist Japanese imperialism. Even warlords in southwest China joined the clamor, though their patriotic fervor was tinged with a self-interested desire to obstruct Chiang Kaishek's nationalist government in Nanjing. The United Front of 1936 allied communists and nationalists against Japan. The development of anti-Japanese organizations meant that when the Japanese army invaded north China in July 1937 to protect its interests in Manchuria, it met fierce opposition.

The war in China was marked by the first atrocities of World War II committed against civilian populations. Japan did not expect the fierce resistance offered by Chinese troops that attacked Japanese forces in and around Shanghai in retaliation for Japan's capture of Beijing and Tianjin. Not until December did the Japanese army capture Nanjing. When the city surrendered, Japanese army spokesmen contended that Chinese troops had taken off their uniforms to mingle with the civilian population, thereby justifying the murder of thousands of Chinese civilians. Frustrated that five months of warfare had not resulted in decisive victory, Japanese officers encouraged their men to loot stores and rape women. The number killed is disputed even today. This horror was dubbed the "Rape of Nanking" by the foreign press.

Shocked by the international outcry over Nanjing and disturbed by the troops' behavior that they had encouraged, Japanese officers decided that indiscriminate rape threatened Japan's reputation and military discipline. To provide for what was deemed the soldiers' physical needs and to combat venereal disease, the army developed "comfort stations," already inaugurated in Shanghai in 1932. Japanese prostitutes were primarily reserved for officers in the rear. To find women for soldiers on the front lines, the military turned to its colonies and then to territories conquered after 1940. Koreans composed 80 percent of the "comfort women" who serviced troops as far away as Burma and the islands of Southeast Asia. In some areas, a woman serviced up to fifty men a day for a modest fee per soldier. Only the end of the war brought release from sexual slavery.

The China war demonstrated the importance and limitations of air power. Owning few planes, the Chinese nationalist army was defenseless against strafing. When Chiang moved his government to Chongqing in the mountains of Sichuan, nearly perpetual fog protected the city from Japanese bombers. The narrow Yangzi gorges precluded an overland attack. Instead, Japanese troops fanned out along the eastern seaboard and along railroad lines in the interior. By the end of 1938, they occupied cities and major towns from Manchuria to Guangdong. In the days before helicopters, their superior air power had less effect in the countryside.

Although Chinese living under Japanese occupation tried to remain inconspicuous, many had to choose between collaboration and resistance. Collaborators set up a provisional government in Beijing in 1937 to administer north China. In 1940, Japan created the Reorganized Government of the Republic of China under Wang Jingwei, a member of Chiang Kaishek's Nationalist party who hoped to win peace with Japan in the name of Greater East Asianism. In 1943, Japan allowed Wang to declare war on the United States and Great Britain. In the countryside, guerrilla warfare led Japanese army units to launch indiscriminate punitive missions against villages thought to be harboring communists. These "rural pacification" campaigns proved ineffective. Although 1 million Japanese troops occupied China's richest regions for eight years, they could not subdue the people or find an exit strategy from a war neither side could win.

Japan expected more than collaboration from its Korean subjects in its war with China. It expanded cotton and wool production at the expense of cereals; it developed hydroelectric power in the north. In 1936, it declared a new policy of forced assimilation: all Korean were to be taught that they too were children of the emperor. Koreans had to worship at Shinto shrines and pray for the emperor's good health. Over six hundred thousand Korean men were drafted to work in Japanese and Manchurian mines, harbors, and factories. Although Japan taught that Korea and Japan were one, it trusted few Koreans to fight its battles. By 1944, upwards of 4 million Koreans worked outside Korea, some as policemen and guards as far away as New Guinea, where they died in battles that made no distinction between combatants and noncombatants.

Japan's aggression in China provoked a response similar to the one that greeted Italy's conquest of Ethiopia in 1936. Both the League of Nations and the United States (which had not joined the League) officially deplored Japan's action. Neither tried to stop it, even though Japanese forces destroyed American property, sank an American warship, and killed American civilians. Fearful of Japan's intentions north of Manchuria, only the Soviet Union provided significant aid to China. It shipped munitions and airplanes to both communist and nationalist forces along with military advisers. Over two hundred So-

viet pilots died in China's defense. In May 1939, the Japanese army in western Manchuria confronted Soviet forces at Nomonhan. The fight cost Japan eighteen thousand men and exposed critical weaknesses in the army's tactics and equipment. Japan sued for peace following the Russo-German Non-Aggression Pact signed in August. In 1941, Japan and the Soviet Union signed a neutrality pact. After Germany invaded the Soviet Union at the end of June, Soviet aid to China came to an end.

The United States relied on sanctions and threats to try to force Japan out of China and check Japan's expansion in Indochina. It placed a series of increasingly stringent embargos on goods to Japan and helped Chiang Kaishek by extending credit with which to buy American arms. When President Roosevelt had the Pacific Fleet move to Pearl Harbor to protect U.S. shipping lanes and intimidate Japan, Japan's navy took it as a threat to its interests in Micronesia and the South Pacific. In September 1940, Japan invaded north Vietnam to secure raw materials for its war machine and cut supply lines running to Chiang Kaishek. When the United States, Britain, and the Netherlands, which controlled the oil fields of Indonesia, cut off trade unless Japan pulled out of China and north Vietnam, Japan felt it had to fight or accept humiliation.

Neither the Allies nor Japan understood the other's motives, and they underestimated their opponents. Japan claimed to be liberating Asia from colonial powers. In 1940, it promoted, though it did not practice, the notion of a Greater East Asia Co-Prosperity Sphere, an economic regional power bloc similar to that envisioned in the Western Hemisphere under the Monroe Doctrine. In Japan's eyes, the United States and Soviet Union had everything they needed for an autonomous defense, but without colonies, Japan did not. Japanese soldiers saw themselves as spiritually superior to the materialistic West; they were hard and high-minded, whereas British and Americans were soft. Public opinion in the United States saw China as a victim of Japanese totalitarian aggression. Madame Chiang Kaishek gave an impassioned speech before the U.S. Congress in which she contrasted China striving for democracy and Japanese warmongers. Henry Luce, son of missionaries in China and owner of Time-Life, flooded his magazines with heart-rending pictures from war-torn China. Editorial cartoons drew on racial stereotypes to mock Japanese for their physical and mental inferiority and portrayed them as vermin to be exterminated.

Japan's desperation to find a solution to its war with China pushed it to open one battlefront after another, many over 3,000 miles from the home islands. To break through what it called the ABCD encirclement (American, British, Chinese, Dutch) and secure the oil crucial for its China campaign, it struck south. It bombed Pearl Harbor in hopes of forcing the United States to negotiate a settlement. Ten hours later, it launched an invasion of the Philippines, a U.S. colony. Britain had expected attack on Singapore to come from the sea; Japanese troops advanced through jungle to capture the city. (The same month that saw the fall of Singapore also saw President Roosevelt sign Executive Order 9066 to place 110,000 Japanese Americans, over half of them U.S. citizens, behind the barbed wire of relocation camps.) Within months, Japan captured Indonesia, the Philippines, Guam, Wake, and the Solomon Islands. The Japanese army took over the rest of Vietnam, forced an alliance on Thailand, chased Britain out of Burma, closed the Burma Road that had carried supplies to Chongqing, and threatened India and Australia. Combined with the islands taken from Germany in World War I, this gave the Japanese a vast empire, albeit mostly over water. (See Map C7.1.)

The empire lacked administrative coherence. After conquering the Indonesian archipelago, Japan divided it between three military commands. In the Philippines, Japan established a republic with a constitution drafted under its supervision, chose the nationalist Jose P. Laurel to be its president, and had the new republic sign an alliance that put land and resources at Japan's disposal. The French Vichy government that collaborated with the Nazis invited Japan to occupy Vietnam, and Japan continued to rely on French administrators until 1945, much to the chagrin of Vietnamese nationalists. In the south, nationalists collaborated with military police and supplied laborers to build boats. When Japan decided to eliminate French rule in March 1945, the nationalists helped, only to suffer betrayal when Japan decided to keep administration in its own hands. Tainted by their association with Japan, noncommunist Vietnamese nationalists lacked credibility in the political strife following the end of the war. On the Malay Peninsula and in Burma, Japan created patriotic associations ostensibly to resist European colonial powers, but in reality to mobilize labor for the Japanese military. In places where Japan ruled through local headmen, the aim was the same: to make each region, each island self-sufficient and

to support Japan's war machine. In some cases, men who were later to lead independence movements against Western imperialism began by collaborating with Japan, as did General Aung San of Burma. When British soldiers retreated to India, units left behind formed the Indian National Army to fight for Indian independence. These instances serve as reminders that South and Southeast Asia welcomed Japan's message of liberation from colonial rule, but not the way it was delivered.

Like Germany, Japan justified its disregard for human life on the basis of racial superiority. Both Ishii Shirō and Joseph Mengele believed that their experiments on human test subjects served a larger purpose: ultimate victory for the master race. The same rationale served for labor policies. Japan saw no reason to provide food, clothing, or basic medical care for laborers from the Malay Peninsula, Philippines, and Dutch East Indies who, having been mobilized to work on construction projects from Micronesia to Thailand, died far from home of malaria, cholera, maltreatment, and starvation. After Japan invaded Java, grain production plummeted, in part because Japan required that fields be planted with textile-related crops. Across the Japanese empire, the dislocation of individuals and families in the name of the Greater East Asia Co-Prosperity Sphere led to starvation and death. As Pramoedya Ananta Toer wrote in his novel *The Fugitive*, "Corpses. Wherever you go, unattended corpses."[1] In contrast to such atrocities stand the good Nazi John Rabe, who saved thousands of Chinese lives at Nanjing, and Sugihara Chiune, who issued visas for thousands of Lithuanian Jews fleeing Nazi persecution.

Japan's arrogant sense of racial superiority helped its enemies. Resistance to Japanese occupation from China to Indonesia to the Philippines contributed significantly to the Allies' counterattack. The British led Indian troops to reconquer Burma, Australians pushed Japan out of New Guinea, Chiang Kaishek's forces inflicted a major defeat on troops in China, the U.S. Army under General Douglas MacArthur advanced through the South Pacific before returning to the Philippines, and the U.S. Navy island-hopped across the Central Pacific.

Much of the fighting in the Pacific and Southeast Asia took place in jungles hated by both sides. After

---

1. Pramoedya Ananta Toer, *The Fugitive*, trans. Willem Samuel (Harmondsworth: Penguin Books, 1990), p. 33.

Map C7.1   World War II in Asia and the Pacific

four months on Bataan peninsula in the Philippines, one-third of U.S. troops were in rain-drenched field hospitals suffering from festering wounds, dysentery, and malaria. Although the Japanese army used the jungle to advantage in taking Singapore, its troops too fell victim to disease in Burma and Malaya. Japanese troops tried to cross the spine of New Guinea from Buna to Port Moresby over mountain passes covered with rain forest. They were thrown back by Australian forces, and both sides struggled through knee-deep mud to engage an enemy seen only sporadically. Communications with headquarters broke

down, and fighting erupted haphazardly when individual units ran afoul of the enemy.

Fighting on so many fronts meant that Japan lacked the ability to provide its troops with adequate supplies. Troops dispatched to far-flung islands and atolls were expected to live off the land. When U.S. submarines sank supply ships, they starved. Because the United States had signed a disarmament pact before the war that abjured submarine warfare as inhumane, Japan did not anticipate attacks on tankers and freighters sailing behind its defensive perimeter. In 1942, Japan received 40 percent of Indonesia's oil. Owing to the war of attrition, it received only 5 percent in 1944, and it received none in 1945. Taxis in Tokyo ran on wood-burning engines, and the air force adulterated scarce fuel with sap from pine roots.

Lacking adequate resources meant that the Japanese army and navy had to rely on men over machines. When Japan built runways on Pacific islands, it used human labor—natives, Koreans, Okinawans, prisoners of war. The Allies used bulldozers. At war's beginning, Japan had well-trained pilots flying the Zero, the most advanced fighter of its day. When those pilots were gone, their barely trained replacements had to fly against planes constantly improved through new technology. Japan lost so many planes trying to defend Saipan in the Marianas that American pilots called the battle "a turkey shoot." After the Japanese fleet lost six aircraft carriers at the battle of Leyte Gulf, the navy asked its pilots to crash their planes into enemy ships. Designated the Divine Wind Special Attack Corps to recall the typhoon credited with repelling Mongol invaders almost seven hundred years earlier, *kamikaze* pilots struck fear in Allied hearts. Another desperate measure was the human torpedo. Nearly five thousand young men sacrificed their lives in a futile effort to stem the Allied tide sweeping toward Japan.

Air power made the decisive difference in battles on sea and land. From the battle of Coral Sea, to Midway, to Leyte Gulf, although enemy ships saw each other's planes, the ships themselves never fought. Even before the attack on Pearl Harbor, the Allies had broken Japanese codes, and at Midway, the United States used its knowledge of Japan's positions and intentions to sink three of Japan's aircraft carriers and damage a fourth. At the end of the battle of Coral Sea, Japan thought it had lost even though it sank more ships than had the Allies. Throughout the war, Japan's admirals sought the decisive sea battle fought with battleships that would turn the tide of war just like Admiral Tōgō's stunning victory over the Russian navy in 1905. Little did they realize that aircraft carriers had made battleships irrelevant.

When Japan destroyed U.S. planes on the ground in the Philippines, it left U.S. troops defenseless against aerial assault. Later in the war, Japan's troops, and later its cities, suffered the same experience once its air force had been decimated. The fall of Saipan in Micronesia—after the navy lost over four hundred planes and every Japanese soldier had died in its defense—put Japan's main islands within range of U.S. heavy bombers. The first raids, carried out at high altitudes, did little but psychological damage. Once General Curtis E. LeMay arrived from Europe, pilots in the Pacific perfected the art of carpet bombing—that is, dropping incendiary bombs at low attitudes—which decimated Japan's wooden cities. In the largest air offensive in history, U.S. planes destroyed the remnants of the Japanese navy, shattered Japanese industry, and dropped 40,000 tons of bombs on population centers. Approximately ninety thousand civilians died in the firestorm that engulfed Tokyo. The plane that carried the atomic bomb to Hiroshima took off from Tinian, just south of Saipan. Its flight was virtually unimpeded.

Even before the fall of Okinawa that sacrificed one-quarter of the island's population to the defense of the homeland, cabinet members began to call for an end to the war. The army rebuffed them. With 5.5 million men relatively unscathed in China and Manchuria, it demanded that all Japanese prepare to make the ultimate sacrifice: to die like "shattered jewels" in protecting the emperor-centered national polity. Recalling President Theodore Roosevelt's mediation of an end to the Russo-Japanese War in 1905 and hoping to keep the Soviet Union neutral, the army finally agreed to let the Japanese ambassador to Moscow ask Foreign Minister Molotov for help. Busy with preparations for the Potsdam Conference, Molotov put him off. On July 26, Churchill and Truman issued the Potsdam Declaration (Stalin did not sign it) demanding that Japan submit to unconditional surrender. Japan was to agree to allow occupation by foreign troops and to renounce all claims to territory on the Asian mainland and Taiwan. Its leaders and soldiers were to be tried for war crimes, and the Japanese people were to choose the form of government they wanted. The alternative was "prompt and utter destruction."

The Potsdam Declaration was both extremely specific and maddeningly vague. Japanese leaders had no way of knowing that destruction was to come via a bomb first tested ten days before. To the distress of the emperor's loyal subjects, the declaration made no mention of him. The cabinet decided to wait and hope for mediation by the Soviet Union. Then, for three days in early August, the atomic bomb, the Soviet Union's declaration of war, and the plutonium bomb sent shock waves through the cabinet. At a meeting on August 14, the emperor instructed the cabinet to surrender. Later, he made a recording to tell the Japanese people that they must bear the unbearable. Despite a plot by junior army officers to steal the recording, it was broadcast at

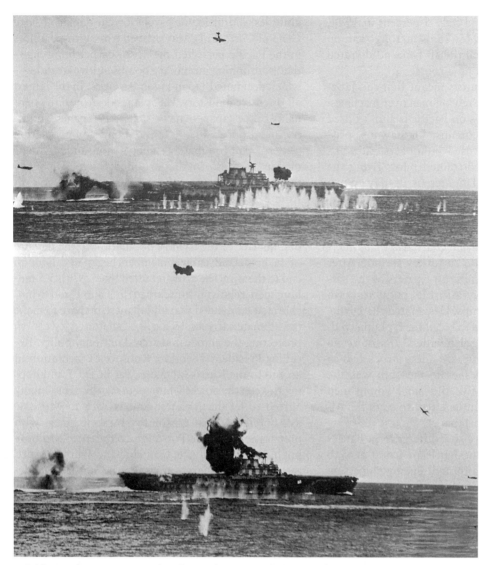

Suicide Bomber. A Japanese bomber makes a suicide dive on the *USS Hornet* on October 26, 1942, off Santa Cruz in the Solomon Islands. *(Bettmann/Corbis)*

noon on August 15. World War II was over, but the debate on why Japan surrendered had just begun—was it the bomb, fear of Russians, or exhaustion?

After the war, Japanese military personnel were prosecuted for war crimes. In Indonesia, the Dutch convicted Japanese who had forced European women to service Japanese troops; they ignored cases involving Indonesian women. Other war-crimes trials made no mention of comfort women. Nor did they include men from Unit 731 who had turned over their data on experiments to test bacteriological weapons performed on Chinese in Manchuria. Instead the trials focused on crimes against humanity broadly de-

fined as the decision to wage war; atrocities such as the Bataan death march in which thousands of American and Filipino soldiers died; the indiscriminate bayoneting of British doctors, nurses, and patients in Singapore; the machine-gunning, decapitation, and drowning of civilians in Southeast Asia; and the massacre of Filipinos in Manila at the end of the war. Japan's treatment of prisoners of war merited special condemnation; soldiers who survived surrender were starved, tortured, and forced to labor for the Japanese war machine in contravention of the Geneva Convention. The war crimes tribunals ignored atrocities committed by Allied forces.

Following World War II, the world split into two camps: the free world dominated by the United States and the Communist bloc led by the Soviet Union. What Winston Churchill called an "iron curtain" between opposing ideologies divided Europe. Forgetting that Japan's early victories had exposed their vulnerabilities, Western powers assumed that their former colonies in South and Southeast Asia would welcome them as liberators. The United States freed the Philippines in 1946. Britain pulled out of Burma and India in 1947. Two years later, the Dutch grudgingly granted independence to Indonesia. France refused to leave Vietnam until defeated in 1954. Civil war in China ended with communist victory. Soviet troops began to enter Korea in August 1945. Hoping to prevent the whole country from falling into their hands, the United States got the Soviet Union to agree to a dividing line just north of Seoul at the 38th parallel. The two nations then sponsored the creation of two separate states on the Korean peninsula. Japan escaped that fate. Under U.S. occupation, it became a bulwark against communism.

War and Revolution, China (1927–1949)

During the two decades from 1927 to 1949, China was ruled by the Nationalist party and its head, Chiang Kaishek. The Nationalist government turned toward the West for help in modernizing the country, but in general was distrustful of intellectuals. In its big cities, above all in Shanghai, China took on a more modern look with tall buildings, department stores, and Western dress. The government had to concentrate most of its energies on military matters, first combating the remaining warlords, then the Communist party bases, then Japan. The Communist party attracted a small but highly committed following. Because of the Nationalists' pressure, it was on the run much of the time until a base area was established in Yan'an in 1935, where Mao Zedong emerged as the paramount leader. During the war with Japan (1937–1945), the Communist party formed itself into a potent revolutionary force, able to mobilize poor peasants into a well-disciplined fighting force. The Civil War of 1947–1949 resulted in the victory of the Communist party.

The large questions behind much of the scholarly work on this period revolve around the outcome in 1949. Why did May Fourth liberalism decline in significance? Could the economic policies of the Nationalists have brought prosperity to China if Japan had not invaded? How much of a difference did the Comintern's often misguided instructions make to the development of the Communist party? How crucial was Mao to the way the policies of the party developed? Why did the Nationalist party and Chiang Kaishek lose the support of the urban middle class?

THE CHINESE COMMUNIST PARTY

With the success of the Bolshevik revolution in Russia in 1917, Chinese intellectuals began to take an interest in Marxism-Leninism, which seemed to provide a blueprint for a world of abundance without exploitation.

Communism appeared scientific, anti-Western, anti-imperialist, and successful: it had just proved itself capable of bringing revolution to a backward country. For the May 1919 issue of *New Youth*, Li Dazhao, the librarian at Beijing University, wrote an introduction to Marxist theory, explaining such concepts as class struggle and capitalist exploitation. Soon intellectuals were also looking into the works of Lenin and Trotsky, who predicted an imminent international revolutionary upheaval that would bring an end to imperialism. Although China did not have much of a proletariat to be the vanguard of its revolution, the nation as a whole, Li Dazhao argued, was exploited by the capitalist imperialist countries. In 1920, Li organized a Marxist study group at Beijing University. At much the same time, Chen Duxiu organized one in Shanghai, where he had gone after resigning his university post in Beijing. Another source of knowledge of European Marxism were the thousands of Chinese students, male and female, who had gone to France in 1919 and 1920 to participate in work-study programs. Most worked in factories, where they were introduced to both strikes and Marxism-Leninism.

The early Marxist study groups were offered financial assistance and guidance by the Comintern. In 1920, soon after the Comintern learned of the existence of Marxist study groups in China, agents were sent to help turn the groups into party cells. This entailed teaching "democratic centralism," the secret to party discipline. Each local cell elected delegates to higher levels, up to the national party congress, with its central executive committee and the latter's standing committee. Delegates flowed up, and decisions flowed down. Decisions could be debated within a cell, but once decisions were reached, all were obligated to obey them. This cell structure provided a degree of discipline and centralization beyond anything in the prior repertoire of Chinese organizational behavior.

Following Comintern advice, thirteen delegates met in July 1921 to form the Chinese Communist party as a secret, exclusive, centralized party. The party broke with the anarchists and guild socialists and asserted the primacy of class struggle. Chen Duxiu was chosen as secretary general. The party agreed to put priority on organizing labor unions and recruiting workers into the party. In Shanghai, the new Communist party oversaw the establishment of a Russian language school, helped organize labor unions, and formed the Socialist Youth Corps.

At the insistence of the Comintern and against the advice of many of the Chinese members, the decision was made in 1922 to ally with the Nationalists. The United Front between the Nationalist and Communist parties was expedient for both at the time, as they could concentrate on their common foes, the warlords. However, it covered over deep differences. The Nationalist military included many staunch anticommunists who were appalled by talk of class warfare. One reason the communists remained in the United Front was that it gave them the opportunity to organize both workers and peasants. Along the route of the Northern Expedition, farmers' associations were established, with membership exceeding 1 million people by the end of 1926.

The United Front ended in the spring of 1927. On March 21, as the Nationalist army neared Shanghai, the Communist-led General Labor Union called for a general strike. Over six hundred thousand workers responded and seized the city. Flush with victory, they began demanding the return of the foreign concessions. On April 11, the head of the union was invited to the home of the leader of the mafia-like Green Gang, where he was murdered. The next day Green Gang members and soldiers loyal to Chiang attacked union headquarters. Soon soldiers were mowing down civilians with machine guns; an estimated five thousand were killed.

The terror quickly spread to other cities. The labor union base of the Communist party was destroyed. Although the party tried to continue working with the left wing of the Nationalist party in Wuhan, Chiang's show of force carried the day. By July 1927 the Soviet advisers had withdrawn from the Nationalist army, and the United Front was over.

That fall, the Communist party tried to organize uprisings in both cities and the countryside, but none met with much success. A failed uprising in Guangzhou led to the execution of three thousand to four thousand worker revolutionaries. From 1927 through 1930, the hunt was on for Communist organizers all over the country; in some areas, the only evidence that troops needed in order to conclude that a young woman was a communist was bobbed hair. The surviving Communist leadership was driven underground and into the countryside. On orders of the Comintern, Chen Duxiu was blamed for these disasters and expelled from the Communist party. Party membership, which had reached about sixty thousand in April 1927, plummeted to fewer than ten thousand within the year.

Mao Zedong's Emergence as a Party Leader

Through the 1920s, Mao Zedong was just one of hundreds of Communist party organizers. He ended up playing such an important role in twentieth-century Chinese history that it is useful to begin with his early experiences.

Mao was born in 1893 in a farming village about 30 miles south of Changsha, the capital of Hunan province. He began helping out on his father's 3-acre farm when he was six. At age eight, in 1901, he entered the local primary school, where he studied for six years. Mao then worked full time on the farm for three years, from ages thirteen to sixteen. When he was fourteen years old, he was betrothed to the eighteen-year-old daughter of a neighbor, but she died in 1910, and Mao left the farm to continue his education. One of his teachers was a returned student from Japan, and from him Mao became fascinated with the writings of Kang Youwei and Liang Qichao. In 1911, at age seventeen, Mao walked the 30 or so miles to Changsha to enter a middle school. Not only was Changsha a large city, but the new provincial assembly was then meeting, and all sorts of newspapers were in circulation. Mao joined student demonstrations against the Qing government and cut off his queue. Then, in October, revolutionary soldiers seized power in nearby Wuhan, and the fall of the Qing Dynasty soon followed. Mao, wanting to be a part of the action, joined the republican army, but after six months of garrison duty in Changsha, he quit to continue his education.

For a year Mao spent his days at the Changsha public library reading world history and Chinese translations of works by such Western writers as Rousseau, Montesquieu, J. S. Mill, Adam Smith, and Charles Darwin. Only when his father refused to support him any longer unless he enrolled in a school that gave degrees did he enter the Hunan Provincial Fourth Normal School, where he studied for five years (1913–1918). The teacher there who had the greatest impact on him was Yang Changji, a social science teacher deeply interested in philosophy, which he had studied during his decade abroad in Japan, Great Britain, and Germany. Mao came to share Yang's dissatisfaction with the physical fitness of Chinese intellectuals, and he wrote an article on physical education that was published in *New Youth* in 1917.

Mao was twenty-four years old when he graduated. When Yang moved to Beijing to take up an appointment at Beijing University, Mao followed him. Yang helped him get a job as a clerk in the library, which made him a subordinate of Li Dazhao, only four years his senior but already well known in intellectual circles, having studied law for six years in Japan and having been offered a position on the editorial board of *New Youth*. That year Li Dazhao wrote about Marxism and the Russian Revolution for *New Youth*.

Before he had been in Beijing a year, Mao had to return home because his mother was ill, but he stopped to visit Shanghai for a couple of weeks on the way. Mao thus missed the excitement at Beijing University during the May Fourth incident. Back in Changsha, Mao took a teaching job and started his own magazine, producing four issues with articles on topics such as democracy, unions, and fighting oppression. Mao also turned his hand to organizing, forming the Hunan United Students Association and organizing a strike of thirteen thousand middle school students against the local warlord.

After his mother died, Mao returned to Beijing to find Professor Yang desperately ill. At the beginning of 1920, Mao's father and Yang both died. When Mao returned to Hunan a few months later, he was appointed principal of a primary school. That seems to have left him some time, as he also organized a cooperative bookstore that proved a commercial success. Professor Yang's daughter Yang Kaihui also returned to Hunan, and by the end of 1920 she and Mao were living together. Two years later, their first son was born, and they spoke of themselves as married.

It was not until 1920 that Mao showed particular interest in Marxism. Part of this new interest came from letters he received from fellow students who had gone to France. When the first meeting of the Communist party was held in Shanghai in July 1921, Mao was one of the two delegates from Hunan. He was sent back to Hunan with instructions to build up the party there and develop ties to labor unions. Mao recruited former classmates, his two younger brothers, and others to help him organize unions and strikes. In early 1923, conforming to party policy, Mao joined the Nationalist party. That June he went to Guangzhou for the third congress of the Chinese Communist party. In December he sent in a pessimistic report on the situation in Hunan, where peasant organizations had been crushed and many factories had closed.

During much of 1924, Mao was away from home, in Guangzhou or Shanghai, doing United Front work. In 1925 he did the opposite, returning to his home village to work with peasants out of the reach of the party authorities. In October 1925, he returned to Guangzhou and took up work for the Nationalist party's propaganda department, becoming the director of the Peasant Training Institute in 1926. During the Northern Expedition, Mao and those he had trained organized peasants in advance of the army. In February 1927, Mao submitted a highly positive report to the Communist party on the revolution among the peasants in Hunan who had seized power from landlords and felt the joy of righting ancient wrongs.

In April 1927, when Chiang Kaishek unleashed the terror in Shanghai, Mao was in Hunan. Following party instructions, he tried to ignite peasant insurrection, but found that the terror had crushed the movement that only recently had looked so promising to him. Mao now wrote a report that emphasized the need to back political ideas with military force, contending, in his oft-quoted phrase, that "political power is obtained from the barrel of the gun." In October 1927 he led his remaining peasant followers into a mountain lair used by secret society members on the border between Hunan and Jiangxi, called Jinggangshan. Mao lost contact with Yang Kaihui, who had just given birth to their third son. He also was out of touch with the party hierarchy. He began to draw in other communists, among whom was nineteen-year-old He Zizhen, from a nearby landlord family, who had joined the party during the Northern Expedition. She and Mao, then thirty-four years old, became lovers and had a child in 1929.

In the mountain area that Mao's forces controlled, he pushed through an extreme form of land reform, redistributing all the land of the rich and requiring all the physically able to work. His troops suffered, however, with little in the way of arms or ammunition, clothes, or medicine.

In January 1929, Mao decided to look for a better-supplied base area that would be less vulnerable to Nationalist attacks. His choice was a border region between Jiangxi and Fujian, where he set up what came to be called the Jiangxi Soviet. The party leadership, which could reach him there, quickly condemned him for his views on rural revolution and the role of military force. Mao fell ill and managed to avoid responding to the party's order that he go to Shanghai. In 1929–1930, Mao did, however, conduct an exhaustive study of rural life in one county in the Jiangxi Soviet, Xunwu County, to learn more about how a party could be built on a peasant base.

In his analysis of landownership, he classified the population into landlords (those who lived off the rents of their lands, subdivided into large, medium, and small landlords), rich peasants (those who rented out some land or made loans but worked the rest themselves), middle peasants (those who worked their own land without borrowing or hiring help), poor peasants (tenants and owners of plots too small to support them), and others, including hired hands, loafers, and those who did such manual labor as boatmen and porters. The vast majority of the population fell into the category of poor peasant or lower. When land was redistributed, many more would receive land than would lose it. In his study of Xunwu, Mao also recorded literacy rates, postal service, shops and services, and even the number of prostitutes.

The Communist party leadership was still trying to ignite urban uprisings and in October 1930 assaulted Changsha. Not only did the attack fail, but the Nationalists arrested Yang Kaihui and had her shot. The three young boys were sent by friends to Shanghai. The youngest died, and Mao did not see the other two until 1946.

THE NATIONALIST GOVERNMENT IN NANJING

The decision of the Nationalist party to purge itself of communists did not delay the military unification of the country, and in 1928 the Nationalists gained the allegiance of three key warlords to reunite the country. It established its capital at Nanjing, not used as a capital since the early Ming Dynasty. International recognition quickly followed, and Western observers were more optimistic about the prospects for China than they had been for decades. Men who had studied in Western countries were appointed to many key government posts, and progressive policies were adopted, such as a new land law limiting rents and a new marriage law outlawing concubinage and allowing women to initiate divorce. (See **Biography: Yuetsim, Servant Girl.**) Over the next several years, most of the foreign powers consented to reductions in their special privileges. Tariff autonomy was recovered, as well as control over the Maritime Customs, Salt Administration, and Post Office. Foreign concessions were reduced from thirty-three to thirteen, and extraterritoriality was eliminated for some minor countries.

BIOGRAPHY   Yuetsim, Servant Girl

Yuetsim, born around 1910, knew nothing about her natal family. All she knew was that she had been kidnapped when she was about three years old and sold, through intermediaries, as a "slave girl." She thought disbanded soldiers then roaming the countryside might have been the ones who kidnapped her.

A Hong Kong family, the Yeos, purchased Yuetsim. Her master's father had been a successful merchant and had three concubines besides his wife. Her master, Mr. Yeo, was the son of the first concubine, and he held a modest government position as a clerk. When his wife had no children, he purchased a prostitute as a concubine, and she gave birth to four children. The wife, who had bound feet, rarely left her room. The family bought little Yuetsim to help the concubine with the housework and care of the children. It is difficult to imagine that a three year old could be of much use to anyone, but by four or five she could at least fetch and carry. Naturally, she never learned to read or write.

Since Yuetsim knew no other life, she put up with the way she was treated. Her mistress, the concubine, was often harsh and contemptuous. In this period, Hong Kong newspapers were filled with agitation against the custom of selling girls into bondage. Yuetsim, however, never heard anything of the movement or of the 1923 law that took the first steps toward outlawing selling girls into service. In December 1929 a further strengthening of the laws against child slavery required owners of slave girls to register them with the government, pay them wages, and free them at age eighteen. Since Mr. Yeo worked for the government and was known to have had a slave girl for years, he had to take some action. He might have married her off, as many masters did, but his concubine was so angry at losing Yuetsim's services that she simply ordered Yuetsim out of the house.

In 1930 one of the officials in charge of the registration of slave girls found a place for Yuetsim in a home for women and girls in need of protection, and she stayed there several years. Finally she went back to the Yeos as a maid, knowing no other place to go. Soon after her return, both the wife and the concubine died. Yuetsim continued to take care of the master and his children.

After the death of his wife and concubine, Mr. Yeo wanted to make Yuetsim his concubine. His children, however, were adamantly opposed and threatened to cut off contact with him if he went through with the marriage. They, after all, had known her all their lives as a humble servant. Although their own mother had been a prostitute before becoming their father's concubine, they thought marriage to a former slave girl would disgrace the family. Mr. Yeo gave in to them.

Yuetsim stayed on anyway. In retirement, Mr. Yeo's fortunes declined, but Yuetsim nursed him in his illnesses and shopped and cooked for him. She was still living with him when she told her story in 1978.

Source: Based on Maria Jaschok, *Concubines and Bondservants: The Social History of a Chinese Custom* (London: Zed Books, 1988), pp. 69–77.

From 1928 on, Chiang Kaishek was the leader of the Nationalists. From a landlord-merchant family near Ningbo, Chiang had aspired to take the civil service examinations, but when they were abolished he went to Japan to study military science, joining the precursor of the Nationalist party while there. His appointment to head the Whangpoa Academy in 1924 was a crucial one because it allowed him to form strong personal ties to young officers in the party's army. Once Chiang, a skillful politician, became fully enmeshed in party and government matters, he proved able to balance different cliques and build personal ties to key power holders. In 1927 he married Soong Meiling, the daughter of a wealthy merchant family and the sister of Sun Yatsen's widow.

To modernize his army, Chiang turned to Germany, attracted by the success the Nazis were having in mobilizing and militarizing Germany. Indeed, Chiang once argued, "Can fascism save China? We answer: yes. Fascism is now what China most needs."[2] Ger-

---

2. Cited in Lloyd Eastman, *Abortive Revolution* (Cambridge, Mass.: Harvard University Press, 1974), p. 40.

man advisers helped Chiang train an elite corps, plan the campaigns against the communist base in Jiangxi, and import German arms. Young officers became members of the Blue Shirts, an organization devoted to the nation and against such New Culture ideas as individualism. Chiang entrusted political training in the army and schools to the Blue Shirts, who also took on secret service work.

Chiang was not a political progressive. He made no attempt at elective democracy, as this was to be a period of "political tutelage." The press was heavily censored, and dissenters and suspected communists were arrested and often executed. To combat the intellectual appeal of the communists and build support for his government, Chiang in 1934 launched an ideological indoctrination program, the New Life Movement. Its goal, he claimed, was to "militarize the life of the people of the entire nation" and to nourish in them "a capacity to endure hardship and especially a habit and instinct for unified behavior" to make them "willing to sacrifice for the nation at all times."[3]

Chiang was a patriot, however, and wanted a strong and modern China. Much progress was made in economic modernization. Life in the major cities took on a more modern look. Conveniences like electricity were gradually changing how all major cities functioned. A professional class, composed of scientists, engineers, architects, economists, physicians, and others with technical expertise, often acquired through study abroad, was gaining influence.

The Nationalists' modernizing programs unfortunately failed to bring improvements to the countryside (see **Documents: The Peasant Exodus from Western Shandong**). Most peasants had seen no improvement in their standard of living since Qing times. The government and private philanthropic organizations sponsored rural reconstruction projects that tried to raise the level of rural education, create facilities for credit, encourage modern enterprises, and form peasant associations, but gains were usually limited to small areas and short periods. Continued population growth to over 500 million by 1930 relentlessly increased the pressure on available land. The advantages brought by modernization—cheaper transportation by railroads and cheaper manufactured consumer goods—were yet to have a positive impact on the rural economy.

3. Cited in Jonathan Spence, *The Search for Modern China* (New York: Norton, 1990), p. 415.

Chiang Kaishek and Soong Meiling. In 1927, Chiang Kaishek married Soong Meiling, the younger sister of Sun Yatsen's widow. Soong came from a wealthy family, had been educated in the United States, and after the Japanese invasion worked hard to gain American support for China. *(Popperfoto/Retrofile)*

China's exports were struggling, silk and tea having lost ground to Japanese and Indian competition, then all exports facing decreased demand due to the worldwide depression of the 1930s.

Shanghai

During the Nanjing Decade, Shanghai emerged as one of the major cities of the world. Since 1910 it had been China's most populous city, and by the 1930s it had about 4 million residents. It attracted Chinese entrepreneurs, especially those willing to collaborate with foreigners. It had China's largest port and was the commercial center of China. In the 1920s and 1930s it had half of China's modern industry.

Shanghai attracted more foreigners than any of the other treaty ports, a high of over thirty-six thousand. The largest number were British or Japanese, as they owned the most foreign companies. Some of Shanghai's foreigners had come in the nineteenth century

DOCUMENTS

The Peasant Exodus from Western Shandong

In the 1930s, those with modern education were well aware of the problems facing Chinese farmers and discussed at length what could be done to solve them. This article was published in the magazine Minjian (Among the People) *in 1937. The author, Hao Pensui, describes what he learned by visiting villages and talking to peasants.*

Toward the northwest of Jinan, in western Shandong, is the district of Yuecheng. . . . Deforestation, dumping, and lack of any river conservancy have prevailed for so many years that the main river bed is narrower than either of its branches. Whereas the Dengjin river is now 32 feet wide and the Zhaonui 48 feet wide the joint stream is only 28 feet wide. No wonder then that since 1930 five out of the seven years have witnessed floods.

The peasants were able to maintain themselves with what little grain store and money savings they had for the first two flood years, but when the fourth and fifth floods came they had absolutely nothing to fall back on. Usurers in the city and at the railway station, who were more resourceful than the village usurers, naturally refused to loan at this time, realizing that they had very little chance of being repaid. . . .

In the winter of 1935 the peasants of Chengnan were reduced to eating the bark from trees and the roots of herbs. . . . Destitute peasants from this large area had no alternative but to rove from one place to another. This further agitated the peasants of Chengnan, who organized themselves to petition the magistrate for relief. The magistrate immediately ordered the shutting of the city gate in order to prevent the entry of over 3,000 peasants into the city. Only a few peasant delegates were permitted to talk to him, resulting in the usual way with the magistrate promising to petition the provincial government for relief from the public granary.

Unending delays and bureaucratic red tape proved once again complete indifference to the acute suffering of the hungry masses. A year's delay meant a year of hunger, and it was not until the spring of 1936 that the peasants received from the public granary 6 kg of unhusked rice per person. . . .

The investigations in one village by the writer of the present article may be taken as a typical example. The village in Chengnan that he investigated is named Zhaozhuang and it had a population of 530 people in 76 families. In the winter of 1935, 25 entire families left the village, and from each of 39 families one to three persons left, leaving only 12 families intact. In all, 230 people left the village that winter. . . .

---

and stayed; others were there for only a few years. Among the merchant families who amassed huge fortunes were the Sassoons, from a family of Jewish traders active in Baghdad and Bombay. David Sassoon began by trading cotton from Bombay to China in the 1870s; his son Elias Sassoon bought warehouses in Shanghai later in the nineteenth century; and his grandson Victor Sassoon turned to real estate, in the 1930s reportedly owning nineteen hundred buildings in Shanghai, including those that are now the Peace and Cypress hotels. Some of the early employees of the Sassoons also made fortunes, including Silas Hardoon and Elly Kadoorie. Hardoon started as a night watchman in the 1870s. Kadoorie's mansion is now the Shanghai Children's Palace.

Because the international districts admitted anyone, no matter what their passport or visa status, Shanghai became a magnet for international refugees. After the Russian Revolution, many of the Russian bourgeoisie fled east via the trans-Siberian railroad. Later they made their way south through Manchuria, many eventually settling in Shanghai, often to find only menial jobs. In the 1930s, thousands of Jews fleeing the Nazis also found refuge in Shanghai, where

The almost annual flood created great confusion among the peasants who were quite unable to effect any organized control. Whatever feeble attempts they did make to turn back the water, such as the building of small mud banks, proved useless in nine cases out of ten. The flood meant the loss of a year's crop, for when the water receded the fields were left in very bad condition, covered with a thick layer of black silt which dried and cracked in a hard crust. Having lost their seed and probably their animals, the peasants had no hope of starting afresh, so after every flood a procession of peasants could be seen from nearly every village abandoning their homes and setting out in search of food. Creaking wheel-barrows piled high with quilts, clothing, and household utensils, were pushed by able-bodied men along narrow paths, each being followed by a group of women and children. Behind them they would leave some houses with the doors sealed with mud, or others with one or two people too old to travel, left to scrape a living as best they could. . . .

The writer himself was in the village of Zhaozhuang in 1936 just two months after the wheat harvest, and his own investigation brought to light the fact that out of the total of 76 families, only nine, at that time, had as much as three months food, 11 only had two months, 19 only one month, and as many as 37 families had already exhausted their supplies. These figures are all the more significant because it was a year in which there was no flood and a good harvest.

Once the writer met a peasant of sorrowful appearance who said,

This year our family harvested about 600 kg of wheat out of which 72 kg were paid for rent, 150 for the repayment of loans in kind, about 108 for taxes, about 60 for the purchase of a working animal, and about 60 to repay recent credit purchases. Thus only about 150 kg remained, and of these 108 had already been consumed by the family. How we are to manage to live with less than 50 kg in hand until the next harvest is hard to conceive. Furthermore, there are still some outstanding debts from credit purchases, some $12 worth of things in the pawnshop to be redeemed and school fees for the boys to be met.

Such a budget reveals the almost hopeless condition of the peasantry in this area, for it not only allows of no leeway to meet such emergencies as flood, drought, and locusts, but it also shows that even in normal years a moderately well-to-do peasant family is being rapidly reduced in its economic status. This explains why the peasant exodus is more or less continuous, regardless of the harvest or the presence of natural calamities.

Source: From *Agrarian China: Selected Source Materials from Chinese Authors* (London: George Allen and Unwin, 1939), pp. 247–251, modified.

they were aided by the wealthy Jewish families already there, such as the Sassoons, Hardoons, and Kadoories.

The foreign presence in Shanghai was visible to all in its Western-style roads and buildings. Along the river an embankment called the bund was built and was made into a park with signs posted that read "No dogs" and "No Chinese."

With its gambling parlors and brothels, Shanghai had a reputation as a sin city. Reportedly about 50,000 women worked in Shanghai as prostitutes in the 1930s. Young women were also drawn into Shanghai to work in textile mills or as servants. In 1930 over 170,000 women worked in industry, about half in cotton mills. The typical prostitute or mill hand was a young, unmarried, illiterate woman recruited in the countryside by a labor contractor. The contractor would supply a small advance payment, often to the girl's parents, and would make arrangements in the city for employment, housing, and food. The women were often kept in conditions of debt servitude. Some factory workers joined unions and engaged in strikes; others put their hopes on getting married and returning to the country. Women in Shanghai, from factory girls and prostitutes to office workers and the wealthy, commonly wore dresses called *qipao*, a compromise between Western and Chinese styles. (See **Material Culture: Qipao**.)

Shanghai also attracted Chinese intellectuals, especially as Nationalist censorship got more severe. If they worked from the International District or French Concession, they were usually safe from the Chinese police. Dissidents, radicals, and revolutionaries chose Shanghai for much the same reasons.

Relocating the Communist Revolution

In 1932 the Central Committee of the Communist party gave up trying to foment urban insurrections and joined Mao in the Jiangxi Soviet. Mao was the chairman of the soviet, but after their arrival, he was on the sidelines, his recommendations often overruled. In the fall of 1934, with the German-planned fifth "extermination campaign" of the Nationalists encircling them with a million-man force, the Communist party leadership, without consulting Mao, decided to give up the Jiangxi Soviet. In October, about eighty-six thousand Communist soldiers, cadres, porters, and followers broke out of the encirclement, the start of the much mythologized year-long Long March in search of a new place to set up a base. Most wives and children had to be left behind (only thirty-five women joined the march). To protect them and the thousand or so sick or wounded soldiers left behind, about fifteen thousand troops remained in Jiangxi. Mao's wife, He Zizhen, although pregnant, was allowed to come, but they had to leave their two-year-old child behind with Mao's younger brother. When Mao's brother, like many of those left behind, was killed in 1935, Mao lost track of the child.

Month after month the Red Army kept retreating, often just a step or two ahead of the pursuing Nationalist troops. Casualties were enormous. The farther west they went, the more rugged the terrain; as they skirted Tibet, they also had to deal with bitter cold. By the time they found an area in Shaanxi where they could establish a new base, they had marched almost 10,000 kilometers. Only about eight thousand of those who began the march made it the whole way, though some new recruits and communists from other base areas had joined en route, to bring the total to nearly twenty thousand. (See Map 25.1.)

To the Nationalists in Nanjing, the Long March must have seemed a huge victory. The Communist party's urban activists had been crushed in 1927–

1928, and now the rural activists had suffered just as devastating a blow, their numbers greatly diminished and the survivors driven into remote and poverty-stricken regions. Those who made the Long March, however, saw it as a victory. That they had overcome such daunting odds reinforced their belief that they were men of destiny with a near-sacred mission to remake China.

It was during the Long March that Mao Zedong reached the top ranks of party leadership. When the marchers reached Zunyi in Guizhou province in early 1935, they paused to hold an enlarged meeting of the Politburo and assess their strategy. Seventeen veteran party leaders were present, including Mao, the Comintern representative Otto Braun, and thirty-year-old Deng Xiaoping to take notes. Blame was placed on Braun and others who had urged positional warfare to defend against the Nationalist attack. Mao was named to the Standing Committee of the Politburo and given new responsibility for military affairs.

From 1936 to 1946 the Communist party made its base at Yan'an, a market town in central Shaanxi where homes were often built by cutting caves into the loess soil cliffs. When the American journalist Edgar Snow visited Yan'an in 1936, the survivors of the Long March appeared to him to be an earthy group of committed patriots and egalitarian social reformers, full of optimism and purpose. They lived in caves, ate simple food, and showed no disdain for the peasants whom they were mobilizing to fight against the Japanese. During the war, too, outside observers were impressed with the commitment to group goals of the Yan'an forces. All through Mao's lifetime the official media promoted this image of the leaders of the Yan'an Soviet as a cohesive group of idealistic revolutionaries.

Mao's standing in Yan'an was high, but he still had rivals. A group of communists who had gone to Russia for training arrived in late 1935 and provoked debate on the errors that had cost the lives of so many party members. Mao realized that he would have to improve his grasp of Communist dialectic and began systematic study. His new secretary, Chen Boda, who had studied in Moscow for several years in the late 1920s, began writing of Mao as a theorist. Mao was becoming more set against the claims of the well educated, even if their education was in Marxism. To contrast himself from the urban intellectuals, Mao would act like a peasant, opening his clothes to look for lice with guests present.

MATERIAL CULTURE

Qipao

In the first decades of the twentieth century, as educated young people came to look on the West as the source of everything modern, they turned to Western styles of dress. This was especially true of those who had worn this style while studying abroad. Some people adopted full Western-style dress, but others tried to develop a style that would be both Chinese and modern at the same time. The so-called Mao suit, first popularized in China by Sun Yatsen, is an example of this sort of hybrid style for men. For women in the early twentieth century, the garment that most successfully modernized Chinese dress was the *qipao*.

The *qipao* is a one-piece dress characterized by an upright ("mandarin") collar, an opening from the neck to under the right arm, and a fairly narrow cut, often with a slit, especially if the skirt reached below midcalf. The *qipao* was much more form-fitting than anything worn in the nineteenth century, but reflected traditional styles in its collar, its slanted opening, and sometimes its fastenings. It could be made in silk, cotton, or synthetics for everyday wear or elegant occasions.

Well-Dressed Young Women. These three young women wear *qipao* with short sleeves and high slits. Notice also their high-heel shoes and curled hair. *(Hulton Archive/Getty Images)*

Mao was victorious over the Soviet returnees in part because he was the better politician but also because he seems to have become truly confident that he was in the right. He began spending more time lecturing party members. He also started to allow or encourage the beginnings of the cult of Mao: in 1937, a portrait of him appeared in the revolutionary newspaper, and a collection of his writings was printed.

It was in this period that Mao took up with Jiang Qing. He Zizhen and Mao's surviving children had gone to the Soviet Union for safety and medical treatment. Jiang Qing, twenty-four years old, had worked as an actress in Shanghai and made her way to Yan'an after the Japanese invasion. Some of the other Communist leaders resented her liaison with Mao, having liked and admired He Zizhen. Mao and Jiang Qing had a daughter in 1940, the last of his four surviving children (six were lost or died).

THE JAPANESE INVASION AND THE RETREAT TO CHONGQING

From the time of the May Fourth protests in 1919, Chinese patriots saw Japan as the gravest threat to China's sovereignty. In 1895, Japan had won Taiwan. In 1905, after an impressive victory over Russia, it gained a dominant position in southern Manchuria. In 1915, by applying pressure on Yuan Shikai, Japan had secured a broad range of economic privileges. The Japanese Army in Manchuria, ostensibly there to protect Japan's railroads and other economic interests, was full of militarists who kept pushing Japanese civil authorities to let the army occupy the entire area. In 1928, Japanese officers assassinated the warlord of Manchuria, Zhang Zuolin, hoping for a crisis that would allow Japan to extend its power base.

Map 25.1   China in 1938

Labels within the map:

SOVIET UNION

MANCHURIA

OUTER MONGOLIA
(Independent 1924)

• Qiqihar   • Jiamusi

• Harbin

Amur

Ussuri

• Baotou

Zhangjiakou
• (Kalgan)

Jinzhou   • Shenyang
               (Mukden)

• Beijing

Tianjin •

KOREA
(Japanese 1910–1945)

• Taiyuan

Yan'an •

Lanzhou •

SHANDONG

Jinan •

Yellow

SHAANXI

Luoyang
Xi'an •   • Zhengzhou

• Xuzhou

• Qingdao

CHINA

• Chengdu

SICHUAN

Chongqing •

Yangzi

Wuhan •

Nanjing •

• Shanghai

Hangzhou •

Zunyi •

Changsha •
         • Nanchang

HUNAN

Jiangxi Soviet under
Mao Zedong and
Zhu De, 1929–1934

Guiyang •

Kunming •

Ji'an

Shantou •

Xiamen
(Amoy)

TAIWAN
(Japanese
1895–1945)

*PACIFIC
OCEAN*

Guangzhou •

Hailufeng Soviet,
1927–1928

BURMA

FRENCH
INDOCHINA

Hong
Kong
(British)

Areas under Communist control before Nov. 1934

Areas under Communist control, 1929–1938

Areas occupied by Japan by end of 1938

← Route of the Long March, Oct. 1934–Oct. 1935
    Main forces from Ji'an

←-- Other forces

Scale:
0   250   500 Km.
0   250   500 Mi.

In 1931, Japanese soldiers set a bomb on the Southern Manchurian Railroad to give themselves an excuse to occupy Shenyang "in self-defense." China did not attempt to resist militarily but did appeal to the League of Nations, which recognized China as being in the right but imposed no real sanctions on Japan. Then in January 1932, Japan attacked Shanghai to retaliate against anti-Japanese protests. By that point Shanghai was such an international city that the Japanese assault and the bombing of civilian residential areas was widely condemned. After four months, the Japanese withdrew from Shanghai, but in Manchuria they set up a puppet regime, making the last Qing emperor the nominal head of Manchukuo ("Manchu land").

Anger at Japanese aggression heightened Chinese nationalism and led to the formation of national salvation leagues and boycotts of Japanese goods. Still, Chiang, like most other military men of the day, did not see any point in putting up a fight when Japanese firepower was so clearly superior. Chiang was convinced that all Chinese would have to be united under one leader before China could hope to thwart Japan.

In 1936 troops that had been driven out of Manchuria by the Japanese were ordered by Chiang to blockade the Communists in Yan'an. When Chiang came to Xi'an, they kidnapped him and refused to release him until he agreed to form a united front with the communists against Japan. These troops did not want to be fighting other Chinese when the Japanese had occupied their home towns. The communists played no part in the kidnapping but joined the negotiations when Stalin urged them to keep Chiang alive and create a nationwide united front against Japan.

The next year, Chiang did put up a fight when the Japanese staged another incident as an excuse for taking more territory. Chiang was probably hoping to inflict a quick defeat to convince Japan that the Nanjing government was a power to be reckoned with so Japan would negotiate with him rather than continue to move into China as though it was unoccupied. Japan instead launched a full-scale offensive, sweeping south. Chiang had to abandon Beijing and Tianjin, but he used his best troops to hold off the Japanese at Shanghai for three months. He asked for an all-out stand, and his troops courageously persisted despite heavy shelling and bombing, absorbing 250,000 killed or wounded (compared to 40,000 Japanese casualties). When Shanghai fell, the Nationalist troops streamed toward the Nationalist capital, Nanjing. After the Japanese easily took Nan-

jing in December 1937, they went on a rampage, massacring somewhere between 40,000 and 300,000 civilians and fugitive soldiers, raping perhaps 20,000 women, and laying the city waste. The seven weeks of mayhem was widely reported in the foreign press, where it was labeled the Rape of Nanking. If this violence was intended to speed a Chinese surrender, it did not achieve its goal.

During the course of 1938, the Japanese secured control of the entire eastern seaboard and set up puppet regimes headed by Chinese collaborators (see Map 25.1). Terror tactics continued, including biological and chemical warfare in Zhejiang in 1940, where bubonic plague was spread and poison gas released. Civilian casualties were also inflicted by the Nationalist government. When the Chinese had to retreat from Kaifeng, Chiang ordered his engineers to blow up the dikes on the Yellow River, creating a gigantic flood that engulfed more than four thousand villages, drowned some three hundred thousand people, and left 2 million homeless. It delayed the Japanese for only three months.

Japan had assumed that once it captured the capital at Nanjing and inflicted an overwhelming defeat on the Nationalist army, Chiang Kaishek would come to terms. When he refused and moved inland, the war bogged down. Rather than persuading the Chinese to surrender, Japanese terror tactics instead intensified popular hatred for the Japanese. China's great distances spread Japanese forces. In north China, Japan concentrated on holding rail lines, and Chinese guerrilla forces concentrated on blowing them up. Guerrilla soldiers depended on local peasants to feed them and inform them of enemy concentrations and movements. They acquired weapons and ammunition by capturing them from the Japanese. Many resistance fighters worked in the fields during the day and at night acted as guides or scouts to help blow up bridges, rail lines, and roads. Peasant cooperation with the guerrillas provoked savage Japanese reprisals, including killing everyone in villages suspected of harboring resistance fighters, which the Japanese called their "kill all, burn all, loot all" policy. Chinese resistance forced Japan to keep about 40 percent of its troops in China even after the Pacific War had begun in late 1941 (see **Connections: World War II**).

The Nationalists' capital was moved inland first to Wuhan, then to Chongqing, deep in Sichuan. Free China, as it was called in the Western press, started with the odds heavily against it. The capital, Chongqing, suffered repeated air raids and faced not only shortages of almost everything, but runaway inflation as high as 10 percent a month, leading to widespread corruption as government workers' salaries fell to a pittance. The army was in worse shape. The army Chiang had spent a decade training had been destroyed. From 1939 on, the bulk of China's 5 million soldiers were ill-trained peasant conscripts. Press gangs would enter villages and seize the able-bodied. As many as a third of the conscripts died on the forced marches to their bases because they were not given enough to eat or medical care. Desertion, not surprisingly, was a huge problem. Another serious disability for Free China was the lack of an industrial base inland. Chinese engineers made heroic efforts to build a new industrial base, but constant Japanese bombing, the end of Soviet aid in 1939, and the closing of the route through Burma in 1942 frustrated their efforts. From 1942 on, American advisers and American aid flown over the mountains from Burma enabled Chiang to build a number of modern divisions, but not an army able to drive the Japanese out of China.

During World War II, international alignments began to shift. After Britain proved unable to defend Hong Kong, Singapore, or Burma from Japanese invasions in 1941–1942, it lost its standing in Chinese eyes as the preeminent Western power. Its place was taken by the United States, which ended up doing most of the fighting against Japan. The American-educated wife of Chiang, Soong Meiling, was popular with the American press and lobbied effectively for China. President Franklin D. Roosevelt, looking ahead, wished to see China become the dominant power in East Asia after the defeat of Japan, and he convinced his allies to include Chiang in major meetings of the Allies at Cairo and Yalta (though Churchill referred to making China one of the Big Four as an absolute farce). It was as a result of this sort of geopolitics that China, so long scorned as weak and backward, became one of the five permanent members of the United Nations Security Council after the war.

THE CHINESE COMMUNIST PARTY DURING THE WAR

During the first few years of the war, there was some genuine cooperation between the Communists and Nationalists. This largely ended, however, when the Communist divisions of the New Fourth Army were attacked by the Nationalists in January 1941 on the grounds that they had not complied rapidly enough with an order to retreat north of the Yangzi. From this point on, the Nationalists imposed an economic blockade on the Communist base area.

Some one hundred thousand people made their way to Yan'an during the war, about half of them students, teachers, and writers. Party membership swelled from forty thousand in 1937 to about eight hundred thousand in 1940. The fight against Japan helped the Communists build a base of popular support. In areas of north China where the Japanese armies had penetrated, peasants were ready to join forces against the Japanese.

Resistance forces were not exclusively Communist. Patriotic urban students fled to these relatively uncontested rural areas where they helped both Nationalist and Communist resistance forces. The Communists, however, were more successful in gaining control of the social, political, and economic life in villages because they gave peasants what they wanted: an army of friendly troops who not only did not steal their crops but also helped them bring in the harvest and implemented popular economic reforms.

Class struggle was not emphasized during the war against Japan, nor was there much confiscation of land. Still, considerable redistribution was accomplished by imposing graduated taxes that led larger landholders to sell land that was no longer profitable. Landlords were more than welcome to help with forming and supplying militia forces, and educated youth from better-off families were recruited as party members. Party propagandists did their best to stoke patriotic passions, glorify the Soviet Union, and convey the message that the Communist party could build a better, more egalitarian future. They called so many meetings that rural folk in Hebei quipped, "Under the Nationalists, too many taxes; under the Communists, too many meetings."[4]

The Japanese did not penetrate as far west as Yan'an, and during the war Mao could concentrate on ideological issues. As the party grew rapidly, Mao sought ways to instill a uniform vision. Neither Marx nor Lenin had seen much revolutionary potential in peasants, viewing them as petty capitalist in mentality, and in Russia the party had seized power in an urban setting. Since the communists in China had failed in the

---

4. Edward Friedman, Paul G. Pickowics, and Mark Selden, *Chinese Village, Socialist State* (New Haven, Conn.: Yale University Press, 1991), p. 41.

cities, Mao reinterpreted Marxist theory in such a way that the peasants could be seen as the vanguard of the revolution. Indeed Mao came more and more to glorify the peasants as the true masses and elaborate the theory of the mass line: party cadres had to go among and learn from the peasant masses before they could become their teachers. Marx was a materialist who rejected idealist interpretations of history. Ideas did not make history; rather, they reflected the economic base, the mode of production, and the relations of production. Mao's vision of revolution, by contrast, was voluntaristic: it emphasized the potential for people, once mobilized, to transform both themselves and the world through the power of their wills.

This "Thought of Mao Zedong" did not win in a free competition of ideas among the survivors of the Long March, but in a power struggle in which Mao proved a master tactician, able to eliminate his rivals one after the other and get the Central Committee to label them deviationists of the right or left. To reform the thinking of both old cadres who had deviated from the correct line and new recruits from bourgeois families, in 1942, Mao launched the first of many rectification campaigns. Cadres had to study documents Mao selected in small groups, analyze their own shortcomings in Maoist terms, listen to criticism of themselves at mass struggle sessions, and confess their errors. Everyone watched the dramatic public humiliations of the principal targets, including the party theorist Wang Ming and the writer Wang Shiwei. People learned to interpret any deviation from Mao's line as defects in their thinking due to their subjectivism and liberalism, characteristics of their petty bourgeois background. One man, for instance, who confessed to being bothered by the party elite's special privileges (such as getting to ride on horseback while others walked) was taught that liberal ideas elevating the individual over the collective lay behind his feelings. Those who balked were punished; some even died. Many of those invited to overcome their errors truly developed a new collective consciousness that greatly increased their usefulness to the party. Others simply learned to be more circumspect when they talked.

The Seventh Party Congress, the first to be held since the 1920s, was held at Yan'an in the spring of 1945. The preamble of the new constitution recognized Mao's new role as sage of the party: "The Chinese Communist Party takes Mao Zedong's thought— the thought that unites Marxist-Leninist theory and the practices of the Chinese revolution—as the guide

The Communist Leadership. Zhou Enlai, Mao Zedong, and Zhu De (left to right) were photographed in the winter of 1944, by which time the Communist party had gained a foothold behind Japanese lines all across north China. *(Popperfoto/Retrofile)*

for all its work, and opposes all dogmatic or empiricist deviations."[5]

THE CIVIL WAR AND THE COMMUNIST VICTORY

The end of the war with Japan set the stage for the final confrontation between the Nationalists and the Communists. When Japan surrendered in August 1945, there were over 1 million Japanese troops in China proper and nearly another 1 million in Manchuria, as well as about 1.75 million Japanese civilians. Disarming and repatriating them took months, as the Nationalists, the Communists, the Americans, the Russians, and even some warlords jockeyed for position. The United States airlifted 110,000 Nationalist troops to key coastal cities like Shanghai and Guangzhou, and 53,000 U.S. Marines were sent to help secure Beijing and Tianjin. The Russians had

5. Cited in Jonathan Spence, *Mao Zedong* (New York: Viking, 1999), p. 101.

entered Manchuria in early August in fulfillment of their secret promise to the United States and Britain to join the eastern front three months after victory in Europe. They saw to it that large stores of Japanese weapons got into the hands of the Red Army—some 740,000 rifles, 18,000 machine guns, and 4,000 artillery pieces—giving them about as much Japanese equipment as the Nationalists got.

From August 1945 until January 1947, the United States made efforts to avert civil war by trying to convince Chiang to establish a government in which opposition parties could participate. The American ambassador brought Mao and Chiang together for several weeks of meetings in Chongqing, but the agreements reached on cooperation led nowhere. Full-scale civil war ensued.

The civil war itself lasted only about two years. The Red Army (now called the People's Liberation Army, or PLA) began to isolate the cities, starting in Manchuria and working south. It lost battles but built support through moderate land reform. When Nationalist soldiers defected, they took their equipment with them, and the PLA incorporated them into its armies. Within a year the Nationalist forces in Manchuria were routed, and the PLA was moving into China proper. In 1948 a two-month battle near the railway center of Xuzhou pitted six hundred thousand of Chiang's troops against an equal number of Communist ones. Although Chiang had air support, his army was smashed, and he lost almost a half-million men. Thus, although the Nationalists had started with much more in the way of modern armaments and several times the number of troops, they fared poorly on the battlefield. In early 1949, Chiang Kaishek

and much of his army and government retreated to Taiwan and reestablished their government there.

The unpopularity of the Nationalists had many roots. Prices in July 1948 were 3 million times higher than they had been in July 1937, and inflation did not let up then. People had to resort to barter, and a tenth of the population became refugees. Nationalist army officers and soldiers were widely seen as seizing whatever they could for themselves rather than working for the common good. Student protests were often put down by violence. When liberals demanded that Chiang widen participation in his government, he had his secret police assassinate them. No amount of American support could make the Chinese want to continue with this government in power.

SUMMARY

What changed between 1927 and 1949? How different was China? More than a half-century of struggle against a Japan intent on imperialist expansion was over: Japan had been thoroughly defeated and had turned against war. The Nationalist party had been defeated by the Communist party and had withdrawn from the mainland. The Communist party itself had changed dramatically. It had broken free from Comintern control and tied itself intimately to the peasantry. Mao had risen to the top position in the party and established his version of Marxism as the correct ideology. The party had grown enormously and acquired extensive experience in redistribution of land, mobilizing peasants, and keeping a tight rein on intellectuals.

Intensified Contact and Divergent Paths

War and Aftermath in Japan (1931–1964)

26

Japan's war in Asia and the Pacific expanded in response to military imperatives and domestic problems. It spurred institutional and economic development; it caused devastation and loss of life. After Japan's surrender, the United States occupied Japan and instituted reforms designed to transform it into a demilitarized democracy. Those that had lasting impact built on trends apparent during the war; others, including Japan's diplomatic relations with the United States, sparked controversy. The despondency of defeat turned into a determination to rebuild. High-speed economic growth began in the 1950s. When the economy reached prewar levels of production in 1956, the government declared the postwar period to be officially over. In 1960 it announced the Income Doubling Plan. The 1964 Tokyo Olympics marked Japan's return to the world order and restored its self-confidence as a nation.

The farther World War II recedes into the past, the more historians emphasize continuities across its divide. Although the impact of the war on individual lives is undeniable, its long-term consequences on the economy and society are debatable. Other questions to consider are: Who was responsible for the war? What impact did the U.S. occupation have on Japan? What enabled Japan's postwar recovery?

ROAD TO WAR (1931–1937)

Military actions exacerbated by rural crises dominated politics in the 1930s. The army demanded support for its takeover of Manchuria in 1931; the navy criticized the limitations imposed by the London Naval Treaty. The armed forces transformed Japan into a militaristic state by forcing the Diet to curtail freedom of speech and approve its war budgets. Anger at capitalist *zaibatsu* for sucking the farmers' blood and at corrupt politicians who put their interests ahead of the nation erupted in abortive coups d'état that exposed factions within the military. Mass organizations drew the farmers' support to the military; farmers also participated in self-improvement drives sponsored by bureaucrats and civilian reformers. Only a few intellectuals dared criticize imperialist policies. For the majority of citizens, being Japanese meant taking pride in the slogan "Asia for the Asiatics," which obfuscated Japan's colonizing project.

Junior Officers and the Citizenry

Radical junior officers drew inspiration from diverse sources. They heard their men's stories of sisters being sold into prostitution to save the family farm from moneylenders. They read in the newspapers of how the *zaibatsu* profited from currency speculation when Japan went off the gold standard in 1931. They studied Kita Ikki's *A Plan for the Reorganization of Japan*. Kita proposed that the "people's emperor" suspend the constitution and have the government confiscate surplus wealth, manage the economy, and provide social welfare and "world knowledge based on the Japanese spirit." When these goals had been accomplished, Japan would liberate Asia, and "the Sun Flag of the Land of the Rising Sun will light the darkness of the entire world."[1] Officers modeled their plans for revolution on the Meiji Restoration. Like men of high purpose (*shishi*), they had to act to remove evil advisers who prevented the emperor from making his will known to the people. They credited violence with purifying the state and mistrusted old men who might tarnish their youthful idealism.

Junior officers responded to and exacerbated factions in the military. Their hero, General Araki Sadao, promoted spiritual training to inculcate devotion to the emperor and martial virtues of loyalty and self-sacrifice. The Japanese spirit (*Yamatodamashii*) sufficed to overcome mere material obstacles. Araki's Imperial Way faction opposed the Control faction's arguments that battles could be won only by rational planning using advanced military technology and sophisticated weaponry. In 1935, an Araki supporter assassinated the Control faction's General Nagata Tetsuzan and electrified the nation with his diatribe

against military men and their civilian toadies who had corrupted army and *kokutai*. On February 26, 1936, junior officers armed with the slogan "Revere the Emperor, Destroy Traitors" led fourteen hundred troops to seize the Diet building and army headquarters, kill cabinet ministers, and call on the emperor to announce a Shōwa Restoration. Horrified at the threat of insurrection, the emperor summoned the army to suppress the rebellion. After a four-day standoff, the junior officers surrendered. They were executed along with their mentor Kita Ikki in a victory for the Control faction.

A symbiotic relationship developed between the military and the old middle class of shopkeepers and factory owners as well as teachers, low-ranking officials, and farmers. The army founded the Imperial Military Reserve Association in 1910, the Greater Japan Youth Association in 1915, and the Greater Japan National Defense Women's Association in 1932. Organized at the hamlet, not the amalgamated village level, the Reserve Association took over community functions such as firefighting, police, road and canal repairs, shrine and temple maintenance, emergency relief, and entertainment. It promoted drill practice, "nation-building" group calisthenics, and bayonet competitions. It hosted lectures by military-approved speakers, and it corresponded with battalion adjutants regarding the welfare and conduct of conscripts. The women's association sank roots in urban as well as rural areas. These associations identified individual with community, community with army, and army with emperor.

Social Reform

In the 1930s, bureaucrats and social reformers focused on devastation resulting from crop failures in northeastern Japan. When students dispatched by Hani Motoko, journalist and founder of the magazine *Woman's Friend (Fujin no tomo)*, reported that farmers knew nothing of modern hygiene and sanitation, spent money foolishly on ceremonies, lazed about, and drank, Hani established settlement houses that taught poor women sewing, cleanliness, etiquette, nutrition, and thrift. The Agriculture Ministry supported similar plans that promoted social education, agricultural cooperatives, economic planning, and moral betterment. The emphasis on thrift and frugality paralleled the nationwide effort by the Home Ministry, social reformers, educators, and women's leaders to increase Japan's savings rate, both to help individuals plan for emergencies and to fund national projects.

---

1. George M. Wilson, *Radical Nationalist in Japan: Kita Ikki 1883–1937* (Cambridge, Mass.: Harvard University Press, 1969), pp. 75, 81.

WARTIME MOBILIZATION (1937–1945)

During eight years of war between 1937 and 1945 (see **Connections: World War II**), government ministries were often poorly informed, disorganized, and overextended. Faced with unexpected challenges, they cobbled together ad hoc measures and made mistakes in prosecuting the war overseas and on the home front. Just as the army and navy competed for resources, the former emphasizing the threat from the Soviet Union while the latter focused on the United States, so did civilian ministries duplicate one another's programs and fight for control of domestic policy. Like Germany, Japan at first refused to mobilize women, a policy that limited the war effort.

Civilian commitment to the war varied. Businessmen supported military goals so long as they did not threaten survival of their firms. Under pressure to conform, citizens greeted news of the first victories with exultation. Dwindling food supplies, higher taxes, and a black market led to forbearance and despair. Malnutrition increased the incidence of tuberculosis (160,000 deaths in 1942), rickets, and eye disease. First children and then adults fled cities for the countryside. When the flower of Japan's youth was summoned to make the supreme sacrifice in the Special Attack Forces (*kamikaze*), many did so gladly; others did not. (See **Documents: Excerpts from the Diary of Hayashi Toshimasa.**)

Unlike other belligerents in World War II, Japan changed its wartime leadership repeatedly. Seven prime ministers served between outbreak of war with China on July 7, 1937, and surrender on August 15, 1945. Executed as a war criminal for having declared war against the United States, General Tōjō Hideki served concurrently as prime minister (1941–1944), army minister, home minister, and munitions minister and filled other posts as he perceived a need. He never directed naval operations, nor did the navy inform him when it fought. Even the army general staff challenged his authority. Civilian bureaucrats, especially in the Justice Ministry, maintained their constitutional autonomy. Only the Shōwa emperor received complete information on military policy and operations, including plans for surprise attacks on American, Dutch, and British bases in 1941. In fear of jeopardizing the throne, he sanctioned military decisions as his ancestors had done for centuries.

Government planning of the economy began in 1931 when the Diet passed the Major Industries Control Law. It promoted cartels and required industries to tell the government their plans. In 1937 came the New Economic Order to make the Japanese Empire self-sufficient. Bureaucrats allocated funds to critical industries, nationalized electrical plants, supervised banks, and spun a web of regulation. The National Mobilization law of 1938 focused research on chemicals and machine technology. Large companies had to introduce on-the-job training for workers. Labor was rationed according to production needs. Military requirements prompted the rise of new industries in fields such as optics, determined techniques used in existing industries such as steel, and stimulated technological innovation. Wartime priorities transformed Japan's industrial structure. Textile industries declined; heavy and chemical industries expanded.

The Home Ministry bent popular culture to the war effort. Foreign words being considered symptomatic of foreign sympathies: *baseball* became *yakyū*. Martial music replaced jazz. Hair permanents were criticized because they were Western and wasted resources. Women had to dress in baggy pants called *monpe*. The Communications Ministry founded the Dōmei News Agency in 1936 to channel national and international news to newspapers. It already controlled radio broadcasts through the national public radio station, NHK. To extend its reach, the ministry distributed free radios to rural villages.

The Education Ministry suppressed academic freedom and promoted patriotism. Professors critical of the war in China and military dominance over politics had to resign. Schoolchildren performed physical exercises to build bodies for the emperor; after 1940 they volunteered for community service projects. Starting in 1941, they took paramilitary training to identify enemy aircraft and practiced charging with bamboo spears. Published in 1937, the textbook *Cardinal Principles of the National Polity* (*Kokutai no hongi*) taught students that the emperor was the divine head of state and benevolent father to the Japanese people. Japanese were superior because of their racial homogeneity. They possessed a distinctive culture and history infused by the radiant presence of the imperial house. No sacrifice was too great to protect this unique heritage.

In the name of national unity, the government suppressed all pacifist new religions under the Religious Organizations Law of 1939. Social reformers and feminist activists joined the Greater Japan Women's Society that sent soldiers to war and disseminated ways to practice frugality. Patriotic Associations united tenant farmers and landlords, workers and businessmen. The ideology of "dedicated work" valorized labor as a public activity in service to the nation. Neighborhood associations organized air raid drills and kept watch for dangerous thought. In 1944 the Home Ministry folded them all into the Imperial Rule Assistance Association.

A dedicated citizenry and long-range planning could not overcome growing shortages. The government struggled to shore up the collapsing economy. Lacking imported technology, companies developed new techniques that took military needs and scarce resources into account. The Zero fighter was crafted with extreme precision and used minimal amounts of steel regardless of the pilot's safety. In addition to the lack of fuel because of disruptions to shipping, the destruction of factories meant fewer manufactured goods such as fertilizer. Food production dropped.

Military conscription created labor shortages in industry and mining. The first to fill the gap were Koreans. In 1943, the government allowed women to volunteer for work in ordnance and aircraft industries. It drafted prisoners of war to work in steel plants and mines. The military ended educational deferments and drafted university students. In 1944, middle school boys started factory work.

The last months of the war brought widespread hardship. Evacuees to the countryside put an extra burden on scarce resources. Nutritional levels fell following the meager harvest of 1944. A few people criticized their leaders in anonymous graffiti and letters to the editor. Worker absenteeism rose, product quality slipped, and work stoppages spread. Although signs of disaffection were slight, they were enough to make politicians and bureaucrats worry about the threat of social revolution. By the time most factions in government were willing to admit defeat, approximately 3 million Japanese had died. Despite evidence of destruction, the emperor's announcement of Japan's defeat on August 15 came as a shock.

OCCUPATION (1945–1952)

Defeat did not bring an end to hardship. The suburban middle class was spared the fate of poor and working-class urban residents who lost everything in firestorms, but everyone was short of food. Farmers were better off, although stunned by defeat that called into question cherished ideals of loyalty, patriotism, and service to the emperor. Occupation by a military dictatorship under General Douglas MacArthur began on August 30, 1945. At first the occupiers considered punishing Japan, perhaps by returning it to an agrarian economy. After the beginning of the Cold War with the Soviet Union and the 1949 communist takeover of China, the emphasis shifted to keeping Japan in the free world.

Despair and Liberation

The war left 6.6 million Japanese soldiers and civilians stranded in enemy territory from Manchuria to Southeast Asia. The Soviet Union sent 575,000 Japanese military personnel and adult male civilians to Siberian labor camps. Soviet soldiers raped and killed women and children. Of Japanese settlers in Manchuria, 50 percent died at the end of the war, many at the hands of Chinese. Japanese settlers in Korea made their way across hostile territory to refugee camps and then onto crowded ships to Japan. Seventy thousand Japanese in the Philippines had to wait until the end of 1946 before seeing Japan; British and Dutch did not return their prisoners of war until 1947. On Pacific islands, Japanese soldiers resorted to cannibalism or starved. The last soldiers came home in the 1970s.

Repatriated soldiers and civilians met a cold welcome in war-devastated Japan. War widows, homeless orphans, and maimed veterans became social rejects. Most shunned were victims from Hiroshima and Nagasaki who were subject to radiation sickness that turned them into pariahs. With the economy at a standstill, there was little work even for the able-bodied. Competition for jobs depressed already low wages. The winter of 1945–1946 was worse than the winters of wartime. Rationed supplies of coal and food were not enough to stave off freezing and starvation. Urban women traveled to the countryside to trade heirlooms for food and patronized the black market.

For some, defeat meant liberation. If life had no meaning, why not drink, take drugs, and steal? In his 1947 novel *The Setting Sun*, Dazai Osamu mourned the loss of prewar values and presented the only choice left: to live for oneself alone. People who celebrated the end to restrictions on freedom of thought and behavior had an easier time coping with material shortages. Defeat vindicated the beliefs of prewar Marxists and socialists who hoped to build a just society out of the rubble of failed capitalist fortunes. The black market flourished at every train terminal,

DOCUMENTS

Excerpts from the Diary of Hayashi Toshimasa

Why do soldiers fight? What do they think about as they wait to die? This diary, written by Hayashi Toshimasa, a graduate of Keiō University who was killed in action on August 9, 1945, affords one answer to these questions and provides glimpses of the camaraderie and resentments that supported members of the Special Attack Forces in their final days.

April 13, 1945

First Lieutenant Kuniyasu was killed in action, as was Second Sub-lieutenant Tani-gawa Takao. Everyone is dying away. The lives of plane pilots are short indeed. I just heard today that Second Sub-lieutenant Yatsunami also died the day before yesterday; he dove straight into the sea while participating in night-training, and his dead body was washed ashore yesterday onto the white beach of Kujuūkuri-hama. Dear Yatsunami! I enjoyed getting together with him again here—the last time was in Mie. Dressed in his nightclothes, he came to my room rather late on the evening of the day before the accident, and we drank beer together. I wonder whether or not it was some kind of premonition. He was very gentle and quiet. When I said, "What a splendid nightwear," he just chuckled and said that it had been made by his wife, whom he just married in January. His wife too suffered the misfortune on this earth of a typical pilot's wife. How is she going to spend the long life that stretches ahead of her?

Tanigawa has a fiancée too, in Kobe. Those who were left behind may be unlucky, but their sacrifice is an offering for Japan's ultimate victory. So I would ask to please continue to live with strength and pride, and in such a way as not to bring shame to the brave men who courageously and willingly died for their country.

April 23

Nighttime flying began. After our flying operation we drank beer at a welcome party for Kamiōseko. I got a little high. Second Sub-lieutenant Kamiōseko and I were enraged at the current situation. It was all about our position as reserve officers in the Imperial Navy. Now I declare! I will not fight, at least not for the Imperial Navy. I live and die for my fatherland, and, I would go so far as to say that it is for my own pride. I have nothing but a strong antipathy for the Imperial Navy—absolutely no positive feelings at all. From now on I can say in and to my heart, "I can die for my own pride, but I would not die—absolutely not—for the Imperial Navy." How terribly we, the 13th class of pilots to come out of the "students mobilized for war" program, have been oppressed by the Imperial Navy! Who exactly is fighting this war now anyway? A full half of my classmates of the 13th class who were bomber pilots on carriers, and my friends, are now already dead.

organized and patrolled by gangsters. Small factory owners made pots instead of helmets, and former soldiers became businessmen. Prostitutes called pan-pan girls who serviced GIs dressed in rayon dresses and nylon hose, curled their hair, and painted their faces in an orgy of self-expression not seen since the 1920s. The dominant themes in popular culture were titillation and sex; the carnal body replaced the *kokutai*, the body politic.

Occupation Goals

As Supreme Commander of the Allied Powers (SCAP —also shorthand for the occupation bureaucracy), MacArthur intended to demilitarize Japan and work through existing institutions to install democracy. The United States kept the Allies out of Japan by putting them on the Far East Commission (FEC) that oversaw SCAP policy, which met in Washing-

June 30

It was raining when I woke up this morning, and I was so glad I could sleep some more that I pulled a blanket over me again. I got up a little after seven, took a late breakfast, and at a barracks I went over some slides designed to help us recognize the different types of enemy ships. Now I have finished with the slides. I returned to my own room, and am writing this and playing a record. Next door, on a blanket spread over the floor, Kamiōseko, Yamabe, Tejima, and Nasu are having fun playing bridge. No change outside—the steady rain continues.

I cannot begin to do anything about everything.

Simply because I shall have to leave this world in the very near future.

I should thank the Navy's traditional spirit, or rather their cliquishness, which drove Eguchi to say: "I want to go to the front soon—I want to die soon," and even drove me into that sort of psychological state. It even drove all the rest of us, university students transformed into pilots, into that same state of mind.

July 31

Today is a sortie day. It is the day for the eight planes of our Ryūsei (Falling Star) squad to carry out a special attack. The fog was extremely thick when I got up. It turned into water that dripped from the leaves and treetops on the mountain.

When I arrived at the airport, the items that were to be carried onto our planes were neatly set out in rows.

Last night, I completely changed everything that I was wearing. I also wound tightly around my waist the thousand-stitch cloth my mother sent me. Then there was the brand-new muffler my aunt in Yudate gave me.—In other words, I put on the very best things I had.

I am all alone and, expecting the sortie command to come along at any moment, I am writing this in an air-raid shelter.

Farewell dear Father, Mother, Brothers and Sisters, and other relatives and friends.

Please continue to live on enjoying very good health.

This time I am going right into Han Christian Andersen's fairyland, and I will become its prince.

And I shall be chatting with little birds, flowers, and trees.

I pray for the eternal prosperity of the great Japanese Empire.

August 9 A clear day

Once again the enemy's mechanized divisions are approaching the home islands.

In one hour and a half I shall leave here for the sortie, as a member of the special attack force. The skies are a breathtakingly deep blue, and there is a sharp touch of autumn.

August 9th!

Today I shall fly one of the very latest in war planes, a Ryūsei, and will slam it into an enemy carrier.

Source: *Listen to the Voices from the Sea: Writings of the Fallen Japanese Students*, comp. Nihon Senbotsu Gakusei Kinen-Kai, trans. Midori Yamanouchi and Joseph L. Quinn (Scranton, Pa.: University of Scranton Press, 2000), pp. 247–250, modified.

ton, D.C. The United States bought off the Soviet Union by handing over islands north of Hokkaido. Only judges for the Tokyo war crimes trials represented countries that had suffered under Japan's war machine. One SCAP faction wanted to restrict Japan's international trade and dispatch the fruits of industrialization to Japan's victims as war reparations. Another consisted of economists and lawyers primed to practice social engineering. By instituting land reform, revising education, promoting labor unions, emancipating women, limiting police powers, and rewriting the constitution, they planned to make Japan fit to rejoin the community of nations.

What was to be done with the Shōwa emperor? He did not sign the instrument of surrender on September 2, 1945; that humiliation was left to a general and a diplomat. Instead, he, the cabinet, and his staff tried to distance him from responsibility for the

Japanese Women Working in an Ordnance Factory. With able-bodied men drafted for the war effort, women had to take their place in industry. *(AKG, London)*

war, taking a stance of plausible deniability on all decisions save the last that ended it. MacArthur dissuaded him from admitting even moral responsibility. Although Britain wanted to try the emperor as a war criminal, MacArthur believed that once the military was gone, the emperor was needed as a bulwark against communism. By refusing to accept responsibility for the war in which so many had died in his name, the emperor also alienated far-right militarists. The issue of his responsibility for the war has continued to rankle at home and with Japan's neighbors. On January 1, 1946, the emperor announced that he was a human being, not a manifest god. Defined by

the new constitution as symbol of the state, he continues to embody a national identity predicated on ethnic homogeneity.

Occupation Reforms

On October 13, 1945, the prime minister appointed a committee at SCAP's urging to consider constitutional revision. Political parties, progressive and socialist groups, scholars, and think tanks drafted constitutions ignored by the prime minister's committee. Its recommendations were so minor that in February 1946, MacArthur ordered his Government

Section to take over the task lest a grass-roots movement for a constitutional convention lead to too much democracy and an attack on the emperor. His people hid their work from the U.S. and Japanese governments, the FEC, and other branches of SCAP. After conferences between SCAP officials and cabinet representatives to debate the draft, it was published in early March 1946. SCAP intervened repeatedly in Diet deliberations to limit discussion and prevent substantial revision. The new constitution replaced the Meiji constitution, to which it was offered as an amendment, when the Upper House approved it in October. The emperor promulgated it on November 3, 1946.

Articles in the constitution define the rights to life, liberty, and the pursuit of happiness in terms of education, health care, police protection, work, and a minimum standard of living. Women received the right to vote. People detained by the police had the right to legal counsel. Freedoms included freedom from arbitrary arrest and unauthorized search and seizure plus freedom of assembly, speech, and religion. The judiciary became separate and independent. The Privy Council was dissolved in accordance with the principle of popular sovereignty. The Diet acquired the sole authority to make laws. Its vote of no confidence sufficed to dissolve the cabinet. Within the Diet, the Lower House of Representatives took precedence over the Upper House of Councilors, which became an elected body.

The new constitution had clauses that MacArthur would have deplored in the U.S. Constitution. Workers obtained the right to organize unions and bargain collectively, professors had the right of academic freedom, and women were guaranteed equal rights with men. Most controversial was Article 9: "The Japanese people forever renounce war as a sovereign right of the nation. . . . Land, sea, and air forces will never be maintained."[2] This wording was later interpreted to mean that armed forces could be created for self-defense. When FEC insisted on a clause that limited the cabinet to civilians, this too was interpreted as implying the existence of a military. In 1950, SCAP wanted Japan to create an army to fight in Korea. Prime Minister Yoshida Shigeru refused. He created a Police Reserve, soon transformed into the Self-Defense Force.

Once the constitution had been promulgated, the Justice Ministry reformed the civil code. The new code emphasized the equality of the sexes and the dignity of the individual. It abolished patriarchal authority in the household, reiterated the freedom of marriage promised in the constitution, and required that all children share the family estate. This was not a burden for middle-class families whose assets consisted of their children's education. For shopkeepers, restauranteurs, and farmers, an equal division of property plus heavy inheritance taxes all too often meant selling off the patrimony.

SCAP quickly imposed additional reforms. The most radical forced landlords to sell their holdings to the government for resale to tenants, a measure met with approval by the Agriculture and Forestry Ministry that had wanted a class of independent farmers even before the war. Absentee landlords had to relinquish all their land; resident landlords were allowed to keep only land they farmed themselves plus an additional five or so acres depending on the region. Although collecting tenant fees had already proved so onerous that many landlords welcomed the chance to sell out, they lamented the loss of their ancestral way of life. By 1950, farmer-owners cultivated 90 percent of Japan's agricultural land.

SCAP also intervened in educational reform. With American schools as the model, a new single-track system of primary school, middle school, and high school replaced the specialized higher schools. Compulsory education was extended to nine years. Teachers embraced the new curriculum that stressed civic virtues of democracy and individual responsibility. Locally elected school boards selected texts, although in later years they did so from a list vetted by the Education Ministry. Parent-teacher associations involved mothers in school activities. New junior colleges, colleges, and universities made higher education available to a wider segment of the population than before. None rivaled Tokyo University, and all required students to pass entrance examinations.

SCAP kept itself above the law. Despite the separation of church and state, MacArthur allowed Christian missionaries to use U.S. government equipment and encouraged the emperor and empress to take instruction in Christianity. Censorship of printed materials and movies continued. Left-wing publications that criticized capitalism faced prepublication scrutiny. In movies, sword fighting and criticism of the emperor were out. Instead, SCAP encouraged movie makers to depict romance between men and women. The first mouth-to-mouth kiss made headlines.

2. Dale M. Hellegers, *We, the Japanese People: World War II and the Origins of the Japanese Constitution*, 2 vols. (Stanford: Stanford University Press, 2002), p. 576.

Economic Developments

Economic reform took many turns. Trustbusters took aim at *zaibatsu* because they had contributed to Japan's war effort (Mitsubishi made the Zero fighter) and because their economic dominance appeared inherently undemocratic. SCAP ordered the holding companies for the ten largest *zaibatsu* dissolved, broke up the Mitsui and Mitsubishi trading companies, forced family members to sell their stock and resign from boards, and purged fifteen hundred executives accused of aiding the war machine. Japanese bureaucrats allowed government assets, including construction materials and machinery, to disappear into the black market or the hands of business cronies. To cover the deficit and the run on savings deposits at war's end, the Finance Ministry printed reams of money. Official prices soared 539 percent in the first year of the occupation, with black market prices ranging from fourteen to thirty-four times higher. Fearing the destabilizing effects of inflation, at the end of 1948, Washington dispatched a banker from Detroit named Joseph Dodge. At Dodge's command, the government collected more in taxes than it paid out. It eliminated government subsidies to manufacturers. Public works, welfare, and education suffered cuts. Dodge curbed domestic consumption and promoted exports. He got the United States to agree to an exchange rate of 360 yen to the dollar. Deflation and economic contraction forced small businesses into bankruptcy.

The Korean War rescued Japan from the brink of depression and laid the foundation for future economic growth. The industrial sector gorged on procurement orders for vehicles, uniforms, sandbags, medicines, electrical goods, construction materials, liquor, paper, and food. Despite the prohibition on the manufacture of war materiel, Japanese companies made munitions. Their mechanics repaired tanks and aircraft. Businesses plowed profits into upgrading equipment and buying advanced technology from the United States through licensing agreements and purchase of patent rights. Industries seeking a way to compete in the expanding world economy incorporated the quality control method that the statistician W. Edwards Deming had introduced to Japan in 1949. By the end of the Korean War, the increase in wages and economic growth had brought food consumption back to pre–World War II levels. Consumers were able to buy household amenities and still put money into savings accounts.

Labor and the Reverse Course

To promote democracy, SCAP had the Trade Union Law issued in December 1945, and workers seized the opportunity to organize. Free to participate in politics, the Japanese Communist party (JCP) and the Japanese Socialist party (JSP) fostered trade unions. By the middle of 1948, unions enrolled over half of the nonagricultural work force, including white-collar workers, especially in the public sector. Other workers organized production control movements to take over businesses, factories, and mines that owners were accused of deliberately sabotaging in revenge for democratization. Like unionized workers, they wanted to get back to work and make a living wage.

Labor union activism led to the "reverse course." Workers united around issues including adequate food, support for working mothers, equal pay for equal work, and democratic elections. Before the postwar election of April 10, 1946, in which women voted for the first time, a rally in Tokyo brought together workers, farmers, Koreans, and ordinary citizens to listen to speeches by Communists, Socialists, and liberals demanding a people's constitution and criticizing the cabinet for obstructing democratic reform. On May 1, International Workers' Day, cities nationwide witnessed demonstrations in support of worker unity and democracy. On May 19, women joined demonstrations demanding that the emperor force the government to deliver food. Students held demonstrations a week later to demand self-government at their institutions. Socialist- and Communist-led labor unions formed in August organized strikes in October. In January 1947, the prime minister warned that striking government workers would be fired. A coalition of labor unions announced plans for a general strike on February 1. MacArthur called it off. In 1948, SCAP had the Japanese government issue regulations forbidding public employees to strike.

The reverse course had additional dimensions. The Cold War led the United States to view its erstwhile enemy as an ally against communism. SCAP compiled lists of "reds" to purge, first from the public sector and later, during the Korean War, from the private sector. Approximately twenty-two thousand workers lost their jobs, and most of the JCP leaders went underground. Previously purged politicians, bureaucrats, and business leaders were rehabilitated. In 1948, the dismantling of the *zaibatsu* came to a halt. The Diet gave the bureaucracy greater control over trade and investment than it had during the war. The

Ministry of International Trade and Industry (MITI) had the Japan Development Bank lend money from the government's postal savings system to private companies. MITI also advised the Bank of Japan on its loans to private banks. It approved the transfer of foreign technology to industries it deemed worthy and provided them with administrative guidance. The Finance Ministry regulated currency transactions by restricting funds individuals and corporations could take or send out of the country.

Before ending the occupation, the U.S. Senate had Japan sign a peace treaty with the Nationalist Chinese on Taiwan that precluded recognition of and trade with the People's Republic of China. The peace treaty and security treaty signed with the United States plus associated agreements signed in 1951 continued the occupation under a different name. After SCAP was dismantled in 1952, one hundred thousand American personnel plus dependents stayed on at military bases that dotted the islands. Extraterritoriality protected them from the Japanese judicial system and removed the bases from oversight by the Japanese government. Okinawa remained under U.S. military jurisdiction until 1972. Under the U.S. security umbrella, Japan was free to pursue economic development, although it had to follow the U.S. lead in international relations. On Bloody May Day 1952, four hundred thousand workers, students, and housewives denounced the security treaty, Japanese rearmament, the status of Okinawa, and government plans to pass an "antisubversive" bill that threatened academic freedom. Political positions were divided between left-wing support for neutrality, democratization, and demilitarization and the conservative affirmation of alliance with the United States.

POLITICAL SETTLEMENT AND ECONOMIC RECOVERY (1952–1964)

A host of political parties contended for Diet seats in the first postwar election of 1946. Yoshida Shigeru pulled together a coalition of conservative parties willing to make him prime minister, but he had to resign when elections the following year gave a significant share of the votes to the JSP. Taking advantage of the JSP's inability to deal with economic crises, Yoshida regained the prime ministership in 1948 and held it until 1954. He recruited former bureaucrats into his party whose administrative experience and skill at in-fighting gave them an edge in faction building. The JSP split over whether to support the U.S.-Japan peace treaty; it reunited in October 1955. The next month, the two conservative parties formed the Liberal Democratic party (LDP). Except for brief interludes, it has continued to dominate the Diet and cabinet. During this period of one-party rule, heads of factions within the LDP selected the prime minister, who rewarded his supporters with powerful and lucrative ministerial appointments.

The LDP promoted economic growth as the nation's highest goal, less to enhance state power than to wean workers from socialism by offering them a better life. Starting in the late 1950s, the LDP spread benefits of the growing economy across all sectors of society through higher wages and a higher standard of living. In 1958, it inaugurated national health insurance. It helped farmers increase productivity by mechanizing production and spreading chemical fertilizers and pesticides. The government paid villages to reorganize landholdings into fewer, bigger plots and individuals to diversify crops. It encouraged companies to locate factories in rural areas and hire farmers. It built roads and sewer systems. It restricted the import of rice and subsidized rice production. Through these programs and the outright purchase of votes, the LDP acquired a lock on rural electoral districts. The appeal of conservative policies to small businessmen and shopkeepers gave it urban votes as well.

The LDP also maintained power by aligning itself with bureaucrats and businessmen. Advisory groups composed of businessmen, bankers, consumers, and union officials consulted with cabinet ministers on policy and proposed legislation. Former bureaucrats either ran for office or joined corporations whose fortunes they had helped guide. Undergirding the web of personal connections was a flow of cash from businessmen to politicians to voters.

Political and Social Protest

Opposition parties in the Diet so little impeded the LDP juggernaut that citizens with grievances sought other forms of protest. Demonstrations against American bases and nuclear testing erupted periodically during the 1950s. The Japan Teachers' Union resisted the centralization of educational policy and personnel practices instituted by the Education Ministry in 1955. The General Council of Japanese Trade Unions (Sōhyō) opposed the Japan Productivity Center set up by Japanese businessmen with U.S. assistance because unions feared it would exploit workers.

When the government decided to switch Japan's chief energy source from coal to oil, the Mitsui Mining Company called for the voluntary early retirement of six thousand workers at its Miike mine in Kyushu. The union responded with a strike marked by violence and death that lasted 113 days. Workers learned that radical calls for class struggle undercut job security, and corporate managers learned that it was cheaper to transfer redundant workers to other operations than to fire them.

The largest political demonstrations in Japanese history erupted from late 1959 to June 1960 over revision and extension of the U.S.-Japan security treaty. Negotiations removed the clause that permitted the use of U.S. troops to quell internal disturbances, but bases remained off-limits to Japanese scrutiny. Indicted as a war criminal and former minister in Manchuria, Prime Minister Kishi Nobusuke rammed the revised treaty through the lower house with the help of police who evicted the JCP and JSP opposition. Outraged at Kishi's high-handed tactics, masses of demonstrators gathered outside the Diet. Sōhyō had already coordinated strikes and mobilized workers against the treaty. The All Japan Federation of Student Self-Government Associations (Zengakuren) organized weeks of agitation. Some 134 groups and organizations including farmers and housewives joined the protest. Kishi had planned to celebrate the revised security treaty by welcoming U.S. President Dwight D. Eisenhower to Japan, but Eisenhower canceled the trip. Daily demonstrations continued at the Diet and in cities across Japan. On June 18, several hundred thousand people surrounded the Diet, but they could not prevent the treaty's automatic ratification at midnight. Kishi resigned five days later. In 1965, Japan signed a peace treaty with South Korea to the outrage of the left wing, which demonstrated against the exclusion of North Korea and the People's Republic of China. The ideological divide between conservatives and progressives sparked political unrest throughout the 1960s.

The constitution's guarantee of social equality and the Civil Code's emphasis on human dignity spurred *burakumin* to renew their struggle for equal rights. Founded in 1955, the Buraku Liberation League (BLL) allied itself with the JCP and JSP to publicize unfair treatment by individuals and institutions. It participated in demonstrations against renewal of the U.S.-Japan security treaty that gained it widespread support. Later protest marches focused nationwide attention on the *burakumin*'s plight. A government commission report in 1965 blamed *burakumin* problems on unwarranted social and economic discrimination. The Diet responded in 1969 by passing the Special Measures Law for Assimilation Projects that decried discrimination without instituting measures to stop it. To ameliorate this defect, the BLL resorted to denunciation campaigns, sometimes escalating to violence and threats that silenced public discussion of *burakumin* problems.

Women's organizations in the 1950s worked to protect children and encourage respect for mothers. Women joined movements to prohibit nuclear testing and to promote world peace for the sake of their children. They demanded clean elections. They elected women to the Diet who pushed for sexual equality and human rights. Women had campaigned for the abolition of state-sanctioned prostitution before the war; their goal became a reality in 1956 when the Diet passed the Prostitution Prevention Law that took effect two years later. While it abolished legal protection for prostitutes, it did not eliminate sex work. Women justified political activism on two grounds: their responsibility for their families and their constitutional rights.

Post-Occupation Economic Development

International and domestic factors promoted economic growth. Under the Potsdam Declaration, Japan was guaranteed access to raw materials it had previously extracted from colonies. Exchange rates remained stable until 1971. The world market was relatively open, and economic expansion across the free market world stimulated a growing demand for manufactured goods. Japan still had infrastructure developed before and during World War II. The most important prewar legacies were human resources—trained engineers, accountants, and workers—and the commitment to achievement through education. The first postwar generation of workers went into factories on graduation from high school, received on-the-job training, and worked long hours for the sake of their companies. Enterprise unions held demonstrations during the yearly spring offensive but interfered as little as possible in production. Management upped basic wages, promised lifetime employment, and distributed raises based on seniority. Workers began to live middle-class lives.

Heavy industries developed in wartime, and new companies that fashioned products for domestic consumption and export saw the greatest expansion.

Demonstrations Opposing the U.S.–Japan Security Treaty. During demonstrations opposing the U.S.-Japan security treaty, men and women marched on the American embassy demanding cancellation of President Eisenhower's visit, the prime minister's resignation, and dissolution of the Diet. *(Bettmann/Corbis)*

Steel producers, shipbuilders, manufacturers of synthetic fibers, and electronics and household appliance makers invested in technologies imported from the United States and in labor-saving mass-production facilities. The government provided low-cost financing that made Japan the largest shipbuilder in the world in the 1950s. MITI protected car and truck manufacturers by forbidding foreign investment in the auto industry and imposing tariffs of up to 40 percent on imported cars. Companies that enjoyed less help from MITI were Matsushita, maker of household appliances, and the electronics innovator Sony. (See **Material Culture: The Transistor.**) Supporting corporate growth were subcontractors that produced quality components for finished products. Between 1947 and 1952, the economy grew at an average annual rate of 11.5 percent. From 1954 to 1971, it grew at over 10 percent a year, to rank second to the United States among free market economies.

Increases in domestic consumption stimulated high-speed economic growth. During the occupation, SCAP broadcast images of American prosperity in the comic strip *Blondie* and other media to promote American values. Department store exhibitions and magazine advertisements illustrated the material life of the conqueror. Once the quality of food had improved, people wanted fashionable clothes. Every household wanted labor-saving devices such as washing machines, refrigerators, and vacuum cleaners. Television broadcasts began in 1953 because the owner of the *Yomiuri* newspaper and key bureaucrats believed that national pride required Japan to have the latest technology. The wedding of Crown Prince Akihito to the industrialist's daughter Shōda Michiko in 1959 swept televisions from retailers' shelves as viewers reveled in the democratic dream of a love marriage. Beginning in 1955, a massive exodus from farms to cities fueled a housing boom of high-density apartment buildings in suburbs. In these years, 90 percent of Japan's production went into the domestic market.

Postwar Culture

The consumption of mass culture stimulated growth in entertainment industries, publishing, and film. Commercial television stations demanded an endless

MATERIAL CULTURE

The Transistor

Every electronic product today relies on transistors, symbol and product of the technological age. Invented by Bell Laboratories in 1948, the early transistors were too unreliable and delicate for consumer applications, and they could not handle high frequencies for the human voice. It took Sony researchers months of experimentation to find a usable combination of materials.

Sony introduced a transistor radio in January 1955, only to discover that it disintegrated in summer heat. The second version, placed on the market in August, had poor sound quality, but it sold domestically owing to its battery's long life. Sony could not compete with American transistor radios until 1957, when it started selling a tiny "pocketable" radio. More important than the radio's size was the technological breakthrough based on the high-performance alloy germanium. In 1960 transistor radios became Japan's second biggest earner on the export market after ships. Teenagers loved carrying the radios to parks and beaches to listen to rock 'n' roll.

Sony introduced the world's first all-transistor television in 1960 and successfully miniaturized it two years later. In 1964, Sony displayed a prototype of a transistorized calculator at the New York's World Fair. Three years later it introduced a desktop calculator.

The transistors in the early radios, televisions, and calculators were huge compared to today's silicon transistors in integrated circuits that work liquid display calculators and watches. People typically buy electronic goods on impulse, indulging in a plethora of gadgetry that fills purses, pockets, and homes.

The TR-63. Sony's first successful transistor radio, the TR-63, could be called "pocketable" only because Sony salesmen wore shirts with extra-large breast pockets. *(Sony Corporation)*

supply of programming. The government-owned NHK had two channels, one devoted to news analysis, dramas, and *sumo* wrestling, the other specializing in education. Magazine and book publishers continued prewar trends without fear of censorship that had kept them from sensitive political topics. Kurosawa Akira directed *Ikiru* (*To Live*), which criticized bureaucratic arrogance. His 1951 film *Rashomon*, which questioned the possibility of knowing the truth, brought international recognition to

Japanese cinema when it won the grand prize at the Venice Film Festival. A series with wider appeal was *Godzilla*, started in 1954, which drew on Japan's sense of victimhood by depicting a monster roused from the deep by nuclear explosion. Misora Hibari captured hearts with her songs of parting and loss. They spoke to the will to survive that had carried women through the hardships of war and occupation. Public intellectuals and writers such as Maruyama Masao and Mishima Yukio questioned

BIOGRAPHY   Daimatsu Hirobumi

Soldier, prisoner of war, women's volleyball coach, and Diet member Daimatsu Hirobumi (1921–1978) gained worldwide fame for his draconian coaching methods when his team won the gold medal at the 1964 Tokyo Olympics.

Hirobumi's wartime experience marked him for life. Conscripted into the army after the attack on Pearl Harbor, he attended an officers' preparatory school in China and fought in China and Southeast Asia. The last months of the war found him in Burma with only raw bamboo shoots for food. Many soldiers died; sheer willpower kept him alive. He ended up a prisoner of war under the British in Rangoon. In revenge for the atrocities that the Japanese army had inflicted on British POWs and the humiliating surrender of Hong Kong and Singapore, British officers subjected Japanese POWs to degrading indignities. Hirobumi later recounted how he cleaned latrines for British and Indian soldiers with his bare hands. Worse, he had to clean female officers' rooms and wash the underwear that they removed before his eyes in a gesture calculated to be emasculating.

Repatriated to Japan after twenty-two months as a POW, Hirobumi found work coaching a women's volleyball team at the Nichibō textile factory in Kaizuka. At that time, volleyball was a popular sport among factory workers because it could be played with just a ball in whatever space was available. In 1954, Nichibō organized a company team with Hirobumi in charge. In 1958 the team won all of Japan's major titles; in 1962 it won the world championship.

Hirobumi's training methods were brutal. He hurled balls at the players until they collapsed from pain and exhaustion. He insisted that they play regardless of injuries. He allowed them only three-and-one-half hours of sleep a night before the Olympics and had them practice for four hours the day of the final match. He also emphasized the incremental improvement of technique, relying on methods similar to quality control circles. His players once complained to the factory management that he was an enemy of women because he worked them unmercifully. He expected them to sacrifice everything for the chance to win, first for the company, then for Japan, just as he had sacrificed himself in wartime.

Eight-five percent of Japan's television sets were tuned to the Olympics the night the Japanese team defeated the Soviet Union in three sets. The women's unprecedented success made volleyball a national obsession. Hirobumi's fame swept him to a seat in the Diet's upper house in 1968. He lost his bid for a second term.

Source: Yoshikuni Igarashi, *Bodies of Memory: Narratives of War in Postwar Japan* (Princeton, N.J.: Princeton University Press, 2000).

---

the ingredients of Japan's national identity. What did it mean to be Japanese if the nation's only goal was economic success? Where laid responsibility for wartime aggression?

New religions provided one answer to these questions. Founded in 1930 and suppressed during the war, Sōka Gakkai (value-creating society) was Japan's largest new religion in the 1960s. Its political arm, the Clean Government Party (Kōmeitō), founded in 1964, became Japan's third largest political party. Today its leaders serve as town councilors and school board officers. It owns land, businesses, and shops. It provides a sense of family and community and aids in finding marriage partners, jobs, loans, and higher education. The *zadankai*, a type of group therapy,

helps followers solve personal problems and gain self-confidence. Sōka Gakkai teaches that the purpose of life is the pursuit of happiness; the three virtues of beauty, gain, and goodness bring happiness; following the teachings of Nichiren and having faith in the *Lotus Sutra* bring virtue. Constitutional guarantees of religious freedom and the population shift from country to town led to an explosion in the numbers of new religions and their membership. Although they criticize the excesses of popular culture and consumerism, part of their appeal lies in their promise of material benefits.

The Tokyo Olympics of 1964 marked the climax of high-speed economic growth and a turning point in Japan's postwar history. (See **Biography: Daimatsu**

Hirobumi.) National and Tokyo metropolitan governments cleaned up and paved city streets; rebuilt stores, schools, and government offices; constructed stadiums at Yoyogi Park; dug new subway lines; laid new roads; and renovated Haneda Airport and connected it to the city by monorail. New hotels became Japan's first postwar high rises. The centerpiece of this vast public works project was the Shinkansen (bullet train), which covered the distance between Tokyo and Osaka in three hours and ten minutes. It was the fastest, most reliable, and safest train in the world.

Japan had been allowed to join the United Nations in 1956, and the Olympics marked the culmination of its reentry into the global community. Worldwide coverage of the games focused attention on Japan as a peaceful modern state. Ichikawa Kon's documentary, *Olympiad*, transformed them into art.

SUMMARY

What changed between 1931 and 1964? What impact did World War II have on Japan, and what was the war's legacy? In 1931, Japan had an overseas empire, took pride in its strong army, and trained its citizens in patriotism. In 1964 it had lost control of even Okinawa, its Self-Defense Force specialized in domestic humanitarian aid, and academics were free to publicly criticize the emperor system for Japan's shortcomings. The war destroyed lives, infrastructure, and, for a time, belief in the Japanese spirit. Japan recovered thanks to the changing international climate of the late 1940s and early 1950s, reforms initiated by the U.S. occupation, protection provided by security agreement with the United States, and U.S. recognition that democracy required economic stability. It must not be forgotten that recovery also built on the bureaucratic, educational, and industrial foundation laid before the war. By 1964 Japan's GDP had surpassed its prewar peak, and purchases by Japanese consumers of the latest electronic technology spurred product development in key export industries. Translators had discovered modern Japanese literature, and art house audiences, Japanese film.

China Under Mao (1949–1976)

By the end of 1949, the Communist party had gained control of almost the entire country, and Mao Zedong had pronounced the establishment of the People's Republic of China (PRC). The party quickly set about restructuring China. People were mobilized to tackle such tasks as redistributing land, promoting heavy industry, reforming marriage practices, and unmasking counterrevolutionaries. Wealth and power were redistributed on a vast scale. Massive modernization projects created new factories, railroads, schools, hospitals, and reservoirs. Ordinary people were subject to increased political control as the central government set policies that determined what farmers would produce, where and how their children would be educated, what they might read in books and newspapers, and where they could live or travel. The most radical phase was the Cultural Revolution, especially 1966 to 1969, when the party itself was attacked by students and workers mobilized to make permanent revolution.

Until the late 1970s, Western scholars had limited access to the PRC and had to rely heavily on analyzing official pronouncements and interviewing refugees. Scholars studied the structure of the government, its policies, its top figures, and their factional struggles. As China has become more open in the past two decades and new sources have become available, research has revealed much more complex pictures of how China fared during the Mao years. Not only can the human dramas be examined with more nuance, but variation from one place to another can be assessed. Mao still fascinates. Can the excesses of the Great Leap and the Cultural Revolution be fully blamed on Mao's inadequate grasp of reality? How could one person make such a difference? The party is also a subject of renewed interest. How did policies set at the center play out at the local level? What means did local cadres (party functionaries) use to get compliance with policies? What were the consequences of vilifying intellectuals? How did day-to-day life change for ordinary people in villages and towns?

THE PARTY IN POWER

From 1950 on, the Communist party, under the leadership of Mao Zedong (to use the phrase of the time), set about fashioning the New China, one that would empower peasants and workers and limit the influence of landlords, capitalists, intellectuals, and foreigners. New values were heralded: people were taught that struggle, revolution, and change are good; compromise, deference, and tradition are weaknesses. People throughout the country were filled with hope that great things could be achieved.

In terms of formal political organization, the Soviet Union's model was adopted with modifications. Rather than a dictatorship of the proletariat, as the Soviet Union called itself, China was to be a "people's democratic dictatorship," with "the people" including workers, both poor and rich peasants, and the national bourgeoisie, but excluding landlords and certain classes of capitalists. The people so defined were represented by a hierarchy of irregularly scheduled People's Representative Congresses.

Real power, however, lay with the Communist party. The People's Liberation Army (PLA) was not subordinated to the government but rather to the party through its Military Affairs Commission. By the end of the 1950s, there were more than 1 million branch party committees in villages, factories, schools, army units, and other organizations. Each committee sent delegates to higher units, including county and province committees, leading up to the three top tiers: the Central Committee with a few dozen members, the Politburo with around a dozen members, and its Standing Committee, which in 1949 consisted of Mao Zedong, Liu Shaoqi, Zhou Enlai, Zhu De, and Chen Yun and later was expanded to include Deng Xiaoping. Mao Zedong was recognized as the paramount leader and was treated almost as though he was an emperor. In 1953, when he was sixty years old, Mao was chairman of the party, chairman of the Military Affairs Commission, and chairman of the PRC. The central government had dozens of ministries, and Mao needed an array of secretaries to handle all the paperwork he had to process. Expert organizers like Zhou Enlai and Liu Shaoqi, both of whom had been active in the party since the early 1920s, coordinated foreign and economic policy, respectively.

The Communist party faced enormous challenges. After forty years of fighting in one part of the coun-try or another, the economy was in shambles. Inflation was rampant. Railroad tracks had been torn up and bridges destroyed. Harbors were clogged with sunken ships. People displaced by war numbered in the millions. Many of those manning essential services had been either Japanese collaborators or Nationalist appointees and did not inspire trust. Chiang Kaishek had transferred much of his army to Taiwan and had not given up claim to be the legitimate ruler of China.

In December 1949, Mao went to Moscow to confer with Joseph Stalin. He stayed nine weeks—his first trip abroad—and arranged for Soviet loans and technical assistance. Soon more than twenty thousand Chinese trainees went to the Soviet Union, and some ten thousand Russian technicians came to China to help set up 156 Soviet-designed heavy industrial plants. To pay for these projects, agriculture was heavily taxed, again on the Soviet model. According to the First Five Year Plan put into effect for the years 1953 to 1957, output of steel was to be quadrupled, power and cement doubled. Consumer goods, however, were to be increased by much smaller increments—cotton piece goods by less than half, grain by less than a fifth.

But China could not create everything from scratch. Ways had to be found to maintain the infrastructure of modern urban life, the factories, railroads, universities, newspapers, law courts, and tax-collecting stations, even as the party took them over. When the Red Army entered cities, its peasant soldiers put an end to looting and rounded up beggars, prostitutes, opium addicts, and petty criminals. They set up street committees, which were told to rid the cities of flashy clothes, provocative hairstyles, and other signs of decadence. But illiterate soldiers were not qualified to run all urban enterprises themselves.

Some enterprises the new state took over outright. By taking over the banks, the government brought inflation under control within a year. The new government took control of key industries, such as the railroads and foreign trade. In other cases, capitalists and managers were left in place but were forced to follow party directives. A large-scale campaign was launched in 1951–1952 to weed out the least cooperative of the capitalists still controlling private enterprises. City residents were mobilized to accuse merchants and manufacturers of bribery, tax evasion, theft of state assets, cheating in labor or materials, and stealing state economic secrets. In the single month of

April 1952, seventy thousand Shanghai businessmen were investigated and criticized. The targets often felt betrayed when their family members and friends joined in attacking them. Once businessmen confessed, they had to pay restitution, which often meant giving shares of their enterprises to the government, turning them into joint government-private ventures. To keep enterprises running, the former owners were often kept on as government-paid managers, but they had been discredited in the eyes of their former subordinates. Smaller manufacturing plants, stores, and restaurants were gradually dominated by the government through its control of supplies and labor.

As the party took control, it brought the advantages of modern life, such as schools and health care, to wider and wider circles of the urban and rural poor. During the 1950s, rapid progress was made in cutting illiteracy and raising life expectancy. Employment was found for all, and housing of some sort was provided for everyone.

Ideology and Social Control

China's new leaders called their victory in the civil war "the liberation." As they saw it, the Chinese people had been freed from the yoke of the past and now could rebuild China as a socialist, egalitarian, forward-looking nation. China would regain its stature as a great nation and demonstrate to the world the potential of socialism to lift the masses out of poverty. Achieving these goals required adherence to correct ideology, identified as "Mao Zedong Thought." Since Mao's ideas changed over time and put emphasis on practice over theory, even those who had studied Mao's writings could never be totally sure they knew how he would view a particular issue. As long as Mao lived, he was the interpreter of his own ideas, the one to rule on what deviated from ideological correctness.

Spreading these ideas was the mission of propaganda departments and teams, which quickly took over the publishing industry. Schools and colleges were also put under party supervision, with a Soviet-style Ministry of Education issuing directives. Numerous mass organizations were set up, including the Youth League, Women's Federation, and Labor Union Federation. Party workers who organized meetings of these groups were simultaneously to learn from the masses, keep an eye on them, and get them behind new policies. Meeting halls and other buildings were festooned with banners and posters proclaiming party slogans.

The pervasive attack on the old led to the condemnation of many features of traditional culture. Traditional religion was labeled feudal superstition. In 1950 the Marriage Reform Law granted young people the right to choose their marriage partners, wives the right to initiate divorce, and wives and daughters rights to property. The provisions of these laws did not go much farther than the Nationalists' Civil Code of 1930, but they had a considerably greater impact because campaigns were launched to publicize them and to assure women of party support if they refused marriages arranged by their parents or left unbearable husbands or mothers-in-law. During the first five years of the new law, several million marriages were dissolved, most at the request of the wives. This campaign should not, of course, get full credit for changes in the Chinese family system, as many other forces contributed to undermining patriarchal authority, such as the drastic shrinkage of family property as a result of collectivization of land and appropriation of business assets, the entry of more children into schools and mass organizations like the Youth League, the mobilization of large numbers of women into the work force, and the public appearance of more women in positions of authority, ranging from street committees to university faculties and the upper echelons of the party.

Art and architecture were also deployed to spread new ideas. The old city of Beijing was given a new look to match its status as capital of New China. The huge walls around Beijing were torn down as outmoded obstacles to traffic. The area south of the old imperial palace was cleared of buildings to create Tiananmen (Gate of Heavenly Peace) Square. (See **Material Culture: The Monument to the People's Heroes.**) On either side of this square, two huge Soviet-style buildings were erected: the Great Hall of the People and the Museum of Chinese History. When huge May Day and National Day rallies were held, China was visually linked to communist countries all around the world.

The Communist party developed an effective means of social and ideological control through the *danwei* (work unit). Most people's *danwei* was their place of work; for students it was their school; for the retired or unemployed, their neighborhood. Each *danwei* assigned housing, supplied ration coupons (for grain, other foodstuffs, cloth, and anything else in short supply), managed birth control programs, and organized mass campaigns. Individuals even needed their *danwei*'s permission to get married or divorced.

MATERIAL CULTURE

The Monument to the People's Heroes

With the communist victory, much of China's old visual culture was rejected and new forms put in its place. Although the old palace was retained and transformed into a museum, it also became the backdrop to a huge new square (Tiananmen Square) where mass rallies could be held. Across from the palace, a new monument was erected after years of careful planning. On the front of this ten-story-high obelisk is a quotation from Mao Zedong in his own hand, and on the back is another written out by Zhou Enlai. At the base, ten bas-reliefs depict major moments in the struggles of the people from the Opium War to the final stage of the "War of Liberation." The art was done collaboratively, rather than by individually recognized artists, and the people depicted were not supposed to look like actual historical actors, but to represent the idealized revolutionary. This "international socialist-realist" style was also seen in posters, book illustrations, and paintings.

Sculptural Frieze on Monument to the People's Heroes. The largest of the friezes is on the front of the monument and depicts the final moment in the civil war when the PLA crossed the Yangzi River. Each of the figures shows a similar heroic determination. *(Wolfgang Kaehler Photography)*

The Korean War and the United States as the Chief Enemy

The new government did not have even a year to get its structures and policies in place before it was embroiled in war in Korea. After World War II, with the ensuing Cold War between the United States and the Soviet Union, the Soviet Union was dominant in Korea above the 38th parallel and the United States below it (see Chapter 29). Mao knew that China's development plans hinged on respite from war. Stalin, however, approved North Korea's plan to invade South Korea, and the invasion occurred in June 1950. In October U.S. forces, fighting under the United Nations flag in support of the South, crossed the 38th parallel and headed toward the Yalu River, the border between North Korea and China. Later that month, Chinese "volunteers," under the command of Peng Dehuai, began to cross the Yalu secretly, using no lights or radios. In late November they surprised the Americans and soon forced them to retreat south of Seoul. Altogether, more than 2.5 million Chinese troops were sent to Korea, as well as all of China's tanks and over half of its artillery and aircraft. A stalemate followed, and peace talks dragged on until 1953, largely because China wanted all prisoners repatriated, but fourteen thousand begged not to be sent back.

This war gave the Communist party legitimacy in China: China had "stood up" and beaten back the imperialists. But the costs were huge. Not only did China suffer an estimated 360,000 casualties, but the war eliminated many chances for gradual reconciliation, internal and external. The United States, now viewing China as its enemy, sent the Seventh Fleet to patrol the waters between China and Taiwan and increased aid to Chiang Kaishek on Taiwan. China began to vilify the United States as its prime enemy.

With Taiwan occupying the China seat on the UN Security Council, the United States pushed through the UN a total embargo on trade with China and enforced it by a blockade of China's coast. Of necessity, self-reliance became a chief virtue of the revolution in China. When the United States helped supply the French in their war to regain control of Vietnam, China supplied Ho Chi Minh and the Vietminh. China became more afraid of spies and enemy agents and expelled most of the remaining Western missionaries and businessmen. A worse fate awaited those who had served in the Nationalist government or army. A campaign of 1951 against such "counterrevolutionaries" resulted in the execution of tens or hundreds of thousands, with similar numbers sent to harsh labor reform camps. This campaign was also used to disarm the population; over five hundred thousand rifles were collected in Guangdong alone.

Collectivizing Agriculture

The lives of hundreds of millions of China's farmers were radically altered in the 1950s by the progressive collectivization of land and the creation of a new local elite of rural cadres. Starting in the 1930s, when the Communist party took control of new areas, it taught peasants a new way to look at the old order: social and economic inequalities were not natural but a perversion caused by the institution of private property. The old literati elite were not exemplars of Confucian virtues but the cruelest of exploiters who pressured their tenants to the point where they had to sell their children. That antiquated "feudal" order needed to be replaced with a communal order where all would work together unselfishly for common goals.

The first step was to redistribute land. Typically, the party would send a small team of cadres and students to a village to cultivate relations with the poor, organize a peasant association, identify potential leaders from among the poorest peasants, compile lists of grievances, and organize struggles against those most resented. Eventually the team would supervise the classification of the inhabitants as landlords, rich peasants, middle peasants, poor peasants, and hired hands. The analysis of class was supposed to be scientific, but moral judgments tended to intrude. How should one classify elderly widows who rented out their meager holdings because they were incapable of working them themselves? Somewhat better-off families of veterans? Families that had bought land only recently using money earned in urban factories? Or families newly impoverished because the household head was a decadent wastrel or an opium addict?

These uncertainties allowed land reform activists to help friends and get back at enemies. In some villages, there was not much surplus to redistribute. In others, violence flared, especially when villagers tried to get those labeled landlords or rich peasants to reveal where they had buried their gold. Landlords and rich peasants faced not only loss of their land but also punishment for past offenses; a not insignificant number were executed. Another result of the class struggle stage of land reform was the creation of a caste-like system in the countryside. The descendants of those labeled landlords were excluded from leadership positions, while the descendants of former poor and lower-middle peasants gained preference.

Redistribution of land gained peasant support but did not improve productivity. Toward that end, progressive collectivization was promoted. First, farmers were encouraged to join mutual aid teams, sometime later to set up cooperatives. Cooperatives pooled resources but returned compensation based on inputs of land, tools, animals, and labor. In the "old liberated areas" in north China, this was accomplished in the early 1940s; in south China, these measures were extended during 1950–1953. From 1954 to 1956 a third stage was pushed: higher-level collectives that amalgamated cooperatives and did away with compensation for anything other than labor. Most of these higher-level cooperatives were old villages or parts of large villages. Once they were in place, economic inequality within villages was all but eliminated.

In 1953 the Chinese state took over control of the grain market. After taking 5 to 10 percent of each collective's harvest as a tax, the government allowed the unit to retain a meager subsistence ration per person; then it purchased a share of the "surplus" at prices it set, a hidden form of taxation. Interregional commerce was redefined as criminal speculation, an extreme form of capitalist exploitation. Trade was taken over by the state, and rural markets ceased to function. Many peasants lost crucial sideline income, especially peasants in poorer areas who had previously made ends meet by operating such small enterprises as oil presses, paper mills, or rope factories. Carpenters and craftsmen who used to travel far and wide became chained to the land, unable to practice their trades except in their own localities.

Rural cadres became the new elite in the countryside. How policy shifts were experienced by ordinary people depended on the personal qualities of the lowest level of party functionaries. In some villages, literate middle peasants who knew a lot about farming rose to leadership positions. In other villages, toughs from the poorest families rose because of their zeal in denouncing landlord exploitation. To get ahead, a team leader had to produce a substantial surplus to serve the needs of the revolution without letting too much be taken away and thus losing his team's confidence. As units were urged to consolidate and enlarge, rural cadres had to spend much of their time motivating members and settling squabbles among them. Serving as a rural cadre offered to farmers with the requisite talents the possibilities for social mobility well beyond anything that had existed in imperial China, since local team leaders could rise in the party hierarchy.

Much was accomplished during collectivization to improve the lot of farmers in China. Schools were opened in rural areas, and children everywhere enrolled for at least a few years, cutting the illiteracy rate dramatically. Basic health care was brought to the countryside via clinics and "barefoot doctors," peasants with only a few months of training who could at least give vaccinations and provide antibiotics and other medicines. Collectives took on responsibility for the welfare of widows and orphans who had no one to care for them.

Minorities and Autonomous Regions

New China proclaimed itself to be a multinational state. Officially the old view of China as the civiliz-ing center, gradually attracting, acculturating, and absorbing non-Chinese along its frontiers, was replaced by a vision of distinct ethnic groups joined in a collaborative state. "Han" was promoted as the correct term for the most advanced ethnic group; "Chinese" was stretched to encompass all ethnic groups in the People's Republic.

The policy of multinationality was copied from that of the Soviet Union, which had devised it as the best way to justify retaining all the lands acquired by the czar in the eighteenth and nineteenth centuries. For China the model similarly provided a way to justify reasserting dominion over Tibet and Xinjiang, both acquired by the Qing but independent after 1911. (Mongolia had fallen away as well, but under the domination of the Soviet Union it had established a communist government in the 1920s, so China did not challenge its independence.)

Identifying and labeling China's minority nationalities became a major state project in the 1950s. Stalin had enunciated a nationalities policy with four criteria for establishing a group as a "nationality": common language, common territory, a common economic life, and a common psychological makeup manifested in common cultural traits. Using these criteria, Chinese linguists and social scientists investigated more than four hundred groups. After classifying most as local subbranches of larger ethnic groups, they ended up with fifty-five recognized minority nationalities making up about 7 percent of the population. Some of these nationalities were clear cases, like the Tibetans and Uighurs, who spoke distinct languages and lived in distinct territories. Others seemed matters of degree, like the Hui, Chinese-speaking Muslims scattered throughout the country, and the Zhuang of Guangxi, who had long been quite sinified. In cases where a particular minority dominated a county or province, the unit would be recognized as autonomous, giving it the prerogative to use its own language in schools and government offices. Tibet, Xinjiang, Ningxia, and Inner Mongolia were all made autonomous provinces, and large parts of Sichuan, Yunnan, and Guizhou were declared autonomous regions of the Zhuang, Miao, Yi, and other minorities. (See Map 27.1.) By 1957, four hundred thousand members of minority groups had been recruited as party members.

Despite the protections given minorities in their autonomous regions, many of them became progressively more Han through migration (see **Biography: Jin Shuyu, Telephone Minder**). Inner Mongolia soon became 90 percent Han Chinese, and the traditional Mongol

BIOGRAPHY   Jin Shuyu, Telephone Minder

Jin Shuyu was born in 1917 to an ethnic Korean family in southern Manchuria near the border with Korea. Her father was a doctor, but when she finished middle school in the early 1930s, Japan had taken over Manchuria, and she, like many of her classmates, ran away into the hills to join the anti-Japanese resistance. The insurrectionaries engaged primarily in guerrilla action, trying to blow up storehouses or convoy trucks and the like. To support themselves, they would kidnap rich people and hold them for ransom. They accepted advice from communist organizers but were not a communist group. Finally, they were hard hit by the Japanese and had to scatter.

Jin's family could not hide her because the Japanese knew she was a "bandit." She therefore decided to try to slip into Korea. She worked first as a servant near the border. After she was able to get forged papers, she went to Seoul, where she got a job teaching middle school. In Seoul she married a Han Chinese eleven years her senior who owned a Chinese restaurant, and the couple soon had children. At the end of the war in 1949, the Japanese ransacked the restaurant. Added to that, they lost all their savings when the banks failed. Yet they were able to borrow enough money to start another restaurant.

In 1949 when the Communists won in China, Jin was thirty-two and wanted to return to China, but her husband was against it. Then the Korean War started. Their restaurant did well, as Seoul was swollen with foreign soldiers who liked Chinese food, but she wanted to return home. Her husband said she could go; he would stay behind until she had sized up the situation. In 1953 she took their children with her across the 38th parallel, then made her way through North Korea back into China. Her husband never followed. They wrote to each other through a cousin in Japan,

and in 1983 they were both able to go to Japan to see each other, the first time in thirty years. Her son tried to convince his father to return with them to China, but he said he still wanted to wait to see how things turned out. She thought he kept on putting off joining them because he was too influenced by the anticommunist propaganda of South Korea, or perhaps because he had taken a new wife and never told them.

Jin's life in China was relatively uneventful. In 1958 she was given a job by her street committee to mind the community telephone. Those who wanted to make a call would pay her a fee and she would let them use it. She also would get people when calls came in for them. Jin's salary was very low, but she got half of the fees people paid to make calls. Moreover, as she told her interviewer in 1958, she enjoyed listening to people talk on the phone, especially young people who often grinned through their calls or bowed and scraped when seeking favors from the people they called.

During the Cultural Revolution, people accused Jin of having a bad class background. She had to locate some of her old comrades to speak up for her, and they said she had distinguished herself in an unofficial anti-Japanese force and should be getting money from the government. After that things were easier because she was classified as an "Anti-Japanese Alliance Veteran" and a repatriated overseas Chinese. She also had some minor privileges as an ethnic minority. However, she told her interviewer, "I'm no more Korean than you are. I became Han Chinese long ago."[1]

Jin's son did well, not only graduating from college but also becoming a college professor, and by the early 1980s Jin lived comfortably. Her only complaint was that her daughter-in-law thought too highly of herself.

---

1. Zhang Xinxin and Sang Ye, *Chinese Lives: An Oral History of Contemporary China* (New York: Pantheon Books, 1987), p. 20.

nomadic culture largely disappeared as ranch-style stock raising replaced moving the herds with the seasons. In Xinjiang, too, in-migration of Han Chinese changed the ethnic makeup, especially in the cities. Manchuria, now called the Northeast, had for nearly a century

been the destination of millions of Han Chinese, a process that continued as the Communists built on the heavy industry base left by the Japanese.

Tibet was a special case. It had not come under rule of any sort from Beijing until the eighteenth century,

Map **27.1**   **Ethnic Groups in China**

and the Manchu rulers had interfered relatively little with the power of the Lamaist Buddhist monasteries. From the 1890s on, Tibet fell more under the sway of the British, but Britain left India in 1947, ending its interest in Tibet. In 1950, when Lhasa would not agree to "peaceful liberation," the PLA invaded. On the recommendation of India, the United Nations would not listen to Tibetan appeals. Tibet had no choice but to negotiate an agreement with the Chinese Communist party. Tibet recognized China's sovereignty and in exchange was allowed to maintain its traditional political system, including the Dalai Lama. From 1951 to 1959, this system worked fairly well. By 1959, however, ethnic Tibetans from neighboring provinces, unhappy with agricultural collectivization, were streaming into Tibet. When massive protests broke out in Lhasa, the army opened fire. The Dalai Lama and thousands of his followers fled to India. The aftermath included more pressure on Tibet to conform to the rest of the People's Republic and the sense among Tibetans that theirs was an occupied land.

Intellectuals and the Hundred Flowers Campaign

In the 1920s and 1930s some of the most enthusiastic supporters of socialism were members of the educated elite (now usually called intellectuals). Professors like Chen Duxiu and Li Dazhao and writers like Lu Xun and Ding Ling saw socialism as a way to rid China of poverty and injustice. Many intellectuals made their way to Yan'san, where they soon learned that their job was to serve the party, not stand at a critical distance from it (see Chapter 25).

After 1949 the party had to find ways to make use of intellectuals who had not publicly sided with it, but rather had stayed in the eastern cities working as teachers, journalists, engineers, or government officials. Most members of this small, urban, educated elite were ready and eager to serve the new government, happy that China finally had a government able to drive out imperialists, control inflation, banish unemployment, end corruption, and clean up the streets. Thousands who were studying abroad hurried home to see how they could help. China needed expertise for its modernization projects, and most of the educated were kept in their jobs, whatever their class background.

Mao, however, distrusted intellectuals and since Yan'san days had been devising ways to subordinate them to the party. In the early 1950s the educated men and women who staffed schools, universities, publishing houses, research institutes, and other organizations were "reeducated." This "thought reform" generally entailed confessing their subservience to capitalists and imperialists or other bourgeois habits of thought and their gratitude to Chairman Mao for having helped them realize these errors. For some going through it, thought reform was like a conversion experience; they saw themselves in an entirely new way and wanted to dedicate themselves to the socialist cause. For others, it was devastating.

Independence on the part of intellectuals was also undermined by curtailing alternative sources of income. There were no more rents or dividends, no more independent presses or private colleges.

In response to de-Stalinization in the Soviet Union, in 1956, Mao called on intellectuals to help him identify problems within the party, such as party members who had lost touch with the people or behaved like tyrants. "Let a hundred flowers bloom" in the field of culture and a "hundred schools of thought contend" in science. As long as criticism was not "antagonistic" or "counterrevolutionary," it would help strengthen the party, he explained. The first to come forward with criticisms were scientists and engineers who wanted party members to interfere less with their work. To encourage more people to come forward, Mao praised those who spoke up. Soon critics lost their inhibitions. By May 1957 college students were putting up wall posters, sometimes with highly inflammatory charges. One poster at Qinghua University in Beijing even dared attack Mao Zedong by name: "When he wants to kill you, he doesn't have to do it himself. He can mobilize your wife and children to denounce you and then kill you with their own hands! Is this a rational society? This is class struggle, Mao Zedong style!"[1]

Did Mao plan this campaign to ferret out dissidents? Or was he shocked by the outpouring of criticism? Whatever the truth of the matter, in June 1957 the party announced a campaign against rightists or-chestrated by the newly appointed secretary general of the party, Deng Xiaoping. In this massive campaign, units were pressed to identify 5 percent of their staff members as rightists. Altogether almost 3 million people were labeled rightists, which meant that they would no longer have any real influence at work, even if allowed to keep their jobs. A half-million suffered worse fates, sent to labor in the countryside. Some of those labeled rightists had exposed party weaknesses, like the thirty reporters who had reported on secret shops where officials could buy goods not available to ordinary people. But other "rightists" had hardly said anything, like the railroad engineer relegated to menial labor for twenty years because someone reported hearing him say "how bold" when he read a critique of the party.

By the end of the campaign, the Western-influenced elite created in the 1930s was destroyed, condemned as "poisonous weeds." Old China had been dominated, culturally at least, by an elite defined by lengthy education. Mao made sure the educated would know their place in the New China: they were employees of the state hired to instruct the children of the laboring people or to provide technical assistance. They were not to have ideas of their own separate from those of the party or a cultural life distinct from the masses. Most of those labeled rightists in 1957 had to wait until 1979 to be rehabilitated (that is, to have their rightist label removed and their civil rights restored).

DEPARTING FROM THE SOVIET MODEL

By 1957, China had made progress on many fronts. The standard of living was improving, support for the government was strong, and people were optimistic about the future. Still, Mao was not satisfied. Growth was too slow and too dependent on technical experts and capital. As he had found from the Hundred Flowers campaign, people's ways of thinking had not been as quickly transformed as he had hoped. Mao was ready to try more radical measures.

The Great Leap Forward

Why was China unable to find a way to use what it was rich in—labor power—to modernize more rapidly? In 1956, Mao began talking of a Great Leap

---

1. Gregor Benton and Alan Hunter, eds., *Wild Lily, Prairie Fire* (Princeton, N.J.: Princeton University Press, 1995), pp. 100–101.

Producing Steel in Henan Province. During the Great Leap Forward, inexperienced workers labored for long hours to produce steel in makeshift "backyard" furnaces. *(Xinhua News Agency, Beijing/Sovfoto)*

Forward. Through the coordinated hard work of hundreds of millions of people, China would transform itself from a poor nation into a mighty one. With the latent creative capacity of the Chinese masses unleashed, China would surpass Great Britain in industrial output within fifteen years.

These visions of accelerated industrialization were coupled with a higher level of collectivization in the countryside. In 1958, in a matter of months, agricultural collectives all over the country were amalgamated into gigantic communes. Private garden plots were banned. Peasants were organized into quasimilitary production brigades and referred to as fighters on the agricultural front. Peasant men were marched in military style to labor on public works projects, while the women took over much of the field work. Those between ages sixteen and thirty were drafted into the militia and spent long hours drilling.

Both party cadres and ordinary working people got caught up in a wave of utopian enthusiasm. During the late summer and fall of 1958, communes, factories, schools, and other units set up "backyard steel furnaces" in order to double steel production. As workers were mobilized to put in long hours on these projects, they had little time to cook or eat at home. Units were encouraged to set up mess halls where food was free, a measure commentators hailed as a step toward communism. Counties claimed 1,000 and even 10,000 percent increases in agriculture production. The Central Committee announced with great fanfare that production had nearly doubled in a single year.

Some Great Leap projects proved to be of long-term value; bridges, railroads, canals, reservoirs, power stations, mines, and irrigation works were constructed all over the country. All too often, however, projects were undertaken with such haste and with so little technical knowledge that they did more harm than good. With economists and engineers downgraded or removed in the antirightist campaigns of the year before, plans were formulated not by experts but by local cadres eager to show their political zeal. Fields plowed deep were sometimes ruined because the soil became salinized. The quality of most of the steel made in backyard furnaces was too poor to be used. Instead it filled railroad cars and clogged train yards all over the country, disrupting transportation.

It was not just the legacy of the Hundred Flowers campaign that kept cadres from reporting failures. The minister of defense and hero of the Korean War, Peng Dehuai, tried to bring up problems in a private letter he gave to Mao at a party conference in July 1959. In the letter Peng began by saying that the Great Leap was an indisputable success, but pointed to the tendency to exaggerate at all levels, which made it difficult for the leadership to know the real situation. He also noted that people began to think that the food problem was solved and that they could give free meals to all. Peng's language was temperate, but Mao's reaction was not. Mao distributed copies of the letter to the delegates and denounced Peng for "right opportunism." He made the senior cadres choose between him and Peng, and none had the courage to side with Peng, who was soon dismissed from his post. Problems with the Great Leap were now blamed on all those like Peng who lacked faith in its premises.

Mao's faulty economics, coupled with droughts and floods, ended up creating one of the worst famines in world history. The size of the 1958 harvest was wildly exaggerated, and no one attempted to validate reports. Tax grain was removed from the countryside on the basis of the reported harvests, leaving little for local consumption. No one wanted to report what was actually happening in his locality for fear of being labeled a rightist. Grain production dropped from 200 million tons in 1958 to 170 million in 1959 and 144 million in 1960. By 1960 in many places people were left with less than half of what they needed to survive. Rationing was practiced almost everywhere, and soup kitchens serving weak gruel were set up in an attempt to stave off starvation. But peasants in places where grain was exhausted were not allowed to hit the roads, as people had always done during famines in the past. From later census reconstructions, it appears that during the Three Hard Years (1959–1962) there were on the order of 30 million "excess" deaths attributable to the dearth of food. Yet neither Mao nor the Communist party fell from power.

Deaths in Hard-Hit Provinces, 1957 and 1960			
Province	1957	1960	Change
Anhui	c. 250,000	2,200,000	780%
Gansu	142,041	538,479	279%
Guangxi	261,785	644,700	146%
Henan	572,000	1,908,000	233%
Hunan	370,059	1,068,118	189%

Source: Based on Roderick MacFarquar, *The Origins of the Cultural Revolution, vol. 3: The Coming of the Cataclysm, 1961–1966* (New York: Columbia University Press, 1997), pp. 2–3.

The Great Leap destroyed people's faith in their local cadres, who in the crisis put themselves and their families first. Another blow to peasants were new curbs on their mobility. Beginning in 1955 a system of population registration bound rural people to the villages of their birth, or in the case of married women to their husbands' villages. When the hasty expansion of the nation's industrial plant was reversed, millions of unemployed workers were sent back to the countryside. To keep them from returning and to keep other peasants from sneaking into the cities, a system of urban household registration was introduced. Only those with permission to reside in a city could get the ration coupons needed to purchase grain there. These residence policies had the unintended effect of locking rural communities with unfavorable man-land ratios into dismal poverty.

It is not surprising that the rural poor would want to move to the cities. Those who got jobs in state-run factories had low-cost housing, pensions, and health care, not to mention a reliable supply of subsidized food. Children in the cities could stay in school through middle school, and the brightest could go farther. In the countryside, only a tiny proportion of exceptionally wealthy communities could come at all close to providing such benefits. In the poorest regions, farmers, forced by the government to concentrate on growing grain, could do little to improve their situations other than invest more labor by weeding more frequently, leveling and terracing fields, expanding irrigation systems, and so on. Such investment often brought little return, and agricultural productivity (the return for each hour of labor) fell across the country.

The Sino-Soviet Split

In the 1920s and 1930s Stalin, through the Comintern, had done as much to hinder the success of the Chinese Communist party as to aid it. Still, in 1949, Mao viewed the Soviet Union as China's natural ally and went to Moscow to see Stalin. Mao never had the same respect for Stalin's successor, Khrushchev. The Great Leap Forward put further strain on relations between China and the Soviet Union. China intensified its bellicose anti-imperialist rhetoric and began shelling the islands off the coast of Fujian still held by the Nationalists on Taiwan, and the Russians began to fear that China would drag them into a war with the United States. In 1958 and 1959, Khrushchev visited Beijing and concluded that Mao was a romantic deviationist, particularly wrongheaded in his decision to create communes. All the assistance the Soviet Union had given to China's industrialization seemed to have been wasted as Mao put his trust in backyard furnaces.

When Mao made light of nuclear weapons—saying that if using them could destroy capitalism, it would not matter that much if China lost half its population—Khrushchev went back on his earlier promise to give China nuclear weapons. There was also friction over India and its support for the Dalai Lama and other refugees from Tibet. Russia wanted India as an ally and would not side with China in its border disputes with India, infuriating Mao. In April 1960, Chinese leaders celebrated the ninetieth anniversary of Lenin's birth by lambasting Soviet foreign policy. In July 1960, just as famine was hitting China, Khrushchev ordered the Soviet experts to return and to take their blueprints and spare parts with them. By 1963, Mao was publicly denouncing Khrushchev as a revisionist and capitalist roader and challenging the Soviet Union's leadership of the international communist movement. Communist parties throughout the world soon divided into pro-Soviet and pro-China factions. As the rhetoric escalated, both sides increased their troops along their long border, which provoked border clashes. China built air raid shelters on a massive scale and devoted enormous resources to constructing a defense establishment in mountainous inland areas far from both the sea and the Soviet border. As the war in Vietnam escalated after 1963, China stayed on the sidelines, not even helping the Soviet Union supply North Vietnam. Meanwhile, China developed its own atomic weapons program, exploding its first nuclear device in 1964.

THE CULTURAL REVOLUTION

After the failure of the Great Leap Forward, Mao, nearly seventy years old, withdrew from active decision making. Liu Shaoqi replaced Mao as head of state in 1959 and, along with Chen Yun, Zhou Enlai, Deng Xiaoping, and other organization men, set about reviving the economy. Mao grew more and more isolated. Surrounded by bodyguards, he lived in luxurious guest houses far removed from ordinary folk. Senior colleagues had not forgotten the fate of Peng Dehuai, and honest debate of party policy was no longer attempted in front of Mao. Any resistance to his ideas had to be done in secret.

By the early 1960s, Mao was afraid that revisionism was destroying the party—that Marxism was being undermined by contamination of capitalist methods and ideas. In 1962 he initiated the Socialist Education campaign to try to get rural cadres to focus again on class struggle. When Liu Shaoqi and Deng Xiaoping rewrote the directives to deemphasize class struggle, Mao concluded that the revisionists were taking over the struggle for control of the party. After gathering allies, Mao set out to recapture revolutionary fervor and avoid slipping in the inegalitarian direction of the Soviet Union by initiating a Great Revolution to Create a Proletarian Culture—or Cultural Revolution for short—a movement that came close to destroying the party he had led for three decades.

Phase 1: 1966–1968

The Cultural Revolution began in the spring of 1966 with a denunciation of the mayor of Beijing for allowing the staging of a play that could be construed as critical of Mao. Mao's wife, Jiang Qing, formed a Cultural Revolution Small Group to look into ways to revolutionize culture. Jiang Qing had not played much of a part in politics before and was widely seen as a stand-in for Mao. Soon radical students at Beijing University were agitating against party officials's "taking the capitalist road." When Liu Shaoqi tried to control what was going on at Beijing University, Mao intervened, had him demoted by a rump session of the Central Committee, and sanctioned the organization of students into Red Guards.

The Cultural Revolution quickly escalated beyond the control of Mao, Jiang Qing, or anyone else. Young people who had grown up in New China responded

DOCUMENTS

Big Character Poster

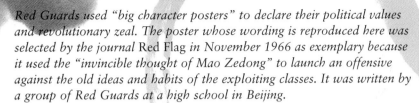

Red Guards used "big character posters" to declare their political values and revolutionary zeal. The poster whose wording is reproduced here was selected by the journal Red Flag *in November 1966 as exemplary because it used the "invincible thought of Mao Zedong" to launch an offensive against the old ideas and habits of the exploiting classes. It was written by a group of Red Guards at a high school in Beijing.*

Revolution is rebellion, and rebellion is the soul of Mao Zedong's thought. Daring to think, to speak, to act, to break through, and to make revolution—in a word, daring to rebel—is the most fundamental and most precious quality of proletarian revolutionaries; it is fundamental to the Party spirit of the Party of the proletariat! Not to rebel is revisionism, pure and simple! Revisionism has been in control of our school for seventeen years. If today we do not rise up in rebellion, when will we?

Now some of the people who were boldly opposing our rebellion have suddenly turned shy and coy, and have taken to incessant murmuring and nagging that we are too one-sided, too arrogant, too crude and that we are going too far. All this is utter nonsense! If you are against us, please say so. Why be shy about it? Since we are bent on rebelling, the matter is no longer in your hand! Indeed we shall make the air thick with the pungent smell of gunpowder. All this talk about being "humane" and "all-sided"—let's have an end to it.

You say we are too one-sided? What kind of all-sideness is it that suits you? It looks to us like a "two combining into one" all-sidedness, or eclecticism. You say we are too arrogant? "Arrogant" is just what we want to be. Chairman Mao says, "And those in high positions we counted as no more than the dust." We are bent on striking down not only the reactionaries in our school, but the reactionaries all over the world. Revolutionaries take it as their task to transform the world. How can we not be "arrogant"?

You say we are too crude? Crude is just what we want to be. How can we be soft and clinging toward revisionism or go in for great moderation? To be moderate toward the enemy is to be cruel to the revolution! You say we are going too far? Frankly, your "don't go too far" is reformism, it is "peaceful transition." And this is what your daydreams are about! Well, we are going to strike you down to the earth and keep you down!

There are some others who are scared to death of revolution, scared to death of rebellion. You sticklers for convention, you toadies are all curled up inside your revisionist shells. At the first whiff of rebellion, you become scared and nervous. A revolutionary is a "monkey king" whose golden rod is might, whose supernatural powers are far-reaching and whose magic is omnipotent precisely because he has the great and invincible thought of Mao Zedong. We are wielding our "golden rods" "displaying our supernatural powers" and using our "magic" in order to turn the old world upside down, smash it to pieces, create chaos, and make a tremendous mess—and the bigger the better! We must do this to the present revisionist middle school attached to Tsinghua University. Create a big rebellion, rebel to the end! We are bent on creating a tremendous proletarian uproar, and on carving out a new proletarian world!

Long live the revolutionary rebel spirit of the proletariat!

Source: From Patricia Buckley Ebrey, ed., *Chinese Civilization: A Sourcebook*, rev. ed. (New York: Simon and Schuster, 1993), p. 450.

Red Guards. In September 1966 a teenage girl Red Guard humiliates the governor Li Fanwu by clipping his hair and forcing him to bow and wear a placard saying he is a member of the Black Gang. *(Li Zhensheng/Asia-Network.co.jp)*

enthusiastically to calls to help Mao oust revisionists. In June 1966 high schools and universities throughout the country were closed as students devoted all their time to Red Guard activities. Millions rode free on railroads to carry the message to the countryside or to make the pilgrimage to Beijing, where they might catch a glimpse of Mao, their "Great Helmsman," at the massive Red Guard rallies held in Tiananmen Square. (See **Documents: Big Character Poster**.)

At these rallies, Mao appeared in military uniform and told the students that "to rebel is justified" and that it was good "to bombard the headquarters." The Red Guards in response waved their little red books, *Quotations from Chairman Mao*, compiled a few years earlier by Lin Biao to indoctrinate soldiers. The cult of Mao became more and more dominant, with his pictures displayed in every household, bus, and train, and even in pedicabs, and his sayings broadcast by loudspeaker at every intersection. From early 1967 on, the *People's Daily* regularly printed a boxed statement by Mao on its front page.

In cities large and small, Red Guards roamed the streets in their battle against things foreign or old. They invaded the homes of those with bad class back-grounds, "bourgeois tendencies," or connections to foreigners. Under the slogan of "destroy the four old things" (old customs, habits, culture, and thinking), they ransacked homes, libraries, and museums to find books and artwork to set on fire. The tensions and antagonisms that had been suppressed by nearly two decades of tight social control broke into the open as Red Guards found opportunities to get back at people. At the countless denunciation meetings they organized, cadres, teachers, and writers were forced to stand with their heads down and their arms raised behind them in the "airplane" position and to listen to former friends and colleagues jeer at and curse them. Many victims took their own lives; others died of beatings and mistreatment.

Liu Shaoqi, the head of state but now labeled the "chief capitalist roader," became a victim of the Red Guards. In the summer of 1967, Red Guards stormed the well-guarded quarters where the party hierarchy lived and seized Liu. Then they taunted and beat him before huge crowds. Liu died alone two years later from the abuse he received. His family suffered as well. Liu's wife ended up spending ten years in solitary confinement. Four other members of his family also

Big Character Posters. Soldiers of the PLA and peasants of the model commune at Dazhai are shown here putting up big character posters in 1970. *(Sovfoto)*

died either of beatings or of mistreatment in prison where interrogators made every effort to get them to reveal evidence that Liu or his wife was a spy. Deng Xiaoping, another target of Mao, fared better; he was sent off to labor in a factory in Jiangxi after being humiliated at struggle sessions.

By the end of 1966 workers were also being mobilized to participate in the Cultural Revolution. Rebel students went to factories to "learn from the workers" but actually to instigate opposition to party superiors. When party leaders tried to appease discontented workers by raising wages and handing out bonuses, Mao labeled their actions "economism" and instructed students and workers to seize power from such revisionist party leaders. Confusing power

struggles ensued. As soon as one group gained the upper hand, another would challenge its takeover as a "sham power seizure" and attempt a "counterpower seizure."

As armed conflict spread, Mao turned to the People's Liberation Army to restore order. Told to ensure that industrial and agricultural production continued, the army tended to support conservative mass organizations and disband the rebel organizations as "counterrevolutionary." Radical Red Guard leaders tried to counterattack, accusing the army of supporting the wrong side. In Wuhan in July 1967, when radicals seized trains loaded with weapons en route to Vietnam, the army supplied their opponents. Then a conservative faction in Wuhan kidnapped two of the radical leaders from Beijing, and the Cultural Revolution Small Group responded by calling on the Red Guards to arm themselves and seize military power from the "capitalist roaders" in the army. Thus began the most violent stage of the Cultural Revolution, during which different factions of Red Guards and worker organizations took up armed struggle against each other and against regional and national military forces. Rebels seized the Foreign Ministry in Beijing for two weeks, and others seized and burned the British diplomatic compound. With communication and transportation at a standstill, consumer goods became scarce in urban areas.

In the first, violent phase of the Cultural Revolution, some 3 million party and government officials were removed from their jobs, and as many as half a million people were killed or committed suicide.

Phase 2: 1968–1976

By the summer of 1968, Mao had no choice but to moderate the Cultural Revolution in order to prevent full-scale civil war. In July he disbanded the Red Guards and sent them off to work in the countryside. Revolutionary committees were set up to take the place of the old party structure. Each committee had representatives from the mass organizations, from revolutionary cadres, and from the army; in most places the army quickly became the dominant force. Culture remained tightly controlled. Foreign music, art, literature, and books (other than works on Marxism, Leninism, and Stalinism) disappeared from stores. Revolutionary works were offered in their place, such as the eight model revolutionary operas Jiang Qing had sponsored. The official line was that it was better to be red than expert, and professionals were hounded out of many fields. High school graduates were sent into the countryside, as the Red Guards had been before them, some 17 million altogether. Although the stated reason for sending them to the countryside was to let them learn from the peasants and give the peasants the advantage of their education, this transfer also saved the government the trouble and expense of putting the graduates on the payroll of urban enterprises or finding them housing when they married.

The dominance of the military declined after the downfall in 1971 of Lin Biao. To the public, Lin Biao was Mao's most devoted disciple, regularly photographed standing next to him. Yet according to the official account, Lin became afraid that Mao had turned against him and decided to assassinate him.

When Lin's daughter exposed his plot, Lin decided to flee to the Soviet Union. His plane, however, ran out of fuel and crashed over Mongolia. Whatever the truth of this bizarre story, news of his plot was kept out of the press for a year, the leadership apparently unsure how to tell the people that Lin Biao turned out to be another Liu Shaoqi, a secret traitor who had managed to reach the second highest position in the political hierarchy.

By this point Mao's health was in decline, and he played less and less of a role in day-to-day management. The leading contenders for power were the more radical faction led by Jiang Qing and the more moderate faction led by Zhou Enlai. In this rather fluid situation China softened its antagonistic stance toward the outside world and in 1972 welcomed U.S. president Richard Nixon to visit and pursue improving relations. In 1973 many disgraced leaders, including Deng Xiaoping, were reinstated to important posts.

The Cultural Revolution's massive assault on entrenched ideas and the established order left many victims. Nearly 3 million people were officially rehabilitated after 1978. Urban young people who had been exhilarated when Mao called on them to topple those in power soon found themselves at the bottom of the heap, sent down to the countryside where hostile peasants could make life miserable. Their younger siblings received inferior educations, out of school for long periods, then taught a watered-down curriculum. The cadres, teachers, and intellectuals who were the principal targets of the Cultural Revolution lost much of their trust in others. When they had to continue working with people who had beaten, humiliated, or imprisoned them, the wounds were left to fester for years. Even those who agreed that elitist values and bureaucratic habits were pervasive problems in the party hierarchy found little positive in the outcome of the Cultural Revolution.

THE DEATH OF MAO

In 1976 those who still believed in portents from heaven would have sensed that heaven was sending warnings. First, Zhou Enlai died in January after a long struggle with cancer. Next, an outpouring of grief for him in April was violently suppressed. Then in July, north China was rocked by a huge earthquake that killed hundreds of thousands. In September Mao Zedong died.

As long as Mao was alive, no one would openly challenge him, but as his health failed, those near the top tried to position themselves for the inevitable. The main struggle, it seems with hindsight, was between the radicals—Jiang Qing and her allies, later labeled the Gang of Four—and the pragmatists—Deng Xiaoping and his allies. In March 1976 a newspaper controlled by the radicals implied that Zhou Enlai was a capitalist roader. In response, on April 4, the traditional day for honoring the dead, an estimated 2 million people flocked to Tiananmen Square to lay wreaths in honor of Zhou. The radicals saw this as an act of opposition to themselves, had it labeled a counterrevolutionary incident, and called the militia out. Yet the pragmatists won out in the end. After a month of national mourning for Mao, Jiang Qing and the rest of the Gang of Four were arrested.

Assessment of Mao's role in modern Chinese history is ongoing. In 1981, when the party rendered its judgment of Mao, it still gave him high marks for his military leadership and his intellectual contributions to Marxist theory, but assigned him much of the blame for everything that went wrong from 1956 on. Since then, Mao's standing has further eroded as doubts are raised about the impact of his leadership style in the 1940s and early 1950s. Some critics go so far as to portray Mao as a megalomaniac, so absorbed in his project of remaking China to match his vision that he was totally indifferent to others' suffering. Some Chinese intellectuals, however, worry that making Mao a monster relieves everyone else of responsibility and undermines the argument that structural changes are needed to prevent comparable tragedies from recurring.

Mao Zedong has often been compared to Zhu Yuanzhang, the founder of the Ming Dynasty. Both grew up in farming households, though Mao never experienced the desperate poverty of Zhu's childhood. Both were formed by the many years of warfare that preceded gaining military supremacy. Both brooked no opposition and had few scruples when it came to executing perceived opponents. Both tended toward the paranoid, suspecting traitorous intentions others did not perceive. But Zhu Yuanzhang cast a shadow over the rest of the Ming Dynasty. As will be seen in the next chapter, within a short period of Mao's death, much of what he had instituted was undone.

SUMMARY

How different was China in 1976 compared to 1949? Although the Cultural Revolution had brought enormous strain and confusion, China was by many measures better off. It was not dominated by any other countries and held itself up as a model to developing nations. The proportion of the population in school more than doubled between 1950 and 1978. Life expectancy reached sixty-seven years for men and sixty-nine years for women, due in large part to better survival of infants and more accessible health care. Unemployment was no longer a problem, and housing was provided for all. Inflation had been banished.

But life was also much more regimented and controlled. There was no longer anything resembling a free press and not many choices people could make about where they would live or what work they would do. Peasants could not leave their villages. Graduates of high schools or universities were given little choice in job assignments. From the experience of repeated campaigns to uncover counterrevolutionaries, people had learned to distrust each other, never sure who might turn on them. Material security, in other words, had been secured at a high cost.

China Since Mao (1976 to the Present)

26

After the death of Mao in 1976, the Chinese Communist party turned away from class struggle and made economic growth a top priority. Gradually the intrusion of the government into daily life abated, leaving people more leeway to get on with their lives in their own ways. Not only did the government permit increased market activity and private enterprise, but it began courting foreign investment and sending students abroad. The infiltration of Western popular culture and political ideas troubled authorities, but with the spread of technologies like telephones, shortwave radios, satellite television, telephones, fax machines, and the Internet, it became nearly impossible for the government to cordon off China from global cultural trends.

The aggregate figures for China's economic growth in the 1980s and 1990s are very impressive, but not everyone has benefited equally. In broad terms, people in cities have gained more than those in the countryside, those in the coastal provinces more than those in the interior, and those entering the job market during these decades more than their parents and grandparents.

Every facet of China's rapid changes since 1976 has intrigued scholars and journalists who have been able to live in China and observe development firsthand. With the collapse of communism in Russia and eastern Europe, many have speculated on the hold of the Communist party in China. Can the party maintain tight control over political expression when communications with the rest of the world have become so much more open? Can it dampen the unrest that results from unemployment, unpaid pensions, and political corruption? Will the disparities between the rich and the poor in China continue to widen? Can the damage to the environment be checked? Is China becoming, as it claims, a country that follows the rule of law? Will China accept the pressure to conform to international standards that comes with its increased participation in international organizations? Is a return to Maoist policies possible any longer?

THE COMMUNIST PARTY AFTER MAO

The pace of change in the quarter-century after the death of Mao was extraordinary. Much of what had been instituted in the 1950s was abolished outright or slowly transformed. The Communist party, however, maintained its large membership and its political power.

In the immediate aftermath of Mao's death, Hua Guofeng took over as head of the Communist party. He was a relatively obscure party veteran singled out by Mao only months before his death. Soon after Mao's funeral, Hua sided with the pragmatists and arranged for the arrest of Mao's wife, Jiang Qing, and three of her closest associates. This "Gang of Four" was blamed for all the excesses of the Cultural Revolution. In 1977, Deng Xiaoping was reappointed to his old posts, and in December 1978 he supplanted Hua as the top official.

Like Mao, Deng had an impressive revolutionary pedigree, going back to the early 1920s when he was active with Zhou Enlai in France, and continuing through the Shanghai underground, the Long March, and guerrilla warfare against Japan. In 1956, at age fifty-two, he became a member of the Standing Committee of the Politburo and secretary general of the party. Twice ousted from power during the Cultural Revolution, he labeled absurd the Cultural Revolution slogan that it was "better to be poor under socialism than rich under capitalism," insisting that "poverty is not socialism."

A pragmatist, Deng Xiaoping took as his catchword "the Four Modernizations" (of agriculture, industry, science and technology, and defense). He openly admitted that China was poor and backward, and he saw no reason not to adopt foreign technology if it would improve the lives of the masses. Thousands of people who had been sent to the countryside were allowed to go home. People everywhere were eager to make up for what they saw as the "wasted years."

Party membership stood at 39 million when Mao died. Deng quickly set about weeding out the leftists recruited during the Cultural Revolution and rehabilitating those who had been persecuted. Deng knew that party members qualified to manage and direct the modernization projects were in short supply. Only 14 percent of party members had finished the equivalent of high school, and only 4 percent had college educations. Moreover, many of those who had gone to high school or college did so during the 1970s when admission was based on political fervor and the curriculum was watered down to conform to the anti-elitist and anti-intellectual ideology of the period. About 15 million party members were sent back to school to learn to read and write. Retirement ages were imposed to reduce the number of elderly party members. Party recruitment was stepped up to bring in younger people with better educations.

Asserting that the influence of the Gang of Four had created "an entire generation of mental cripples," Deng pushed for reform of universities. Intellectuals responded to the more open atmosphere with a spate of new magazines and a new frankness in literature. In 1978, the Democracy Wall in Beijing attracted a wide variety of self-expression until it was shut down the following spring.

Television coverage was extensive in 1979 when Deng Xiaoping visited the United States and discussed deepening commercial and cultural ties between the United States and China. The need to modernize was also brought home that year when the People's Liberation Army did poorly in its invasion of Vietnam (in retaliation for Vietnam's invasion of Cambodia). In 1980, with Deng Xiaoping's sponsorship, the first Special Economic Zone was created at Shenzhen, just across the border from Hong Kong. By the early 1980s China was crowded with foreign visitors. Thousands of Western teachers were brought to China to teach English and other foreign languages. Christian churches reopened, as did Buddhist and Daoist temples. People began wearing more varied colors, giving the streets a very different look from China in the 1960s.

Economic restructuring placed many party cadres in positions where corruption was easy and tempting; they were the ones to supervise distribution or sale of state and collective assets. Between 1983 and 1986 some 40,000 party members were expelled for corruption, and in 1987 the number reached 109,000.

Not everyone in the party was happy with the rapid changes or with the new interest of young people in the West. In 1983 the party launched a campaign against "spiritual pollution" to warn against overenthusiasm for things Western. After political unrest at several universities in 1986, the party revived a campaign from the early 1960s to "learn from Lei Feng," a model of the selfless party member devoted to advancing China's development. Still, an even bigger political protest movement occurred in 1989, with huge demonstrations at Beijing's Tiananmen Square (see Color Plate 30). After its bloody suppression, the 48 million party members had to submit self-evaluations in order to weed out sympathizers. About 1 million were sent to the countryside to learn from the masses.

By the early 1990s, the collapse of communism in eastern Europe and the Soviet Union added to Deng Xiaoping's determination to persist in economic reform. In Deng's view, the Soviet Union broke up because central planning had not produced prosperity. To show his support for market reforms in 1992, Deng went south to visit the Special Economic Zones. He told people not to worry if policies were capitalist or socialist, only whether they would make China more prosperous. Soon the party constitution was rewritten to describe China as a "socialist market economy" and to declare "the essential nature of socialism" to be "to liberate and develop productive forces." Joint ventures grew more and more common in the 1990s, with businessmen from Hong Kong, Taiwan, and South Korea especially active. Local elections that allowed people to elect some of their leaders were changing the nature of political participation.

By the year 2000, there were some 63 million party members, about 83 percent of whom were male, half high school graduates or better, and about 6 percent members of minorities. Corruption remains the most serious problem for the party (see **Documents: Reporting on Corruption**).

RESTRUCTURING THE ECONOMY

Deng Xiaoping's economic policies set in motion an economic boom that led to the quadrupling of average incomes by 2000. In a manner reminiscent of Japan in 1947–1971, the economy grew rapidly every year, sometimes at more than 10 percent. Overall poverty declined sharply. According to the World Bank's statistics, the population below the poverty line fell from 250 million in 1978 to 80 million in 1993 and then to 27 million in 2001. Life expectancy has continued to rise (to seventy-one for men and seventy-five for women in 2007), as has the average height of Chinese, both reflecting improvements in nutrition.

Encouraging Capitalist Tendencies

In the countryside the most important reform was the dismantling of collective agriculture. In the early 1980s, Deng Xiaoping instituted a "responsibility system" under which rural households bid for land and other assets that they could treat as their own (though the

land was legally held on leases of up to fifty years). In turn they agreed to provide specified crops; whatever the household produced above what it owed was theirs to keep or sell. Sideline enterprises like growing vegetables and raising pigs or chickens were encouraged, as were small businesses of all sorts, ranging from fish farming and equipment repair to small factories producing consumer goods for export. Rural industry boomed. By 1995 township and village enterprises employed 125 million workers. Especially in the coastal provinces, where commercial opportunities were greatest, the income of farmers rapidly increased.

Deng Xiaoping abandoned Mao's insistence on self-sufficiency and began courting foreign investors. Special Economic Zones were created; the best known were Shenzhen on the border with Hong Kong and Pudong across the Huangpu River from Shanghai. These zones offered incentives to foreign firms, including low taxes, new plants, and a well-trained but cheap labor force. China had to bring its legal system more into line with international standards to court these foreign investors, but the payoff was substantial since joint ventures pumped a lot of capital into the Chinese economy and brought up-to-date technology.

Foreign manufacturers were attracted to the low labor costs in China, and both set up factories to produce goods for the Chinese market (such as vehicles) and contracted with Chinese manufacturers to produce consumer goods for Western markets (such as clothing, toys, watches, and computers). Guangdong, with the best access to the financial giant Hong Kong, did especially well in the new environment. Between 1982 and 1992, 97 percent of Hong Kong's thirty-two hundred toy factories relocated to Guangdong. By 1996, China was the world's largest garment maker, accounting for 16.7 percent of world garment exports. In 1997 it manufactured 1.55 billion shirts. The market for shoes, too, came to be dominated by China, which in 1998 made 6.3 billion pairs of leather shoes and about 1 billion pairs of sports shoes. By 2004 China had become the world's top exporter of computer and related equipment and components. By 2006 it was the world's leading supplier of seafood.

Shrinking the State Sector

During the 1980s and 1990s, people who worked for the state found that reform meant that they could lose their jobs. Between 1990 and 2000 some 30 to 35 million workers were shed by state-owned

DOCUMENTS

Reporting on Corruption

The Chinese government has repeatedly announced campaigns against corruption. To publicize the tough measures it is taking, it has encouraged newspapers to report arrests, trials, and convictions. This article reports on progress made in catching those guilty of graft at both high and low levels.

Nine Top Officials Caught in the Net

The Chinese government has been fighting a wave of top-level corruption cases that threaten to undermine its legitimacy. Government and Party leaders have been arrested in major cities in the past year. From 2003 to October last year, a total of 67,505 government officials were punished for corruption. More than 17,505 were prosecuted and sanctioned in the first eight months of last year alone.

Some officials arrested for corruption last year who were above the ministerial level:

1. Liu Zhihua, 58, Beijing's former vice-mayor, who was in charge of Olympic construction was sacked in June for corruption and was expelled from the Communist Party of China (CPC) last December.

   The investigation also found that Liu's lifestyle was corrupt and depraved and he abused his power in order to contract projects for his mistress and sought large illegal profits.

2. Wang Shouye, 64, former deputy commander of the navy of the Chinese People's Liberation Army (PLA) was expelled from China's national legislature in June for "loose morals." He abused his power by requesting and accepting bribes.

   Wang fell from power after one of his mistresses turned him in. She had been in an "improper relationship" with Wang "for a long time."

3. Chen Liangyu, former secretary of the Shanghai Municipal Committee of Communist Party of China (CPC), was sacked in September for his involvement in the misappropriation of at least a third of a 10-billion-yuan ($1.2 billion) social security fund.

   The city's labor and social security department chief, a district governor, and several prominent businessmen were also detained for questioning over the scandal.

4. Qiu Xiaohua, 49, former head of the National Bureau of Statistics, was removed from his post in October for his suspected involvement in the 10-billion-yuan ($1.25 billion) Shanghai social security fund fraud.

5. He Minxu, 51, former vice-governor of Anhui, was expelled from the Communist party of China and removed from office for taking bribes and abusing power.

   He was found to be guilty of taking bribes worth several million yuan and offered cheap land, tax cuts and job promotions to people who paid their way.

6. Wang Zhaoyao, 63, former deputy secretary of the Provincial Communist party of Anhui Province, went on trial in November.

   Wang is accused of taking bribes amounting to more than 7 million yuan ($893,000) and failing to account for property worth more than 8 million yuan ($1.02 million).

7. Wang Wulong, 64, former deputy chief of the provincial legislature of Jiangsu Province, was dismissed in July from his government post on charges of corruption.

   He allegedly took 5.35 million yuan ($668,000) and HK$200,000 from real estate developers in return for favors in land deals, according to a legislative source.

8. Du Shicheng, 56, the deputy Party secretary of Shandong Province was sacked last month and is being investigated for "serious discipline violations."

   Du has also been stripped of his post of secretary of the Municipal Party Committee of Qingdao, a coastal city in Shandong.

9. Zheng Xiaoyu, 61, former head of China's drug administration, is being investigated on suspicion of taking bribes to allow companies to get around drug approval standards.

   Zheng was removed from his post in June 2005.

China Daily, January 11, 2007.

Shenzhen. In the quarter century since the fishing village of Shenzhen was made a "special economic zone," its population has grown to about 9 million, and its skyline has been transformed by the rapid construction of high rise buildings and factories. *(Chang W. Lee*/The New York Times/*Redux Pictures)*

enterprises under pressure to become profitable. Still, few state enterprises could compete with private or collective enterprises. The mines run by the Ministry of Coal could not produce coal as cheaply as the eighty thousand small mines operated by local governments and private individuals. By 1992 the ministry had a debt of 6 billion yuan and needed to lay off 1 million miners. More jobs had probably been created at the small mines, but those jobs lacked the benefits and pensions of the state jobs.

The province of Liaoning in northeast China can be taken as an example. In the 1990s about half of the 10 million people who worked in state-owned enterprises there lost their jobs. The mayor of Shenyang tried to find buyers for the city's bankrupt factories, but no one wanted to take on their obligations to retirees. The situation was even worse farther north. In the cities of Heilongjiang at the end of the 1990s, up to 60 percent of urban population was either unemployed or not being paid. Bankrupt companies paid neither salaries nor pensions, but they were not

dissolved because the government did not want to take over their obligations.

The military is another part of the state sector that has shrunk considerably. The PLA peaked at 4.75 million troops in 1981. Many were later moved to the People's Armed Police, a domestic force. By 2000 soldiers on active duty were thought to number about 2.5 million. The PLA also divested itself of many of the factories it owned and operated, even many military ones. Some factories that once produced tanks have been converted to produce buses or trucks; others have been abandoned.

Regional Disparities and Internal Migration

Deng Xiaoping announced early on that he was willing to tolerate growing inequalities, saying it was acceptable that "some get rich first." Because most of the industrial growth was in the coastal provinces, regional inequalities increased. (See Map 28.1.) Some regions

Restructuring the Economy 479

Map **28.1**   **Population Density in China**

of the country, especially regions far from good roads, remain extremely poor. In Shanxi province, the uplands are occupied by about 9 million people, a third of whom fall below the poverty line. In the late 1990s, half the boys and most of the girls in this area did not attend school. About 80 percent of the adult women were illiterate.

When internal controls on migration collapsed in the early 1980s, the coastal regions were flooded with job seekers willing to live in shantytowns or a dozen to a room to get a chance to share in the wealth that the market economy was bringing to the fortunate regions (see **Biography: Cheng Junyu, Migrant Worker**). In the 1980s about 10 million migrated to the dozen largest cities. In 1992 city authorities estimated that 100 million migrant laborers were working away from home or roaming China in search of work. Crime in cities grew, much of it blamed on migrants. In Guangdong internal migrants, especially those who could not speak Cantonese, became an exploited class, hired for the worst work, kept on the job for ten or twelve hours a day, seven days a week, and unable to protest without losing their jobs. In the 1990s, as newly un-

employed workers from state factories took jobs migrants had previously taken, cities began to deport larger numbers of migrants back to the countryside.

For poorer areas in the countryside, the costs of dismantling the communes have been considerable. Health care has become harder for poor people to obtain. Communes had paid the so-called barefoot doctors. Their replacements, village doctors with little more education, now have to support themselves by charging high prices for the drugs they dispense, making antibiotics beyond the reach of many peasants. Diseases that had been under control, such as hookworm and tuberculosis, have made comebacks. When poor people fall ill, their families usually have to borrow money to put down a deposit before a hospital will admit them.

There has been some trickle-down effect from the booming areas to the poorer ones. The Pearl River Delta in Guangdong imports pigs and rice from Hunan and Sichuan, helping their economies. The millions of migrant laborers from those provinces also help, sending home whatever they can spare from their wages. Yet it is often the poorer areas that are most

BIOGRAPHY   Cheng Junyu, Migrant Worker

Cheng Junyu was born in 1986, a decade after Mao died, in the small hamlet of Caoping in Sichuan province to a family of farmers who raised pigs and grew crops. When she was three, a younger brother was born. Two years later her father took a job in a nearby coal mine because it paid better than farming. When she was nine, her mother left the family, and Junyu began skipping school two or three days a week to tend the fields. When she was thirteen, her father, suffering from black lung, had to quit the mine, and Junyu became the family's main provider. An aunt said she would take Junyu to the city to find work.

Their first stop was Chongqing, the largest city in their province. Her aunt arranged a series of jobs for Junyu as a maid, a waitress, a cook in a mining camp, and a cashier. The aunt took a cut of her wages and also sent money home to her father. After Junyu and her aunt relocated to booming Guangdong province, Junyu got a job as a cook for a foreign factory owner and within weeks talked him into letting her work at the factory, which made small generators. At that point she broke with her aunt and became independent.

Even though Junyu had little formal education, the factory owner quickly recognized that she was intelligent and gave her other jobs to do. She helped him with shippers and suppliers and kept track of parts, inventory, and costs on a computer. Junyu was able to bring her younger brother to town, and the factory owner agreed to pay for him to attend a three-year technical school.

Junyu went back to visit her father and other relatives once or twice a year—the 600-mile trip taking her thirty-six hours on a train and eleven hours on a bus. Although she earned only US$206 per month in 2006, she was able to send $50 to $100 to her family every month. This was enough money for her father to build a new five-room house with concrete floors but no plumbing; the only heat came from a small charcoal burner kept in the living room. Still, it was the most impressive house in the village. Junyu's money was also used to buy a color television, but it still stayed in its box, as television broadcasts had not yet reached the region.

Most of the young people in Junyu's village had, like her, left to find better-paying work elsewhere, though few with so much success. Many factory jobs paid only $100 per month, leaving much less to send home. For the village, however, the money sent back by the young people was a lifesaver. Junyu's father's younger brother wanted to give up working in the mine, where he earned about $65 a month, but his seven- and nine-year-old children were too young to send out to work. So it was his wife who would go, leaving the boys with him and joining Junyu at the generator factory. Keeping the family financially afloat required breaking it up.

Once her brother finishes school and can become the family wage-earner, Junyu would like to go back to school to get a high school diploma.

Based on Alwyn Scott, "Bridging Two Worlds: A New Life for Susie Cheng," *Seattle Times*, July 9, 2006.

---

pressed by cadres. In 1998 and 1999 peasant riots protesting the imposition of new fees and taxes by local officials were common in Hunan.

Environmental Degradation

Under Mao, Chinese were encouraged to harness nature to increase production. Little thought was given to the ecological consequences of terracing mountains, plowing grasslands, reclaiming wetlands, damming rivers, or killing all the sparrows. Soil erosion, desertification, and massive flooding were among the results. With the rapid expansion of industry since 1978, air and water pollution have been added to China's environmental woes. A 1998 World Health Organization study concluded that seven of the ten most polluted cities in the world were in China. Air quality in cities will not improve soon as China depends on coal for 75 percent of its energy, and cars are rapidly replacing bicycles. Air pollution contributes significantly to death rates from respiratory diseases. The water supply in much of the country is unfit to drink. Water pollution comes from untreated sewage as well as industrial

天津城埋伏地雷

Color Plate 25
Boxer Print. The Boxers spread word of their invincibility through woodblock prints like this one, which shows their attack on the treaty port city of Tianjin.

(British Library)

Color Plate 26
People of the Five Nations: A Sunday. This woodblock triptych published in 1861 showed Japan how westerners dressed and entertained themselves in the foreign settlement at Yokohama.

(Arthur M. Sackler Gallery, Smithsonian Institution, Washington, DC:
Gift of Ambassador and Mrs. William Leonhart, S1998.96a–c)

Color Plate 27
Gas Lights. Gas lights illuminating the streets of Tokyo became
a favorite subject for modern woodblock print artists.

(Edo Tokyo Museum/Tokyo Metropolitan Foundation for History and Culture Image
Archives/DNP Archives.com)

Color Plate 28
Magazine covers for *Kagaku chishiki* (Scientific
Knowledge) by Sugiura Hisui from 1931–1935
illustrated the wonders of science and technology
for young readers.

(The National Museum of Modern Art, Tokyo)

Color Plate 29
Raising Mao Zedong's Thought. This 1967 poster is titled "Revolutionary Proletarian Right to Rebel Troops, Unite!" The books they hold are the selected works of Mao Zedong. The woman's armband reads "Red Guard."

(David King Collection, London, UK)

Color Plate 30
Goddess of Democracy. During the 1989 demonstrations in Tiananmen Square, art students provocatively placed a 37-foot tall statue labeled the Goddess of Democracy facing the portrait of Mao Zedong.

(Jeff Widener/AP Wide World Photos)

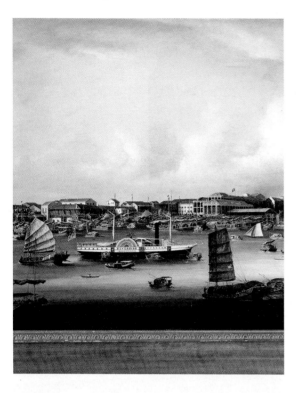

Color Plate 31
Hong Kong After the Opium War.
Framed by Chinese junks, a paddle wheel steamship makes its way past hastily built government buildings and merchant storehouses.

(Photograph Courtesy Peabody Essex Museum)

Color Plate 32
Industrial Plants. This photo depicts industrial plants stretching along Japan's Pacific coast, transforming what had once been scenic views of mountains and water into a modern landscape.

(Corbis)

Migrant Workers. China's rapid economic development has brought not only prosperity to the cities but also millions of peasants looking for better lives. The migrant workers shown here in January 2004 sit beneath a billboard, waiting to be hired. *(Agence France Presse/Getty Images)*

effluent and agricultural runoff. Paper mills, chemical plants, and tanneries dump their wastes in rivers, making the water not only unsafe to drink but also often ruining it as a source for irrigation.

Not only is the quality of water at issue but the supply as well. In the north, so much water has been diverted from the Yellow River that it runs dry for longer and longer periods each year. So much water gets brought up from underground that the water table is dropping steadily in many places.

In the Yangzi region, floods have gotten worse because of tree cutting and soil erosion coupled with dams that have reduced floodplains. Development projects of all sorts have led to the paving over of more and more arable land, leading to questions about how China will be able to feed its growing population in the decades to come.

Environmental activism is growing in China, with more than two thousand officially registered environmental nongovernmental organizations (NGOs). These groups protest dam construction, file lawsuits against polluters, promote conservation, and publicize new threats to biodiversity. In June 2007 about ten thousand residents of Xiamen, alerted by cell phone calls, took to the streets to protest a huge new chemical plant that they considered too dangerous for an urban area. The national government increasingly recognizes the seriousness of environmental issues and implements tougher laws, but enforcement lags at the local level, where officials face competing demands for jobs and development.

Consumer Culture

In the early 1980s, although people began to have more disposable income, there was not yet much to buy, even in city department stores, which were well stocked with thermos bottles and inflatable children's toys but not with the TVs and tape recorders customers wanted. By the 1990s this had changed. Disposable incomes of urban households steadily increased, and more and more factories were turning out consumer goods. Like people elsewhere in the world, Chinese bought TVs, stereos, clothes, furniture, air conditioners, and washing machines. Shopping streets of major cities abounded in stores well stocked with imported as well as domestically produced goods. Between 1986 and 1995, the number of refrigerators per hundred households went from 62 to 98 in Beijing, 47 to 98 in Shanghai, and 14 to 83 in Xi'an. Acquisition of washing machines made similar gains. Telephone service lagged, but Chinese responded eagerly when pagers and cellular phones became available. By 2000 there were 26 million cellular phones in China. By 2006 there were 126 million Internet users, up from 8 million in 2000.

In the 1990s many grew rich enough to buy imported cars, build lavish houses, and make generous gifts to all the officials they dealt with. In 1978 there had not been a single privately owned car in China; by 1993 there were over 1 million, and by 2007 the number had reached 13 million, with 4 million new cars being produced every year.

Consumer culture also came to the countryside, though there it is limited by the much lower level of disposable income. In the 1980s, as farm incomes grew, farmers began building new homes, buying better food, and purchasing consumer goods such as TVs, furniture, and clothing. Villages without electricity built small local generators. With migrant workers bringing home knowledge of city life and with television bringing everyone images of modern living, families in the countryside steadily added to the list of goods they considered essential. Chinese, like people in more developed countries, were identifying more with the goods they consumed than with politics.

SOCIAL AND CULTURAL CHANGES

Education

Education at all levels had deteriorated during the Cultural Revolution, when it was considered more important to be red than to be expert. An important symbolic reversal of these policies occurred in 1977 with the reinstitution of college entrance examinations. Soon those graduating from college could also apply to study abroad in Europe, the United States, or Japan, which led to a craze for studying foreign languages. In the 1990s there were as many as one hundred thousand studying in the United States at any given time.

Only a tiny proportion of Chinese reached college, however. In the 1980s there was room for only a quarter of the elementary school students to continue to middle schools and for only 2 percent to enter college. In the cities, the competition for places in middle and high school and college put children under great pressure.

Educational opportunities had always been better in the cities than in the countryside, and in the 1990s the disparity seemed to grow. During the Cultural Revolution, when the educated were ousted from their jobs, teaching positions were filled by peasant teachers paid like other workers on the commune through work points (redeemable largely in shares of the commune's grain). With the dismantling of the communes in the early 1980s, other ways had to be found to pay teachers. The most common method was to charge parents fees, which could run 200 to 300 yuan per year for elementary school and as high as 1,000 yuan per year for middle and high school, too much for most peasants. Sometimes rural schools tried to make ends meet by having the students work, peddling apples on the streets or assembling firecrackers in their classrooms. After a blistering analysis of the disadvantages faced by rural children in Hunan province published in *China Youth Daily* in 2005, the government announced that rural school fees would be eliminated by 2007. By the end of the 1990s, universities were also charging fees, generally about 10,000 yuan per year. Bitter complaints about how these fees kept out children from rural areas led to the introduction of scholarship programs in 2006.

The Arts

During the decade of the Cultural Revolution, intellectuals learned to keep quiet, and ordinary people were fed a dull and repetitive diet of highly politicized stories, plays, and films. With the downfall of the Gang of Four, people's pent-up desire for more varied and lively cultural expression quickly became apparent. A literature of the "wounded" appeared at the end of the 1970s, when those who had suffered during the Cultural Revolution found it politically possible to write of their experiences. Greater tolerance on the part of the government quickly resulted in much livelier media, with everything from investigative reporters exposing corruption of cadres, to philosophers who tried to reexamine the premises of Marxism, to novelists, poets, and filmmakers who experimented with previously taboo treatments of sexuality.

Television as a cultural force expanded enormously as TV sets became a readily available consumer good and programming became diverse enough to capture people's interest. China severely restricted the showing of foreign films in theaters, but people still saw them because VCRs or DVD players became common and the pirating of videotapes and DVDs made them inexpensive. Western music of all sorts found fans, and China developed its own rock bands capable of filling a stadium for their shows. Cinema reached new artistic heights and found a large audience abroad as well as in China (see **Material Culture: China's New Cinema**).

Gender Roles

The Communist party, from its beginnings in the 1920s, had espoused equality for women, and women were eligible to join the party on the same terms as men. Moreover, the party pushed for reforms in marriage practice that were generally seen as improving women's situations, such as giving them the right to initiate divorce. The reality never came up to the level of the rhetoric, but women did play more active roles in the revolution than they had in earlier eras of Chinese history.

After 1949 official rhetoric encouraged people to think of men and women as equal. With collectivization, women were mobilized to participate in farm work, and efforts were made to get girls enrolled in schools. Images of tough women who could do jobs traditionally done by men were part of everyday propaganda. Women did increase their presence in many jobs; the proportion of elementary school teachers who were women increased from 18 percent in 1951 to 36 percent in 1975 and continued to increase in the reform era to 49 percent in 1998.

When Western scholars were first able to do research in China in the early 1980s, it was not the advances women had made that struck them most forcefully, but how far the reality lagged behind the rhetoric. Girls and women were certainly more visible outside their homes than their counterparts had been in the nineteenth century, but men still occupied most positions of power and the better-paid jobs. In rural areas, the work points women earned by working for the collective were given to the family head, not to them as individuals. The reform era seemed at that point to be taking things backward. With fees charged by elementary schools, poorer families did not send their daughters to school for as long as their sons. New opportunities opened up by the expanding economy favored males. Young men could join construction companies and do relatively well-paid work far from home; young women could work in textile, electronic, and toy factories for lower wages. For those who did not want to leave their hometowns, employment patterns were also skewed by gender. The women often did the field work, while the men got the better-paid skilled work.

In the cities girls were more likely to stay in school as long as boys did, but once the state withdrew from the hiring process, their degrees were worthless. New female graduates of high schools or colleges tended not to get jobs that were as good as the ones their male classmates got, something that happened less frequently when state bureaus made job assignments. The decline in the state-owned factories has hurt both men and women, but women complain that they are the first to be laid off.

Population Control and the One-Child Family

From 1957 to 1970, China's population grew from about 630 million to 880 million. Public health measures promoted in the 1950s deserve much of the credit for reducing the death rate and thus improving life expectancy, which increased dramatically from forty years in 1953 to sixty in 1968 and sixty-five in 1984. As a consequence, population growth accelerated, and even the horrible famine of 1959–1962 could make only a temporary dent in its upward course. Mao had opposed the idea that China could have too many people, but by the time Mao died, China's population was approaching 1 billion, and his successors recognized that China could not afford to postpone bringing it under control.

Since the late 1970s, the government has worked hard to promote the one-child family in the cities and the one- or two-child family in the countryside. Targets were set for the total numbers of births in each place and quotas then assigned to smaller units. Young people needed permission from their work units to get married, then permission to have a child. In the early 1980s, women who got pregnant outside the plan faced often unrelenting pressure from birth control workers and local cadres to have abortions. In the 1990s, the campaign was relaxed a little, making it easier for families with only daughters to try again for a son.

The preference for boys remains so strong that China faces a shortage of young women in coming decades as female fetuses are more likely to be aborted (after being identified by ultrasound) and girl babies are more likely to be made available for adoption. In the mid-1990s, China quietly began to allow unwanted children, primarily baby girls, to be adopted by foreigners, and by the end of the century, more orphans

MATERIAL CULTURE

China's New Cinema

During the Mao period, feature films were produced by state-run studios under the Ministry of Culture. Particularly during the Cultural Revolution, most movies had predictable plots and stereotyped characterizations, and even within China would not have had much of an audience except for the lack of other forms of entertainment and distribution of free tickets. After the graduation of a new generation of directors from the Beijing Film Academy beginning in 1982, films of high artistic level began to be made, and by the 1990s, Chinese films were regularly screened at international film festivals. Heart-wrenching, visually stunning melodramas like *Ju Dou* (1990), *Raise the Red Lantern* (1991), and *Farewell My Concubine* (1993) often ran afoul of censors at home but found appreciative audiences abroad. Some of these movies dramatized a long sweep of modern Chinese history, as did some quieter, less exoticized movies like *Blue Kite* (1993) and *To Live* (1994).

During the 1990s, Chinese filmmakers produced around fifteen hundred films, perhaps a dozen of which were widely circulated abroad. Standards of quality continued to improve. *Shower* (1999), a comedy about ordinary people with no exotic past or political turmoil, won both the best picture and best director awards at the Seattle International Film Festival. *Not One Less* (2000) succeeded with children from a remote area as its main characters. *Blind Shaft* (2003) focused on itinerant miners and illegal privately run mines. Big-budget movies were also made through international collaborations. The highly profitable *Crouching Tiger, Hidden Dragon* (1999) was made by a Taiwanese director (Ang Lee), but its leads include Hong Kong, Taiwan, and mainland Chinese actors, and the funding came mostly from overseas.

Searching Through the City. The thirteen-year-old heroine of the film *Not One Less* had to figure out how to find a ten-year-old boy in a large city she had never visited before. *(Kobal/The Picture Desk)*

Female Workers. Young women are in high demand for the assembly lines of China's light industry. These women, making musical instruments, earned about $130.00 per month in 2007. Efforts to improve salaries, benefits, and job security have been frustrated not only by China's labor laws but also by foreign investors who do not want to see their profits diminish. *(Patty Chen/Reuters)*

were adopted from China into the United States than from any other country.

Almost everyone agrees that China needs to limit population growth. The 2000 census reported a population of 1.27 billion (excluding Taiwan and Hong Kong; 1.3 billion with them). Population control policies are not without consequences, however. By the 1990s, with increased prosperity, people talked about the pampered only children in the cities whose parents would take them to Western fast-food restaurants and pay for all sorts of enrichment experiences. Not only will this generation grow up without siblings, but their children will have no aunts and uncles. Planners are already worrying about how they will take care of their aging parents, since one young couple could well have four elderly parents to support.

Family Life

Both changing gender roles and population control policies have had an impact on family organization and family dynamics. So too have many other policies put into effect by the government since 1949.

Ancestor worship, lineages, and solidarity with patrilineal kin were all discouraged as feudal practices. The authority of family heads declined as collectives took over property and allocated labor. As both women and children spent much more time away from the home, the family became less central in their lives. Coerced marriages became less common, and in the cities at least, people did in fact choose their own spouses much of the time.

The reform era has not turned the clock back on these changes in family structure and authority. Scholars who have studied families in rural areas have shown that although patrilineal stem families are still quite common—the newly married couple living with or very near the husband's family—the older couple has much less power over the younger one. Even in the countryside young people are likely to have decided to marry on their own and seek a companionate marriage. They may extract a hefty bride price from the husband's family, but they use it to purchase things they want for their home. If a new house is built or an extension added, they will work hard to give themselves more privacy. Although the man's parents may push for grandsons, the younger couple often are quite comfortable with birth control policies and are happy with only one or two children, even if they are daughters. They are more concerned with the happiness of their nuclear family than with family continuity. Although divorce is still very rare in the countryside, women believe that the ability to threaten divorce gives them more voice in family decision making.

CRITICAL VOICES

From early in the reform period, people found ways to express political criticism. The first big character posters were pasted on Democracy Wall in Beijing in the fall of 1978. Many of those who participated were blue-collar workers with high school educations, and Deng gave them his blessing. Soon a twenty-eight-year-old electrician named Wei Jingshen courageously pasted up a call for the "fifth modernization":

> What is true democracy? Only when the people themselves choose representatives to manage affairs in accordance with their will and interests can we speak of democracy. Furthermore, the people must have the power to replace these representatives at any time in order to prevent them from abusing their powers to oppress the people. Is this possible? The citizens of Europe and the United States enjoy just this kind of democracy and could run people like Nixon, de Gaulle, and Tanaka out of office when they wished and can even reinstate them if they want to, for no one can interfere with their democratic rights. In China, however, if a person so much as comments on the now-deceased "Great Helmsman" or "Great Man peerless in history" Mao Zedong, the mighty prison gates and all kinds of unimaginable misfortunes await him. If we compare the socialist system of "democratic centralism" with the "exploiting class democracy" of capitalism, the difference is as clear as night and day.[1]

Wei was soon to know those prison gates himself. By April 1979 he had been arrested and Democracy Wall shut down. Wei spent most of his time from

then on in prison, with long stretches in solitary confinement, until he was exiled to the United States in 1997.

Wei's fate did not deter intellectuals from speaking up. In 1986 the physicist Fang Lizhi told students that the socialist movement "from Marx and Lenin to Stalin and Mao Zedong, has been a failure" and advocated adopting the Western political system.[2] That year students at 150 campuses demanded greater freedom, less corruption, and better living conditions in their dormitories. After the protests were suppressed, Deng had party secretary general Hu Yaobang dismissed from his post because he had been too conciliatory toward the students.

In the spring of 1989, huge student protests erupted in Beijing. The protest began modestly in April with a parade honoring the memory of recently deceased Hu Yaobang, viewed as the strongest voice in the government for political reform. Buoyed by the positive reaction of the Beijing citizenry, student leaders gradually escalated their activities and their rallying cries. They called for more democratic government: Make officials disclose their income and assets! Renounce the use of mass political campaigns! Abolish prohibitions against street protests! Permit journalists to report protest activities! End corruption! Many evoked the ideas of the May Fourth movement, claiming that China had still not achieved science and democracy. When Deng Xiaoping called the students' actions "counterrevolutionary turmoil," they did not tone down their rhetoric. When the momentum seemed to be flagging, a couple of thousand students staged a hunger strike to testify to their sincerity and determination.

On May 17, 1989, with the international press present to cover the visit of the Soviet premier Gorbachev, Tiananmen Square was filled not merely with students from every university in Beijing, but also with people from other organizations, even government units like the Foreign Ministry, the Central Television Station, the National Men's Volleyball Team, and the Public Security Bureau Academy. Workers in their work clothes held banners inscribed with the names of their factories.

The students themselves had no experience with democracy, and the leaders who emerged often disagreed

---

1. Wm. Theodore De Bary and Richard Lufrano, *Sources of Chinese Tradition: From 1600 Through the Twentieth Century* (New York: Columbia University Press, 2000), p. 498.

2. Richard Baum, *Burying Mao: Chinese Politics in the Age of Deng Xiaoping* (Princeton, N.J.: Princeton University Press, 1994), p. 201.

on the best tactics. Chai Ling, a female student, was one of the most zealous of the leaders. She told an American reporter in late May that she hoped for bloodshed, because the Chinese people would not open their eyes until the government brazenly butchered the people. She complained about other leaders who were talking to government officials in the hope that violence could be avoided. She claimed to feel sad that she could not tell the other students "straight out that we must use our blood and our lives to wake up the people."[3]

The public's support for the students was a humiliation to Deng and the other leaders, who declared martial law as soon as Gorbachev left and dismissed the more conciliatory Zhao Ziyang from his post as secretary general of the Communist party. When truckloads of troops attempted to enter the city, the citizens in Beijing took to the streets to stop them. Successful against these unarmed soldiers, they were exhilarated by this evidence of "people power." On June 3–4, seasoned troops were brought into central Beijing through underground tunnels, and tanks and artillery soon followed. Many unarmed citizens still tried to halt their advance, but the armored vehicles got through the blockades after bloody clashes and successfully ended both the protest and the occupation of the square. At least several hundred people lost their lives that night, many of them ordinary citizens trying to stop the soldiers from entering central Beijing.

Demonstrations against the government suppression of the Tiananmen protestors erupted in several other Chinese cities. All around the world people expressed shock and outrage. Yet to party hardliners, this bloody suppression was essential because the entire power structure was in jeopardy. In their view, allowing nonparty forces to interject themselves into the decision-making process was a greater threat to stability than was corruption.

Suppression of this movement, coupled with compulsory political study classes at universities, kept political discussion subdued within China for the next several years. In the 1990s no single issue united critics of the government. Some activists tried to organize workers who were facing unsafe conditions or were not being paid. Farmers often protested the arbitrary addition of taxes.

The government was more alarmed by the political potential of a school of Qigong teachings. Until then, the government had pointed with pride to the elderly who early each morning could be seen in parks practicing the stretching and balancing exercises called Qigong, believed to nurture the practitioners' *qi* (vital energy). Masters of Qigong often attributed all sorts of powers to their techniques. In the 1990s one such teacher, Li Hongzhi, developed Falun Gong, a form of Qigong that drew on both Buddhist and Daoist ideas and promised practitioners good health and other benefits. Many from the party and PLA, as well as their wives and mothers, were attracted to this system of knowledge beyond the understanding of Western science. When in 1999 Li organized fifteen thousand followers to assemble outside the party leaders' residential complex in Beijing to ask for recognition of his teachings, the top leadership became alarmed and not only outlawed the sect but also arrested thousands of members and sent them for reeducation. The potential of Falun Gong to reach the masses and offer an alternative to the party was seen as particularly threatening.

TAIWAN

In 1949, when the victory of the Communist party in the civil war seemed imminent, Chiang Kaishek and large parts of the Nationalist government and army evacuated to the island of Taiwan, less than a hundred miles off the coast of Fujian province. Taiwan had been under Japanese colonial rule from 1895 to 1945 and had only recently been returned to Chinese rule. The initial encounter between the local population and the Nationalist government had been hostile: in 1947, the government responded to protests against the corruption of its politicians by shooting at protesters and pursuing suspected leaders, killing, it is estimated, eight thousand to ten thousand people, including many local leaders. In part because of the support the United States gave Chiang and his government as the Cold War in Asia intensified, the Nationalists soon stabilized their government and were able to concentrate on economic development. After Chiang Kaishek died in 1975, he was succeeded by his son Chiang Chingkuo (Jiang Jingguo). During his presidency in the late 1980s, Taiwan succeeded in making the transition from one-party rule to parliamentary democracy.

---

3. Geremie Barmé, *In the Red* (New York: Columbia University Press, 1999), p. 329.

| Comparisons of China, Taiwan, and Other Countries | | | | |
Country	GDP per Capita (in U.S. dollars)	Life Expectancy (years)	Literacy Rate	Fertility Rate	Population (millions)
United States	44,000	78.0	99%	2.1	301
Japan	33,100	82.0	99%	1.2	127
Taiwan	29,500	77.6	96%	1.1	23
China	7,700	72.9	91%	1.8	1,322
India	3,800	68.6	61%	2.8	1,130
Vietnam	3,100	71.1	90%	1.9	82

Source: *World Factbook,* 2007.

During the 1950s and 1960s, the United States treated Chiang's Republic of China as the legitimate government of China and insisted that it occupy China's seat at the United Nations. When relations between the United States and the PRC were normalized in the 1970s, Taiwan's position became anomalous. The United States and the PRC agreed that there was only one China and that Taiwan was a part of China. The United States maintained that any unification of China should come by peaceful means and continued its military aid to Taiwan. China insisted that countries that wanted embassies in Beijing had to eliminate their embassies in Taiwan. As China joined more and more international organizations, Taiwan was frequently forced out.

This loss of political standing has not prevented Taiwan from becoming an economic power. In 2006, Taiwan's per capita income for its 22 million citizens was about $29,000, placing it next after Japan in Asia and way beyond China. Several factors contributed to this extraordinary economic growth. The Nationalists started with the advantage of Japanese land reform and industrial development. They also benefited from considerable foreign investment over the next couple of decades, especially from the United States and Japan. But hard work and thoughtful planning also deserve credit for Taiwan's growth. The government of Taiwan gave real authority to those with technical training. Economists and engineers, including many trained abroad, became heads of ministries. Through the 1950s, emphasis was placed on import substitution, especially by building up light industry to produce consumer goods. The 1960s saw a shift toward export-oriented industries, especially electronics, as Taiwan began to try to follow along behind Japan, moving into stereos and televisions as Japan moved into cars. In 1966 the first tax-free export processing zone was set up, attracting foreign capital and technology. By the 1980s, there was adequate wealth in Taiwan to develop capital-intensive industries such as steel and petrochemicals.

Over the past twenty years, there has been increasing contact between Chinese in Taiwan and the PRC. In 1987, when Taiwan lifted restrictions on travel, thousands of people from Taiwan visited the mainland. The scale of Taiwan's investment in its giant neighbor has been a staggering $100 billion since 1987. In the early 2000s, nearly 1 million Chinese from Taiwan were living on the mainland, more than four hundred thousand of them in and around Shanghai. This movement reflects the relocation of Taiwan's semiconductor and personal computer manufacturing plants to the mainland, where wages are much lower. Trying to adjust to this exodus of manufacturing jobs, Taiwan's own economy has been strained.

In 1996, Taiwan held its first open elections for the presidency and the National Assembly. In 2000, the Nationalist party lost the general election for the first time, losing to the Democratic Progressive Party, long associated with Taiwan independence. In 2008, however, the Nationalist party was returned to power after promising improved ties to the mainland.

CHINA IN THE WORLD

After China split with the Soviet Union in the early 1960s, China severely limited its contacts with the rest of the world. It provided some assistance to African countries and to Maoist revolutionary groups but had too great a fear of spies to encourage people to maintain ties with relatives abroad. Mao's death changed this. China sought entry into international

MAKING COMPARISONS   Food Cultures

Much is shared in the food cultures of East Asia. Throughout the region, food is offered to ancestors and gods. The two most popular sources of carbohydrates are rice and noodles eaten from individual bowls. Soybeans are used to make bean curd, bean curd skin, soy sauce, and various bean pastes. Food is served in small enough pieces so that no cutting needs to be done at the table. Fuel-efficient ways of cooking, such as stir-frying and steaming, are widely used. Chopsticks are a ubiquitous utensil for picking up food. Since water normally had to be boiled before it was drunk, simple soups became a major way to consume fluids. At the same time, in all three countries much farmland has been devoted to tea and a significant share of rice used to make alcoholic drinks.

The explanation of these common features is in most cases diffusion of Chinese foodstuffs and food customs to Korea and Japan. These were not customs that elites purposely set out to adopt or teach to commoners but rather ones that spread as a by-product of contact. Rice had spread to Korea by 1000 B.C.E. and to Japan by 900 B.C.E. Chopsticks, found in some Shang tombs in China, spread to Korea and Japan during the early centuries C.E. Soybeans were native to both China and Korea, but the ways they were prepared as sauces and bean curd must have spread from China. Foodstuffs that were introduced to China from farther west, such as wheat, barley, and sesame seeds, in time also spread to Korea and Japan. Tea is thought to have spread via monks who studied in China.

In premodern times, most people ate locally produced foods, so there would be considerable differences from place to place in what people ate, depending on the local climate and terrain. Japan, with its long seacoasts suitable for fishing, made the most use of products of the sea, not only fish and shellfish but also seaweed. Many dishes associated with Japan today—sushi, buckwheat noodles (soba), and tempura—appeared only in the eighteenth century. In China, much of the fish consumed came from rivers and lakes rather than from the ocean. In ancient China, millet was the most common grain in the north, but with the introduction of wheat from the west and improved transport of rice from the south, it gradually came to play a lesser role in people's diet. Wheat became the basic grain in the north, and meals frequently included steamed rolls, rarely seen in the south.

Beginning in the fifteenth century, New World foods such as potatoes, sweet potatoes, yams, tomatoes, corn, chili peppers, and peanuts spread to the countries of East Asia. In all three countries, sweet potatoes became a common "poor people's food." In China it is believed that New World crops contributed to increased food supply and therefore to rapid population growth because they could be cultivated on steep, rainy slopes or sandy coastal soils that had previously been viewed as worthless.

What about differences? Korean food is the spiciest, especially the pickled cabbage called kimchi (though in China the regional cuisines of Sichuan and Hunan are also spicy). Japanese eat more food at room temperature and are perfectly content with cold rice in their lunch boxes. In all three countries, a banquet or other elegant meal might include eight or ten distinct dishes, but the presentation differs. In China the guests help themselves to food from large plates in the center of the table. In Korea and Japan each guest has a small plate for each of the foods.

The past century has brought many changes in food culture to all three countries. Railways, hothouses, and refrigeration have added to the variety of foods available all year. Restaurants serve versions of Western and other foreign food, and some originally foreign foods such as bread and ice cream have been fully incorporated into everyday eating habits. Yet for most people their own country's cuisine remains a source of pride and pleasure.

organizations, invited overseas Chinese to visit and participate in China's development, and began sending its officials on trips around the world.

It took a while for China to readjust its foreign policy. In the 1970s it supported the murderous Khmer Rouge government in Cambodia and was incensed when Vietnam invaded Cambodia. In February 1979, Deng Xiaoping ordered the army to invade Vietnam to pressure it to withdraw from Cambodia. Despite absorbing large numbers of casualties, China failed in its objectives and soon withdrew.

In the 1980s, China worked to improve its relationship with Western countries, partly to reduce the threat from the Soviet Union. In 1984, the British government agreed to return Hong Kong to China when the ninety-nine-year lease on the New Territories expired in 1997. China promised to let Hong Kong maintain its own political and economic system for fifty years.

In the 1990s, to help expand its economy, China joined the World Bank, the International Monetary Fund, and the Asian Development Bank, which offered both low-interest loans and various types of technical and economic advice, but also required that China report its economic situation more openly. In 2001, China was admitted to the World Trade Organization. Some setbacks occurred in the next few years, such as the SARS epidemic and scandals about tainted food, medicine, and toys, but these were overshadowed by expectations for the 2008 Olympics to be held in Beijing. Just as hosting the Olympics in 1964 was seen to mark Japan's reemergence as a great power, China is expecting the 2008 Olympics to showcase how it has been transformed in the last three decades.

SUMMARY

How different is China early in the twenty-first century than it was at the death of Mao three decades earlier? In the more modernized coastal provinces, the standard of living is much higher. Knowledge of the outside world is much more extensive. Inequalities are also more extreme: some Chinese have grown fabulously wealthy, while others have not been able to find work or cannot afford to send their children to school or to pay for medical care. The party is no longer as dominated by a single person as forms of collective leadership have been developed, and leaders now can rise as much because of their technical expertise as their political fervor. Nevertheless, the Communist party still dominates the government and has its hands in much of what goes on in the country. The Chinese state does not interfere in everyday affairs to the extent it used to, but it still has tremendous coercive force.

Korea (1945 to the Present)

Liberation from Japanese colonialism resulted in division of the Korean peninsula. North and South formed separate states in 1948—the North under the auspices of the Soviet Union and the South under the United States—and fought the bloody Korean War between 1950 and 1953. Divided at the demilitarized zone (DMZ) close to the 38th parallel, the two states began a race for superiority in military and economic strength with policies and politics, social change, and culture reflecting their relationships with the dominant powers and indigenous preferences. Each developed in distinctive ways, the North under a cult to the leader that supports a family dynasty, the South moving from dictatorship to democracy with a pluralistic society and a popular culture that has attracted fans across East Asia. Even today, despite intensified contact between the two nations, they continue to follow divergent paths.

Was the division of Korea in 1945 simply a matter of foreign interference in Korea's affairs, or did it reflect internal differences? Was the Korean War an act of aggression by the North or the continuation of civil conflict? What is responsible for the divergent political and economic systems? What constitutes the Korean inflection of modernity? What are the chances of Korean reunification?

NATIONAL DIVISION AND THE KOREAN WAR (1945–1953)

Rather than divide Japan at the end of World War II, as had been done to Germany, the Allies divided Korea. As soon as Stalin declared war against Japan, Russian forces invaded the Korean peninsula. A week later, after Japan had surrendered, the United States rushed troops to Korea and won Soviet acquiescence to dividing the peninsula at the 38th parallel. Both Russians and Americans were greeted by the spontaneous organization of people's committees (PCs) at the local level that spanned the political spectrum. The Soviets used the PCs as a basis for reconstructing civilian rule, but General Hodge, who established a U.S. military government for South Korea, did not. Each side picked a leader who reflected its ideology, the Soviets recruiting the socialist Cho Mansik as an interim leader in the North and the Americans bringing Syngman Rhee back from the United States to rule the South.

After liberation, millions of Koreans living in Japan and Manchuria flooded back to the peninsula, many radicalized by their experiences during the colonial period. In North Korea, former collaborators were excluded from leadership roles, but in South Korea, collaborator businessmen and landlords formed the Korean Democratic party (KDP). Communists jailed by Japan were released, and one of them, Pak Hŏnyŏng, formed the Korean Communist party (KCP) in Seoul, expecting that the city would be the capital of a united Korea.

In North Korea, several communist groups greeted Soviet commanders: the domestic Communists, the Yan'an Communists who had fought with Mao Zedong in the Chinese civil war, Koreans holding Soviet citizenship, and the Manchurian guerrilla fighters who had fought alongside Kim Il Sung. The thirty-two-year-old Kim Il Sung and his supporters arrived in North Korea from Siberia on September 19, 1945. The Soviets established a northern branch bureau of the KCP and introduced Kim at a large public meeting in Pyongyang, where he praised Stalin and supported Cho Mansik. With Soviet support, Kim replaced Cho in January 1946 because Cho had opposed Stalin's agreement with the United States to set up a trusteeship for Korea at the Moscow Conference in December.

The U.S.-Soviet division of Korea between the communist North and the capitalist South soon reflected political and social differences between Koreans. In South Korea, violent protests by workers and peasants began in late 1945. A railroad strike and mass demonstrations broke out in the autumn of 1946 in Pusan and Taegu, followed by farmers' riots against Hodge's grain policies in Chŏlla and Kyŏngsang, leaving two hundred police and a thousand civilians dead. U.S. authorities blamed the communists, put an end to the PCs, and declared martial law. Pak Hŏnyŏng and other communists fled to North Korea, while landlords, businessmen, and Christians from the North moved to the South.

In North Korea, Kim Il Sung became chairman of the Provisional People's Committee (PPC) and eclipsed Pak Hŏnyŏng. In 1946 the PPC carried out land reform to eliminate the landlord class and redistribute land to sharecroppers. Kim nationalized all industries with little opposition because Japanese factory owners had left the country. He reduced working hours

to eight hours per day, banned child labor, created a labor federation, declared equal rights for women, established universal education through the eleventh grade, and founded Kim Il Sung University. He made his guerrilla allies from Manchuria his chief aides and created the Korean People's Army (KPA).

In South Korea, local rivalries, distrust of the central administration, and resentment of outsiders fueled civil conflict. In April 1948, the people of Cheju Island rebelled against a repressive right-wing governor and his Northwest Youth gangs who had infiltrated the police. Two regiments of the Korean army assigned to fight the guerrillas on Cheju rebelled at Yŏsu on the southern coast and murdered hundreds of police and landlords. U.S. forces helped suppress both rebellions. Forty-five thousand people died on Cheju, forty thousand fled to Japan, and seventy thousand were placed in concentration camps. Fed by tenant anger at high rents, guerrilla war spread throughout the South. The Rhee regime's suppression campaign during the winter of 1949–1950 killed around six thousand people.

As the Cold War intensified between the United States and the Soviet Union, political divisions hardened. The United States supported Syngman Rhee's plan to hold elections across the peninsula in 1948, but the Soviets refused to allow elections in the North because its population was only half that of the South. Following a separate election in the South on May 10, 1948, the Republic of Korea (ROK) was proclaimed on August 15. A constitution modeled on the U.S. Constitution was adopted. A National Assembly was elected, and it chose Syngman Rhee as its first president. On September 10, 1948, North Korea established the Democratic People's Republic of Korea (DPRK) with Kim Il Sung as chairman of the National People's Assembly. The Soviet Union withdrew its forces from Korea in December, and the United States withdrew most of its forces in 1949.

Korean War (1949–1953)

Neither North nor South Korea expected the division to be permanent. Both Kim Il Sung and Syngman Rhee began conducting cross-border raids in 1949, hoping to provoke the other into an all-out war. Despite the escalation in conflict, the United States prevented Rhee from invading the North lest he drag the United States into war with the Soviet Union. When Kim met with Stalin in Moscow in March to seek support for invasion of the South, Stalin refused to allow it.

Map **29.1** Korean War

Korean War Refugees. While armies fought up and down the peninsula, civilians tired to get out of their way. Five million refugees left their homes, many to end up on the opposite side of the DMZ. Hundreds of thousands of families remain divided between North and South to this day. *(Frederic Brown/AFP/Getty Images)*

Having sent Korean troops to support the communists in their war for China, Kim Il Sung had a new ally in Mao Zedong, but Mao said that the timing for an invasion was premature.

In 1950, Kim Il Sung gained reluctant acquiescence from his big-power supporters for an invasion of the South. Stalin promised to supply weapons, planes, and pilots only because he wanted to avoid a direct challenge to the United States. Mao sent perhaps as many as eighty thousand experienced Korean troops who had fought in the Chinese civil war to North Korea. On June 25, 1950, Kim launched his invasion with seven divisions and 258 Soviet tanks against the four front-line divisions of the ROK Army, which had no tanks. North Korean forces overran the South Korean military and pushed south all the way to Pusan.

The United States played a major role in the war that followed. President Truman viewed the invasion as a plot by Stalin to spread communism, and he dis-

patched U.S. forces to Korea as a "police action" rather than declare war. He also used the absence of the Russian delegate from the UN Security Council to win approval of a UN force under the command of U.S. General Douglas MacArthur. Truman had already signed a policy document early in 1950, NSC 48, that committed the United States to the containment of communism within its present boundaries in Asia and "where feasible" to reduce communist power in Asia.

Truman's determination to roll back communism led to China's intervention. The initial contingent of U.S. forces with remnants of the ROK Army was barely able to defend the Pusan perimeter until General MacArthur turned the tide of battle by launching an amphibious attack at Inch'ŏn, near Seoul, on September 15. Kim was forced to withdraw his main forces north across the 38th parallel. Truman authorized MacArthur to follow him into North Korea.

Oblivious to Chinese signals passed through India, General MacArthur ordered his troops to the Yalu River with the promise that they would be "home by Christmas." Instead Mao Zedong committed an army of Chinese "volunteers" that overran U.S. positions. The Chinese recaptured Seoul, only to lose it once again. In 1951 the fighting stabilized along a front that eventually became the Demilitarized Zone (DMZ) near the 38th parallel (see Map 29.1). The battle back and forth across the front raged for two more years at the cost of many casualties until all parties except Syngman Rhee signed an armistice in 1953. To this day there is still no peace treaty.

More than 3 million North Koreans, 1 million South Koreans, 1 million Chinese, and fifty-two thousand U.S. soldiers died in the conflict. South Koreans suffered another four hundred thousand casualties and Americans one hundred thousand. North Korean and Chinese casualties are unknown. Both sides and their big-power supporters committed atrocities against soldiers, POWs, and civilians. Both North and South suffered such extreme devastation that the industrial capacity built during the colonial period and expanded after 1945 lay in ruins.

THE DEMOCRATIC PEOPLE'S REPUBLIC OF KOREA (1953 TO THE PRESENT)

Kim Il Sung set the basic lineaments of the political system in North Korea even before the Korean War, and they have scarcely changed since. He maximized political power in his own hands as the supreme leader; he developed a militarist policy based on arming the entire population; he initiated a revolutionary social policy; and he launched periodic terrorist acts. His regime experienced a roller-coaster economic ride under a command economy with a downward plunge in 1991 following the withdrawal of Soviet support upon the collapse of communism in the Soviet Union and Eastern Europe.

Economic Development

After the end of the Korean War in 1953, Kim Il Sung relied on aid from the Soviet Union and China. He invested primarily in heavy and defense industries to create the basis for economic independence and a national arms industry. He postponed the production of consumer goods to the indefinite future, called on the public to accept sacrifice for the greater good of the nation, and compensated by providing cheap housing and food, free education, and free medical treatment.

In the mid-1950s, Kim embarked on a rapid farm collectivization plan aimed at converting all farmers to proletarians receiving wages on state farms. The plan was never fully implemented and ended with smaller collectives at the village level. Broad fields were created out of small parcels to enable the use of tractors and chemical fertilizer. In the early years, the program fostered tremendous gains in productivity, and its drawbacks did not appear until decades later. These included severe soil erosion, the replacement of age-old farming experience with bureaucratic managers, and restrictions on people's freedom to move or change jobs. When the withdrawal of Soviet support in 1991 led to shortages of fuel oil, agricultural production plummeted.

Blessed with more extensive mineral reserves, North Korea enjoyed higher growth in industrial production than did the South through the mid-1960s. After that, aid from the Soviet Union and China declined; also, the five- and six-year plans could not solve problems of bottlenecks in the production process, insufficient technological development, and excessive investment in weapons. Kim Il Sung's solution was to use a moral appeal to workers for greater sacrifice and to undertake mass mobilization efforts such as the Thousand-League Horse campaign of 1958. It was similar to the Great Leap Forward campaign in China, but was not designed to supplement factories with backyard steel furnaces, nor did it result in massive starvation (see Chapter 28). Instead workers were required to work extra hours, and students were taken out of classrooms to work.

By 1970 the economy needed an infusion of new technology. It had done well in the second industrial revolution in terms of chemicals, steel, locomotives, and internal combustion engines, but it did not develop the electronics industries based on the transistor that are the hallmark of the third industrial revolution. Kim opened trade relations with the West in 1972 to import advanced machinery and even complete factories from Europe and Japan on credit. Lacking anything to export, he defaulted on his international debt in 1975. Most trade with the West evaporated. Despite technological shortfalls, problems with quality control, and wastage of energy, per capita GNP in North Korea probably stayed equal to that in the South at least to 1983.

While much of the rest of the world pursued economic interdependence, North Korea insisted on trying to produce whatever it needed itself. This autarkic policy has led to increasing hardships for the population. One sign of economic difficulty came in 1987 when Kim Il Sung was forced to abandon construction on what was to be the tallest building in East Asia, the 105-story Ryugyŏng Hotel. He then decided to shift investment to light industry and consumer products to improve living conditions. He even opened talks with South Korea on economic and humanitarian cooperation and sent food aid to flood victims in South Korea. In 1988 he began informal talks with U.S. representatives. In 1990 they reached an agreement to establish trade offices with consular functions in both countries.

The collapse of communism in the Soviet Union in 1991 left North Korea without a patron and without socialist trading partners. Oil supplies dropped because Russia demanded cash payment, and factories operated at only a fraction of capacity. North Korea opened a free economic trade zone in the Rajin-Sŏnbong area in the northeast in 1991, but no foreign investors responded. The floods of 1995 and 1996, followed by drought in 1997, reduced the country to near-famine conditions, and up to 2 million people lost their lives. Denizens of Pyongyang and the army fared well, while the rest of the civilian population suffered from malnutrition and disease. For the first time, the government allowed people to leave their homes without permission to forage for food and to cultivate small private plots and sell the products in farmer's markets.

Declines in industry and agricultural production have had a devastating effect on the North Korean population. Illegal emigration into China's northeast province (the former Manchuria) increased, even though China has a policy of returning refugees. Worldwide charitable organizations, South Korea, China, the United States, and Japan supplied perhaps a fifth of North Korea's food in the 1990s.

After Kim Il Sung's death in 1994, Kim Jong Il took cautious steps to open the economy. He established the Diamond Mountain tourist center for South Koreans, the Uiju free trade zone south of the Yalu River, and the Kaesŏng industrial park. He permitted construction of rail lines and roads across the DMZ from South Korea to Kaesŏng and the Diamond Mountains. He welcomed investment by South Korean companies to build factories that would hire cheap North Korean labor and make products for export. He also counterfeited the currency of other nations and exported ballistic missile technology to enemies of the United States.

State and Society

The new proletarian state aimed at remaking economic relationships. It banned collective bargaining, instead allowing only single state trade and farmers' unions. Kim Il Sung borrowed Mao Zedong's "mass line" strategy in 1960 to force party cadres to consult with workers and farmers in devising production plans. Faced with a dearth of proletarians, he admitted farmers to the Korean Workers' party (KWP) and converted them to proletarian class consciousness by indoctrination and self-criticism. Unlike Mao, he never launched periodic mass mobilization campaigns to purge party cadres and bureaucrats who had lost their revolutionary ideals.

Kim Il Sung divided society into a new status hierarchy. The nuclear masses included KWP party members, government officials, military officers, anti-Japanese guerrilla fighters, and martyrs who died in the Korean War. The non-nuclear masses included nonparty workers, peasants, and clerical workers. The lowly mixed masses were outcasts with tainted backgrounds: descendants of the bourgeoisie, landlords, capitalists, and dissidents. By 1962, Kim had executed all Catholic priests and Protestant ministers. Christians who had not fled to the South went to reeducation camps. Instead of equal treatment for all, Kim turned the status structure upside down, reviving hereditary privilege for the elite and hereditary stigma for the despised.

Kim locked all individuals into a variety of state-run mass organizations. Because of labor shortages, he encouraged women to work and had the state provide child-care facilities for working parents. He replaced the home with communal mess halls, gave women the right to divorce, and incorporated women into the military. Despite these measures, few women had the opportunity to take on political responsibilities.

Expansion of Personal Power

Kim Il Sung's creation of a personality cult defines the North Korean regime. In becoming a family-centered corporate state, Kim Il Sung's Korea resem-

North Korean Soldiers Performing for Kim Jong Il and Madeleine Albright. Above the soldiers are 25,000 placard holders who construct precisely timed mosaics that demonstrate both North Korea's bellicosity and subordination of the individual to the group. *(www.imbc.com <http://www.imbc.com> @ MBC & IMBC Co. Ltd. Seoul, Korea)*

bles Syria more than it does the Soviet Union or China. Its cultural conservatism means that it is closer to the Chosŏn dynasty than is South Korea. In 1972, Kim introduced a new constitution that created a new office of president, which gave him control of all government agencies. More shocking for ideologically committed communists, he subordinated the KWP to his command and left it out of many of his policy decisions. As signs of his megalomania, he also built gigantic statues of himself and adopted grandiose titles such as "supreme leader," "fatherly leader," "the Great Sun," "the supreme mind of the nation," and "genius of mankind."

Kim also began to displace Marxism-Leninism with *chuch'e* (self-reliance) as the country's leading ideology. A person who has *chuch'e* has imbibed the correct thought from which will naturally spring correct action in any and all situations: the making of music and steel, getting up in the morning and being a good citizen, being modern and Korean. *Chuch'e* is what makes North Korea proudly independent, self-contained, and the center of the world. In 1973, Kim borrowed from dynastic tradition by grooming his

son, Kim Jong Il, to succeed him. He gave him responsibility for running most state affairs when he appointed him secretary of the KWP and member of the Military Commission in 1980. Although Kim Jong Il has never taken over his father's position as president, he has taken the personality cult to new heights. He is most commonly known as "dear leader" and enjoys hearing massed thousands of children sing his praises and watching elaborately choreographed mass spectacles.

Anyone who might challenge Kim Il Sung's supremacy was purged. At first the purges focused on members of the party. They started with Pak Hŏnyong and the domestic Communists after the Korean War. After Stalin died in 1953 and Khrushchev denounced Stalin for creating a cult of personality in 1956, Kim purged members of the Russian and Yan'an factions who accused him of doing the same thing. He also purged three generals after the failure of his military ventures against South Korea and the United States in 1968 (a commando attack on the ROK presidential mansion and the capture of the intelligence-gathering ship *USS Pueblo*) and 1969 (the downing

BIOGRAPHY   Kang Chol-hwan, Survivor of a North Korean Prison Camp

Kang Chol-hwan and his family exemplify the potential for mobility in the twentieth century, going from one country to another, from one occupation to another, and from privilege to a concentration camp. Kang Chol-hwan's grandmother migrated to Japan from Cheju Island in the 1930s at the age of thirteen. At the age of twenty, she joined the Japanese Communist party and married a man from Cheju. Their son, Kang's father, was born in the early 1940s. After the end of World War II, Kang's grandfather did what many resident Koreans in Japan did—he opened a pachinko parlor in Kyoto. To stay in what is a somewhat shady business, he made friends with *yakuza* (gangsters). In the 1960s, the grandmother persuaded her reluctant husband to move the whole family, including her brothers, to Pyongyang. They were treated as celebrities on the ship, were greeted by Kim Il Sung when they arrived, and were provided with a first-class apartment in the capital. The grandmother was elected to the Supreme People's Assembly, and the grandfather was appointed to the Office of Commercial Affairs. Kang's parents married in 1967, and he was born soon after.

One day in 1977, the grandfather disappeared, never to return, shipped off to a concentration camp for treason without a word to his family. Shortly after, at the age of nine, Kang returned home to find that security agents were sending him, his grandmother, his father, and his uncles to a concentration camp because of his grandfather's crime. His mother was left behind with no way to communicate with the rest of the family. When Kang and the others arrived at Yodok camp, they were placed in a hut with earthen walls and floor. Whole families lived together in rags and filth. The camp included two thousand or three thousand people; every year about a hundred died from hunger and disease. Minor violations were punished by a trip to the sweatbox for as long as three months. There the prisoner had to crouch on his knees in darkness without moving or speaking. If he did either, he was beaten. Many failed to survive.

Kang spent ten years in the camp and was able to avoid the worst punishments. His work assignment was to carry ore from the mines. He hunted rats, frogs, snakes, and insects to supplement the starvation rations of cornmeal and cabbage soup. One of his uncles attempted suicide twice. Adults worked in the gold mine for thirteen hours a day, and many died from cave-ins. Women caught engaging in sex were humiliated in public or physically abused. Any babies born in the camp were taken away. The entire camp had to turn out for executions. One prisoner who tried to escape was dragged to his death behind a car. The rest of the prisoners had to file past and touch his corpse as a warning not to try escaping themselves.

After a decade in the camp, Kang and his family were released by an amnesty, but they were not allowed to return to Pyongyang. Instead they were sent to the countryside where they were subjected to strict surveillance. Kang finally left his family behind and bribed his way across the border to China. Eventually he made his way to South Korea. Many other refugees have followed him, only to find that starting over is never easy.

Source: Chol-hwan Kang and Pierre Rigoulot, *The Aquariums of Pyongyang* (New York: Basic Books, 2001).

of a U.S. reconnaissance plane). In the late 1960s, hundreds of thousands of party members received punishment for violating party rules. The prison camps received new influxes of political prisoners in the 1970s (see **Biography: Kang Chol-hwan, Survivor of a North Korean Prison Camp**). Today they house economic refugees who have had the misfortune to be recaptured and returned to their homeland.

International Relations

Until the collapse of the Soviet Union in 1991, Kim Il Sung tried to stay on good terms with both of his giant communist neighbors. He remained neutral during the Sino-Soviet split and signed mutual defense treaties with each. Surprised and alarmed when Mao invited President Nixon to visit Beijing in

1972, he allowed members of families separated by the Korean War to meet for the first time since 1953. He even signed a joint pledge for peaceful reunification with the president of South Korea.

This détente did not last long. After 1973, Kim Il Sung constructed secret tunnels across the DMZ large enough to accommodate an invasion. North Korea kidnapped Japanese citizens for their passports and language expertise. To demonstrate support for South Korea, President Reagan shipped it cruise missiles and F-16 fighters and increased the number of troops in the joint U.S.-ROK Team Spirit military exercise of 1981. Kim supported the Soviet Union's invasion of Afghanistan as a means of ensuring military aid. Possibly in return for that favor, a Soviet interceptor in August 1983 shot down a South Korean airliner, KAL Flight 007, which had strayed into Russian territory. The next year the Soviet Union shipped more military equipment in return for docking and overfly rights. In 1986 it promised to construct a nuclear power plant in the North.

In 1989 and 1990, North Korean officials indicated a willingness to normalize relations with the United States and Japan, open trade with South Korea, support peaceful coexistence, reduce defense expenditures, and introduce market reforms. They also voiced their objection to U.S. nuclear weapons on South Korean soil, joint ROK-U.S. Team Spirit exercises, and the thirty-seven thousand U.S. troops stationed in South Korea. In 1991, Kim Il Sung signed a denuclearization pact with South Korea. The United States eased tensions when it announced withdrawal of all U.S. nuclear weapons from Korean soil and cancelled joint Team Spirit exercises with South Korea.

North Korea's Nuclear Challenge

Between 1964 and 1986, North Korea built several gas-graphite nuclear reactors in the Soviet style at Yŏngbyŏn north of Pyongyang, for research and electrical generation. All produced the by-product plutonium, which could be used to manufacture hydrogen bombs. In 1985, the Soviet Union induced Kim Il Sung to sign the Nonproliferation Treaty (NPT), which required inspections by the UN International Atomic Energy Agency (IAEA) to prevent military use of fissile material. The IAEA never followed through on the inspections.

The 1990s saw protracted negotiations over North Korea's nuclear power program. Kim Il Sung offered to replace his gas-graphite reactors with new light-water reactors, which produce less plutonium as a waste product. Concerned that Kim planned to develop nuclear weapons, the United States ignored the offer and considered taking punitive action. American generals warned that a second Korean war would result in three hundred thousand to five hundred thousand military and millions of civilian Korean casualties on both sides. The next crisis came when Kim threatened to pull out of the NPT. Sent by President Bill Clinton, former president Jimmy Carter went to Pyongyang and reached an agreement with Kim to freeze the processing of nuclear waste to extract plutonium at Yŏngbyŏn in return for light-water reactors. Kim also told Carter he was willing to carry out the North-South denuclearization agreement, pull back forces from the DMZ, match South Korea in reducing troops by 1 million men, and accept the presence of U.S. troops in Korea. He died before negotiations could be continued.

His son, Kim Jong Il, signed the Agreed Framework with the United States in 1994. Under this agreement, South Korea and Japan assumed the cost for the light-water reactors, and the United States was to provide 500,000 tons of heavy oil annually to replace energy lost from the inactive reactors. A neutral agency, KEDO (Korean Energy and Development Organization), was established to administer construction. North Korea remained a party to the NPT and promised to allow the IAEA to inspect facilities not subject to the freeze when the light-water reactors were completed but before the nuclear components were installed.

The Agreed Framework was only partially implemented. The United States delayed delivery of heavy oil, and the economic crash of 1997 rendered the ROK incapable of financing construction of a light-water reactor. In 1998, North Korea test-fired a Taep'odong missile over Japan, an act repeated in 2006.

The early twenty-first century saw increased tension between North Korea and the United States. After the destruction of the twin towers in New York City by the Islamic terrorist al-Qaeda organization on September 11, 2001, President Bush voiced hostility to what he called the "axis of evil," a group of "rogue states" that included North Korea. When in 2002, U.S. intelligence discovered the North's clandestine plan to build atomic weapons from enriched uranium (supplied by Pakistan), Bush declared that the North would have to abandon its nuclear weapons program before the United States offered any material aid. North Korea expelled IAEA inspectors and withdrew from the NPT. Bush threatened to launch a preemptive strike against North Korea. In 2006, North Korea tested a plutonium bomb. Under pressure from China, North Korea re-joined six-nation talks with China, Russia, the United States, South Korea, and Japan. In 2007, Kim Jong Il agreed to shut down his nuclear weapons program in return for a guarantee that other nations will respect North Korea's sovereignty, help in building light-water reactors, and move toward normal diplomatic relations.

THE REPUBLIC OF KOREA: DICTATORSHIP AND PROTEST (1953–1987)

During the Cold War, dictators ruled South Korea. As in the North, they suppressed civil liberties and tried to promote economic growth through heavy-handed state planning that fostered inefficiency and corruption. Although they never developed personality cults, they killed, jailed, and tortured thousands of their opponents. The only way for protesters to voice opposition was outside the system, but they repeatedly forced changes in leadership.

The Dictators

Syngman Rhee constructed a dictatorship based on the police, a new army, and a centralized bureaucracy that appointed district magistrates. In 1949 he passed a National Security Law that allowed imprisonment for treason of anyone who supported, abetted, or praised an "enemy state" (that is, North Korea), terms so vague that Rhee immediately began to use the law against his political rivals. He railroaded bills through the National Assembly. He used officials and police to intimidate voters during elections. He distributed favors to politicians, gagged newspapers, jailed critics, and had them tortured. Whatever he had learned in America about respect for law, democracy, and civil liberties he forgot once he returned to Korea.

A combination of student protest followed by a coup d'état brought South Korea's longest-reigning dictator to power. On April 19, 1960, college students marched in opposition to Rhee's attempt to fix his reelection. Many died when the police fired into the crowd. Lacking the army's support, Rhee retired to Hawai'i. His successor proved unable to handle

either the students or the economy. A year later, on May 16, 1961, former Japanese army officer General Park Chung Hee took control in a coup. Two years later, under pressure from the United States, Park donned civilian garb, abolished the supreme council, and held elections. By relying on the civil bureaucracy, police, army, and Korean Central Intelligence Agency (KCIA), he won the presidential elections of 1963 and 1967 and majorities for his Democratic Republican party (DRP) in the National Assembly.

When Park nearly lost the presidential election of 1971, he took new measures to stay in power. In 1972 he revised the constitution to allow the president to appoint one-third of the members of the National Assembly, guaranteeing him a two-thirds majority and the ability to declare martial law at any time. Decree No. 9 banned any criticism of the president, and he also forbade all labor union activity. To eliminate his strongest political challenger, in 1973 Park authorized the KCIA to kidnap Kim Dae Jung from his hotel room in Tokyo and dump him in Tokyo Bay. Sharp U.S. protest forced Park to bring Kim back to Seoul and put him under house arrest. In 1979 labor protest erupted in Pusan and the free export zone of Masan. Park was about turn the army on the demonstrators when the head of the KCIA shot and killed him.

A second military dictatorship followed. General Chun Doo Hwan, chief of the Army Security Command, declared martial law, closed all universities, banned political activity, suspended the National Assembly, and arrested hundreds of students and opposition politicians. When students in Kwangju in Chŏlla province protested en masse on May 18, 1980, and citizens took over the city, elite paratroopers clubbed, bayoneted, and murdered people on the streets. Although the exact number will never be known, it appears that over two thousand civilians died. Chun Doo Hwan made Kim Dae Jung the scapegoat for the Kwangju massacre and had a kangaroo court sentence Kim to death. (Again, U.S. pressure saved his life.)

Chun's repression of dissent continued. He revised the constitution to establish a seven-year term for the presidency. He banned hundreds of politicians from political activity and won a sham presidential election in February 1981. Four years later Chun lifted the ban against most politicians but dismissed a half-dozen dissident professors, expelled 1,363 university students, forcibly conscripted 465 students into military service where several were murdered on duty, and subjected others to brainwashing in concentration camps. Chun took revenge on his critics in the

Kim Dae Jung (Kim Taejung), Opposition Politician and Later President of South Korea, 1997–2002. Here, on August 14, 1980, Kim Dae Jung appears on trial on the phony charge of fomenting the Kwangju uprising of May 1980, for which he received the death penalty. *(Han'guksa vol. 19 [Seoul: Han'gilsa, 1994], p. 29)*

media by dismissing hundreds of newspaper and broadcast reporters, banning 172 periodicals, closing down 617 publishing companies, and taking over the Munhwa Broadcasting Corporation (MBC). He required all newspapers to run his picture every day.

The most massive demonstrations in Korean history erupted when Chun Doo Hwan gave signs of reneging on his pledge to retire at the end of his seven-year term. Forced to retreat, he nominated General Roh Tae Woo, a commander in the Kwangju massacre, to be his party's nominee for president. He authorized Roh to announce direct elections, restoration of freedom of the press, and reinstatement of Kim Dae Jung's right to run. President Reagan had put pressure on Chun to back down, but the main force for democracy came from students who had fought against dictatorship for decades and elements of the urban middle class who joined the democratic struggle at its end.

Building a New Economy

South Korea's economy did not fare well during the Korean War. To compete with the North, Syngman Rhee adopted a land reform policy that created a class

of conservative small property owners who voted for Rhee and subsequent dictators. Eleven billion dollars of U.S. civil and military aid kept the economy afloat. Rhee distributed U.S. dollars to favored businessmen in return for political contributions. His import-substitution policy cut the cost of imported goods, but the country's economic growth rate remained so low that U.S. officials viewed the ROK as a basket case incapable of serious development. They proposed turning South Korea into a supplier of agricultural products and raw materials in exchange for Japan's manufactured goods, a policy Rhee opposed.

Military dictators ignored the principles of free market capitalism and adopted a developmentalist strategy. Park Chung Hee controlled the banks to direct foreign exchange and have loans made at preferential low interest rates to labor-intensive export industries, such as textiles, to take advantage of South Korea's low wages. He allowed the most efficient companies to become huge conglomerates (*chaebŏl*) and protected them from bankruptcy. Park devalued the currency to promote exports, protected companies with tariffs and non-tariff barriers, banned the sale of export items on the domestic market, and prevented foreign investors from owning more than 49 percent of businesses. After repressing strikes for higher wages, he created a single national trade union to block labor activism. He maintained subsistence income for the new class of smallholding farmers by buying their rice crops at high prices and distributing it to low-wage urban factory and white-collar workers below cost, using tax revenues to make up the difference. He also built multistory apartment houses for squatters and the homeless poor.

The South Korean government used foreign policy to raise money for investment. In return for normalizing relations with Japan in 1965, it received $800 million in grants and loans. As a result, the economy grew about 9 percent per year for almost two decades, with most of the investment in industry, not agriculture. During the Vietnam War, South Korean troops fought alongside U.S. forces. In return for its fifty thousand soldiers and equipment, the ROK received $1 billion in compensation. Just as Japan had prospered from the Korean War, so did South Korea prosper by sending steel and transport to Vietnam.

In the early decades, state-managed economic growth did not bring many benefits to workers. In the late 1960s, workers in the electronics, chemical, steel, and automobile industries struck against low wages. The nation was particularly shocked in 1970 at the self-immolation of Chŏn T'ae'il, a worker in the Peace Market in Seoul (a warren of garment sweatshops) who protested the mistreatment of young girls. In 1971, Park established the New Village Movement complete with training camps to mobilize both farmers and workers on behalf of peaceful worker-employer relations.

Despite criticism from foreign advisers, in 1973, Park decided on a big push: forced industrial development to increase exports and raise per capita income. He initiated his heavy and chemical industry (HCI) program to develop steel, ships, automobiles, petrochemicals, and electronics to build capacity in weapons production and increase national power. When the Middle Eastern oil-producing nations raised oil prices in 1973 and 1974, he refused to derail industrialization and borrowed from abroad to keep factories going. By the end of the decade, South Korea was exporting machinery, steel, chemicals, freighters, and tankers. In the 1980s, it moved into electronics, following Japan and the United States into the third industrial revolution. While economic growth paid the most handsome dividends to the conglomerates (*chaebŏl*), it also put money in the pockets of workers.

Social Change and Official Arts

The Korean War did as much to dissolve the old status system as had Japan's colonization projects. By dislocating the population, it tore people from their old relations of dependency and control. Although former *yangban* from the southwest still claimed social prestige, they lacked economic clout and political power. The development of industry in the 1960s brought a massive migration of the rural population to Seoul and other cities. The largest, most cohesive institution became the military. During the long years of military preparedness following the war, male conscripts learned drills, discipline, patriotism, and anticommunism. Large corporations required workers to have completed military service before being considered for employment. They counted military service as work experience that justified higher pay and faster promotion for veterans, and veterans received extra points on employment tests. Through universal conscription, men became incorporated into the nation as equal citizens.

By constructing the labor market as masculine, military dictatorships marginalized women in the workplace. Although close to 80 percent of women finished high school and 25 percent attended college by the 1970s, educated women were limited to secretarial or white-collar jobs. They were segregated from men, received less training, and were given lower wages for similar work. With no chance for promotion, they were usually forced out once they married or at an earlier age than men. Women also worked in factories. With encouragement by the state, the textile industry hired hundreds of thousands of young women in the early 1970s, but only as temporary and cheap unskilled labor. During the Factory New Village Movement in the mid-1970s and early 1980s, the state encouraged factories to set up classes for working women to teach them etiquette, deportment, and womanly accomplishments such as flower arranging and embroidery. According to the Ministry of Labor, "Women workers need common sense, civility, thrift, wisdom as well as their duty as workers because they are mothers of future generations."[1]

While training women to be housewives and mothers, military dictatorships also tried to limit their fertility. The state provided financing for women's

---

1. Seungsook Moon, *Militarized Modernity and Gendered Citizenship in South Korea* (Durham, N.C.: Duke University Press, 2005), p. 75.

MATERIAL CULTURE

Modern Traditional Handicrafts

Traditional handicrafts are big business in today's Korea. Stores in Seoul near what was once the main U.S. army base sell massive chests, divans, tables, and other furniture, not just to foreigners but also to Koreans who wish to decorate their houses to look like *yangban* mansions. There customers can also buy lacquered wood vases inlaid with mother-of-pearl, elaborately carved folding screens, paintings of Korean tigers, and fine Korean silk. They can wander through Madong village, a suburb of Kyongju, where families of potters make Korea's famous celadon glazed ceramics and view climbing kilns fired with pine wood that produce the crackle. They can visit the National Folk Museum to see how people lived centuries ago. They can visit shops where artisans craft long-stem bamboo pipes.

Given the convenience of mass-produced cigarettes, few people smoke long pipes anymore, except in movies and television dramas set in the Chosŏn dynasty. The pipes vary in the length of the stems made from polished bamboo. The mouthpiece and bowl are made of metal, highly decorated to increase the pipe's quality and hence its price. Collectors cherish a finely made pipe in the old style; tourists enjoy the novelty.

Handicrafts constitute the antithesis of modern mass production. Reflecting the anonymity of the craftsperson rather than the individuality of the artist, they posit a diversity of regional styles against the homogenization of globalization. To revive and protect Korea's traditional arts, the

The Older the Smoker, the Longer the Pipe. Enjoying a well-deserved retirement, these two men, photographed in 1950, display their pipes and their respectable status. *(Hulton Archive/Getty Images)*

government issued the Cultural Properties Protection Law in 1962 and the Culture and Arts Promotion Law of 1972. In this way, it asserted that Korea has a distinctive heritage and a source of national pride.

---

organizations such as the Korean National Wives' Association and the Korean Federation of Housewives' Clubs to encourage women in rational management of the household. Concerned that unchecked population expansion threatened economic growth, in the 1960s the state promoted family planning by encouraging women to use IUDs, seen as more rational than less permanent means of birth control. In the 1970s, the state promoted female sterilization, with 48 percent of all fertile women being surgically sterilized by 1988. Women had the patriotic duty to have children, but not to have too many.

The dictators used arts and culture to foster a sense of nationhood and promote patriotism. In 1959 each province started to sponsor an annual folk fes-

tival to support a sanitized version of traditional arts. Performances of masked dance drama, for example, failed to include lines critical of *yangban*, the old ruling class. In 1962, Park introduced the Cultural Properties Protection Law to designate tangible and intangible cultural assets, folk cultural properties, and monuments. The Ministry of Culture and Information appeared in 1972. Following the lead of economic planners, it drew up a five-year plan for cultural development. This included support for film, translations of literature from Chinese into *Han'gŭl*, funding for archaeological research, and refurbishment of famous sites. It also subsidized traditional handicrafts (see **Material Culture: Modern Traditional Handicrafts**).

International Relations

Following the Korean War, South Korea grew increasingly frustrated with its reliance on the United States for defense. In 1958, the United States had placed over two hundred nuclear weapons on South Korean soil, with missiles aimed at China and the Soviet Union as well as North Korea. Within a decade, President Lyndon B. Johnson refused Park's request for military retaliation after North Korean commandoes tried to assassinate Park on January 21, 1968. Two days later, Johnson again took no action when North Korea captured a U.S. intelligence ship, the *USS Pueblo*, and kept its eighty-two crew members in detention. In 1969, President Nixon did not retaliate when North Korea shot down a U.S. EC-121 reconnaissance plane. In July, he announced his "Nixon Doctrine," which shifted responsibility for self-defense to Asian nations, and in February 1970 he removed twenty thousand of the sixty-two thousand U.S. troops in Korea to cut U.S. costs. Alarmed, Park had his agents bribe U.S. congressmen to grant more funds to the ROK—the "Koreagate" scandal. Park perceived Nixon's rapprochement with Mao's China in 1971 as capitulation to the communist enemy. He decided to negotiate directly with Kim Il Sung and induced him to sign a joint communiqué for peaceful reunification on July 4, 1972. This initiative soon collapsed.

DEMOCRACY IN SOUTH KOREA (1987 TO THE PRESENT)

General Roh Tae Woo deserves great credit for bringing democracy to South Korea. He won the election in 1987 despite gaining only 35.9 percent of the vote because the opposition splintered into regional blocks. In the National Assembly, his new Democratic Liberal party (DLP) won only a minority of seats, but it managed to attract enough opposition members to function. Workers seized the initiative to found a new, independent National Federation of Trade Unions in defiance of the government-controlled Korean Federation of Trade Unions. It did not include school-teachers because Roh refused to let them unionize. Chun Doo Hwan had founded a private foundation to control Roh after the election, but his hopes were dashed when Roh jailed fourteen of Chun's brothers and relatives for embezzlement and corruption. Chun retired in disgrace to a Buddhist monastery.

Kim Young Sam's single-term presidency (1992–1997) removed the curse of military interference in politics. He purged high-ranking military officers who had served dictators and stripped the Agency for National Security (the old KCIA) and the Military Security Command of the power to investigate domestic politicians. In 1995, he held the first local elections for provincial governors, city mayors, county magistrates, and local assemblies in Korean history. Even more courageously, he prosecuted former presidents, Chun Doo Hwan and Roh Tae Woo, for treason, mutiny, and corruption. The results of the trial sent Chun to jail for life and Roh for seventeen years. When several cabinet members and his two sons went to jail for evading military service and receiving bribes, his popularity plummeted. Regional power bases and shifting patron-client groups could not compete with new political parties. In 1997, the chairman of the Millennium Democratic party, Kim Dae Jung, won the presidential election with the help of the United Liberal Democratic party, the first opposition victory in ROK history. Kim set up a Human Rights Commission to protect people from the oppression he and others of the dictators' opponents had suffered, and he created a Ministry of Gender Equality. Kim also had to deal with the Asian financial crisis and backlash from his trip to Pyongyang. His reputation worsened when his son and many officials were prosecuted for taking bribes. Independents and defectors from the major parties formed a new liberal party, Our Open party. Roh Moo Hyun, from Kim's Millennium Democratic party, was elected president in 2002, but conservatives forced him out of the party. They then joined with the opposition One Nation party to impeach him for publicly endorsing Our Open party in the April 2004 national assembly elections. Incensed by the pettiness of the impeachment, the electorate proceeded to give Our Open party a parliamentary majority. After decades of dictatorship, democracy has become firmly entrenched in South Korea.

Economic Crisis and Recovery

Following decades of central planning under the dictators, Kim Young Sam's advisers advocated globalization and the adoption of liberal, free market principles. The results were dire. Reduced tariffs and cheap imports undersold home industries. Encouraged to cut costs to increase efficiency, companies laid off workers. Owing to the inflow of foreign capital, the *chaebŏl* glutted the market with autos, semiconductors, and steel and doctored their books to hide indebtedness from banks. By 1996, South Korea's national debt almost doubled to $109 billion, of which two-thirds was short-term debt.

In 1997, the Asian financial crisis spread from Thailand to South Korea, and the economy crashed. By calling in short-term loans, foreign lenders drove a half-dozen *chaebŏl* and their suppliers into bankruptcy. South Korea was saved from defaulting on its national debt only because the International Monetary Fund (IMF) provided a record bailout package of $55 billion. When the IMF imposed a brutal retrenchment policy by raising interest rates from 12 to 27 percent per annum to stabilize the currency, more companies failed, and thousands of workers were laid off. The unemployment rate rose from less than 2 percent to 7.6 percent in September 1998. Female workers were often the first to be fired. National per capita income dropped from $10,000 to $7,000. The government had to sell eleven state-owned industries, including the prized Pohang Iron and Steel Company (Posco), to private owners to raise funds.

Recovery began in the fall of 1998 when the government defied IMF dictates by lowering interest rates to increase business investment. The *chaebŏl* gobbled up the loan money and left little for small businesses. When the *chaebŏl* supported unprofitable member companies, Kim Dae Jung allowed foreign companies majority ownership in failing Korean businesses to save them from bankruptcy. The government announced a new initiative to provide every home with broadband access to keep South Korea competitive in the twenty-first century. Although South Korea still suffers from technological gaps and the loss of jobs to low-wage countries like China, it sells electronics, appliances, and cars across the world.

Opening Up International Relations

In addition to opening South Korea's political process, Roh Tae Woo mended relations with the communist states of the Soviet Union, Eastern Europe, and China. In 1988, South Korea hosted the Summer Olympics in Seoul, and Roh invited communist states to send athletes. Kim Il Sung sought to ruin the games by having two agents blow up South Korean Flight 858 from the Middle East to Seoul. The explosion killed all on board but did not keep any nation out of the games. Instead of retaliating, Roh sent officials to Pyongyang in 1989 to persuade Kim Il Sung to allow Chung Ju

Yong of Hyundai Corporation to open a tourist area in the Kŭmgang (Diamond) Mountain area just north of the DMZ. He also punished activists under the National Security Law for traveling to North Korea without his permission to discuss peaceful reunification. In 1991 he gained Soviet and Chinese support to admit South Korea to the United Nations, forcing Kim Il Sung to abandon his previous opposition and accept admission to the United Nations as well.

Upon becoming president of the ROK in 1997, Kim Dae Jung inaugurated a new "sunshine policy" to seek rapprochement with North Korea. In 2000 he persuaded Kim Jong Il to hold a summit meeting in Pyongyang. Although Kim Dae Jung won the Nobel Peace Prize, it was later revealed that he had paid a bribe of $500 million to Kim Jong Il to enable the talks. When Kim Jong Il took no further measures to ease tension, Kim Dae Jung's reputation was further damaged. Opposition to the sunshine policy has increased following Kim Jong Il's saber rattling. South Koreans support reconciliation with the North, but having observed what reunification did to the West German economy, they are not eager to absorb their neighbor.

THE KOREAN INFLECTION OF MODERNITY

South Korean society has changed significantly since 1945. Arranged marriages began to decline, as marriage brokers were used for introductions only. College men and women arranged group "meetings" or group dating to enable couples to pair off for dates and "love marriages," even though they sought parental approval first. Wives were still subordinated to husbands and mothers-in-law, but middle-class married couples obtained some distance from parents who bankrolled large rental deposits for modern apartments. Couples put intense pressure on their children to gain entry into the best colleges. Middle-class wives were virtually abandoned by their overworked white-collar husbands who stayed out drinking until midnight, but they took to making money in the real estate or stock markets. As women became conscious of gender discrimination and were frustrated by unhappy marriages, books and movies from the 1990s began to portray (and reflect) married women seeking sexual liberation with lovers.

DOCUMENTS

Selections from the Sexual Equality Employment Act

Following the passage of the Equal Employment Law in the late 1980s, women pressed for laws that would protect them from discrimination in the workplace and ensure them equal pay for equal work. The result was the Gender Discrimination Prevention Act and the Sexual Equality Employment Act, both modified repeatedly in subsequent years. These sections reflect landmarks in the struggle for workplace equality. They also illustrate the various ways employers discriminated against women and the problems women have faced in trying to pursue a dual career as an employee and a working mother.

The purpose of this Act is to contribute to the improvement of the status of working women and promotion of their welfare by securing equal opportunity and treatment between men and women in all employment in conformity with the ideal of equality in the constitution, to protect maternity and develop vocational abilities.

Article 6 (Recruitment and Employment)

(1) In recruiting and employing workers, business owners shall give the same equal opportunity to women as men.

(2) In inviting or employing female workers, business owners shall not demand any physical conditions, such as appearance, height, weight, etc., or marital status, which are unnecessary for carrying out the duties for which the business owner desires to employ them.

Article 6-2 (Wage)

(1) Business owners shall pay the same wage for all work of the same value in the same business.

(2) Criteria for same value work shall be technique, endeavor, responsibility, working condition, etc. which are required for carrying out any duties, and in determining such criteria, the business owner shall hear the opinion of the person representing workers of the grievance settlement organ as prescribed in Article 14.

(3) Any enterprise undertaken separately by the same business owner for the purpose of wage discrimination shall be considered as the same business.

[This Article Newly Inserted by Act No. 4126, Apr. 1, 1989]

Article 6-3 (Money, etc., Other Than Wage)

The business owner shall not discriminate against working women in payment of any money or lending of any funds to assist the employees in their living, in addition to their wage.

[This Article Newly Inserted by Act No. 4976, Aug. 4, 1995]

Article 8 (Age Limit, Retirement, and Dismissal)

(1) No business owner shall discriminate against working women in favor of men by reason of sex, with respect to the age limit and dismissal of workers.

Modernity brought diversity in employment opportunities; democracy made it possible for workers to unionize and demand reform. Young women decided they would rather work in the service industry where they could wear pretty clothes and sell cosmetics to their peers. Not for them were repetitive factory jobs. Educated young men preferred white-collar jobs. Their elders had a hard time adjusting to the restructuring caused by the Asian financial crisis and the outsourcing of jobs overseas. The factories that

(2) No business owner shall enter into any labor contract stipulating as the cause of retirement a working woman's marriage, pregnancy, or childbirth.

Article 8-2 (Prevention of Sexual Harassment at Work)

(1) A business owner shall take the following measures to prevent sexual harassment at work and to create conditions under which the workers work in safe and sound circumstances:

　a. Conduct of education necessary to prevent sexual harassment at work;

　b. Change of post, disciplinary action, or other equivalent measures for a person who causes sexual harassment to another worker at work.

(2) A business owner shall not penalize the victim in connection with sexual harassment at work.

[This Article Newly Inserted by Act No. 5933, Feb. 8, 1999]

Article 11 (Childcare Leave)

(1) If a working woman or worker who is her spouse taking her place, who has an infant under one year of age, applies for a leave to care for her or his infant (hereinafter referred to as "childcare leave"), the business owner shall permit it, except in such cases as prescribed by the Presidential Decree.

(2) The childcare leave as referred to in paragraph (1) shall be less than one year.

(3) The business owner shall not treat unfavorably any working woman by reason of childcare leave as referred to in paragraph (1), and the period of childcare leave as referred to in para-

graph (2) shall be included in the length of her or his service.

(4) The method and procedure of the application for the childcare leave, and other necessary matters, shall be determined by Presidential Decree.

Article 12 (Nursing Facilities)

(1) In order to support the employment of workers, the business owner shall install nursing facilities necessary for suckling, nursing, etc. (hereinafter referred to as "workplace nursing facilities"), and report it to the Minister of Labor.

[This Article Wholly Amended by Act No. 4976, Aug. 4, 1995]

Article 19 (Burden of Proof)

The burden of proof in settling any dispute related to this Act shall be borne by the business owner.

[This Article Newly Inserted by Act No. 4126, Apr. 1, 1989]

Article 23 (Penal Provisions)

(1) Any business owner who violates the provisions of Articles 6-2 (1) and 8 shall be punished by imprisonment for not more than two years, or by a fine not exceeding ten million won.

(2) Any business owner who violates the provisions of Articles 6, 6-3, 8-2 (2), 11 (1), and (3) shall be punished by a fine not exceeding five million won.

[This Article Newly Inserted by Act No. 4126, Apr. 1, 1989]

Source: Korean Women's Association United (KWAU): www.women21.or.kr.

remain have had to welcome mature women into tasks once reserved for men. Starting in 1983, when a telephone operator filed suit against company policy that forced her to retire at age forty-three, women have figured in one court case after another to gain equal employment rights with men. Passed in the late 1980s, the Equal Employment Law itself became a target for reform because it did not require equal pay for equal work or require punishment for noncompliant employers. In the 1990s, pressure from women's

MAKING COMPARISONS   Popular Religion

In today's South Korea, there are an estimated three hundred thousand shamans (*mudang*) who placate the gods, comfort the spirits of the dead, intimidate evil spirits by walking barefoot on knife blades, and help politicians decide whether relocating their ancestors' tomb will win elections. They maintain websites offering online fortunetelling. Young shamans keep blogs.

Although there are probably not as many shamans in any other East Asian country today, the popular religious traditions of China, Japan, and Korea share a wide range of ideas and practices. Intermediaries between the visible and invisible worlds have long histories in China and Japan as well as in Korea. Much of our knowledge of Shang China comes from the bones cracked by diviners trying to communicate with ancestors and gods. In the northern kingdom of Koguryŏ, shamans exorcized the vengeful spirits of people executed by the king and performed divination by reading cracks on turtle shells. The gold crowns worn by Silla kings and queens resemble headdresses worn by shamans in Siberia and Manchuria. The earliest ruler in Japan described in Chinese records from the third century also functioned as an intermediary. Her tradition continues in the founders of new religions who by channeling gods have gained the power to speak in public and in mediums who communicate with spirits. Some of Japan's mountain priests (*yamabushi*) have the power to leave their bodies to roam through the invisible world, a power also granted Chinese shamans. Today in Taiwan, shamans are summoned to carry bribes to the king of the underworld on behalf of the recently deceased.

Local deities have figured prominently across the landscapes of popular religion. Over time the Chinese spirit world came to be organized like the visible world, with a king of hell, local rulers, bureaucrats, and police officials. Demons plague the living. There are gods for specific problems such as illness, various Daoist immortals, and gods who were once historical human beings. Others were once ghosts or the spirits of mountains and rivers. Cities have protective deities. If they do not do their job, they can be dismissed and new city gods brought in to take their place. Some temples are dedicated to the goddess of mercy and overseer of families and children; others focus on the goddess of waters; and then there is Guandi, the red-faced god of war and patron of business. Koreans saw gods in mountains, waters, trees, tigers, bears, and founding kings. In the third century C.E., rulers inveighed against blood sacrifices to local gods, a prohibition repeated in the twelfth century. Japanese too worshipped the numinous in nature. From the sixteenth century on, men who strove for self-perfection or power worshipped the god in

themselves. When commercial development in the eighteenth century brought surprising prosperity to entrepreneurs, those not so favored assumed that the newly rich had control of fox spirits who stole the wealth of others.

Propitiation of the dead is another characteristic of popular religion. Regardless of whether Confucian ancestral rites carry religious significance, practices performed by ordinary Chinese placed the ancestors squarely in the spirit realm. Families came close to bankruptcy to pay for elaborate funerals that sent a father and mother to the afterlife in a style far above their standing in the visible world. They assumed that parents vitally concerned about the family before they died would continue to be so after death; they also believed that life after death replicates this life on another plane. To keep ancestral spirits from turning into unhappy ghosts, they had to be provided with paper furnishing, paper money, and food.

In Korea and Japan, one reason for funerary rites was to eliminate the dead person's dangerous influence. Buddhism spread during the Koryŏ dynasty in part because its funerals dealt with the havoc that the dead caused the living. Travelers, infants, and single men and women were likely to hold grievances. Women who had been mistreated by their communities might return as vengeful spirits. Since ghosts afflicted only those who had known them in life, it was particularly important to treat dead relatives with respect.

Fear is not the only reason to placate the spirits; they also bring this-worldly benefits. Rulers summoned shamans in Koryŏ Korea and diviners in Heian Japan to bring about the release of water-giving dragons during droughts. In all three countries, women pray for safe childbirth; men and women pray for prosperity, good health, and long life. The object of their prayers may be a god; it may also be a Buddha, or in China a Daoist immortal or deified hero. Since no one knows which will be efficacious, better to ask them all.

Xunzi in China's Warring States questioned the efficacy of praying to gods for rain or other benefits, and ever since his time skeptics have associated popular religion with ignorance. In China under Mao, popular religion was looked on as a useless "feudal superstition," and most temples were converted to other uses. Old people were allowed to continue making offerings or praying to gods, but the young were educated to view such behavior as silly and wasteful. Since the death of Mao, popular religion has been revived. It is especially strong in Fujian and Guangdong, undoubtedly because those provinces have strong connections to Chinese outside the PRC, where religious traditions have been maintained.

A Comparison of Living Standards in North and South Korea 2005		
	South Korea	North Korea
Population	48.2 million	22.5 million
Life expectancy (at birth)	78	64
Infant mortality rate (per 1,000 live births)	5.0	42.0
Fixed line and mobile telephones (per 1,000 people)	1,286.0	21.1
Internet users (per 1,000)	684	No data available
Paved roads (% of total)	74.5	6.4

Source: World Bank, http://www.worldbank.org/data/countrydata/countrydata.html.

associations and labor unions forced the government to first pass and then amend equal opportunity laws (see **Documents: Selections from the Sexual Equality Employment Act**). There is now a ministry in charge of gender equality and the family.

The growth of income and wealth led to a consumer culture and conspicuous consumption in clothing, appliances, pianos, and luxury apartments. South Koreans today have wide access to goods and technology, while residents of North Korea lag significantly behind. The table on this page compares the two countries in terms of their standards of living and access to technology.

Korean poetry and literature in the vernacular came into its own in the postwar period. Many authors were consumed with the Korean War, social justice, and the evils of dictatorship. In 1957, Sŏnu Hwi wrote *Flowers of Fire*, which traces the history of the Ko family from the March First demonstrations of 1919 through the Korean War. Ch'ae Mansik's *Peace Under Heaven* portrays an evil landlord, and the famous "Five Bandits" poem of Kim Chiha condemn bureaucrats and businessmen. Hwang Sunwŏn wrote of the poor in the 1970s, and Hwang Suk-young wrote about personal problems and Korean soldiers in the Vietnam War in *The Shadow of Arms* (1985). Pak Kyŏngni's lengthy *The Land* (1980) was a bestseller, and short-story writers such as Kang Sŏkkyŏng, Kim Chiwŏn, Pak Wansŏ, and O Chŏnghŭi left their mark with descriptive and contemplative stories of anomie under industrialization.

Another response to urban anonymity has been the spread of new religions. Christianity, Buddhism, and Ch'ŏndogyo continue to attract adherents, but many Koreans are attracted to more activist ministries. Korean medical missionaries work in war-torn areas across the world, including Ethiopia and Afghanistan. Reverend Sun Myung, founder of the Unification Church, has sought to bring happiness to thousands through his mass wedding ceremonies.

In the late 1990s, the "Korean Wave" hit China, Taiwan, Southeast Asia, and Japan. It has since made inroads in the United States, Europe, and South America. Dominated by TV dramas, music, and film, it has popularized Korean fashion, food, cosmetics, and electronic goods. Korean soap operas and their stars are household names in Asia. In the West, Korean films have won awards at international film festivals. Despite Hollywood's global hegemony, Korean films gain the larger share of the Korean market. Released in 2005, director Yoon Jong-bin's *The Unforgiven* critiques compulsory military service and the harsh military subculture through the eyes of three conscripts. Korea also has a thriving industry in romantic comedies (*Please Teach Me English*, 2003) and animation (*Empress Chung*, 2005). Recorded on DVD, they have even infiltrated North Korea.

South Korean Soap Opera. Starring the popular Hyun Bin and Sim Sun-ah, the romantic comedy titled *My Lovely Kim SamSoon* depicts an "average" single woman of 29 who dreams of romance but thinks she has to settle for happiness through work. *(Hulton Archive/Getty Images)*

SUMMARY

How has Korea changed in the last sixty years? Based on the political division carried out at the end of World War II, it has become two separate countries with opposing political, economic, and social systems. Although repressive regimes once dominated both the communist North and the bureaucratic capitalist South, North Korea has remained a nationalistic hereditary monarchy under *chuch'e* ideology, while military dictatorship in South Korea was transformed into democracy. Society in both North and South has changed through social leveling and the partial liberation of women, albeit in different ways. The North turned the social order upside down, while the South created a new society of urban capitalists and white- and blue-collar workers. Religion was replaced by hero worship and patriotism in the North, while in the pluralistic South people follow varied practices. Both North and South Korea have gained new standing on the world stage—the North through the threat posed by its nuclear program, the South through its economic prowess and popular culture.

Contemporary Japan (1965 to the Present)

Japan's desire for peace was marked in 1965 by demonstrations against the Vietnam War. Protest provoked by public policy decisions and industrial pollution was also a sign that by the late 1960s, the consequences of Liberal Democratic party (LDP) domination and high-speed economic growth could no longer be ignored. The 1970s brought political scandals, diplomatic crises, and economic opportunities in the midst of setbacks. Minorities and working women demanded political initiatives to ameliorate their condition. Economic adjustments positioned Japanese companies to expand in export markets. In the 1980s, Japan had the world's second largest economy, and the euphoria of seemingly unstoppable growth led to a bubble in overpriced investments. When it burst in 1990, the economy deflated. Although social problems increased, most Japanese people enjoyed low crime rates, clean cities, superb public transportation, and unprecedented prosperity.

Why did the Japanese economy rise so far and fall so fast? Are protest and demonstrations worth discussing, given the power of the LDP and bureaucrats? Which social trends will prove enduring, and which will prove beneficial?

POLITICAL PROTEST AND ENVIRONMENTAL POLLUTION

The 1960s saw student movements worldwide, and Japan was no exception. Students joined citizen's movements to protest Japan's support for the American war in Vietnam under the U.S.-Japan Security Treaty at the same time that they attacked educational policies. At some universities, they criticized what they viewed as assembly-line-style courses. At Tokyo University, medical students protested a top-down reorganization of the program that ignored their concerns. In January 1968, they went on strike. When university administrators refused to hear their grievances

Opponents of Narita Airport. Waving staves and wearing helmets, opponents of Narita Airport battled riot police protected by heavy shields, helmets, and padded armor. *(Corbis)*

and expelled their leaders, students in other departments struck in sympathy. They wanted curriculum control, amnesty for students arrested in confrontations, and exclusion of riot police from campus. To make their point, they barricaded the central building. The administration cancel entrance examinations for 1969. On campuses across Tokyo, students launched sympathy strikes. On January 19, 1969, eighty-five hundred riot police retook the campus in a two-day battle broadcast live on TV. The Diet passed a University Control Bill giving the Education Ministry enhanced authority to punish students. Radical student groups went underground.

Japan's rise to prominence in world affairs and the increase in air travel led the LDP and Transportation Ministry to decide on a new international airport for Tokyo in 1965. Farmers who owned land at the proposed site outside Narita protested because expropriating their land destroyed their livelihood, secrecy surrounding the decision demonstrated that popular opinion counted for naught, and the airport might be used to support the American war effort in Vietnam. Farmers petitioned prefectural and national ministries; they rallied support in the Diet among the opposition parties. When these measures failed, they built barricades and fortresses; they dug ditches to trap bulldozers; they chained themselves to fences. Radical student union Zengakuren helped with agri-

cultural work and publicity. Citizens in peace, antinuclear, and environmental movements joined them because they were fighting against government indifference to the social costs of economic growth. Plans called for the airport to be built in six years; it took twelve. The government reduced the number of runways from three to one; a proposal in 1998 to add a second also faced opposition. Having learned its lesson, the government later built Osaka International Airport on an artificial island in the bay.

At the end of the 1960s, the left and right wings attacked capitalism and materialism. Mishima Yukio created a paramilitary organization and received permission to join Self Defense Force (SDF) military maneuvers. In 1970, he called on the soldiers at SDF headquarters to remember the sacrifices made in World War II and rally behind nationalist goals by overthrowing the government. When they laughed at him, he committed ritual suicide. Between 1970 and 1972, students in the Red Army robbed banks and post offices, hijacked a plane to North Korea, and machine-gunned travelers in Tel Aviv's Lod airport in support of Maoist revolution and Palestinian rights.

Less dramatic but longer lasting, citizens' movements arose in response to industrial pollution. In the 1950s, local and prefectural governments encouraged industrial development that spread pollution from cities to towns and made Japan the most

A Victim of Mercury Poisoning. Held by her mother, this sufferer has a malformed hand along with other physical deformities characteristic of the Minamata disease. *(AP/Wide World Photos)*

polluted nation on earth. By the early 1970s, about half the population complained of suffering from pollution (see Color Plate 32). Citizens' movements mobilized hundreds of thousands of ordinarily apolitical residents to sign petitions, visit industrial sites, display posters, and launch education drives to rally support in stopping potential polluters from building in their neighborhood. They warned against trusting promises by industry and local government that a proposed factory would not pollute, and they rejected charges that fighting to protect the individual's quality of life is egotistical.

Between 1932 and 1968 at Minamata in southern Kyushu, a Chisso factory produced acetaldehyde, a key ingredient in making plastics through a process that released methyl mercury as a by-product. Dumped into the water, mercury concentrated in marine life and then attacked brain cells in domestic animals and humans. Victims suffered progressive debilitation, often leading to a vegetative state and death. In 1959, a Kumamoto University research team traced the cause to the Chisso factory. The team lost its government funding. With support from the Ministry of International Trade and Industry, Chisso hired researchers

who proved mercury was not at fault. Workers at the plant and community leaders blamed the victims' poor diet and unsanitary living conditions for their afflictions. In 1965, another outbreak of the disease in Niigata on the Japan Sea was traced to mercury discharged by a chemical factory. Despite efforts by company officials and government bureaucrats to undermine the investigators' credibility, the Niigata outbreak lent weight to the Minamata case. The victims launched petitions, demonstrations, and sit-ins. They attracted support from doctors, lawyers, filmmakers, journalists, and academics. In 1971, they sued Chisso. The verdict against the company in 1973 brought it to the verge of bankruptcy. The victims then sued the government. The Environmental Agency refused to comply with the court's recommendation to settle. In 1995, the cabinet accepted an out-of-court settlement that denied government responsibility for either the disease or delay in acknowledging the problem. In 2004, the Supreme Court placed responsibility for having failed to prevent the disease on the central government and Kumamoto prefecture, but local officials still urge victims not to apply for compensation.

Diseases caused by pollution in Minamata and elsewhere exposed the costs of high-speed economic growth and the way politicians and bureaucrats insulated themselves from citizens. Despite free elections, pollution victims had to protest outside regular government channels. Owing to their demands, the government instituted stringent pollution controls in the 1970s and began spending a larger portion of the gross national product (GNP) on antipollution measures than any other developed nation. By 1978, air and water pollution had declined, and manufacturers had learned how to profit from measures to keep the environment clean.

STRAINS OF THE 1970s

Having enjoyed the economic benefits of supporting the United States during the Cold War, Japan was unprepared for the international crises that punctuated the 1970s. When President Richard Nixon announced in 1971 that the United States would no longer accept fixed exchange rates that overvalued the dollar, the yen rose 14 percent. Nixon intended to make Japanese exports to the United States more expensive and less competitive. Japanese companies survived by taking advantage of lower costs for imported raw materials. The second shock came in 1972 when Nixon recognized the People's Republic of China without notifying Japan in advance. Prime Minister Tanaka Kakuei followed Nixon to China seven months later. In 1978, China and Japan signed a peace and friendship treaty. The first oil shock came when the Organization of Petroleum Exporting Countries (OPEC) embargoed oil to countries that had supported Israel in the 1973 war. Dependent on oil for 80 percent of its energy, Japan had to pay premium prices on the world market. Inflation rose, companies reduced energy use by cutting production, and consumers stopped spending. During the remainder of the decade, Japan built nuclear power plants. Japanese companies so rationalized energy use that when OPEC raised prices again in 1978–1980, they had a competitive advantage over less efficient firms in their prime export markets.

To retain dominance in the Diet and cabinet, the LDP catered to its core constituencies, sometimes to the point of scandal. Tanaka Kakuei had Japan National Railroad (JNR) build a bullet train line through the mountains to his constituents in Niigata, at the cost of $60 million a mile. It provided government contracts for his cronies in the construction business and fattened the purses of real estate developers. Tanaka's excesses were so blatant that public outcry drove him from office in 1974. In 1976 an investigation by the U.S. Senate disclosed that President Nixon had arranged for Lockheed Aircraft Corporation to pay Tanaka almost $2 million to have All Nippon Airways buy Lockheed planes. Despite the stench of corruption, LDP politicians held on to power because voters believed that the opposition parties were too ideologically driven and too fragmented to be trusted with national policy.

Industry had to make traumatic adjustments. Some adjustments arose from increasing protectionist pressures, exemplified in a 1979 report to the European Economic Community Executive Committee that called the Japanese "work maniacs who live in houses little better than rabbit hutches."[1] Nixon demanded that Japan reduce its textile imports through voluntary restraints. The increase in oil prices hurt petrochemical and energy-intensive industries. The market for tankers declined, which hurt steel. The shipbuilding industry survived by consolidating and moving into new fields such as ocean drilling platforms. The government helped workers with wage subsidies, retraining programs, and relocation expenses. To compete with low-labor-cost countries, the steel industry developed specialty high-value-added products. Automobile and electrical manufacturing grew. In 1980, Japan produced more cars than any other country. Big electrical companies made generating plants and electric motors for trains; small firms made office equipment, household appliances, and entertainment items.

Although lifetime employment became a watchword, it covered less than half the work force. Toyota, for example, had permanent workers who received regular salary increases based on seniority and fringe benefits; during good times, it hired temporary workers who were terminated when necessary. Over two hundred independent contractors made parts and components for cars in accordance with guidelines and timetables established by Toyota. Their workers enjoyed no job security. Women returning to the labor force after raising children typically worked at part-time or temporary jobs in small, often marginally profitable companies.

---

1. "Europe Toughens Stand Against Japan's Exports," *New York Times*, April 2, 1979, D:1, 5.

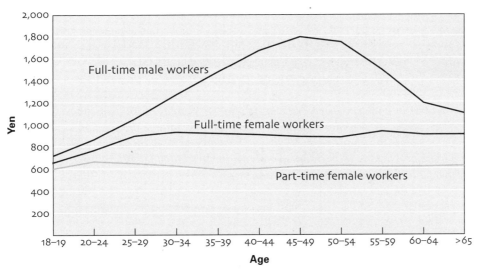

Figure 30.1   Hourly Wages for Japanese Workers, by Age, 1989 *(Mary C. Brinton, Women and the Economic Miracle: Gender and Work in Postwar Japan [Berkeley: University of California Press, 1992], p. 47.)*

A white-collar worker joined a firm straight after college and expected to stay with it for life. For indoctrination into company culture, first-year recruits lived in dormitories where they learned to maintain constant contact with their coworkers by working together and drinking together after work. Since only family men were deemed suitable for promotion, most workers soon married, perhaps to an "office lady" (OL) who understood that the company came first. A popular movie series, *It's Tough Being a Man (Otoko wa tsurai yo)*, which debuted in 1969, commented on the conformity engineered by the straitjacket of company life through the eyes of an itinerant peddler who rejected job security for the byways of modern Japan.

Husbands and wives lived in separate worlds. Rural-based factory workers left farm work to parents, wives, and children. Only 2 to 5 percent farmed full time. For the urban middle class, a wife's job was to provide a stress-free environment for her husband. She managed the household, raised the children (preferably two), and did household repairs. The husband handed her his paycheck; she gave him an allowance, allocated money for food and other expenses, and saved the rest. Mothers devoted themselves to their children's education, earning the opprobrium of being *kyŏiku mama* (education mothers, implying an obsession with their children's educational success). When children needed extra help, mothers sent them to afterschool schools. Mother consulted with teachers, attended Parent-Teacher Association meetings,

volunteered at school, and supervised their children's nutrition, health, and homework. For the professional housewife, her child was her most important product. (See **Documents: Fujita Mariko, " 'It's All Mother's Fault': Child-Care and the Socialization of Working Mothers in Japan."**)

Continuing Social Issues

Women's career choices were limited. They typically worked after graduating from high school or junior college; to the mid-1980s almost 90 percent of companies rejected female graduates of four-year colleges because they had to be placed on a management track. Instead, women were hired as clerical or assembly line workers with the understanding they would retire at marriage or when they turned thirty. In the late 1960s women got the courts to agree that this practice constituted sex discrimination. In the early 1970s the courts forbade mandatory retirement because of pregnancy or childbirth or at a younger age than men. Women objected to being kept from managerial positions and to well-meaning restrictions on the hours they could work and the kinds of work they were allowed to do. In response, the Diet passed the Equal Employment Opportunity Act of 1985. Although it urged employers to put women on the same track as men, it made no provisions for sanctions if they did not. In 1976, women's earnings stood at 56 percent of men's; in 1988, they declined to

DOCUMENTS

Fujita Mariko, "'It's All Mother's Fault': Child-Care and the Socialization of Working Mothers in Japan"

Various sectors in postwar society have made a fetish of conformity. This essay by a college professor provides a glimpse of how women enforce the standards for being a professional housewife. What are the conflicts between working and being a mother? How do women interact across the work divide? What is the role fathers are expected to play in child rearing?

A woman should recognize herself as the best educator of her child. An excellent race is born from excellent mothers. . . . Only women can bear children and raise them. Therefore mothers should be proud and confident in raising their children. It is also a fundamental right of children to be raised by their own mothers. . . .

—1970 Family Charter by the Committee on Family Life Problems

I live in a small-scale *danchi* (apartment block) built for national governmental employees in the southeastern part of Nara City. The complex consists of three four-story buildings which house about 70 families. The occupants are mostly young and early middle-aged couples, though some are tanshin-funinsha (husbands who reside away from their families due to the relocation of their jobs). The ages of the children in this complex range from babies to junior-high-school students. There are only a handful of high school students. Therefore, the mothers' ages range roughly between 25 and 45.

Because the rent is substantially lower than in private housing, there is not much economic pressure for the wives to work. This explains the fact that the majority of wives are full-time housewives. The mothers of older children may engage in occasional part-time jobs. As far as I know, those women who work full-time are without children. If a couple has preschool children, the wives most certainly stay at home to raise them.

As soon as my neighbors found out that I had a toddler, they assumed that I was a full-time housewife and mother. They never thought to ask whether I worked outside the home. Because I did have a job, they often found me walking alone without my son and they would always ask, "Where is Hosaki today?" indicating their expectation that I would always be with my child. The situation was complicated because at the time I was a part-time lecturer at a university and I did most of my work at home.

50 percent. Companies still refuse to promote women at the same rate as men. Rather than pay women equal wages, some companies do not hire women at all. Full responsibility for home and children makes it hard for women to work past childbirth. Once the children are in school, mothers take part-time jobs. Although the working woman in Japan is imagined to be single, most are married women over age thirty-five.

Despite decades of denunciation tactics, *burakumin* still faced economic hardship and discrimination. Under the Special Measures and Enterprise Law concerning Assimilation of 1969, national and local governments put sewage systems, paved streets, better housing, schools, hospitals, and fire stations in ghettoes. In 1976, the Justice Ministry agreed to restrict access to family registers that could be used to trace individuals back to the "new commoners" category established in 1871. Private detective agencies then published lists giving addresses for *burakumin* ghettoes. Their customers were companies, especially the largest and most prestigious; individuals; and colleges. In 1977, the overall unemployment rate was around 3 percent, but 28.5 percent of Osaka *burakumin* were unemployed. Those with jobs worked in small enterprises for low wages. Although most

My neighbors found this kind of work pattern very difficult to understand because to them work means regular employment between 8:00 AM and 5:00 PM. Telling them that my son was at day care was tricky because they would wonder what I was doing at home during the day instead of being at work. Only after I took a full-time teaching position, which keeps me away from home most of the time, were my neighbors convinced that I was actually working.

The fact that working mothers and non-working mothers do not belong to the same circle of friends became clear to me when I spent a day with my son instead of sending him to day care. I took him to the neighborhood playground where he played in the sand box by the other children. Since he did not have toys of his own (I did not know the children were supposed to bring their own toys), a mother told her son to let my son use his toys. Several mothers were present; they talked among themselves and politely ignored me. I said a few words to them and they replied, but that was the end of our conversation. I basically watched my son, and later played with him when he wanted to play ball. After half an hour, one of the mothers finally asked me whether I lived in the same apartment complex. The question astonished me because I had frequently seen them in the neighborhood. But, as far as they were concerned, I was a total stranger.

Our son frequently became ill his first year in Japan, perhaps due to lack of immunity to the viruses he was exposed to at day care. Soon after enrolling our son at Sakura Day Care, we asked the director if she had a list of baby-sitters, or if she would introduce us to people who would be willing, with pay, to take care of our son when he became sick. Her answer made us realize how unusual our request was in Japan: she was truly astonished by our question and replied that she had never heard of such people.

Our neighbors frequently offered the folk belief that "boys are more susceptible to all sorts of illness than girls when they are young" to explain my son's frequent sicknesses. But as soon as they found out that my work required me to spend two nights a week away from home, they started to use my absence to explain my son's illness. They thought Hosaki was lonely and thus became ill. No one openly criticized me for working until they found out about my absence. Then, they were quick to criticize the mother, making her absence the cause of illness, although the times of Hosaki's illness and my absence did not coincide and although his father was with him and took care of him. They sympathized with the father, who was, from their point of view, unduly burdened while the "selfish" mother was neglecting her duty of childcare.

Source: *Journal of Japanese Studies* 15:1 (Winter 1989): 70–71, 72–73, 80, 86, 87, 89, modified.

burakumin lived next to factories, they never received more than temporary or part-time work.

Ainu and Okinawans launched movements in the 1970s to assert pride in their ethnic identities. Ainu protested that the 1968 celebration for the centenary of Hokkaido's colonization ignored them and their suffering. Kayano Shigeru opened an ethnographic museum in 1972 and wrote on Ainu language, folktales, and practices of daily life. In 1994, he became the first Ainu elected to the Diet. He and other culturalists sought to restore seasonal ceremonies and protested plans to turn Hokkaido into an energy source for the rest of Japan with an oil-generated power station. The United States returned Okinawa to Japan in 1972, but left its bases on the islands. The local economy depended on servicing them and catering to Japanese tourists in search of a tropical experience at home. Okinawan music, dance, and crafts attracted aficionados on the mainland because they were seen as both a variant on primitive Japanese folk arts and an exotic island culture. Okinawa's most famous export is karate. Although the national government has spent lavishly on construction projects, it hires natives only in low-level jobs. *Burakumin*, Ainu, and Okinawan poverty rates and school dropout rates have been higher than the national average. Negative stereotypes abound, with the usual consequences for marriage and employment.

Koreans resident in Japan (637,000 in 1999) faced special disabilities in fighting discrimination. As long as Korea was part of Japan's empire, Koreans were Japanese citizens. The postwar constitution defined Japanese citizens as those born of Japanese fathers, and Koreans became permanent resident aliens. Although celebrities and spouses of diplomats found the naturalization process easy, working-class Koreans did not. They also suffered a division between supporters of North Korea, who followed a separatist path, and supporters of the South, who tried to preserve vestiges of Korean identity while sending their children to Japanese schools. Children and grandchildren of Korean residents who grew up in Japan and spoke only Japanese paid taxes, but they could not vote. They had to be fingerprinted for their alien registration cards. After years of protest, that requirement changed in 1991, and resident Koreans were allowed to vote in local elections. Still, Japanese refused to marry Koreans, employers to hire them, and landlords to rent to them. Resident Koreans who protested were told they should go back to Korea.

Japanese nationalists ignored all evidence to the contrary in praising the virtues of their uniquely homogeneous race. The debate on Japaneseness (*Nihonjinron*) arose in response to the protest movements of the late 1960s, universalizing social science theories that pigeonholed Japan solely in terms of economic development, and foreign criticism of Japan's economic policies. The more Japanese people ate, dressed, and lived like people across the developed world, the more they had to be reminded that they possessed a uniquely distinctive culture. According to *Nihonjinron*, "we Japanese" speak a language intrinsically incomprehensible to outsiders, think with both sides of the brain, and have intestines too short to digest Australian beef. "We Japanese" innately prefer consensus and harmony, and we put the interests of the group above the individual.

Despite social problems, by the mid-1970s most Japanese people enjoyed unprecedented levels of prosperity. Income and salary disparities remained relatively narrow, and 90 percent of the population considered itself to be middle class. The proportion of total income spent on food declined, while quantity, quality, and variety increased. The older generation ate rice, vegetables, and fish. Young people ate meat, dairy products, and spaghetti. Although Japan maintained the highest savings rate in the industrialized world,

people had discretionary income to eat out, go to movies, and take vacations.

THE ROARING 1980S

Japan's recovery from the shocks of the 1970s put it on a collision course with its major trading partner, the United States. Japan adjusted to oil and pollution crises by building fuel-efficient, less-polluting cars. When stricter pollution emission requirements, consumer demand for higher quality, and increased gasoline prices caught Detroit by surprise, Japan's automobile makers seized the American market. To make Japanese goods less competitive, President Ronald Reagan devalued the dollar in 1985. Japan discovered that it was twice as rich as before. The yen bought twice as much oil, and since Japanese manufacturers had already streamlined production techniques, they needed half as much to make their products as their American competitors did. When Honda raised the price of the Accord by a thousand dollars, American manufacturers raised their prices as well.

American negotiators demanded that Japan import more foreign products. Japan had lower tariffs on manufactured goods than other industrialized countries, but it protected farmers by restricting food imports. It also had non-tariff structural barriers to trade—regulations to ensure quality and safety, the requirement that car buyers show proof of an off-street parking space, a multilayered distribution system, and zoning that favored shops over supermarkets and discount stores. Despite reluctance to disturb a system that provided employment and political support, the LDP and the bureaucracy gradually reduced restrictions. Australian cheese appeared in supermarkets. Shakey's Pizza, McDonald's, Kentucky Fried Chicken, and family-style restaurants invaded Japan in the late 1970s. Seven-Eleven spawned a boom in convenience stores. In 1983, Disneyland opened its first international venue near Tokyo. In 2000 it welcomed 16.5 million visitors, the largest number for any theme park in the world.

Trade surpluses and a strong currency generated more capital than Japan could absorb domestically. With unemployment rates at about 3 percent and labor costs rising, companies built factories in low-wage countries on the Asian mainland. To get around protective tariffs, antidumping measures, and quotas, they built high-technology factories in developed countries, and Toyota became a multinational corporation. In

1982 industrial plants, equipment, and capital goods constituted 43 percent of Japan's exports. Japanese capital serviced the U.S. debt. Japan became the world's largest supplier of loans to developing countries and the chief donor of foreign aid, and it supplied 50 percent of lendable capital to the World Bank.

The electronics industry had two modes of expanding overseas. In setting up production facilities, first in Southeast Asia in the mid- to late 1970s and then in developed countries in the 1980s, parent companies retained complete control of local subsidiaries. The managerial staff was Japanese; the workers were local. The U.S. Semiconductor Industry Association accused Japan of dumping in 1985; in an agreement a year later, Japan agreed to voluntary quotas. Corporations then instituted cooperative ventures with partners in the United States and Europe to develop new technology or combine specialties. Automobile manufacturers followed suit: Toyota and General Motors, Nissan, Honda, and Ford operate joint ventures and exchange components at factories from Australia to Brazil to Europe and the United States.

Japanese capital investment deepened ties with Asian neighbors, while nationalist sentiment strained diplomatic relations. Japan dominated China's Special Economic Zones and invested heavily in Korea and the Pacific Rim, leading pundits to claim that it had succeeded in creating a Greater East Asia Co-Prosperity Sphere. In 1982 the Education Ministry approved a textbook for middle school and high school students that minimized Japanese aggression in China. This led the PRC, North and South Korea, and other Asian nations to denounce resurgent Japanese nationalism. Japan's aggression and its refusal to acknowledge the suffering it inflicted on Korean women were still issues in the textbooks prepared for 2005. Asians and some Japanese criticized visits by prime ministers to Yasukuni Shrine, where war criminals are enshrined. Textbook revision and Japan's refusal to apologize for waging war roiled popular opinion even as government leaders drew closer together. When the president of South Korea visited Japan for the first time in 1984, demonstrations erupted in Seoul.

The government faced domestic problems as well. The LDP did not want to raise taxes to cover deficit spending that started in 1973. Among the culprits were subsidies for farmers, public corporations—Japan National Railroad (JNR) and Nihon Telephone and Telegraph (NTT)—and national health insurance, which initiated free care for the elderly in 1972. Following the lead of Prime Minister Margaret Thatcher

in Britain, a commission set up in 1981 promoted privatizing public corporations to relieve the government of drains on its resources and undermine the strength of the railroad workers' union. Although allowed to bargain collectively, unions in the public service sector did not have the right to strike, nor did they have incentive to boost productivity. In 1975 railroad workers shut down JNR for eight days in a strike to win the right to strike.

The conservative triumvirate of the free market world consisted of Margaret Thatcher, Ronald Reagan, and Nakasone Yasuhiro, Japan's prime minister from 1982 to 1987. Nakasone privatized JNR and NTT and took the government out of the business of selling tobacco and cigarettes. Beginning in 1982 the elderly had to contribute payments for health services. Nakasone urged a return to family values, especially the obligation of the younger generation to care for elders. He attributed Japan's economic success to its ethnic homogeneity and funded research into Japan's distinctive identity. He also called for internationalization so that government leaders would learn how to reduce trade friction and businessmen would feel comfortable with foreigners. His promotion of corporate capitalism made Japan a major player at the Group of 7 conferences of industrialized nations, while he lectured the United States on its social and economic failings exemplified in racial diversity and the lack of a work ethic.

The Good Life

For many people, old and young, the good life meant material possessions. It meant automated bread-making machines, three-dimensional TV, and self-heating canned sake. It meant laughing at Itami Jūzō's movies about funeral practices, food, tax evasion, new religions, and gangsters. The good life made it easy to buy books and magazines (1.45 billion and 4.01 billion, respectively, in 1987). (See **Material Culture: Manga**.) Whether a meaning for life could be found in a late capitalist society divided Japanese writers. Murakami Haruki captured the absurdity of modernity in his novels *A Wild Sheep Chase, Hardboiled Wonderland*, and *Sputnik Sweetheart*. Yoshimoto Banana's *Kitchen*, a novella popular with college students, depicted a dysfunctional family and individuals alone in a postmodern world. Nostalgia for simpler times under the occupation sold 4 million copies of *Totto-chan, The Little Girl at the Window* by the fast-talking television celebrity Kuroyanagi Tetsuko.

MATERIAL CULTURE

Manga

Japanese comics called manga attained their present form in 1959 when they became a source of entertainment and information for all ages. Early manga were printed on cheap paper and sold at a price working poor could afford. The first generation born after World War II grew up reading them and continued the habit through college and into their working lives. Manga gave them a chance to laugh at the restrictive conditions that enforced conformity while warning them that failing to work hard and toe the corporate line would lead to mockery. Manga and their close cousins, animated films, became the domain of Japan's most creative minds.

From the 1960s to the mid-1990s, manga offered escapist fantasies, often violently pornographic, for white-collar workers on their daily commute. Science-fiction manga appealed to children and teenagers. Manga taught history to students studying for entrance exams. *Barefoot Gen* graphically illustrated the horrors of the atomic bomb explosion over Hiroshima. Cookbooks and biographies could be found in the form of manga. Manga explained energy policy, the value-added tax, investment strategies, and the principles of superconductors. *Japan Inc.: An Introduction to Japanese Economics in Manga* (1986; in English 1988) sold over 1 million copies in hardcover.

Manga reached their peak of sales in 1994. Publishing houses devoted one-third of their total output to manga and sold 5.33 million copies a year. Shibuya, the crossroads for youth culture in Tokyo, contained manga superstores where the clerks dressed as manga characters. Manga and the Japa-

Manga. Manga provided education and entertainment. *The Manga Introduction to Superconductors* explained new technology in 1987 through the eyes of three young salaried workers who visit a research laboratory. *(*The Manga Introduction to Supercomputers *by Takashi Hashimoto and Fumio Hisamatsu)*

nese publishing industry are currently in decline. Former readers thumb cell phones with Internet connections or play handheld computer games.

Rejecting materialism meant seeking the roots of Japanese identity. A self-styled Kyoto philosopher creatively interpreted the prehistoric Jōmon era as a time when Japanese lived in harmony with nature and each other in a community of man and gods. Mystically transmitted through the emperor system and buried deep within every Japanese, the national essence could be recapitulated by a visit to the *furusato* (home village). JNR's "Discover Japan" and "Exotic Japan" advertising campaigns promoted visits to thatched roof farmhouses foreign to urban residents. Villages striving to overcome depopulation revived agricultural festivals to attract tourists; castle towns put on daimyo processions. On Yaeyama in the Ryukyu Islands, a new tradition of weaving sashes for betrothal gifts became a way to assert a folk identity and sell souvenirs to tourists.

The search for origins scarcely concealed new and, to conservative eyes, troubling trends among Japanese youth. In 1978 the "bamboo shoot tribe" (*takenoko-zoku*) of middle and high school students dressed in outlandish and expensive costumes started appearing

Gyaru. Following constantly evolving fashions, gyaru (gals) can be divided into various subcultures depending on whether their faces are darkly tanned with white makeup or white with black makeup, their hairstyles, the mix of Japanese and western apparel, and their shoes. *(Peter M. Wilson Photography)*

every Sunday near trendy Harajuku in Tokyo. Late at night, gangs of motorcycle riders roared through residential neighborhoods, disrupting the sleep of salary men. In 1985 newspapers started reporting an increase in incidents of bullying, some leading to murder or suicide, in elementary through high schools. The "new breed of human beings" rejected the work ethic, harmony, and consensus of their elders. They took part-time jobs that did not require the commitment of a regular position. Since many of them lived with their parents, their income bought luxury items rather than necessities. They splurged on designer clothes, meals and entertainment, and trips abroad. Married couples demanded bigger living spaces and better plumbing. They wanted a shorter work week and longer vacations. Rather than put up with low initial salaries and long hours of after-work socializing, a few workers switched jobs, and some husbands went home to their wives.

Despite these problems, Japan's economy appeared unstoppable. In 1988, the per capita GNP surpassed that of the United States. The United States cited unfair trade practices and Japan's free ride under the American security umbrella as explanations. In 1989, Morita Akio, chairman of Sony, and Ishihara Shintarō, mayor of Tokyo in the twenty-first century, published *The Japan That Can Say No*. It criticized U.S. business practices and claimed that Japan bashing was the result of racial prejudice. It also castigated the Japanese government for fearing reform and Japanese people for being soft. Banks awash with yen urged capital on borrowers. Japanese art purchases led to an outcry that the cream of Western heritage was being shipped to Asia. Mitsubishi bought Rockefeller Center in New York City. Sony bought Columbia Pictures. Real estate costs rose so high that land in Tokyo was valued at three times the entire United States. The tripling of the stock market inflated a speculative bubble.

MALAISE IN THE 1990s

For the LDP, political problems began in 1989. The Shōwa emperor died at the beginning of the year. For having remarked that the emperor bore some responsibility for the military's behavior during World War II, Nagasaki's mayor was shot by a right-wing fanatic. The new emperor took Heisei, translatable as "achieving peace" or "maintaining equilibrium," for his era name. Prime Minister Takeshita Noboru inaugurated a value-added tax of 3 percent that infuriated consumers. Two months later he resigned because of publicity surrounding 150 million yen he had received from Recruit Cosmo, an employment information firm with investments in real estate and publishing. LDP faction bosses had difficulty identifying an untainted successor. Uno Sōsuke lasted barely six weeks before a palimony suit by his mistress brought him down. In the election that summer, the JSP under the female leadership of Doi Takako ran an unprecedented number of women candidates and gained control of the upper house. It also did well in the more powerful lower house in 1990.

The LDP faced challenges from members of its own party. Frustrated by elderly faction bosses who monopolized the prime ministership, younger politicians split the LDP. In 1993, Hosokawa Morihiro from the Japan New party became prime minister when the LDP suffered defeat in elections for the lower house. The worst rice harvest in two hundred years forced him to allow rice imports from Asia for the first time since World War II. Farmers were outraged. He too was caught in a financial scandal. Two more non-LDP prime ministers followed him, neither capable of dealing with Japan's economic woes. The government's tardy response to the Kobe earthquake on January 17, 1995, which killed over 520,000 people and left over 300,000 homeless, received much criticism. In 1996 a chastened LDP returned to power, and faction bosses picked the next prime minister. In 2001 they chose a third-generation Diet member, Koizumi Jun'ichirō, who promised liberals he would make structural reforms needed to bolster the economy and pleased conservatives by his call to revise the pacifist constitution.

Koizumi inherited a stagnant economy. The speculative bubble of the late 1980s collapsed when a recession in the developed world sent sales tumbling, and competition from low-labor-cost countries eroded corporations' market share. The stock market lost nearly 40 percent of its peak value in 1990 and 65 percent by August 1992. Corporations that had borrowed billions of yen to buy land or expand their businesses discovered that their debts exceeded their rapidly depreciating assets. Mitsubishi had to sell Rockefeller Center at a loss. The Asian economic turmoil of 1997 caused by speculators' dumping Asian currencies caused another recession in Japan. Two brokerage houses and a bank went bankrupt, leading to fears of depression. Economic growth, which had limped along at barely 1 percent per annum between 1992 and 1995, went negative in 1997. In 2002, bad loans ballooned to $1.3 trillion, and government debt climbed to 150 percent of the GDP. Except for an occasional quarter of slight expansion, deflation stalked Japan.

The LDP scrambled to stimulate the economy. In the 1980s it tried to revitalize rural communities by building culture halls and art museums and encouraging production of traditional handicrafts as souvenirs. In the 1990s it poured money into dams, roads, and postmodern public buildings. In 1991, the Tokyo metropolitan government moved into massive new headquarters that soared above office buildings and hotels, many half empty. Koizumi halted a project to turn a saltwater swamp into farmland, while the government paid farmers not to plant rice. His decision to privatize the post office threatened the Finance Ministry's control over the $3 trillion in postal savings accounts kept outside government budgets that it used to finance public works projects, prime the stock market, and buy government bonds. Proposals to streamline the bureaucracy, reduce regulatory oversight, and eliminate positions foundered on bureaucratic inertia. Near-zero interest rates and government support for nonperforming loans failed to stimulate business investment. The Education Ministry made universities more responsive to the interests of industry and eliminated irrelevant fields in the humanities and social sciences. In 2004, national universities became independent entities.

Japan faced international criticism of its role in world affairs. The United States grumbled when Japan refused to commit troops to the Gulf War in 1991 even though Japan's military spending ranked third below the United States and Russia. Six months after the war, Japan sent six minesweepers to the Persian Gulf amid debate fueled by antiwar sentiment in the postwar generation over whether their dispatch violated constitutional restrictions. Japan also paid $10 billion toward the cost of the war and permitted its troops to participate in peacekeeping missions in Cambodia and East Timor. After terrorist attacks in the United States on September 11, 2001, the Diet passed an antiterrorism law that allowed Japanese troops to provide rear-echelon support for the war in Iraq in 2004.

Social Problems for the Twenty-First Century

Japan's social problems also defied easy solution. In the 1980s, American social scientists praised Japan's educational system for producing literate students who scored higher on mathematics tests than did Americans. Japanese critics feared that schools were turning out soulless automatons with weak characters and no sense of national identity, unable to think for themselves, and lacking the creativity to put Japan in the lead of technological innovation. Preteenage rebels disrupted classrooms and terrorized teachers. In a series of high-profile crimes, youths killed classmates, tortured the homeless, and murdered elderly neighbors. Labor shortages in the 1980s in the sex trade and the dangerous, dirty, and low-paying work of construction and stevedoring brought men and women from Taiwan, the Philippines, Iran, and other countries to work as prostitutes and day laborers. About half entered illegally because the Labor and

Justice ministries refused to acknowledge the need for their services. Immigration of Latin Americans of Japanese ancestry was encouraged because it was thought that they would assimilate to the dominant culture. In 1999, 1.56 million foreigners lived legally in Japan out of a total population of 126.6 million. Tokyo became a more cosmopolitan city, but mainstream Japanese were quick to accuse foreigners of robbery, rape, and drug trafficking.

Economic stagnation and rising unemployment had social consequences. Corporations stopped competing to hire college graduates, and unemployment rose to an official rate of 5 percent in 2001. This figure excluded part-time workers who had lost their jobs, most of them women. The government reduced the duration and value of unemployment benefits. Job security guarantees covered just over 15 percent of workers in 2002. "Pay for performance" started to replace the seniority system of merit raises. Tokyo, Yokohama, and Osaka had long had a floating population of farm men from the north who spent the winter working as day laborers and congregated in flophouses. In the late 1980s, permanent dropouts started to swell their numbers. Osaka laborers caused the worst rioting in nearly twenty years in 1990 in reaction to police harassment. Homeless people appeared as well. Once in the public eye, sleeping on benches and in pedestrian tunnels near train terminals, they and their blue tarp camps have been moved to less conspicuous locations.

The search for meaning in a materialistic world took new paths. Right-wing militants who rode sound trucks blaring martial music and decorated with posters calling for return of the northern territories held by Russia attacked offices of the Asahi publishing company because of articles showing disrespect for the emperor. Adherents of new religions such as the Unification Church and Mahikarikyō sought a sense of community and a merging of the individual ego in a larger entity. Aum Shinrikyō attracted students from Japan's elite universities, lawyers, and businessmen. In March 1995, feeling persecuted by the Justice Ministry, its followers released Sarin, a poison gas, in the Tokyo subway system adjacent to National Police headquarters, killing twelve people and incapacitating thousands. The LDP tried to revise the 1951 Religious Corporations Law to bring government oversight to the fundraising, educational activities, and business-related income of the 183,970 registered religious organizations. Opposition by Sōka

Gakkai's political arm and other religious organizations kept the 1951 law intact.

Starting in the late 1960s, LDP politicians urged women to have more children; thereafter they lamented the selfishness of young women who put consumerism ahead of maternal responsibilities. National health insurance, a 99 percent literacy rate, sanitary housing, and nutritious diets contributed to one of the lowest infant mortality rates in the world at 5 per thousand in 1989 and longevity rates for men reaching into the mid-seventies and for women into the eighties. Women had 1.3 children apiece, well below the 2.2 necessary to maintain the population. Couples who wanted a higher standard of living or worried about the costs of their children's education limited their family size regardless of political propaganda.

In 2000, 16 percent of the population was age sixty-five or older, giving Japan the oldest population in the industrialized world. It is projected to grow to 25 percent by 2015, when 25 percent of the national budget will have to be spent on social welfare. Through the 1990s, corporations had plentiful sources of investment capital at low interest rates because Japan had the highest rates of personal savings in the world. With more retired people, the savings rate will drop.

The government wants to limit its costs for hospitals and nursing homes by having children care for parents. Elder sons with the traditional responsibility for parental care have trouble finding marriage partners because women increasingly prefer to take care of their own parents. Some farmers now marry brides from the Philippines.

Although marriage is still the norm, it too has changed. The average age of marriage for women crept from twenty-two in 1950 to over twenty-six in 2000. Crown Princess Masako delayed marriage for a career in the Foreign Ministry until she was twenty-nine. So many women opt for four years of higher education that the former junior colleges have become universities even though the decline in the college age population means that more are having trouble meeting their enrollment targets. In hopes of better futures than they perceive possible in Japan, some women seek academic degrees and employment abroad. Women want careers, and they have become increasingly choosy about whom they will marry and under what conditions. Older women have been known to divorce their retired husbands because they cannot stand having "that oversized garbage" underfoot every day.

SUMMARY

How has Japan changed over the past forty years? It has become a mature industrial society whose strength pulled it through the doldrums of the 1990s. Although inbred politics has induced voter apathy, it is a functioning democracy: in 2007, the LDP lost control of the Diet's upper house. Its cities are among the world's cleanest and safest. Despite discrimination against women and minorities, most of its citizens enjoy a comfortable life. Japanese foods are eaten in Europe and the United States; Japanese fashions and popular music are followed in Asia. Introduced in 1980, karaoke is performed around the world. Ōe Kenzaburō won the Nobel Prize in literature in 1994 for his writings that express universal truths regarding the human condition. Japanese politicians infuriate their Asian neighbors by calling the emperor a living god and Japan a divine nation while participating in Asian economic conferences. Lingering memories of the war and Japan's wariness of China's growing economic and military strength has not prevented Japan from trading more with China than with the United States, even as it offers support for the global war on terrorism.

East Asia in the Twenty-First Century

IT SHOULD COME AS NO SURPRISE IN OUR increasingly global world that the countries of East Asia are now more connected than ever before. Hundreds of thousands of Korean, Taiwanese, and Japanese businesspeople live in China to manage the manufacturing operations they have located there, and they regularly fly back and forth to their home countries. Thousands of Chinese, often there illegally, live in Japan, some as students or businesspeople, others as laborers. Cheap international phone service, as well as the ubiquity of e-mail and the Internet, make it easy for those living outside their home countries to keep in contact with friends and relatives back home, creating diasporas different from the immigrant communities of earlier times.

For two decades, Japanese, Korean, and Taiwanese tourists have been visiting China, often on package tours, and today Chinese who have prospered during the reform period are reciprocating by visiting nearby countries in increasing numbers. Popular and classical music no longer respect national boundaries. Singers and instrumentalists often have large followings throughout East Asia, adding to the huge popularity of karaoke in the region. Popular TV serials are often dubbed to be shown in other East Asian countries.

Japan, Korea, Taiwan, and China all participate in contemporary global culture. Currently the Korea wave is inundating Japan, Taiwan, and China. A soap opera, *Winter Sonata*, and its star, Bae Yong-joon (called Yon-sama in Japan), have such a powerful appeal that when he visited Japan, middle-age women threw themselves in front of his car and swarmed his hotel. On Internet sites, young women fed up with Japanese men can try to meet Korean men (without realizing that Korean and Japanese men have similar attitudes toward women). *Winter Sonata* was also the rage in Uzbekistan and Egypt. In China, "Korea" stands for fashionable or stylish. To Chinese ears, even American hip-hop sounds better in Korean. Episodes of *The Marrying Type*, a sitcom about three single professional women in Seoul, were so popular that they were sold on pirated DVDs. Shanghai's animation studios are set to rival Japan's. One project calls for a Japanese company to produce the script and direction, a South Koran company to handle three-dimensional graphics, and the animation to be done in Shanghai. Japan's experimental music is the world's leader in something called "noise." A Japanese wedding company is exporting Japanese-style weddings to Shanghai. Young people in Japan study Korean and Chinese; Chinese is as popular in Korea today as English is in China. Japanese too is studied in the rest of East Asia, although given Japan's wartime legacy, not with the same enthusiasm.

East Asia has leaped to the forefront of electronic technology. In China cell phones and fiber optics have lowered the costs of telephones and electrical transmission. Computers have given Internet access to about 59 million people (3 percent of the Chinese population), and the figure may grow to 250 million in 2008. Microsoft opened a research laboratory in the Haidian District of Beijing, where some 810,000 Chinese research scientists and engineers live. Oracle, Motorola, Siemens, IBM, Intel, General Electric, and Nokia (which produces mobile phones) run research facilities in China to develop new products as well, opening the door to innovative and independent research to young scientists. In 2010, Shanghai will host a World Expo; visitors will be rocketed from the airport to the exhibition by magnetic levitation trains traveling at speeds of up to 270 mph.

Aware that unlimited contact with the outside world poses a political threat to the regime, the Chinese leadership has ordered operators of Internet sites to monitor government bans against rumors, libel, subversion, sabotage of national security, the promotion of cults and feudal superstition, pornography, violence, and gambling. Foreign movies, popular songs, and chain stores from Japan, South Korea, and the

United States have penetrated the country. Whether the leadership is right to fear their liberalizing effect remains to be seen.

Modern communications have impacted both Koreas. In the South, it seems that everyone (especially teenagers) has a cell phone. Nearly every house has computers and Internet access. The movie industry has produced an internationally renowned generation of directors, producers, and actors. Thousands of young students travel to the United States to get an education, and interest in China is growing rapidly. North Korea has tried to insulate itself from the communications revolution and the cultural effects of globalization, but clandestine access to the Internet has already proved subversive to the closed society by cracking open the window of information from the world outside.

Contemporary Japanese culture in the form of Japanese comic books (manga), computer cartoon and video games, animation (anime), designer clothing, pop music, new dance steps, and paraphernalia has become a major export industry. In Japan, 53 million people are connected to the Internet, and cell phones are ubiquitous. Japan leads the world in new and innovative products and designs in electronics. Most of these innovations aim at the young and create new job opportunities outside the rigid hierarchies of big business, opening possibilities for individual creativity and entrepreneurship.

Signs of American culture abound in East Asia. Fast food restaurants—McDonald's, Burger King, KFC, and Starbucks—are found in cities of any size. Designer boutiques from the United States and Europe have taken over floors in major department stores, and Asian designers have penetrated the West. American teenage clothing and music styles are everywhere, but no more than Japanese Nintendo games, Pokémon, and the Hello Kitty fad among American youth. Baseball and basketball are played in East Asia (baseball is now a Japanese national sport, albeit with its own special variations). Japanese and Korean ballplayers have joined several American major league teams. The seven-foot-six-inch-tall Yao Ming plays basketball for the NBA. In 2002, South Korea and Japan jointly hosted the World Cup soccer tournament. In 2008, Beijing will host the summer Olympics. No matter what the political differences, cultural convergence (albeit with national variations) has gone too far to stop.

Japan, South Korea, and Taiwan are all democratic countries with freely elected governments, but that has not saved them from political problems. Chief among these is corruption arising from businessmen who offer bribes and kickbacks to further their companies' interests. Despite the highly publicized executions of party officials for corruption, it is a growing problem in China and North Korea as well. Kim Jong Il is notorious for living off the fat of the land. Although both the Chinese Communist party and the Korean Communist party govern in the name of the people, their officials are often as unresponsive to people's needs as are the officials of Japan's powerful Liberal Democratic party (LDP). The leader-follower factions of the LDP meet behind the scenes to choose prime ministers, and it has slighted the issue of most pressing concern to the middle class—scandals surrounding the pension system. South Korean political parties have shown no lasting power. They consist of leader-follower groups that shift allegiance from one party to another. The nefarious national security law still remains on the books. In Taiwan an independence movement backed by native Taiwanese had its candidate elected president in 2000. In the most recent election, voters supported the candidate promising economic benefits from close ties with the mainland.

Although the 1990s were a difficult period for East Asian economies, double-digit growth in China has raised South Korean, Taiwanese, and Japanese economic boats. China is South Korea's biggest export market, and since 2004, Japan has traded more with China than with any other country, including the United States. The booming Chinese economy has lifted Japan out of a fifteen-year recession and has helped South Korea recover from the Asian financial crisis. Korean and Japanese companies are eager for access to Chinese consumers and labor, while China welcomes all the foreign investment it can get. Taiwan has invested heavily in China, in terms of both hard cash and human capital, with 1 to 1.5 million Taiwanese, including many managers, working there. More than 100 million Chinese men and women toil in China's factories, and the Pearl River Delta of Guangdong has become the world's manufacturing center. When Abe Shinzō became prime minister of Japan in 2007, his first overseas visit was to China, not to the United States. Chinese Prime Minister Wen Jiabao has visited South Korea and Japan to push for strengthened economic ties. "The future trend in East Asia is economic integration," said Huang Dahui, professor of international affairs at People's University in Beijing. "Without Sino-Japanese cooperation, real integration is impossible."[2] In this growing economic interdependence, the balance is tilting in China's favor. For the United States this means that its purchase of Chinese products is not only the largest contributor to the trade deficit but also that China is also the largest purchaser of U.S. national debt. Someday China will decide that it would be better off investing its surplus cash in infrastructure—roads, railways, education.

China has begun to show many of the problems that Japan and South Korea have experienced: bank loans forced by the state to insolvent companies; collusive and corrupt agreements between bureaucrats and businessmen; maintaining inefficient state enterprises as a substitute for welfare payments to workers. The gap between rich and poor, between flourishing coastal urban regions and backward rural areas in the interior, and between skilled and unskilled workers is growing. Millions of underemployed and homeless migrant workers from the countryside fill urban slums. Strikes by workers have increased, only to be met by government repression. Owners of coal mines ignore safety measures that could save thousands of lives annually; owners of brick factories kidnap children for slave labor; and the lack of quality control has become an international scandal. Industrial pollution may be killing as many as 750,000 Chinese every year. China now produces more greenhouse gases than the United States. China's leaders are trying to address these problems with the help of Japanese technology and foreign pressure.

There has been talk about the possibility of creating a regional free trade bloc in East Asia like the European Community, but there are serious obstacles. The Chinese economy has by far the highest growth rate based on a huge population and low wages and stands to gain the most from unrestrained trade until its wage rates rise. North Korea needs economic assistance from China so long as its economy remains moribund, but its intense nationalism precludes domination by any foreign economy. South Korean business is shipping its factories to China, but the public fears the loss of industry and the resulting economic decline. Japan has much to gain from exports of high-tech products and investment in factories in China, but lingering Chinese resentment of Japanese atrocities in World War II, Japan's military alliance with the United States, and suspicion of Japanese rearmament could put a brake on further integration. All nations except North Korea continue to benefit from exports to the United States and, although on a smaller scale, to Europe. Trade with Southeast Asia and Latin America is growing. The potential for exports to Russia and surrounding states in return for oil and gas could be enormous if political and bureaucratic obstacles to free trade in those countries could be removed.

One obstacle to continued economic growth may be demographic. Education for women, urbanization, and industrialization have brought about a collapse in birth rates. Japan's birth rate has been stuck at approximately 1.3 births per woman for so long that it now has the world's oldest population. In 2005 the population officially started to decline, and politicians worry that Japan will lose half its population by 2100. At 0.9 births per woman, Hong Kong has the world's lowest fertility. Taiwan and South Korea both have fertility rates lower than Japan's, with Korea's falling to 1.08 in 2005. Owing to the official "one child" policy in China, the fertility rate there is 1.7. Because so much of China's large population still resides in the countryside, where sons are the chief form of old-age insurance, there is a serious sex imbalance. By 2020 the number of twenty- to forty-five-year-old men will exceed women by 30 million. Given that young, unattached males are the most likely to cause trouble, the sex imbalance could have political consequences.

The declining birth rates in Japan and South Korea have also led to labor shortages and aging bachelors. To some extent, sex selection techniques are to blame, but women are also more choosey in whom they marry and whether they marry. In both countries, the myth of ethnic purity has made it difficult to welcome immigrants in any number with the exception of guest workers. To find brides for farmers, Japan turns to the nearby Philippines; Korea turns to Vietnam because the two countries share a common Confucian tradition.

South Korea and Japan also share high rates of suicide. Both countries have extremely competitive economies where the pressure to succeed in school and business is intense. The number of people committing suicide in Japan has topped thirty thousand a year for ten straight years. Young people blame the school problems of bullying and poor grades; the middle-aged cite employment issues; and the

2. Bruce Wallace and Mark Magnier, "China, Japan Patching Up Diplomacy," *Los Angeles Times*, Saturday, February 17, 2007, p. A5.

elderly blame health concerns. In South Korea, the number of suicides has more than doubled in the past decade, and its rate of 24.7 per one hundred thousand people was higher than Japan's (24.2) in 2005. Although it is not responsible for the majority of suicide deaths, the most disturbing trend in both countries is the increase in the number of group suicides. The culprit is the Internet, where people contemplating suicide can meet and then use e-mail and cell phones to plan their demise. On the other hand, homicide is relatively rare throughout East Asia.

Despite economic and cultural convergence, memories of World War II continue to roil international relations in East Asia, where suspicions about Japanese attitudes and policies remain strong. Japan refuses to correct distortions in school textbooks about its conduct in China and mistreatment of Koreans during the colonial period, to apologize publicly and pay reparations to the comfort women, and to share advanced technology in some industries. Not only do Japanese revisionist historians deny the Nanjing massacre, but some have put the blame for starting the war on China. Although Japanese businessmen would prefer that prime ministers not pay homage to the war dead at Yasukuni shrine because of its effect on trade, nationalists insist that such homage is owed the men who sacrificed themselves for a sacred cause.

As China's economic clout increases, it is becoming increasingly dominant politically, not just in East Asia but in world affairs as well. Its relations with Tibet remain troubled because of ongoing nationalistic resistance to the Chinese, but Chinese migration has overwhelmed the smaller Tibetan population. China has taken advantage of the "war on terror" to suppress what it says are Uighur Muslim separatists in the northwest. Despite international disapproval, China's relations with the military dictators of Myanmar and the government in Sudan have remained close. Throughout Southeast Asia, China has put on a "charm offensive," building government buildings for the fledgling East Timor government and an aqueduct and major highways in the Philippines. As it moves aggressively to buy raw materials from South America and Africa, infrastructure projects promote the idea that China is a friendly partner. The biggest concern for the United States is China's growing military strength. At present, China has a large army capable of defending against invasion, but its outmoded weaponry and its weak navy and air force cannot support expansion abroad so long as the United States is committed to the defense of Japan and Taiwan.

Japan's fear of North Korea's nuclear weapons and missiles has pushed public sentiment toward rearmament and nuclear weapons. Six hundred books have been published on North Korea in Japan, most of them extremely hostile. Initial attempts to negotiate with North Korea to pay reparations for the damage done by Japanese colonialism backfired when Kim Jong Il admitted kidnapping Japanese as a means of recruiting Japanese language instructors. The public, the media, and Japanese nationalists have responded with demands for a hard line against North Korea—no peace treaty, no economic aid without a full accounting of all the abductees. Nationalists also argue that until Japan has a legitimate military, it will not be a truly independent nation.

The U.S. military presence in East Asia has had a strong stabilizing effect. It has prevented Japan's rearmament and has stemmed both the growing Taiwanese desire for independence and China's ability to take Taiwan by force. It has blocked a North Korean invasion of the South and a southern invasion of the North. If the United States finds a way to reach a negotiated solution of problems with North Korea, it might be able to maintain a beneficial presence in East Asia. Otherwise, the United States could spark an even more disastrous Korean war, or East Asia might decide to solve its own problems without U.S. interference. South Korea, Taiwan, and Japan are at a crossroads. In terms of security, they face east, allied militarily with the United States and Australia. In terms of prosperity, they now face west as they strengthen economic cooperation with China.

CREDITS

Chapter 16

p. 322: Fang Bao's "Random Notes from Prison," from *The Search for Modern China, A Documentary Collection* by Pei Kai Cheng, Michael Lestz, and Jonathan Spence. Copyright © 1999 by W.W. Norton & Company, Inc. Used by permission of W.W. Norton & Company, Inc.

Chapter 17

p. 286: Excerpt adapted from Saikaku Ihara, "Sensible Advice on Domestic Economy" from *The Scheming World*, translated by Masanori Takatsuka and David C. Stubbs (Rutland, Vermont: Charles E. Tuttle Company, 1965), pp. 54–57. Reprinted by permission of Tuttle Publishing.

Chapter 18

p. 318: J. Mason Gentzler, ed., *Changing China: Readings in the History of China from the Opium War to the Present.* Copyright © 1977 by Preager Publishing. Reproduced with permission of Greenwood Publishing Group, Inc., Westport, CT.

Chapter 19

p. 392: J. Mason Gentzler, ed., *Changing China: Readings in the History of China from the Opium War to the Present.* Copyright © 1977 by Praeger Publishing. Reproduced with permission of Greenwood Publishing Group, Inc., Westport, CT.

Chapter 20

p. 350: Excerpt adapted from "Fukuzawa Yukichi's Escape from Asia, March 16, 1885," translated by Hidehiro Okada, The Centre for East Asian Cultural Studies, comp. *Meiji Japan Through Contemporary Sources*, Vol. 3, 1869–1864 (Tokyo: The Centre for East Asian Cultural Studies, 1972), pp. 129–133.

Chapter 21

p. 358: Excerpt adapted from Don Baker, "The Great Transformation: Religious Practive in Ch'ondogyo" in Robert E. Buswell, Jr., ed., *Religions of Korea in Practice* (Princeton, NJ: Princeton University Press, 2007). Reprinted by permission.

Chapter 22

p. 380: Excerpt adapted from Andrew Gordon, *The Evolution of Labor Relations in Japan: Heavy Industry, 1853–1955* (Cambridge: Council on East Asian Studies, Harvard University, 1985), pp. 116–119. Reprinted by permission of The Asia Center.

Chapter 23

p. 389: Excerpts from Louise Yim and Nym Wales (Helen Foster Snow) in Nym Wales, *Song of Arirang* (Ramparts Press, 1941), p. 27, 39, 56. Reprinted by permission.

Chapter 24

p. 410: Excerpt from Lu Xun, "Sudden Notions" in *Lu Xun: Selected Works*, translated by Yang Xianyi and Gladys Yang (Peking: Foreign Languages Press, 1980), II: pp. 125–27. Published again in 2003, ISBN: 7119034081. Reprinted by permission.

Chapter 25

p. 432: Excerpt adapted from Hao Pensui, "Minjian," translated in *Agrarian China: Selected Source Materials from Chinese Authors* (London: George Allen and Unwin, 1939), pp. 247–51. Reprinted by permission.

Chapter 26

p. 446: Excerpt adapted from Hayashi Toshimasa, "Journal Entries," in Nihon Senbotsu Gakusei Kinen-Kai, *Listen to the Voices from the Sea: Writings of the Fallen Japanese Students*, translated by Midori Yamanouchi and Joseph L. Quinn, S.J. (Scranton: The University of Scranton Press, 2000), pp. 247–250 [ISBN: 0940866854]. Reprinted by permission of The University of Scranton Press.

Chapter 29

p. 506: Selections from the Sexual Equality Employment Act, translated on www.women21.or.kr, Korean Women's Association.

Chapter 30

p. 516: Excerpt adapted from Mariko Fujita-Sano, " 'It's All Mother's Fault': Childcare and the Socialization of Working Mothers in Japan," *Journal of Japanese Studies,* 15:1 (Winter, 1989), pp. 70–73, 80, 86, 87, 89. Reprinted by permission of Mariko Fujita-Sano.

INDEX

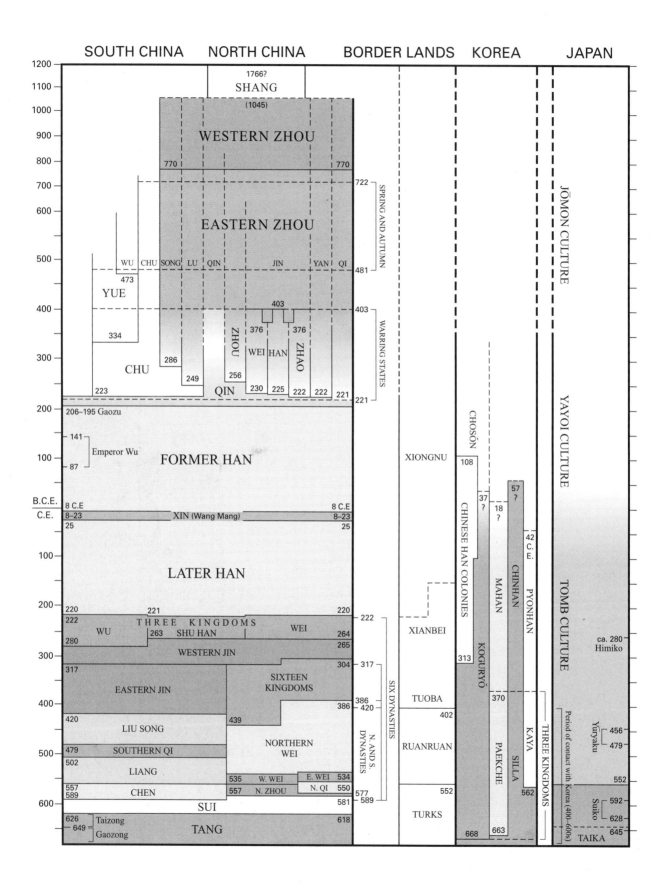